STALIN'S USABLE PAST

STANFORD-HOOVER SERIES ON **AUTHORITARIANISM**

Edited by Paul R. Gregory and Norman Naimark

STALIN'S USABLE PAST

A Critical Edition of
the 1937 Short History of the USSR

DAVID BRANDENBERGER

Stanford University Press | Hoover Institution, Stanford University

Stanford, California

Stanford University Press
Stanford, California

Printed in the United States of America on acid-free, archival-quality paper

Library of Congress Cataloging-in-Publication Data available on request.

Library of Congress Control Number: 2023058003

ISBN 9781503637863 (cloth)
ISBN 9781503638990 (ebook)

Cover design: Jason Anscomb

Contents

THE SHORT HISTORY OF THE USSR

List of Illustrations

Maps

Acknowledgments

This critical edition has benefited from a number of long- and short-term grants provided by the International Research and Exchanges Board, with funds supplied by the National Endowment for the Humanities and the United States Department of State under the auspices of the Russian, Eurasian, and East European Research Program (Title VIII); the National Endowment for the Humanities; the Department of State's Fulbright Program; and the School of Arts and Sciences at the University of Richmond.

Aspects borrow from the third chapter and appendix of my 2002 monograph NATIONAL BOLSHEVISM: STALINIST MASS CULTURE AND THE FORMATION OF MODERN RUSSIAN NATIONAL IDENTITY. I would like to thank Harvard University Press and the Davis Center for Russian, East European and Eurasian Research, for permission to reprint portions of that book. I would also like to acknowledge my gratitude to a number of friends and colleagues who have contributed to the analytical framework used in this book—M. V. Zelenov, A. M. Dubrovsky, Lars Lih, Erik van Ree, Peter Blitstein, Kevin M. F. Platt, Ronald Grigor Suny, Geoffrey Roberts, David Hoffmann, K. A. Boldovsky, Samantha Schwartzkopf, George Enteen, and Terry Martin. I am also grateful to A. K. Sorokin at the former Central Party Archive in Moscow. At Stanford University and the Hoover Institution, I'd like to express my gratitude to Norman Naimark and Paul Gregory, and at Stanford University Press, I'd like to thank Margo Irvin, Gigi Mark, Katherine Feydash, Cindy Lim, Elliott Beard, and Kate Wahl.

A Note on Conventions

The transliteration of titles, terms, surnames, and geographic locations in this volume's introduction, endnotes, and index adhere to a simplified version of the conventions practiced by the US Library of Congress. Some Slavic first names have been rendered in their English spellings to improve readability (Alexander rather than Aleksandr), as have some last names (Khmelnitsky rather than Khmel'nitskii). Terms and place-names are spelled according to their Soviet-era Russified variants to avoid anachronism (Kiev rather than Kyiv; Belorussia rather than Belarus). Exceptions occur in quotations taken from other sources and in the bibliographic citations, which strictly adhere to the US Library of Congress's transliteration conventions.

Within the text of the Short History of the USSR itself, the transliteration of titles, terms, surnames, and geographic locations follows an arcane and somewhat idiosyncratic house style practiced by the Co-Operative Publishing Society of Foreign Workers in the USSR in the late 1930s. Peculiarities in grammar, punctuation, and capitalization (including the title of chapters and subchapters) also stem from this original house style.

Struck-out characters, words, sentences, and entire paragraphs in this critical edition capture the excision of material that was written originally by A. V. Shestakov and his brigade of authors. Italics denote editorial interpolations into the text. Additions and deletions to the text are annotated in each case to clarify their authorship and provenance. Because of the need to reserve italics for these editorial interpolations, this critical edition renders all book titles, dramatic emphases, and foreign expressions in small capital letters. Square brackets denote notations added by the editor of this critical edition.

Terms and Acronyms

For a complete list of the terms, historical events, and personalities referred to in this volume, see the index.

barshchina   peasant labor owed to landlord in lieu of obrok

Bolsheviks   colloquial term for Vladimir Lenin's faction of the RSDLP and later the CPSU(B)

bourgeoisie   middle-class economic entrepreneurs, merchants, and business owners

boyar   medieval Muscovite noble

Comintern   the Third Communist International, an international coordinating body of socialist parties

CPSU(B)   Stalin-era English-language acronym for the Communist Party of the Soviet Union (Bolsheviks). More accurately the Russian Communist Party (Bolsheviks) between 1918 and 1925; the All-Union Communist Party (Bolsheviks) between 1925 and 1952; and the Communist Party of the Soviet Union between 1952 and 1991

Dashnaks   Armenian Revolutionary Foundation

imam   Muslim community leader

International   international coordinating body of socialist parties

komsomol   All-Union Leninist Communist Youth League

kulak   "prosperous" peasant

Cheka secret police (1918–1922)

Mensheviks colloquial term for non-Leninist factions of the RSDLP

Muscovy medieval Russian principality centered on Moscow

Mussavatists Azerbaidzhani Muslim Democratic Equality Party

Narodniki revolutionary agrarian populist movement

NKVD secret police (1934–1946)

obrok peasant payment-in-kind owed to landlords

Oprichnina Ivan the Terrible's privy council and personal guard

petty bourgeoisie small-scale, lower-middle-class craftsmen and shopkeepers

Politburo CPSU(B) Central Committee Political Bureau

pomeshchik tsarist-era landed noble

RSDLP Russian Social Democratic Labor Party

Rus medieval Slavic principality centered on Kiev

smerd medieval term for poor peasant

soviet prerevolutionary strike committee; postrevolutionary governing council

SRs Socialist-Revolutionary Party

subbotnik voluntary Saturday work

uyezd county

Veche medieval Slavic governing council

Varangians Scandinavian Viking-like groups

volost district

voyevodas tsarist-era regional governors

Whiteguards anti-Bolshevik forces during Civil War (1918–1921)

WEIGHTS AND MEASURES

center approx. 112 lbs. (50.8 kg)

dessiatin approx. 2.7 acres (10,925 sq. m.)

pood approx. 36 lbs. (16.3 kg)

verst approx. 3,500 ft. (1 km)

STALIN'S USABLE PAST

INTRODUCTION TO
THE CRITICAL EDITION

A t the height of the Great Terror in July 1937, Joseph Stalin took a break from the purges to edit a new history textbook. Published that September, this SHORT HISTORY OF THE USSR finalized a major turnabout in Soviet mobilizational propaganda.[1] Breaking with two decades of Bolshevik sloganeering that styled the October Revolution of 1917 as the beginning of a new era, Stalin's new catechism established a thousand-year pedigree for the Soviet state that stretched back through the Russian empire and Muscovy to the very dawn of Slavic society.

Officially credited to Andrei Shestakov and an "All-Union Government Editing Commission," Stalin's textbook was designed to supply the Soviet Union with what historians refer to today as a "usable past"—a mobilizational narrative designed to unite society around a common set of political beliefs.[2] What is more, by connecting the Soviet present to the epic trials and tribulations of the past, the book resolved the party's long-standing dilemma over how to rally together a population that was too poorly educated to be inspired by Marxism-Leninism alone. Appearing in million-copy print runs through 1955, this new narrative governed how Soviets were to understand the past not only in public schools and adult indoctrinational courses but also on the printed page, the theatrical stage, and the silver screen.

Despite its Stalin-era fame, the SHORT HISTORY faded from popular memory after it was withdrawn from circulation in 1956. This historical amnesia was compounded by the fact that archival documentation associated with the textbook was classified as a state secret until the fall of the Soviet Union in 1991. While working at the former Central Party Archive in Moscow during the mid-1990s, I investigated the origins of this textbook, taking note of the outsized role that party leaders like Stalin and Andrei Zhdanov played in its development.[3] A few years later, after my resulting book appeared in print, a new tranche of documents from Stalin's personal archive was declassified that allowed scholars to appreciate for the first time the general secretary's centrality to the shaping of this history. Most valuable among these materials turned out to be several sets of publisher's galleys that Stalin personally edited during the summer of 1937—archival documents that lie at the core of this critical edition.[4]

The importance of Stalin's intervention into the writing of this official history is hard to exaggerate. It was Stalin who identified the priorities that shaped the early stages of the narrative's development. It was Stalin who sanctioned his court historians' departure from earlier, more materialist approaches to the subject. It was Stalin who consistently demanded a more and more etatist, russocentric logic to prerevolutionary history. It was Stalin who insisted on an ultravanguardist theme within the text's discussion of the formation of the Bolshevik movement, its struggle for power, and its subsequent building of a socialist society. And it was Stalin who enforced the priority of that agenda during his own meticulous editing of the text, frequently expanding upon others' work with lengthy textual interpolations of his own.

As important as the SHORT HISTORY was for Soviet society under Stalin, surprisingly little until now has been written about it.[5] Filling a major gap in the scholarly literature, STALIN'S USABLE PAST both analyzes the text and places it within its proper historical context. In so doing, this critical edition pursues three key objectives: it identifies the ideological origins of this new historical line, it defines the nature and scope of Stalin's personal involvement in the narrative's construction, and it documents in unprecedented detail the dictator's plans for the transformation of the Soviet historical imagination.

1. HISTORICAL CONTEXT

Propaganda and Agitation. The USSR is often regarded as the world's first propaganda state. As is well-known, in the wake of the October Revolution of 1917, politically charged rhetoric and imagery came to dominate the press, the schools, and mass cultural forums from literature to cinema and the fine arts. Elements of this mobilizational agenda ought to be contextualized in the age of mass politics, which, starting in the mid-nineteenth century, increasingly forced ruling elites to base their authority and legitimacy on print media, public spectacle, and populist campaigning. Other elements of this propaganda drive stemmed from Marxism-Leninism, which predicted that the revolutionary transformations associated with the shift from capitalism to socialism would be accompanied by a revolution in popular consciousness. Members of this new society were to demonstrate a correspondingly new world view, and Lenin and Stalin believed that it was the responsibility of the Bolshevik-led dictatorship of the proletariat to cultivate it.

Early Soviet propaganda attempted to promote this new sense of socialist identity through an array of approaches that reflected Marxism-Leninism's commitment to historical and dialectical materialism. Internationalism replaced earlier stresses on nationalism and patriotism. Tsarist-era russocentrism was supplanted by a thorough condemnation of Great Russian chauvinism and a stress on liberating and enfranchising the former colonial peoples of the Romanov empire. Interest in individual heroes and villains gave way to a new focus on class consciousness and class conflict. Experiments in propaganda, agitation, and mass mobilization were conducted simultaneously alongside those in journalism, literature, art, music, dance, theater, cinema, design, architecture, education, and other forms of mass communication. Entire new genres of avant-garde expression in these fields came into being during the first decade after the revolution.

But if the new themes and forms of expression often proved transformative within the creative intelligentsia, they were less impactful across society itself. Even the best of this work, whether in art, theater, or education, tended to be difficult for the uninitiated to interpret, due to its iconoclasm and antiestablishment militancy. Less accomplished examples tended to be abstract, bloodless, and schematic. As a result, poorly educated Soviet citizens struggled to understand the propaganda that was supposed to be leading them to rethink the ways they understood themselves and the society in which they lived. Frustrated, the party leadership repeatedly intervened in Soviet mass culture during these years in an attempt to identify a more successful way of conveying its revolutionary message.

The "Revolution from Above." Crisis gripped the Soviet Union as it entered into its second revolutionary decade. As Stalin consolidated power within the party hierarchy, he and his comrades-in-arms rejected the hybridized market system of the New Economic Policy (1921–1928) in favor of an administrative command economy that precipitated a frenetic period of shock industrialization and collectivization. These policies resulted in an array of other mass upheavals in culture, class and ethnic relations, the workplace, and everyday life. Such revolutionary transformations strained Soviet society to the breaking point.

Amid this countrywide chaos and dislocation, the party leadership struggled to maintain order and bolster social mobilization. Unwilling to admit that their "revolution from above" was poorly conceptualized, Stalin and his comrades-in-arms blamed problems with implementation and follow-though both on political enemies and on their own poorly educated and insufficiently class-conscious population. Particularly after Stalin's famous 1931 letter to the journal PROLETARSKAIA REVOLIUTSIIA, propaganda and indoctrinational efforts in Soviet society were reconstructed to stress the accessibility and motivational power of the official line. According to the party leadership, propaganda had to be more dynamic and inspirational and agitation more evocative and persuasive. In an effort to provide groundwork for the revolutions of the present and future, history now acquired a new role within official Bolshevik messaging, leading the party leadership to invest heavily in what is often referred to today as the "search for a usable past."

Stalin first spoke of the need for a new textbook devoted to the prerevolutionary history of the USSR on March 5, 1934, at a Politburo meeting devoted to the deficiencies of the public schools' history curriculum. There, the official historical line came under fire for its materialist schematicism and focus on anonymous social forces—an approach promoted during the 1920s by the first dean of Soviet historiography, Mikhail Pokrovsky, which was being increasingly recognized as inaccessible and unevocative.[6] Responding to critical reports by Central Committee Secretary Andrei

Zhdanov, Commissar of Education Andrei Bubnov, and the Central Committee's Department of Culture and Propaganda Chief Alexei Stetsky,[7] Stalin issued a series of directives that Stetsky would paraphrase a week later at the Communist Academy:

> Comrade Stalin brought up the issue of the teaching of history in our middle schools at the last meeting of the Politburo [. . .] Everyone present is most likely aware that about three years ago history had been practically expelled from our schools [. . .] History, at long last, has been restored. In the past year, textbooks were created. But these textbooks and the instruction [of history] itself are far from what we need, and Comrade Stalin talked about this at the Politburo meeting. The textbooks and the instruction [of history] itself are done in such a way that sociology is substituted for history [. . .] What generally results is some kind of odd scenario [NEPONIATNAIA KARTINA] for Marxists—a sort of bashful relationship—[in which] they attempt not to mention tsars and attempt not to mention prominent representatives of the bourgeoisie [. . .] We cannot write history in this way! Peter was Peter, Catherine was Catherine. They relied on specific classes and represented their mood and interests, but all the same they took action. They were historic individuals [and even though] they are not ours, we must give an impression of the epoch, about the events which took place at that time, who ruled, what sort of a government there was, what sort of policies were carried out, and how events transpired. Without this, we won't have any sort of civic history.[8]

A more conventional political history narrative, in other words, was to supplant the Marxist-inspired schematicism of the previous decade. Coinciding with the era's explosion of mobilizational patriotic rhetoric in the press, the new official historical line was to capture the public's imagination and promote a unified sense of civic identity—something that the previous decade's proletarian internationalist ideology had failed to do.[9]

Assigned the task of presenting a follow-up report to the Politburo later in the month, Bubnov quickly convened a meeting of handpicked historians and geographers at the Commissariat of Education to discuss the crisis. His remarks followed Stalin's closely, criticizing the excessively schematic, "sociological" approach to history laid out in the present generation of textbooks. Theory dominated the discussion of history, Bubnov said, leaving events, personalities, and their interconnection to play only a secondary role. As a result, "an entire array of the most important historical figures, events, wars, etc., slip by unnoticed . . . Under such conditions, we are vastly overencumbered by what can be referred to as the sociological component and lack—almost entirely in some places—what could be referred to as pragmatic history." Bubnov then noted that he had been reviewing old tsarist-era history textbooks and advised his audience that, "although they may not be written at all from our point of view, it is necessary to remember how people put them together."[10] Nadezhda Krupskaia—Bubnov's deputy and Lenin's widow—seconded his point, noting that children have difficulty applying abstract paradigms to concrete events and therefore risked passing through the public school system without ever acquiring a true sense of historical perspective.[11]

Days later, on March 20, the Politburo reconvened, inviting an elite group of historians to its ongoing textbook discussion. One of those present, Sergei Piontkovsky, recorded in his diary a riveting account of the proceedings:

We went into the hall single file [. . .] In all, there were about a hundred people in the room. Molotov chaired the session and Bubnov delivered a report on textbooks [. . .] Stalin stood up frequently, puffed on his pipe, and wandered between the tables, making comments about Bubnov's speech [. . .] Krupskaia spoke in Bubnov's defense [. . .] After Krupskaia, Stalin took the floor . . . Stalin spoke very quietly. He held the middle school textbooks in his hands and spoke with a small accent, striking a textbook with his hand and announcing: "These textbooks aren't good for anything [NIKUDA NE GODIATSIA] . . . What the heck is 'the feudal epoch,' 'the epoch of industrial capitalism,' 'the epoch of formations'—it's all epochs and no facts, no events, no people, no concrete information, not a name, not a title, and not even any content itself. It isn't any good for anything." Stalin repeated several times that the texts weren't good for anything. Stalin said that what is needed are textbooks with facts, events, and names. History must be history. What is needed are textbooks on antiquity, the middle ages, modern times, the history of the USSR, and the history of the colonized and enslaved peoples. Bubnov said, perhaps not [the history of] the USSR, but the history of the peoples of Russia? Stalin said—no, the history of the USSR. The Russian people in the past gathered the other peoples together and have begun that sort of gathering again now.[12]

Although Stalin's commentary did not immediately translate into a shift in regime propaganda, the general secretary was clearly rejecting a "multiethnic" history of the region in favor of a historical narrative that would implicitly focus on the Russian people's state building during the preceding millennia. He was also demanding that the historical line be more concrete and accessible. Dismissing the abstract, sterile nature of a 1933 text on feudalism, Stalin noted offhandedly: "My son asked me to explain what was written in this book. I took a look and also didn't get it." Alexei Gukovsky, one of the text's authors, later recalled Stalin's conclusion: "The textbook has to be written differently—what is needed is not general models, but specific historical facts."[13]

Returning to his advocacy of "pragmatic history" at a subsequent gathering at his commissariat on March 22, Bubnov tried to apply the new directives to the task of textbook writing. Facts, dates, and heroes required proper arrangement and emphasis. Agreeing, Grigory Fridliand, the chair of Moscow State University's History Department, noted that students had learned more effectively under the tsarist system than they had in recent years because history lessons at that time had revolved around the easily understandable paradigm of heroes and villains. "This is an issue of the heroic elements in history," Fridliand argued. Today, "a schoolchild, closing his textbook, doesn't remember a single distinct fact or event. In the tsarist school, they beat those textbooks into our heads, but all the same, an entire array of those facts have not slipped from my mind to the present day. But our contemporary schoolchild is not memorizing a single event." Admitting that Soviet texts would not be able to use the tsarist pantheon of heroes, Fridliand concluded that "the issue is how to select some new names, which the bourgeoisie intentionally left out of its textbooks." "Not forgetting," added Bubnov, "the old names that we still have use for." The correct balance between tradition and innovation, then, was to be the essence of the debate, with the goal being a more accessible, evocative official line.[14]

Aftershocks of these discussions reached the central press that April. PRAVDA echoed the now-familiar criticism that textbooks in circulation discussed abstract sociological phenomena like class conflict without specific historical examples. While conceding that the material was essentially Marxist-Leninist, one writer concluded sarcastically that "they are textbooks without tsars and kings. . . . they're 'class warfare' and nothing else!"[15] Later in the month, articles in ZA KOMMUNISTICHESKOE PROSVE-SHCHENIE argued that effective historical instruction was best pursued through the presentation of animated, engaging descriptions of the past. Colorful discussions of major figures, events, wars, revolutions, and popular movements were endorsed as the most effective way of illuminating the nature of class, the state, and historical progress for the uninitiated. Existing texts, according to their critics, not only excluded specific individuals from their descriptions of the past but also slighted historical events in favor of abstract theories that tended to bewilder those they were supposed to inspire.[16] Theory needed to be deemphasized in favor of a more conventional narrative that would contribute directly to mobilizational efforts on the popular level.

The Commission. The party leadership's demands, formalized in a May 15 joint Central Committee and Council of People's Commissars resolution entitled On the Teaching of Civic History in the Schools of the USSR, amounted to a reversal of the previous decade's party line. Calling for the renewed study of what had been disparaged during the 1920s as "naked historical facts," the resolution emphasized the centrality of "important historical phenomena, historic figures, and chronological dates" in students' understanding of the past. The decree likewise underscored the need for history lessons to be composed of material suitable for those with little educational background and urged scholars to break with "sociological" trends that were now referred to sarcastically as the "childhood disease" of Marxist historiography. To facilitate this new pedagogical requirement, university history departments in Moscow and Leningrad were reopened for the express purpose of training new teachers.[17] A supplementary Central Committee decision specifically defined the emphases and relative weight of the history curriculum in the public schools.[18] Although some commentators regard this shift in priorities as an "abandonment of revolutionary innovation in favor of traditional techniques and forms" (an assessment that echoes Nicholas Timasheff's description of the era as "the Great Retreat"), it's better to think about it as a form of neo-traditionalism, in which tried-

and-true practices from the past were repurposed to support modern mobilizational objectives.[19]

This supplementary Central Committee resolution also announced the formation of a number of editorial brigades composed of experienced historians who were to take on the task of writing heroic new history narratives designed for mass consumption. Indicative of the importance of this textbook project, a Politburo commission consisting of Stalin, Zhdanov, Stetsky, Bubnov, Lazar Kaganovich, and Valerian Kuibyshev was formed to supervise the work.[20] As decreed on May 15, the new texts were to emphasize famous personalities, events, and dates and deemphasize arcane, "sociological" styles of analysis.[21] History, in other words, was to provide society with an array of cultural landmarks that would aid in the promotion of a newly unified sense of group identity.

Although the party and state decrees were quite explicit about the need to prioritize accessible, evocative approaches to history at the expense of the previous decade's orthodox materialism, they were less clear about other elements of the new line. Behind the scenes, Stalin and Bubnov had stressed the need to focus more attention on prerevolutionary Russian state building and an array of leaders associated with that effort. Elements of this etatism were reflected in the public sphere later that spring and summer, as the central press followed Stalin's lead in promoting the concept of Soviet patriotism.[22] But official directives on the writing of history were vague and ambiguous. Worse, much of the present official line on the past—especially in society at large—tended to characterize Russian history's first millennia before 1917 in almost exclusively negative terms as a story of exploitation, imperialism, and colonialism. Historians thus struggled to grasp how they were to stress the new etatist agenda without rehabilitating prerevolutionary tsarism.

As decreed, the brigades immediately began working on new elementary and advanced textbooks on the history of the USSR, as well as on the history of antiquity, the Middle Ages, modern times, and the colonial world. According to the resolutions, abstracts were to be completed by their respective editorial brigades by the end of the summer and the manuscripts themselves nine months after that. In light of the importance of the elementary text on the history of the USSR, it was decided that two versions would be developed in parallel by two separate teams of historians: a Moscow-based brigade under Isaak Mints and a Leningrad group under Alexander Malyshev.[23] Maxim Gorky referred to this new generation of textbooks in his address at the first congress of the Soviet Writers' Union several months later, indicating the high priority the initiative enjoyed.[24]

In fact, the priority afforded the project almost led to its undoing. The first in a long wave of scandals broke in August 1934, when the brigade working on the advanced text on the history of the USSR, led by Nikolai Vanag, was shaken by Stalin, Zhdanov, and Sergei Kirov's circulation of unpublished observations concerning their abstract.[25] Savaging Vanag's work, the party bosses declared that the brigade had "not fulfilled its task nor even understood what that task was." Focusing on the issue of imperialism, they observed that the brigade had skirted the nature of tsarism's relationship with both the non-Russian peoples and Russia's European neighbors. Not only had the brigade failed to characterize the tsarist state as internally oppressive and externally reactionary (both "a prison of the peoples" and "the international gendarme"), but no effort had been made to assimilate non-Russians into the narrative. Similarly slighted were Western thinkers' positive influence on nineteenth-century Russian revolutionaries and Western capital's predatory colonial ambitions within the Russian empire. According to the party hierarchs, only a dual emphasis on capitalism and imperialism could adequately convey the importance of 1917 in both class and ethnic terms. Stylistically, Vanag's abstract was also deemed inappropriate for use in the public schools, since "the task is to produce a TEXTBOOK in which each word and definition is well chosen rather than irresponsible journalistic articles that babble on and on irresponsibly." Concepts like feudalism and prefeudalism had been "lumped together," as had reaction and counterrevolution. Even the term "revolution" had been used indiscriminately. Stalin, Zhdanov, and Kirov rebuked Vanag and his brigade for such shortcomings and ordered them to remember their responsibility "to teach our youth scientifically grounded Marxist definitions."[26]

At first glance, these observations seemed to suggest that contrary to expectations, surprisingly little had changed regarding the party leadership's expectations for the official historical line. They insisted upon a materialist approach to history based on Marxist theory. They stressed the international nature of the Russian revolutionary movement. They demanded a prominent role in the narrative for the non-Russian peoples of the empire. And they even appeared to affirm Pokrovsky's famous critique of prerevolutionary Russia as a "prison of the peoples" and the "international gendarme." That said, a closer reading of the observations suggests that they are actually better understood as the beginning of a major departure from the historiography of the 1920s. For instance, although the observations insisted on attention being cast on the non-Russians, this was to be done within the context of a newly unified narrative on the prerevolutionary history of the USSR—an approach to the subject that privileged the Russian people and assimilated their non-Russian brethren into an inherently russocentric historical continuum. What is more, although the observations appeared to approvingly invoke two of Pokrovsky's famous maxims about prerevolutionary Russia, both had been altered in important ways. First, Pokrovsky's slogans had been subtly reworded from "Russia—a prison of the peoples" and "Russia—the international gendarme" to "tsarism—a prison of the peoples" and "tsarism—the international gendarme." This shift in semantics transformed the nature of the critique from a broad condemnation of the ethnically Russian empire to a much more narrow indictment of its ruling class. Second, the references in the observations to "tsarism as the international gendarme" ought to be interpreted in light of Stalin's nuancing of that thesis in a personal memorandum to the Politburo in July 1934. In this letter, Stalin noted that Soviet historians had long been wrong in their vilification of tsarist Russia's reactionary role in the early nineteenth century. According to Stalin, because all European powers had been forces of reaction in the nineteenth century, Russia did not deserve to be singled out for special condemnation.[27]

Such clarifications, of course, are more understandable in hindsight than they were at the time. Indeed, it is possible that no one outside of Stalin's inner circle understood his developing position on the issue, insofar as the party leadership declined to publish any explanatory directives on the subject for some eighteen months. Perhaps the party bosses thought their position was more obvious than it was. Perhaps they themselves struggled to codify it into more systematic recommendations. In any case, the development of a new narrative on the prehistory of the USSR repeatedly ground to a halt as the textbook brigades struggled with the task of converting the party hierarchs' hints, winks, and nods into articulate historiographical positions. Ultimately, if the historians were supposed to finish the drafting of their respective texts by the summer of 1935, it should come as no surprise that none of the manuscripts were completed on time.[28]

Confusion over the official line often led to disastrous results. For instance, when Commissariat of Education authorities finally managed to forward the drafts of the elementary texts on the history of the USSR to the Central Committee for vetting later that fall, they were met with vicious critique. Boris Volin, the head of the Central Committee's department of schools, took a particular disliking to the draft prepared by Mints's Moscow-based brigade and lashed out in his report at Bubnov for his poor leadership of the brigades:

> I find the work that Bubnov has done on the book to be extremely deficient, as evidenced by some, if not all of my marginalia . . . (1) the text is dull, written without style, and will not interest schoolchildren; (2) the textbook surprisingly digresses into discussions of figures from Greek, Roman, Scythian, and feudal times, etc., which may complicate the children's mastery of our own history; (3) there is very little information and few drawings referring to the culture of the Slav-Russians [SLAVIANE-RUSSKIE] (art, architecture, weaponry, writing); (4) there is much repetition about slavery, serfdom, and so on . . . There is no way the book can be published in this form. The textbook needs very serious revisions.[29]

Stalin was no more impressed with the manuscript than Volin. Skimming it some weeks later, he noticed with disfavor that a seventeenth-century campaign by Kuzma Minin and Dmitry Pozharsky to rebuff Polish and Swedish invasions during the so-called Time of Troubles—an initiative that ultimately allowed the Romanovs to come to power—had been included in a section on counterrevolution. Stalin scribbled in the margin, "Huh? The Poles and Swedes were revolutionaries? Ha-hah! Idiocy!"[30]

The other elementary textbook, drafted under the leadership of Zalman Lozinsky after Malyshev was arrested in February 1935, fared little better. Mints prepared a long report on the manuscript for Stalin in which he argued that the text was really more of a reader than a systematic and rigorous textbook. Identifying dozens of problems with the narrative and its chronological emplotment, he also noted that the manuscript failed to provide a Marxist explanation for many historical events. In the early chapters,

Lozinsky did not identify the shift from classless "primitive communism" to stratified slaveholding society. Later, "the defeat of the peasant wars is attributed to the weakness of their armed uprisings. And this is in spite of the fact that the main purpose of this course is to explain to schoolchildren that it was only the proletariat, under the leadership of the Bolshevik party, that was able to be victorious." Still later, Lozinsky failed to explain the origins of the Socialist-Revolutionary Party and how Lev Trotsky had come to play such a role in Russian social democracy.[31]

The advanced text on the history of the USSR produced under Vanag, Boris Grekov, Anna Pankratova, and Piontkovsky proved equally unsatisfactory. Reconceptualized after the circulation of the observation by Stalin, Zhdanov, and Kirov, the manuscript was completed only in the second half of 1935. Mints subjected it to a close reading and identified scores of shortcomings in the narrative.[32] Then, according to Vanag's wife, A. E. Salnikova, Stalin read the draft with care and made comments in the margins of several of the chapters before inexplicably allowing the manuscript to languish in his chancellery until late 1935.[33] At that point, the draft was sent to Vadim Bystriansky, the director of the Leningrad party committee's Institute of Party History. Apparently acquainted with the party bosses' thus far unpublished observations, Bystriansky argued that Vanag and his brigade had failed to address the issues that Stalin, Zhdanov, and Kirov had raised some eighteen months earlier. He also noted that the brigade's schematic understanding of historical materialism undermined important lessons that were to be learned from the past—particularly in regard to the subject of Russian state building:

> In this textbook, there is an array of examples of "crude sociology," where the presentation of civic history is replaced by superficial sociological generalizations. [. . .]
>
> One of the most serious shortcomings of the text is that is authors do not show the progressive meaning of "the gathering of the Russian lands" and "the formation of the core of the Russian national state." The textbook refers only to the Muscovite princes' depredation and violence, meaning that students will not be able to understand that the formation of the Russian tribe's national state was a step forward in historical development.

In this connection, a false and incorrect picture is given of the events at the start of the 17th century. [The pretenders] False Dmitry I and False Dmitry II are cast as the leaders of peasant uprisings, even though these adventurers only exploited the rebellious masses to further their own corrupt interests.

The positive dimensions of Minin and Pozharsky's struggle for the liberation of the country from its occupation by foreigners—the Poles and Swedes—and for the formation of a national state (pages 120–124 of the ab-br[eviated] text) are also not shown. Here you instead find a sort of "leftist internationalism"—the failure to understand that communists do not have to distance themselves from positive appraisals of their country's history.

There's no clear picture of the imposition of serfdom [. . .] No clear reason is given for the defeat of the peasant wars—the lack of leadership from the vanguard [proletarian] class. The progressive role of Peter the Great's reforms is utterly missing, despite Lenin and Stalin's completely clear statements on the issue. Only the negative aspects of the Petrine reforms and their impoverishment of the masses are given without showing their progressive meaning.[34]

Bystriansky's damning report almost certainly ruined the Vanag text's prospects for publication.[35] But his review and others like it proved destructive in other ways as well, complicating what was already uneven party oversight. First, they were issued privately to individual editorial brigades rather than circulated more widely among all the scholars engaged in this search for a usable past. Second, instead of being systematic and thorough, the reviews tended to randomly list factual, interpretive, and stylistic objections with little rhyme or reason. As such, they offered little help with the ongoing task of identifying the correct theoretical red thread and how to weave an overarching narrative around it. Third, these reviews were utterly inconsistent in the way that they dealt with controversial issues, such as the role of the non-Russian peoples, in this thousand-year narrative.[36]

In the wake of these debacles, Zhdanov convened a group of high-ranking party functionaries, establishment historians, and consultants on January 17, 1936, to determine whether anything could be salvaged either from the Vanag text or the two elementary histories of the USSR.[37] This group decided that it would be best to start again from scratch and called for its membership to write a series of articles for Pravda and Izvestiia later that month that would explain both the party leadership's official position regarding the manuscripts' deficiencies and its broader ambitions for historical pedagogy. Particular emphasis was to be placed on the creation of a usable past populated by recognizable heroes that would advance the cause of Russian state building. Open criticism of Pokrovsky at this meeting acquired considerable momentum, propelled by Nikolai Bukharin, as well as by Bystriansky and Karl Radek.[38]

Zhdanov concluded after the meeting that new leadership was needed as the search for a new textbook resumed. On January 21, he proposed that his working group be transformed into a blue-ribbon commission under the joint authority of the Central Committee and the Council of People's Commissars.[39] Working in tandem with Bukharin, Zhdanov took a close look at a denunciation of Pokrovsky's "school" that Bukharin was drafting and included parenthetical mention of it in his mission statement for the commission. Stalin agreed with the criticism of Pokrovsky and expanded it further when he edited the piece before its publication.[40] Days later, Zhdanov's initiative was ratified by a joint party and state decree that recognized the new commission and tasked it with resolving the ongoing crisis, either by appointing new textbook brigades or holding a public competition to identify a superior manuscript.[41] Pravda and Izvestiia accompanied this news with a barrage of editorials, articles and publications (including Stalin, Zhdanov, and Kirov's 1934 observations) that were to clarify aspects of the new historical agenda. These articles devoted almost as many column inches to an indictment of Pokrovsky and the previous decade's schematicism as they did to the case for a newly animated, accessible style of etatist storytelling.[42]

Publication of the party leadership's observations and their criticism of Pokrovsky unleashed a firestorm within the historical discipline that has been detailed elsewhere.[43] Many of the scholars taking part in this pogrom evidently did so in hopes of obscuring their own ties to the late scholar, who had died of cancer in 1932.[44] More important, however, were the motives behind the campaign itself. Pokrovsky was pilloried in the press as the personification of a historiography that no longer corresponded to the party leadership's needs, whether because of its inaccessible schematicism or because of its tendency to describe the Russian national past as remarkable only for its traditions of tyranny, backwardness, and chauvinism. Although the late academician's work had never elicited such criticism during his lifetime, the political and historiographical climate had changed and Pokrovsky made an ideal scapegoat. Most of Pokrovsky's critics attacked him only in caricature, unconcerned with anything more than a straw-man characterization of his scholarship. In essence, the anti-Pokrovsky campaign was to demonstrate by negative example that new history writing had to be based more in fact and personality, as well as more accessible and more patriotic.

For historians, the publication of the observations by Stalin, Zhdanov, and Kirov was almost as confusing as the sudden volte-face regarding Pokrovsky. Not only was the critique of Vanag's 1934 abstract difficult to understand without access to the abstract itself, but as noted earlier, the observations assumed an ambiguous position in regard to several prerevolutionary controversies, particularly concerning the overall role of the tsarist state and the non-Russian minorities. The confusion that this publication caused is visible in an secret police informant's account of a conversation with the Leningrad historian Boris Romanov in 1936. According to the informant, Romanov had apparently sought out Vanag's advice on how to emplot the new narrative. From the report, it appears that Romanov understood that the state was to play a central role in new accounts of the Russian national past and that the non-Russian peoples were to play a supporting role in this story rather than to preside over their own separate histories. That said, perhaps in light of Vanag's recent experience, Romanov confessed to being intimidated by the task of organizing the new narrative. Using the metaphor of an orchestral conductor, he wondered aloud about how one might sequence the eventual work:

> The main thing is how to arrange the contents, the "symphonic score," if you will, as that is the most important thing. A conductor must be found who will not hesitate to follow his own intuition. Will he be able [to cue] the entrance of every one of the peoples in the USSR at the right moment in time? The USSR is now a single entity—one has to show how this happened. One would have to be able to organize the historical performance in such a way that each [non-Russian] people enters when it is necessary, so that the student, the schoolchild, reading, and listening, does not sense any false

notes. He must hear with his inner ear that the entrance of each individual people—even if it does not correspond to historical fact—conveys the impression of playing a part in an orchestra on cue. Until now, you know, it's been like an artificial Christmas tree, the branches being stuck in here and there as one pleases. It can't be like that now. They used to be stuck in one of two ways: "the [non-Russian] people were conquered," [that is,] they were conquered by the Russian autocracy, or they rose in rebellion. Sometimes, neither way worked and they were tossed aside like a bad branch. But now, a conductor must be found who can compose a plan—a score. Who that is—I have no idea. But it is important that he knows—it's necessary that he has a sense. Let him take advantage of every Musabekov et al., who knows the history of his [non-Russian] country; even if they don't know it, it's not important. Important is the emplotment.[45]

Romanov's long, rambling statement indicates that, although he theoretically understood that the prerevolutionary history of the USSR was to be structured around the Russian national past, he had no idea how to do it in practice. Shestakov would recall later that his brigade's progress had also been stymied by the need to resolve complex interpretive issues.[46]

The Competition. When Zhdanov's new commission met to discuss resuming the textbook campaign in mid-February, it discussed the feasibility of holding a public competition to solicit a maximally diverse array of texts on the history of the USSR.[47] Hoping that this unconventional approach would provide a breakthrough, the commission nominated a panel to judge the competition and assigned Bukharin and Bubnov the task of authoring an official announcement.[48] Once they were done, Zhdanov then inexplicably cut down their draft article into the core of a joint resolution of the Central Committee and the Council of People's Commissars entitled On the Organization of a Competition for the Best Primary School Textbook for an Elementary Course in the History of the USSR with Brief References to General History.[49] Perhaps Zhdanov believed that releasing both an announcement and the resolution would be redundant. Perhaps Bukharin's own declining fortunes had compromised his authority to author a signed article of such importance. In any case, the competition was announced anonymously on March 4, 1936, through a terse government decree containing little in the way of concrete instructions. Instead, it referred interested parties to the articles discussed previously that had appeared in the press in late January and early February.[50] Four days later, PRAVDA reiterated the rationale of the project: "In the country of the victorious proletariat, history is to become a mighty weapon of civic upbringing [GRAZHDANSKOE VOSPITANIE]." "Our generations," the paper continued, "must create unwavering revolutionaries—communists, fighters, and builders—according to the heroic templates of the past and present."[51]

As hoped, the competition campaign caught the attention of not only professional historians but others as well, ranging from the celebrated playwright Mikhail Bulgakov to an utterly unknown mechanic named Alexander Lokhvitsky. Many of these contestants—collective farmers, workers, and rural schoolteachers—appear to have done little more than cobble together material from a variety of earlier Soviet and prerevolutionary textbooks.[52] Others, however, attempted to craft narratives that would answer the party's call for a new approach to the subject. Here, they struggled with the ambiguity of the leadership's directives, as had the brigades between 1934 and 1935. Confusion reigned, for instance, over the role that the non-Russian peoples were to play in the new history. According to Zhdanov's personal secretary, A. N. Kuznetsov, many historians were grappling with the most elementary of questions: was the narrative to be presented as a "single Russian historical process, with the inclusion of the history of individual peoples who played a major role in the development of that process, or should Cent[ral] Asia, the Transcaucasus, etc., be treated in individual historical sketches?" According to Kuznetsov, "Com[rade] Radek recommended presenting a single historical process, including the individual peoples at the specific points at which they enter into contact with Russia. But there is hesitation and ambiguity and almost all the authors are finding this to be a stumbling block." Equally delicate were questions of judgment such as "whether or not tsarism brought 'progress' to the Transcaucasus and Central Asia through its conquests (the process of centralization, the development of capitalism, etc.)," a question that apparently had been provoked by spurious references in Stalin, Zhdanov, and Kirov's observations to the old regime as a "prison of peoples." Related queries concerned whether Slavophilism ought to receive a positive or negative evaluation and precisely which events were to script the new periodization. Kuznetsov noted that although the authors were "wrestling with these issues," their difficulties stemmed from the fact that solutions to such ticklish questions were not to be found by consulting either official history journals or authorities in the field.[53]

In response to the confusion, Bukharin drafted an article that spring that clarified elements of the party hierarchy's ambitions "on the historical front." According to Bukharin, the goal was a popularized narrative revolving around etatist priorities, particularly the formation and development of the Russian state (GOSUDARSTVO ROSSIISKOE), "both as an entity and as a 'prison of the peoples.'" Equally important was the process by which the imperial Russian state was "transformed by revolution into a socialist union." While Marxist stages of historical development were to be included, this was to be accomplished while avoiding the abstraction of the previous decade. As Bukharin put it, "the autocracy must be displayed in all its institutions: the army, courts, church, bureaucracy, etc., and princes, ministers, governors, generals, gendarmes, priests, etc., must be given as real historic personages [ZHIVYE ISTORICHESKIE TIPY]."[54] Unfortunately, Bukharin's increasingly vulnerable position in the party likely explains why his article never appeared in print, preventing it from conveying this timely advice to the competition's contestants.

Despite this air of uncertainly, some forty drafts were eventually submitted for official consideration by late 1936.[55] Most, written by amateurs, appear to have been dismissed with a minimum of formality. Others, however, required more serious vetting at a time when outside factors complicated this process. Solid manuscripts, like that of V. N. Astrov, a researcher at the Voronezh Provincial Museum of Regional Studies, had to be discarded when their authors fell victim to the ongoing purges. The Leningrad editorial brigade, initially shaken after the ouster of Malyshev in early 1935, had to endure the arrest of his replacement Lozinsky in mid-1936. Vanag was arrested at about the same time, leaving his group of senior historians without a leader.[56]

Commission panelists surveying the submitted manuscripts quickly noticed that the drafts' interpretation of controversial issues varied significantly, even among the most professional of them. This is clear from a December 1936 memorandum in which Bubnov described Zhdanov's impressions of the ongoing search. Although the Central Committee secretary was willing to concede that some of the textbook drafts that had come across his desk were "a big step forward in comparison to the last period (from 'sociologizing' texts to Marxist ones)," he still had to concede that "none of the texts can be considered satisfactory." Concerned that historians were still "avoiding certain questions," Zhdanov highlighted this observation with his own interpretation of Russia's acquisition of its southerly possessions. Seizing upon the debate over how best to characterize Russian imperialism, he focused on Ukraine and Georgia, which found themselves in the seventeenth and eighteenth centuries caught between the Polish-Lithuanian Commonwealth and the Russian, Ottoman, and Safavid empires. Zhdanov recommended that the Ukrainians' and Georgians' need to subordinate themselves to one of these regional powers should be styled as a choice of evils that favored their coreligionists in Moscow. Turning to the Transcaucasian kingdom for example, Zhdanov averred, "At that time (in the developing historical context), an independent Georgia wasn't meant to be." The same judgment apparently applied to Ukraine. Perhaps realizing the heresy implicit in this neocolonial position, Zhdanov added that unification with Russia "was not an absolute good, but of two evils, it was the lesser one."[57] Zhdanov reversed other basic historiographic positions as well, even rehabilitating aspects of church history. Monasteries, for instance, were apparently not exclusively sites of exploitation, insofar as they had contributed to the growth of the state. These directives, like others, reflected overarching etatist sympathies—as Zhdanov noted to Bubnov in a moment of unusual frankness, "the most important historical factor is 'the gathering of Rus.'"[58]

Careful work that December and in early January 1937 allowed the panel and its consultants to narrow the field to seven superior manuscripts. These included submissions from Shestakov's editorial brigade at Moscow's Bubnov Pedagogical Institute; Vanag's former group, including Pankratova, Konstantin Bazilevich, Sergei Bakhrushin, and Anastasia Fokht; Lozinsky's former Leningrad group, consisting by then of only Viktor Bernadsky and Tatiana Karpova; Mints's Moscow group, then including only Militsia Nechkina and Evgenia Genkina; a group known as "The East," consisting of Sergei Dubrovsky and Berta Grave; another duo consisting of PIONERSKAIA PRAVDA correspondent Sergei Gliazer and publishing house editor Olga Zhemchuzhina; and, finally, a teachers' collective from Moscow's Krasnopresnensky district under the direction of Pavel Gorin.[59]

Difficulties emerged, however, when the panelists and consultants tried to rank the seven manuscripts. Although there was a general consensus that the eventual selection would require substantial revisions before publication, deciding which manuscript had the fewest liabilities became the subject of major debate. In particular, most of the submissions were judged to be insufficiently popularized for their intended audiences.[60] At the final meeting of the panel in late January 1937, heated debate erupted over its final recommendations and associated questions of historical interpretation and methodology. Bubnov, following Zhdanov, presented a report in which he chastised the seven collectives in a strikingly uncongratulatory way. Beginning with the general complaint that historians had failed to break completely with their "Pokrovskian" sociological schematicism, Bubnov listed an array of specific interpretive errors. First of all, their dismissive treatment of church history—particularly the tenth-century christening of Kiev Rus—ignored the progressive nature of literacy and culture that had been received from Byzantium.[61] Similarly slighted were progressive aspects of the consolidation of the Muscovite state and the reforms of Peter the Great. Criticism of the incorporation of Ukraine and Georgia into the Russian empire, according to Bubnov, was ahistorical, in that these societies' alternatives to alignment with their northerly Orthodox Christian neighbor were uniformly unattractive.[62] Unsurprisingly, most of the controversies concerned positions that were incompatible with the party hierarchy's increasingly statist views of the historical process.

Despite its caustic tone, Bubnov's report received the jury's endorsement as its concluding resolution. Bubnov and Central Committee member Yakov Yakovlev preserved much of its harsh language when they attempted to adapt it into a communiqué for publication in the press. The competition's results were so marginal and flawed, they averred, that no first or second prize was to be awarded. Only a joint third prize would be given to Shestakov's group and either the Gliazer-Zhemchuzhina team or Mints's brigade. Once revised, these manuscripts would serve as textbooks on the history of the USSR for the third and fourth grades.[63]

Unexpectedly, Zhdanov rejected the Bubnov-Yakovlev communiqué when it was forwarded to him in late January, despite its resemblance to the jury's earlier report. Perhaps he found the document's tone too poisonous. The process then ground to a virtual standstill for about a month, perhaps

FIGURE 1: Andrei Shestakov, 1930s.
Collection of the author.

because of the approach of the infamous purge-era Central Committee plenum of February and March 1937. Only once the plenum concluded did the party leadership return to the ongoing question of the history curriculum. Frustrated with the sluggish progress on the textbook front, Stalin apparently discussed the possibility of reediting tsarist-era textbooks with Solomon Lozovsky in mid-April, speaking fondly of one authored by Pavel Vinogradov.[64] Assigned the task of vetting this material, Stetsky reported back that such a retreat would be an exercise in futility:

> The prerevolutionary editions of Russian history textbooks (Ivanov, Platonov, Ilovaisky, and others) aren't suitable for use. All these textbooks promote religious-monarchist notions; in fact, the falsification of history in this sense strengthens particularly with the start of Catherine II['s reign]

[. . .] The history of the peoples of the USSR is not illuminated at all. The presentation ends abruptly at the end of the nineteenth century. Reworking these textbooks would be just as difficult as publishing new textbooks.[65]

At about the same time, Stalin also met with Yakovlev and Bystriansky to discuss several issues of historical interpretation. This conversation proved decisive, as it allowed Yakovlev the insight necessary to craft a second, more acceptable communiqué on the results of the textbook competition. In contrast to the first draft that he had written with Bubnov, Yakovlev's second was more constructive and focused on the modern period rather than the controversial feudal epochs. As before, no first prize was to be awarded, but Shestakov's text now merited a second prize and would be reworked into an official textbook. The groups under Mints, Pankratova, Gorin, and Moshe Gudoshnikov were to be awarded "incentive prizes" that would serve as motivation to reedit their work into supplementary readers.[66]

Editing Shestakov's SHORT HISTORY OF THE USSR. Although Shestakov's brigade was likely thrilled to have won the competition, they enjoyed only a brief respite.[67] Shortly after the disclosure of the results, Zhdanov, with Stalin's consent, organized a new committee to supervise what were to be major revisions before the textbook's publication that fall.[68] This new committee, in turn, recruited a number of senior historians to assist in the matter. Most were scholars who had been trained under the old regime; they were drafted both because of their experience with narrative history and because the ranks of the younger Marxist historians had been thinned by the Cultural Revolution, Stalin's letter to PROLETARSKAIA REVOLIU-TSIIA, the fall of the Pokrovsky "school," and the ongoing party purge.[69]

But if this three-year search for a usable past appeared to be nearing its conclusion, the party leadership again proved unable to articulate its overarching strategy for the historical front. This is clear from a disorganized list of revisions that Zhdanov and Yakovlev presented to Shestakov on April 19, 1937. Indeed, the list is telling enough to present in its entirety:

It is essential to include in the textbook:
1) the 150 million DESIATINS (h[ect]a[res]) of land that the peasantry gained from the landlords . . .
2) the liquidation of Russia's economic, political, and cultural backward-

ness as a result of the victory of the Great Proletarian Revolution and the liberation of our motherland from its half-colonial dependency on bourgeois Europe—in general, underscore the difference between conditions in Russia before 1917 and after;

3) strengthen throughout [the textbook] elements of Soviet patriotism and love for the socialist motherland . . .

4) must introduce the growth of electricity, coal, and oil;

5) show the best factories and mills, electric stations, canals . . . ;

6) underscore that during the 1918–1920 intervention [by foreign powers], the landlords restored their power everywhere . . .

7) point out that the landlords and capitalists had an interest in the intervention;

8) the Trotskyites—the enemies of the people—must be shown to be enemies not only of the CPSU(B), but genuine enemies of the people;

8) [SIC] edit methodically those places [in the text] where the role of the party is discussed;

9) . . . work through the issue of the peasant wars better and eliminate exaggerations about their organization, etc.

10) bring up the Byzantine issue;

11) explain better the cultural role of Christianity;

12) provide [something] on the progressive meaning of the centralization of state power;

13) clarify the issue of 1612 and the interventionists—and, by the way, about the name False Dmitry

14) introduce Sviatoslav's line "I'm coming against you"

15) provide something more on the German knights, using Marx's chronology on the Battle on the Ice, Alexander Nevsky, etc.;

16) don't include medieval West[ern] Europe;

17) strengthen the history of individual [non-Russian] peoples;

18) remove the schematic design of certain lessons;

18) [SIC] make corrections on Khmelnitsky;

20) and on Georgia;

21) [and on] the reactionary nature of the Streltsy rebellion.

Zhdanov and Yakovlev gave Shestakov and his brigade until May 19 to rework their manuscript.[70]

The fact that Zhdanov and Yakovlev's recommendations were laid out in such a chaotic way likely confused Shestakov and his brigade. Were they to treat the list as identifying twenty-two discrete errors in need of correction? Or were they to treat the list as the basis for more extensive, systematic revisions? In the end, Shestakov and his brigade decided to read the document literally as a list of nearly two dozen concrete mistakes. In so doing, they failed to realize that Zhdanov and Yakovlev were clumsily trying to stress the need for a larger, more patriotic vision of the USSR based on the accomplishments of the revolution and the construction of a socialist economy. This etatist narrative was to identify continuities stretching back into the prerevolutionary period and underscore the celebration of state-building efforts and institutions as well as the priority of leadership, economic development, societal unity, and national defense. This narrative was to be populated by an array of heroic, patriotic protagonists, committed to both state and society. It was also to feature antagonists, who were to be identified as enemies of the people rather than just wrongdoers.

It is possible that Shestakov's confusion over official priorities was compounded by other reviews solicited from the historians Evgeny Morokhovets, Mikhail Zinovev, and Fokht. These critiques, too, tended to focus on individual, concrete factual errors rather than engage with the manuscript in a more holistic sense, although they did agree that it lacked a broader theoretical framework. Even if it paid lip service to what had been articulated in the 1934 observations by Stalin, Zhdanov, and Kirov, the textbook in their assessments had not been structured as a truly Marxist historical narrative.[71]

Working around the clock, Shestakov and his brigade managed to finish their revisions and have their manuscript laid out in publisher's galleys by the end of May or early June. Stalin took a quick look at two copies of the prototype textbook and objected chiefly to their narrative digressions and excessive promotion of his personality cult.[72] Other copies were sent to Zhdanov and other members of the party leadership. Still others were shared with a group of consultants, including the senior historians Bakhrushin, Bazilevich, Bernadsky, Bystriansky, Grekov, Nikolai Druzhinin, Vladimir Picheta, and Stepan Veselovsky.[73]

Zhdanov presented the results of this second review to Shestakov around June 20. As the historian would tell his brigade the following day:

"There are many reviews and requests for corrections. We have been given five days for corrections and then five days for the preparation of a new set of publisher's galleys." Continuing, he outlined what had learned from Zhdanov:

> There is an array of imprecise explanations and biases in the textbook's presentation and it is too schematic and lacks spirit [. . .] The personality of Ivan Kalita should not be entirely negative. The marriage to Sophia Paleologue should either be explained or skipped. More content and detail [is needed] on the Slavs. The influence of Pokrovsky is visible in the discussion of trade. [Material] on the typography under Ivan is done poorly, as is that on the manufactory under Alexei Mikhailovich. The material on the Narodniki needs to be stronger; more is needed in greater clarity in regard to feudal decentralization; the concepts of obrok and barshchina are confused. The time under Ivan Kalita needs to be illuminated in political terms, more needs to be said about the 17th century. Use the reviews by Bakhrushin, Bykhovskaia, Bubnov, Bazilevich, Grekov [. . .], and others for these corrections.[74]

If Zhdanov's general recommendations remained—as before—disorganized and vague, the professional reviews that he passed on to Shestakov and his brigade were more systematic.[75] As a rule narrow and concrete rather than broad and conceptual, they were nevertheless explicit about the need to strengthen the overarching aspects of the historical narrative dealing with state building. Accounts of the growth and systemization of prerevolutionary Russia and the creation of a sense of continuity over the course of the preceding millennia were important. Such historical dynamics, according to these specialists, would endow the USSR with a sense of authority and legitimacy that October 1917 and subsequent revolutionary transformations had been unable to provide alone. Unfortunately, there were so many suggestions offered by the reviews that only a fraction of them could be incorporated into the brigade's frantic, last-minute revisions.

Wary of missing their deadline, Shestakov and his brigade completed their revisions in the allotted time and submitted their manuscript in the form of publisher's galleys to Zhdanov's committee on July 1, 1937.[76] One copy was sent to Stalin; others were circulated to members of the party leadership. Bubnov eagerly read the galleys in early July and returned to

Zhdanov recommendations that focused on three things. First, the text-book's narrative needed to be framed in more grandiose, triumphalist terms. Second, it needed to strengthen the Marxist analysis of a number of historical junctures, from the rise of Moscow to the nature of the Petrine reforms. Third, Shestakov and his brigade needed to expand their coverage of historical protagonists such as Ivan the Terrible and Alexander Suvorov. On the whole, Bubnov's review reflected the stress on "pragmatic history" that he had been advocating for since 1934.[77]

Vladimir Zatonsky, a Ukrainian party boss and the commissar of ed-ucation for that republic, adopted a more critical point of view. First, he thought that the book was insufficiently Marxist in its critique of prerev-olutionary Russian state building. Commentary on Peter the Great, for in-stance, needed to be more exacting when it explained that the emperor's reforms contributed first and foremost to the "formation and strength-ening of the landlords' and merchants' national state." Second, Zatonsky found the textbook to embrace a russocentric point of view in its narration of the prerevolutionary period. According to Ukrainian party boss, during the redrafting of the Shestakov text, the simplification and popularization

FIGURE 2: Stalin at his writing desk, late 1930s.
RGASPI, f. 558, op. 11, d. 1650, l. 20.

of the narrative had taken place at the expense of the non-Russian peoples. Denouncing a historical narrative that virtually ignored the Ukrainians and Belorussians, much less the other non-Slavic peoples of the USSR, Zatonsky raged: "It hasn't turned out to be a history of the USSR at all so far. Basically, it is a history of the Russian state. For decorum, a few pages at the beginning are given on the Transcaucasus, Central Asia, Kazakhstan, and Siberia."[78]

As Bubnov and Zatonsky was poring over the textbook, Stalin also sat down to vet his own copy of Shestakov's galleys. He appears to have worked on the text alone—perhaps at his dacha on July 6, insofar as his Kremlin office calendar indicates that he did not hold any meetings on that day. Generally speaking, Stalin seems to have liked what he read, although that did not stop him from making literally hundreds of factual, interpretive, and stylistic alterations to the narrative. This editing—which is analyzed in detail in the following section—stressed a broad array of priorities including the strengthening of the text's statist and russocentric thematics. Stalin then evidently met with Zhdanov to pass along his markup of the galleys and explain the nature of his revisions. Available documentation does not indicate when this meeting took place, but it may well have occurred at the general secretary's dacha on July 12, when his office calendar again indicates that he was not receiving guests in the Kremlin.[79]

Zhdanov then apparently retired to his office at the Old Square Central Committee building to spend much of the next week poring over Stalin's editorial revisions and integrating them together with those of his own, mostly drawn from the reviews that he had solicited from Bakhrushin, Bazilevich, Bernadsky, Bystriansky, Druzhinin, Grekov, Picheta, and Konstantin Sivkov. At the end of this intensive editing, Zhdanov appears to have had an assistant prepare a master set of corrections by gluing blank pages of notepaper into the margins of an unbound copy of the manuscript, where both Stalin's and Zhdanov's comments were recopied in neat handwriting. Zhdanov then almost certainly met with Stalin one more time in late July to go over these final revisions to the text. The resulting set of loose-leaf, edited galleys was apparently then recopied again and passed along to the State Instructional-Pedagogical Publishing House in early August for typesetting.[80]

In late August, on the eve of going to press, a third set of publishers' galleys of Shestakov's SHORT HISTORY was circulated among members of the party hierarchy by Zhdanov's secretariat. Kliment Voroshilov attempted to remove passages that exaggerated his revolutionary pedigree and civil war service, but was overruled. Zhdanov, acting on the suggestions of his personal secretary, shifted a reproduction of Viktor Vasnetsov's famous portrait of Ivan the Terrible to the front of the text's fifth chapter. He also struck out the names of all the editorial brigade members (with the exception of Shestakov), a change that meant that when the textbook rolled off the presses a few weeks later, its title page would be graced only by Shestakov's name and the phrase "approved by an All-Union Governmental Commission."[81] This, of course, was a misnomer: not only had Stalin and Zhdanov repeatedly overruled the commission's decisions and rewritten much of the manuscript themselves, but almost a third of the commission's original members were under arrest by the time the book appeared in print. The purges would claim all but two of those who remained during the coming year.[82]

As published in 1937, Shestakov's SHORT HISTORY OF THE USSR consisted of 223 pages of text with fifteen chapters, six maps, a chronological table, and 111 pictures. In its final form, the SHORT HISTORY offered its audience a narrative that stretched from prehistoric times to the Stalin Constitution of 1936.[83] Stalin had declared in 1934 that "Peter was Peter and Catherine was Catherine," and unsurprisingly, Shestakov's text devoted unprecedented attention to the study of historical personalities associated with the old regime, from military commanders to the ruling dynasts themselves. Tsars like Ivan the Great and Ivan the Terrible epitomized state building, the latter also symbolizing the importance of vigilance in the struggle with sedition. Many elements of the narrative revolved around the theme of national defense, such as Alexander Nevsky's 1242 defeat of the Teutonic Knights and Minin and Pozharsky's 1612 expulsion of the Poles from Moscow. So dominant were these new themes that the previous decade's Marxist attention to periodization and stages of historical development now appeared only obliquely in the narrative.[84] Such priorities meant that Zatonsky's premonition had come true—the SHORT HISTORY was indeed little more than a Russian historical narrative, charted linearly from Kiev Rus through Muscovy and the Romanov empire to the Soviet Union. The non-Russian peoples appeared in the narrative only when discussions of broader imperial trends—such as territorial conquests, colonial expansion, and peasant revolts—required it. As would befit a story composed chiefly of events drawn from the Russian national past, Russian surnames dominated the list of rulers, military leaders, scientists, writers, popular heroes, and revolutionaries mentioned in the text. Non-Russian names, to the extent that they appeared at all, most frequently figured into discussions concerning foreign invasion and domestic insurrection.[85]

Pragmatic history in the sense that it conferred the legitimacy of a thousand-year pedigree upon the Soviet experiment, the Shestakov text also successfully finessed one of the most delicate paradoxes associated with such a storyline: how could a historical narrative geared toward the valorization of state authority explain the rise of a successful antiestablishment revolutionary movement? Worse, how could the text's narrative voice switch sides, so to speak, and shift its sympathies to the Bolsheviks' attempts to overthrow the state after spending seven chapters not only celebrating Russian state building but also downplaying the significance of peasant rebellions? And how could the text provide positive coverage of any element of Russian society after the empire descended into absolute reaction in the wake of the 1825 Decembrists' revolt?

Shestakov approached these challenges to emplotment in three ways that Stalin and Zhdanov developed more explicitly in their editing of the textbook. First, Shestakov embraced the Marxist doctrine of historical materialism, according to which progress and development are charted in terms of society's relationship to the means of production. According to this theory, in prerevolutionary times, nonproletarian historical figures—even feudal princes, tsars, and emperors—could be considered progressive if they contributed to important historical developments such as the centralization of the state, the expansion of the empire, the systemization of the economy or the defense of realm.

Second, Shestakov proposed that although historic peasant rebellions could be used to gauge levels of popular discontent and exploitation, they were not—in a Marxist-Leninist sense—particularly progressive or revolutionary. Peasants, according to Marx and Lenin, lacked the education and class consciousness that workers would acquire later in the nineteenth century. This meant that peasant rebellions were unable to bring about revolutionary change on their own, did not directly anticipate the nineteenth-century working-class struggle that culminated in the Bolshevik movement, and did not require special celebration or praise within the official historical line.[86]

Finally, Shestakov found a way to shift attention away from the state to progressive social forces after the country's descent into nineteenth-century reaction by obliquely relying on Lenin's famous 1913 dictum that there were effectively two nations within every capitalist society. According to Lenin, every reactionary bourgeois nation that defended the state, its exploitative economy, and its oppressive apparatus was flanked by a more democratic one that consisted of commoners and those who supported their cause.[87] This allowed Shestakov to focus on the Decembrists in 1825 and then segue in quick succession to Alexander Pushkin and Nikolai Gogol and then to Vissarion Belinsky, Alexander Herzen, and Nikolai Chernyshevsky, characterizing all of them as progressive, patriotic, and critical of the tsarist establishment. Each provided Shestakov with opportunities to retreat from his heretofore etatist narrative while at the same time foreshadowing an incipient interest in free-thinking European philosophers like Marx and Engels. From Marx and Engels, the text's pivot to Georgy Plekhanov, Lenin, and the origins of Bolshevism was completely straightforward.[88] Deft and subtle, the shift that Shestakov scripted into the events of 1825 was perfectly orchestrated, ultimately allowing the party hierarchy to claim a pedigree that was at once statist and revolutionary.

The publication of Shestakov's SHORT HISTORY in September 1937 was an event that is hard to exaggerate in importance. Massive fanfare in the press hailed the textbook as no less than "a great victory on the historical front." Held to be free of the "sociologizing" tendencies that had plagued the Soviet historical sciences for years, it was welcomed as "a wished-for gift on the twentieth anniversary of the Great Socialist Revolution." Reviews described the narrative as an example of "concrete history," comprising "facts, the dates of events, and animated personages who had in one way or another taken part in the historical process." Moreover, the textbook's presentation was disingenuously praised for its treatment of the prerevolutionary history of all the Soviet nations rather than just that of the Russian people.[89]

Publicity surrounding the book's release made it clear from the start that it was to have a role much greater than that of a standard third- and fourth-grade textbook. The journal Istorik-Marksist proclaimed the text to be a template for all future historical publications.[90] Bolshevik went even further, endorsing the text for use with the widest of possible audiences:

> Not only millions of children and young people will learn according to it, but so too will millions of workers and peasants and hundreds of thousands of party activists, propagandists, and agitators. Without a doubt, the Short History of the USSR will be not only a school textbook, but a handbook for every party member and nonparty Bolshevik who wishes to understand the past in order to grasp the present and predict the future [. . .] [U]ntil other more detailed Marxist texts on the history of the USSR appear, there is no doubt that this will be the fundamental study aid for adult readers and students in party, komsomol, and trade union schools.[91]

In the end, Bolshevik's prediction did not stray far from the mark. Shestakov's Short History came to be used not only in primary schools, but secondary ones as well. Red Army and party training courses relied on the text, as did discussion circles involving ordinary Soviet citizens.[92] Konstantin Shteppa, who taught at Kiev State University at the time, recalled later that, "until the late 1930s and early 1940s, it was the only material on Russian history for courses in these and even in the higher [collegiate-level] schools." "Only by means of this little book," Shteppa added with a touch of bitterness, "was it possible to orient oneself regarding the demands of Party policy with respect to any historical question, phenomenon, or event."[93]

But despite such glowing appraisals, it was not an ideal text. Shteppa cursed the Short History for being unimaginative and Rankeian in nature.[94] Shestakov himself was already cautioning audiences some two months before the text even appeared that they would have to teach aggressively to compensate for the density of the curriculum. That this speech was immediately published in Istoricheskii zhurnal indicates the level of official concern in regard to the text's accessibility.[95] Be that as it may, the fanfare with which the new curriculum was launched rendered Shestakov's Short History the paradigmatic statement on Soviet history during the late 1930s.

Massive print runs resulted in the release of some 6.5 million Russian-language copies before the end of 1937, with 5.7 million more being printed over the course of 1938. Translated into dozens of union languages, 3 million more copies were printed in Russian alone in 1939.[96] At the same time, the SHORT HISTORY formed the basis for other, more advanced textbooks, such as the three-volume HISTORY OF THE USSR released by Pankratova, Bazilevich, Bakhrushin, and Fokht in 1940.[97] These texts, in turn, shaped the official historical line represented in scholarly monographs and articles, as well as in the press and mass cultural venues such as film, theater, and opera.[98] Such a saga indicates Shestakov's 1937 SHORT HISTORY to have marked a decisive breakthrough in Stalin's search for a usable past.

2. THE TEXT

The critical edition. This critical edition of the SHORT HISTORY OF THE USSR highlights both the content of the textbook and Stalin's editing of its prototype during the summer of 1937. It aggregates the dictator's revisions from July of that year with all other known editing of the text between his intervention and the textbook's later publication that September. Laid out in a way that draws attention to each textual correction, interpolation, and excision, this editing is also annotated to indicate source and authorship.

Incorporation of the archival record into this critical edition involved extensive work deciphering the handwriting not only of Stalin but also of Zhdanov and at least one of his assistants. It also involved the close analysis of a number of other reviews of the Shestakov text that Zhdanov relied upon when making his corrections. Once the core text of this critical edition was assembled and annotated, it was compared to the first September 1937 printing of the textbook to identify all other minor technical changes made at the State Instructional-Pedagogical Publishing House on the eve of its production. Finally, all those revisions were transposed into the textbook's official 1938 English translation to produce the most authentic critical edition possible.[99] Subsequent changes to the text through 1955 are analyzed in the appendix at the end of this volume.

Stalin as editor in chief. As noted earlier, the archival record indicates that Shestakov and his brigade submitted their final prototype draft—their second set of publisher's galleys—to Stalin for vetting in early July 1937. Although the general secretary had taken a quick look at their first galleys in either May or early June, he spent a considerable amount of time editing the new set.[100] Once he was done, he apparently discussed his revisions with Zhdanov, who then worked to integrate the general secretary's editing together with the recommendations of several historians and party bosses who he had drafted to help review the text. Zhdanov then apparently had an assistant compile all the corrections together before meeting Stalin for a second time. There, the two again carefully went over the revisions to the text.[101] After the State Instructional-Pedagogical Publishing House laid out in type a third set of galleys that August, Zhdanov and a handful of other party bosses took one final look at the SHORT HISTORY before authorizing its publication.[102]

Stylistic editing. Stalin's revisions to the Shestakov textbook reveal him to have been a demanding editor who disliked historical writing that focused on minutiae at the expense of the big picture. He also had little patience for wordiness, metaphorical language, hyperbole, digressions, and literary devices like foreshadowing. Isaak Mints described the experience of working with Stalin in 1935 on the editing of THE HISTORY OF THE CIVIL WAR IN THE USSR in terms that inform the general secretary's revisions to the SHORT HISTORY two years later: "Stalin was pedantically interested in formal exactitude. He replaced 'Piter' in one place with 'Petrograd,' 'February in the Countryside' as a chapter title (he thought that suggested a landscape) with 'The February Bourgeois-Democratic Revolution,' [and] 'Land' as a chapter title (a 'modernism,' he called it) with 'The Mounting Agrarian Movement.' Grandiloquence was mandatory too. 'October Revolution' had to be replaced by 'The Great Proletarian Revolution.'"[103] This and other aspects of Stalin's work on the SHORT HISTORY display the hallmarks of an experienced but nonprofessional editor. As is well known from his personal library and archive, Stalin fancied himself a wordsmith of sorts and read with pencil in hand, compulsively reworking the phrasing of passages in draft documents and even published books that he felt could be expressed more efficiently or effectively. This means that the vast majority of Stalin's alterations to the Shestakov text are best categorized as line editing. Only rarely did Stalin revise the text in a more complex way as professional editors do, reorganizing the narrative, the argument, or the analysis. And although it is true that Stalin did alter a number of the book's central themes, even this was done in a rather crude and inconsistent way. In the end, despite the fact that Zhdanov helped Stalin some in regard to analysis and stylistics, the end result of this editorial process was a heavily revised textbook that demonstrated less of the subtlety or accessibility than one would expect from such intensive effort.

Political and ideological editing. As pedantic as Stalin was when it came to stylistics and terminology, many of his editorial interventions were politically charged. First, Stalin consistently strengthened etatist aspects of this historical narrative, stressing aspects of Russian history connected to the construction and consolidation of central political authority. This put the communist leader in the awkward position of defending the historical legacies of not only the tsars and their servitors but the Russian Orthodox Church as well. It also led Stalin to delete gratuitous, compromising, and salacious detail about these historical protagonists, inasmuch as he believed that Marxists ought to focus on such figures' progressive contributions to their historical epochs rather than their failings as individuals.

This emphasis on the centralization of power and leadership also led Stalin to systematically stress the importance of the party leadership in the history of the Bolshevik revolutionary movement. An important element of Leninism, this vanguardism led Stalin to emphasize over and over again the initiative, decisiveness, and follow-through of the central party apparatus at the expense of local activists, regional party organizations, and others at the grass roots.

Other aspects of Stalin's editing reiterated this deep commitment to Marxism-Leninism. He strengthened the historical materialist core of the narrative, stressing stages of Marxist socioeconomic development that were often only implicit in Shestakov's prototype text. He also highlighted Marx's and Lenin's contention that only a working-class party could truly change the world, insofar as rural, agrarian populations lacked the education, ideological vision, political consciousness, and organization to overthrow the established order. Stalin stressed this thesis in Shestakov's narrative again and again, highlighting a theoretical red thread running throughout the book that explained why the premodern Russian peasantry's frequent revolts against tsarist authority were forever doomed to failure.[104]

Stalin's commitment to Marxism-Leninism probably also explains another dimension of his editing of the SHORT HISTORY—his systematic deletion of elements of his own personality cult from later chapters of the text. Stalin's removal of excessive biographical detail and acclaim—which sometimes even equated his role in the Bolshevik movement with that of Lenin—is present throughout his editing. Similar celebratory material about Lenin was also occasionally deleted. Such editing indicates that Stalin was neither craven nor single-minded about the promotion of his cult. Instead, he appears to have been preoccupied by something entirely different: the task of enhancing the historical agency of the central party vanguard.

Somewhat less orthodox from a Marxist-Leninist perspective was Stalin's pivot in the text away from proletarian internationalism toward russocentric autarchy. Despite routine lip service to slogans such as "Workers of the World, Unite!" the general secretary downgraded or deleted portions of Shestakov's SHORT HISTORY dealing with world history and events in foreign lands—even those describing worker unrest abroad or international support for the Bolshevik revolution. At the same time, Stalin highlighted the singularity and uniqueness of Russia's thousand-year experience with statehood and its unprecedented transformation into the Soviet Union after 1917 under the leadership of the Bolshevik party. The end result of these editorial interventions was the consistent assertion of a sense of Russo-Soviet exceptionalism that was underrepresented in party ideology and propaganda before 1937. Although this approach to the history of the USSR can be traced back to Stalin's doctrine of Socialism in One Country and that concept's Leninist origins, the Shestakov narrative presented a much more autarchic, sui generis vision of Russo-Soviet state building than Lenin ever anticipated.[105]

Similarly controversial from a Marxist standpoint was Stalin's emphasis on the theme of national unity across the span of Russo-Soviet history. Despite Marx and Engels's maxim from the COMMUNIST MANIFESTO that "the history of all hitherto-existing society is the history of class struggle," Stalin proved eager in his editing to stress the importance of national unity and warn of the implications of social discord, disharmony, and dissent.

In light of the importance of Stalin's political and ideological revisions to this narrative—changes that ultimately transformed the text into an official line on USSR history during the preceding millennium—a chapter-by-chapter overview of the prototype text that Shestakov presented to Stalin in July 1937 follows. This overview also details Stalin's and Zhdanov's edits and alterations to each chapter. In so far as Stalin and Zhdanov made literally thousands of editorial changes to the SHORT HISTORY, these sketches address only the most important of them.

Introduction

When Shestakov and his brigade submitted their textbook to Stalin's chancellery for vetting in July 1937, they handed it in in the form of a bound set of publisher's galleys entitled AN ELEMENTARY HISTORY OF THE USSR WITH SHORT ACCOUNTS OF WORLD HISTORY. On its title page, Shestakov and the history department at the Andrei Bubnov Pedagogical Institute in Moscow were credited with its compilation. On the obverse side of the title page, a list identified the individual brigade members. For a frontispiece, Shestakov chose a sketch by Vasily Svarog of Stalin, Lazar Kaganovich, Sergei Kirov, Yan Rudzutak, Viacheslav Molotov, and Grigory Ordzhonikidze surrounded by children at Moscow's Gorky Park.[106]

In the volume's introduction, Shestakov stressed the uniqueness of the USSR—its size, its natural resources, its prosperity, and so on. He and his brigade described the USSR as a happy country composed of eleven republics and inhabited by some 170 million people hailing from 120 different ethnicities. Stressing the socialist nature of the society, Shestakov noted that there were no longer any hostile classes in the USSR and that its inhabitants were committed to the common good. This society, the historian continued, was the result of a Bolshevik-led revolution waged by the parents of the schoolchildren for whom the textbook had been written. The introduction then concluded that it was necessary to study the past in order to uphold the USSR's revolutionary agenda and accomplishments.

When Stalin opened his copy of Shestakov's galleys in July 1937, he immediately began to reframe the whole text. Starting with the book's title, he cut it down to A SHORT HISTORY OF THE USSR. He also crossed out Shestakov's institutional affiliation and Svarog's frontispiece. Unsurprisingly, Zhdanov seconded these changes, also deleting the list of Shestakov's collaborators.[107] On the eve of the textbook's printing, editors at the State Instructional-Pedagogical Publishing House added a line to the title page explicitly noting that that the SHORT HISTORY enjoyed the endorsement of an all-union government commission.

Within the introduction itself, Stalin deleted several literary flourishes including the whimsical declaration that the USSR was a "happy" country. Factually, he reduced the official number of Soviet ethnic groups from 120 to 50.[108] He also added a number of Marxist-sounding phrases about how "there is no exploitation of man by man" in the USSR and how the revolution had been won by workers and peasants under the leadership of the party vanguard—editing that led him to delete Shestakov's sentimental mention of the parents of the textbook's grade school readership. Finally, Stalin edited several turns of phrase to underscore the socialist essence of the USSR and its constituent republics.

Chapter 1: Our Country in the Distant Past

Shestakov and his brigade began the first chapter of their textbook with prehistoric human society. Adhering to Marx's understanding of historical materialism, the narrative began with primitive hunter-gatherer society and then segued to the emergence of clans and tribes. Social stratification increased over time and clan and tribal leaders eventually became a ruling elite, establishing administrative institutions to enforce their power.

Shestakov and his brigade then surveyed the earliest states to rule over what would eventually become Soviet territory. They traced the origins of modern Georgia to Urartu, where local elites ruled over Georgian and Armenian peasants. Similar attention was cast upon the forerunners of the Central Asian republics. The rulers of these states were described as cruel and continuously at war with one another. Amid all this strife, however, the societies experienced economic growth and diversification as well in line with the laws of Marxist historical materialism.

The textbook then turned to the Scythian nomads who ruled the steppe along the northern coast of the Black Sea, where Greek merchants had established a number of ports. According to Shestakov, these Scythians challenged Greek hegemony in 107 BC, when the slave Savmak led a brief, unsuccessful uprising. Both the Scythians and Greeks were then eclipsed by the arrival of new waves of nomads from the east—the Huns, Khazars, and Bulgars. In time, these groups came into conflict with an array of Slavic agriculturalists in the region—the forefathers, according to Shestakov, of the modern Russian people. The Slavs waged ceaseless war against the Khazars and Bulgars, as well as the Byzantine Greeks; in the west, other Slavs challenged the dominance of local Germanic tribes and Viking-like Scandinavian Varangians. As the Slavic tribes grew in strength and number, they too experienced growing social stratification; by the eighth century AD, a Slavic nobility had emerged to preside over some fifteen towns that traded with Byzantium in agricultural goods and slaves.

Stalin approved much of the way Shestakov and his brigade framed the first chapter of this manuscript, having rejected a more detailed account in earlier publisher's galleys in late May or early June.[109] He particularly underscored the primordial roots of the Soviet republics in the Caucasus and Central Asia and the autochthonic claims of the Georgian, Uzbek, Tadzhik, and Turkmen peoples. For Stalin, these peoples' ethnogenesis in this region reinforced their claim to these lands, implicitly downgrading competing pan-Turkic, pan-Islamic or Persian influence.[110] Perhaps for this reason, Stalin interpolated a line reinforcing modern Georgia's debt to Urartu while also deleting a line about how this state ruled over local Armenian tribes, so as to not offend the latter's descendants.[111] Stalin made no changes to Shestakov's discussion of the early Slavic tribes, evidently satisfied by how they were described as defending their primordial lands.[112]

Unsurprisingly, Zhdanov shared Stalin's assumptions about the permanence of the region's ethno-political order in his editing of the chapter. To that end, he deleted mention of the Caucasian and Central Asian states' continuous internecine warfare. He then gently corrected Shestakov's anachronistic russocentrism by noting that the Slavic tribes were the forefathers of not only the Russian people, but the Ukrainians and Belorussians as well. At the same time, Zhdanov scaled back Shestakov's exaggeration of these agriculturalists' prosperity and urbanization, perhaps in consultation with his historical consultants.

Chapter 2: The Kiev State

Shestakov's second chapter shifted to focus more centrally on the Slavic tribes. According to the historian and his brigade, the tribes living in the Novgorod region were conquered in the ninth century AD by the Varangians. These Scandinavian warriors plundered the area for tribute and slaves and then transported their booty in longboats down the Dnieper to sell in Byzantium. In the ensuing century, the Varangians extended their power south, where they founded the state of Kiev Rus and intermarried with the local Slavic population.[113] In time, their now-Slavic heirs grew strong enough to even lay siege to the Byzantine capital of Constantinople.

Shestakov and his brigade spent much of their narrative on Kievan rulers such as Prince Igor and their state building, military campaigns, and extraction of tribute from the surrounding area.[114] Later, Igor's widow, Princess Olga, took an interest in Byzantium and its Christian religion during her sorties south. Secular revelations about rulership and religious ones about the divine right of kings apparently led her to break with the Slavs' pagan traditions and personally convert to Byzantine rite Christianity. Later, in 988, her grandson Prince Vladimir grasped the wisdom of her decision and converted the whole Kievan polity to Christianity.[115] According to Shestakov, Vladimir's baptism of Kiev Rus was met with protests that he suppressed by force of arms. Over time, the presence of Byzantine clerics and craftspeople in Kiev led to the spread of Greek culture and literacy. Iaroslav the Wise, Vladimir's heir, oversaw the assembly of a code of laws according to Byzantine models. This accomplishment was overshadowed, however, by a poorly fought war against the Poles which resulted in the sacking of Kiev. Only a popular uprising dislodged these invaders and allowed Iaroslav to reclaim his throne. Ultimately, Shestakov concluded, modern readers owed Kiev's Byzantine-inspired chroniclers a debt of gratitude, insofar as it was their recordkeeping that allowed their descendants to learn "about the history of our motherland."[116]

As princely power in Kiev increased, so too did social stratification and the impoverishment of its population. According to Shestakov, if early on, the prince had been obliged to rule alongside a popular assembly known as the Veche, he had become strong enough to ignore that democratic institution. Predictably, as the prince and his noble retinue grew in power and wealth, the exploitation of the commoners grew as well—something Marxists would have recognized as a hallmark of the prefeudal slave-owning mode of production.[117] This predictably led to an increase in popular unrest.

In the twelfth century, internecine fighting among the heirs to the throne led to the economic decline of Kiev and the emergence of several new centers of feudal power. In the west, Galicia Volynia took shape, balanced in the north by the rise of Suzdal-Rostov. To the northwest, Novgorod reasserted its dominant role in regional trade. There, the democratic tradition of the Veche persevered, keeping kept both the powerful nobility and the moneyed merchantry in check. Over time, cautioned Shestakov, the nobles and their merchant allies nevertheless succeeded in undermining the Veche. A series of popular protests against excessive taxation sparked an uprising that temporarily dislodged this Novgorod elite in 1209, but such reversals were only fleeting.

In 1240, the Swedes attacked Novgorod. Rallying to the defense of their region, the Novgorodians assembled an army under the command of Prince Alexander, who dealt the invaders a major defeat at the river Neva. Two years later, the German Livonian knights invaded the region and attempted to impose their Catholic rite on the local population. Again, Prince Alexander (now known as Nevsky) came to the rescue. Detailing how Alexander defeated the German forces in the Battle on the Ice, Shestakov then noted that he expelled them from the Novgorod region for good.

When Shestakov and his brigade shifted their attention to the principality of Rostov-Suzdal, they noted that the region's non-Slavic population stubbornly resisted Kievan and Novgorodian inroads. Long considered a backwater, this region rose to relative prominence in the twelfth century, when a series of influential princes moved their seat of power first to Vladimir and then Moscow. That said, they struggled to control their constituent princelings and nobles and collapsed into internecine warfare by the end of the century. Only a few decades later the region—paralyzed by what Marx called feudal fragmentation—was overrun by invading Tatar-Mongolian forces.

When Stalin turned to chapter 2, he sanctioned much of Shestakov's work. That said, when vetting the galleys' treatment of Vladimir's decision to baptize his subjects, the general secretary underscored the "heathen" nature of Kiev's pagan beliefs and declared that Vladimir's choice of the Byzantine rite had been progressive in Marxist-Leninist terms. "Compared with idolatry," he wrote, "the introduction of Christianity marked a step forward in the development of Russia."

Marxist-Leninist theory also led Stalin to clarify the ineffectiveness of the frequent popular uprisings during these centuries. According to Stalin, the grassroots rebellions had failed to overthrow princely power because they were "spontaneous" and lacked "political consciousness and organization." Such observations about the limits of grassroots action would continue in subsequent chapters. Stalin completed his editing of the chapter with a handful of stylistic changes—among them replacing Shestakov's hyperbolic anachronism about the "history of our motherland" with the more neutral "history of the Eastern Slavs."

Zhdanov made an array of more workmanlike changes to the chapter. Perhaps in consultation with his historical advisers, he added detail on the Varangians' Dnieper trade route to Byzantium, the consolidation and christening of Kiev Rus, and the functioning of the Kievan Veche. He strengthened the reputation of Iaroslav the Wise by deleting mention of his military fiasco against the Poles. He likewise explained Novgorod's renewed rise as a center of international trade. In detailing the region's invasion by the German crusaders in 1242, Zhdanov noted that the Livonian order had plundered not only local Slavic settlements, but those of other tribal groups as well. Zhdanov also mitigated the story of Kiev's decline and eclipse by clarifying that it was this region that supplied the Slavic migrants who later helped bring Rostov-Suzdal to prominence. Finally, he added several sentences to the end of the chapter about how the ceaseless internecine warfare divided the local nobility and ruined the peasantry. Feudal fragmentation and its weakening of regional unity and governing institutions, averred Zhdanov, proved fatal when the Slavic lands were subsequently confronted by a Tatar-Mongol invasion.

Chapter 3: Eastern Europe under the Rule of the Mongol Conquerors

Shestakov and his brigade opened their third chapter with a discussion of the rise of the Mongol empire. Emerging from Central Asia in the early thirteenth century, the Mongol forces overran Kiev in 1240 and defeated Slavic principalities that Shestakov anachronistically termed "Russian." Over the course of the next two hundred years, the Mongols and their Tatar allies would plunder the region, subjugating the "Russian" princes and forcing them to aid the Golden Horde in its collection of tribute. The Russian Orthodox Church was also induced to instruct its parishioners to submit to their new Tatar overlords.

Moscow emerged as a regional capital during these difficult years. Prince Ivan "Kalita" ("Money Bags") was especially successful in this regard, using his role as a Tatar vassal to enrich himself and expand the size of his holdings. According to Shestakov, Kalita's descendants continued to follow this pattern, accumulating land, wealth, and power for their seat in Muscovy. By 1380, Kalita's grandson, Dmitry, was even able to challenge the hegemony of his Tatar overlords on the Don River at the Battle of Kulikovo Field. This victory allowed the prince, subsequently known as Dmitry Donskoi, to temporarily throw off the so-called Tatar yoke. And although Donskoi's victory was a fleeting one, it bolstered the rise of his Muscovite principality.

As the Golden Horde began to decline in the late fourteenth century, Lithuanian and Polish polities to Moscow's west grew; in 1386, a royal marriage united them into the Polish-Lithuanian Commonwealth. According to Shestakov, although Russian, Belorussian, and Ukrainian peasants had never lived easy lives, those who had fallen under the control of the Polish and Lithuanian overlords were reduced to the status of serfs and forced to convert to Catholicism. Only continuous warring with the German Livonian order kept this aggressive new state from attacking Moscow, which was reasserting its independence from the Golden Horde during those same years.

When Stalin turned to chapter 3, he focused on issues associated with Muscovite state building. Ivan Kalita, according to the general secretary, was to be understood as having accumulated wealth for both himself "and his principality." This, according Stalin, meant that, although the grand prince may have been greedy and unscrupulous, he nevertheless had the best interests of Muscovy in mind. Stalin reinforced this point by adding a new conclusion to the section: "Thus, resorting to every means, Kalita gathered the disunited Russian principalities into a single state with Moscow at its centre." Such anachronistic russocentrism should come as no surprise, as Stalin and his advisers had been stressing the "gathering of the Russian lands" since at least 1934. In Marxist terms, Stalin's editing was equally eye-catching, as it highlighted the ongoing transition from feudal fragmentation to manorial and then patrimonial feudalism.

Aside from state building, Stalin continued to be concerned about Shestakov's use of terminology. Emphasizing the diversity of Chingiz Khan's forces, he exchanged the term "Mongol" for "Tatar-Mongol" in several places. In commentary on these invaders' conquest of Central Asia, Stalin noted that they had subjugated the "eastern Turco-Mongolian peoples" rather than some nonexistent feudal "Turkish state." Other terminological corrections were more subjective. Once the Tatar-Mongol forces had conquered the Caucasus in 1240, Stalin stressed that they "attacked the Russians from the east," exaggerating Shestakov's anachronistic russocentrism. He later repeated his use of this teleological ethnonym in his discussion of Kalita's assembly of "Russian principalities" into a single state before completing his editing with purely stylistic changes that Zhdanov complemented with more of his own.

Chapter 4: The Rise of the Russian National State

The fourth chapter of the SHORT HISTORY began with a discussion of the formation of a major state centered on the principality of Moscow. Shestakov and his brigade attributed the maturation of this state-building project to Ivan III, who aspired to strengthen his polity's defenses against the Tatars, Poles, and Lithuanians. At first, neighboring principalities such as Novgorod resisted this incorporation and allied with Muscovy's enemies to frustrate Ivan's ambitions. That said, the tsar, as Ivan was by then styled, eventually succeeded in incorporating them into what Shestakov termed "the Russian national state," a Marxist concept associated with patrimonial feudalism that connected state building and centralization with the fate of the broader society.[118] Ivan subsequently proved able to defend Muscovy from the Poles and Lithuanians and finally broke all ties with the Golden Horde in 1480.

As a Marxist, Shestakov conceded that Ivan's state-building program came at considerable cost. In particular, it resulted in the increased exploitation of the peasantry at the hands of Ivan's nobility. As they had for generations, the peasants responded to this oppression by migrating elsewhere in search of less onerous conditions. This frustrated Muscovy's landowners—the boyars and the monasteries—who began to insist on measures to impede their movement. In 1497, Ivan III decreed that peasants would be allowed to move from one master to another only on a single day of the year—a decision that effectively completed their enserfment.

Stalin agreed with Shestakov's labeling of Muscovy as a centralized "Russian national state" that was different in structural, functional, and ideological terms than its predecessors. Enthusiastic about Ivan III's declaration of complete Muscovite independence from the Golden Horde, Stalin strengthened the textbook's appraisal of the tsar by dubbing him the "victor" in his final standoff with the khan on the Ugra River in 1480. Stalin also added to the text the triumphalist conclusion that it was thanks to Ivan that the Tatar-Mongol yoke, "which Russia had borne for over two hundred years," was finally thrown off. He then concluded his editing with a focus on terminology and left Zhdanov to attend to stylistics.

Chapter 5: The Expansion of the Russian National State

The fifth chapter of Shestakov's SHORT HISTORY continued its focus on development of the centralized "Russian national state" under Ivan the Terrible. Shestakov and his brigade began the chapter with a biographical sketch of the "terrible tsar," noting that his difficult childhood at court led him to claim the title of autocrat, monopolize power, and govern without consulting his boyars. Shestakov's emphasis on Ivan's troubled relationship with his boyars hinted at Muscovy's transition from the Marxist stage of patrimonial feudalism to estate-representative feudalism, when the ruler of an increasingly complex state is forced to rely on noble and economic elites. According to Shestakov, when Ivan reached his majority, he took up his ancestors' interest in expanding the Russian state and made war on the neighboring khanates of Kazan and Astrakhan. Both victories resulted in massive bloodbaths, particularly after the siege of Kazan. Both also resulted in the colonization of new lands and the exploitation of new non-Russian populations.

Unsuccessful campaigns against the Baltic Germans, the Polish-Lithuanian Commonwealth, and Sweden led Ivan to conclude that he was being betrayed by his own nobles. According to Shestakov, he decided to form a personal guard—the Oprichnina—to suppress opposition to his autocratic rule. The black-clad members of this guard enabled Ivan to strengthen his sway, both at home and abroad. Frustrated by failed military campaigns in the west, Ivan turned to expand eastward into Siberia, making Muscovy one of the largest states in the world.

In Marxist terms, Ivan's centralization was accomplished at great cost. An ever-expanding need for taxation led Ivan and his nobles to strip the already impoverished peasantry of the right to leave even the most oppressive of masters, finalizing their enserfment. Many peasants responded to this oppression by fleeing to the state's southern borderlands in order to join the freebooting Cossacks of the steppe.

In his revisions to this chapter, Stalin supported Shestakov's general characterization of Ivan the Terrible and his reign. That said, he took steps to reduce the text's attention to the tsar's cruelty. In his editing of the first set of textbook galleys that May or June, Stalin had deleted a reproduction of Ilya Repin's famous canvas depicting Ivan's murder of his first son, presumably believing it to be gratuitous. Now, he deleted a similarly prejudicial line about Ivan's forces massacring the population of Kazan in 1552. Instead, he stressed the tsar's progressive transformation of the Russian national state into a multiethnic empire.[119]

Although not a total historical whitewash, this editing is best seen as at least a partial rehabilitation of Ivan the Terrible. Stalin confirmed the overall state-building lesson that the chapter was intended to convey by interpolating into the text a concluding line that credited Ivan with an epic sense of foresight. According to the general secretary, "He thus, as it were, completed the work, started by Ivan Kalita, of gathering together the scattered appanage principalities into one strong state." Such a positive assessment

FIGURE 3: Stalin's deletion of I. Repin's "Ivan the Terrible and His Son Ivan on 16 November 1581" (1883–1885), May-June 1937. RGASPI, f. 558, op. 3, d. 374, l. 109.

should not, however, be interpreted as characterizing Ivan as a singularly enlightened renaissance prince. Aside from leaving plenty of negative detail about Ivan's reign in the text, Stalin agreed with Shestakov that the tsar had completed the enserfment of the peasantry.[120]

Following the general secretary's lead, Zhdanov took steps to further rehabilitate the chapter's main protagonist. Deleting Shestakov's colloquial reference to Ivan as "the terrible tsar," Zhdanov insisted that the autocrat be referred to by his more traditional epithet. He also objected to the description of the Oprichnina guards as dressing exclusively in black and ordered the hyperbole stripped from the text. Finally, he toyed with the idea of reversing the order of the chapter's opening illustrations to foreground a noble portrait of the tsar by Viktor Vasnetsov—a decision he finalized in August 1937.[121] The end result was a depiction of the tsar who—like his ancestors—was brutal but historically progressive in his expansion of the Russian state. In aggregate, Stalin and Zhdanov characterized Ivan as anticipating what Marx termed the apogee of feudal power—absolutism.

Chapter 6: The Peasant Wars and Revolts of the Oppressed Peoples in the Seventeenth Century

Chapter 6 of Shestakov's history concerned Muscovy's long and difficult seventeenth century. According to the historian, the period began with a dynastic crisis, insofar as during the reign of Ivan the Terrible, the tsar had accidentally killed his first son, Ivan, and saw his second, Dmitry, die in childhood. This left his third son, the mentally disabled Fedor, to rely on the Oprichnik Boris Godunov to rule after Ivan's death in 1584. When Fedor died in 1598 without an heir, Godunov took the throne for himself.

Godunov's reign was disrupted first by natural disasters and then a series of peasant revolts. Then the Polish-Lithuanian Commonwealth challenged Godunov's rule by supporting a pretender to the throne who claimed to be Ivan's long-dead son Dmitry. When Godunov suddenly died in 1605, this pretender and his Polish allies occupied Moscow. According to Shestakov, False Dmitry's rule was no less turbulent than Godunov's: he was soon murdered, his Polish supporters exiled, and a boyar named Vasily Shuisky elected to the throne. Shuisky, in turn, was challenged by the peasant rebel Ivan Bolotnikov, whose uprising inspired similar revolts among non-Russian populations living along the Volga and in Siberia. Shuisky responded by suppressing Bolotnikov's rebellion and further intensifying the exploitative nature of serfdom.

Shortly thereafter, another pretender also claiming to be the dead Dmitry appeared in Muscovy with a large Polish army. Although he died soon thereafter, the Muscovite boyars felt so threatened by the ongoing peasant unrest that they deposed Shuisky, swore allegiance to the Polish-Lithuanian crown prince, and welcomed his forces into Moscow. This in turn triggered a national uprising against the Poles in 1611 under the leadership of the Nizhny Novgorod merchant Kuzma Minin and the provincial noble Dmitry Pozharsky. In 1612, the two expelled the Poles from Moscow; in 1613, they enabled Mikhail Romanov to be elected to the throne.

Tsar Mikhail and his heir Alexei faced continued peasant unrest during the decades that followed. According to Shestakov, multiple uprisings in 1648 triggered a further intensification of serfdom, which resulted in still more rebellions in both Russian and non-Russian areas. At the same time that peasants in Muscovy were challenging the tsar, peasants on the neighboring Ukrainian steppe were rebelling against their Polish-Lithuanian overlords. One such uprising was led in 1648 by the Cossack landowner Bogdan Khmelnitsky. When Khmelnitsky subsequently tried to come to terms with his Polish opponents, his peasants deserted him for the lowborn rebel Maxim Krivonos. Rejoining the struggle somewhat later in 1654, Khmelnitsky realized—according to Shestakov—that Ukraine had no independent future and that he would need to choose the lesser of two evils: annexation by his Russian coreligionists to the north or Polish Catholic suzerainty from the west. Khmelnitsky's decision to align with Muscovy, according to the text, secured for him and his Cossack elite not only security but also an array of privileges at the expense of their more humble brethren.

In the years that followed, Muscovite peasants continued to flee south to seek refuge with the Cossacks in the borderlands. Discontent among their ranks in 1670 led to a massive uprising under Stepan Razin. Such unrest led the state to dispatch governors and armed detachments to reenforce its rule over the Russian and non-Russian inhabitants of the Siberian steppe. Russian merchants and priests followed to complete this subjugation, exploiting the commoners' naïveté and extending the oppressive practice of serfdom whenever possible.

Shestakov then provided a broader analysis of the seventeenth-century Russian state. Agriculture formed the backbone of the economy and relied on the ever-increasing exploitation of the enserfed peasantry. Industry and trade were underdeveloped, in part because Russia lacked a merchant fleet and warmwater ports. In political terms, the Russian state functioned as it had for centuries. The tsar presided over a boyar council but made most decisions autocratically. A clumsy, slow, and corrupt bureaucracy administered the country in tandem with an array of equally corrupt regional governors. This led the state to rely on noble and economic elites to maintain its authority—a hallmark of Marx's estate-representative stage of feudalism that Shestakov referred to as the "landlords' and merchants' national state." The textbook then concluded the chapter with a discussion of seventeenth-century Russian culture. According to Shestakov, much of the country languished in what he described as backwardness. The church suppressed secular institutions such as the press and theater and instructed its subjects that "all power comes from God." As a result, commoners divided what little free time they had between the church and the tavern.

It is somewhat surprising that when Stalin turned to chapter 6, he did not object to either its length or its level of detail. Perhaps he felt that a focus on peasant exploitation, enserfment, and rebellion was necessary after the preceding chapters' undisguised focus on political elites and state building. That said, Stalin expressed concern over whether Shestakov had drawn the right Marxist-Leninist conclusions from the chapter's subject matter. This led him to clarify in several places that all seventeenth-century peasant rebels were to be considered monarchists rather than revolutionaries— they sought to overthrow Shuisky, for instance, "to put a 'good' tsar in his place," rather than to abolish the political system as a whole. What is more, even if they had wanted to alter the system, they would have failed because of their lack of visionary leadership and class consciousness. They were, in a sense, their own worst enemies. Stalin made this clear in his revisions to the discussion of Bolotnikov's defeat, where he deleted nearly a whole paragraph on the rebels' heroic last stand in order to characterize their defeat in much colder, more analytical terms. Their uprising's tragic end, according to Stalin, is not surprising. The peasants at that time had no such ally and leader as the working class. Besides, the peasants themselves lacked political consciousness. They did not fight against tsarism and landlordism, but against the bad tsar and the bad landlords. They wanted a "good" tsar and "good" landlords.

Stalin repeated this conclusion in regard to the Razin rebellion as well, using the same Marxist-Leninist argumentation:

> During the Razin rebellion, as was the case during Bolotnikov's rebellion, the peasants did not have an organized working class for their reliable ally. Nor did they understand the aim of the rebellion; they could wreck the landlords' mansions and kill the landlords, but they did not know what to do further, what new order to introduce. This was the cause of their weakness.

Stalin would repeat this thesis about the connection between societal change and education, class consciousness, and vanguard leadership again and again in subsequent chapters.

Aside from these ideological interpolations, Stalin made several other important clarifications in the chapter. First, he deleted a picture of a Siberian serf auction, apparently believing it to be superfluous alongside the chapter's already extensive attention to the peasantry's exploitation. Second, he deleted mention of Tatar and other non-Russian support for Bolotnikov as the rebel marched on Moscow, keeping Russian events at the center of the narrative. Zhdanov followed suit, deleting a picture of Khmelnitsky's campaign against the Poles to support the contention that the Cossack forces were unable to fend for themselves without Muscovite help. Third, Stalin underscored the role that the church played in preserving the Russian people's "backwardness"—a signal that the dictator no longer believed the church to be playing a progressive role in Muscovite history. Finally, Stalin rewrote Shestakov's moniker "the landlords' and merchants' national state" into "the Russian landlords' and merchants' state"—a correction that stressed both the ascendency of these economic groups and the Russian empire's newly multiethnic character.[122]

Chapter 7: Russia in the Eighteenth Century.
The Empire of Landlords and Merchants

Shestakov's seventh chapter surveyed the results of the so-called Petrine revolution over the course of the eighteenth century. He and his brigade began with Peter the Great and his wars against Russia's neighbors. According to the textbook, much of the impulse behind Peter's famous embassy to Europe stemmed from his struggle to expand and modernize his country's military capacity. Returning home to suppress a rebellion of his royal musketeers (the Streltsy), Peter reorganized his armed forces to attack Sweden and gain access to the Baltic Sea. Initially disastrous, this war led Peter to further reform his approach to military supply and provisioning. Increases in taxation and police control over the populace—particularly in the south and among the Bashkirs, according to Shestakov—were also by-products of Peter's wars. In 1703, he secured an outlet to the Gulf of Finland on the Neva and began construction of a new port and capital that involved the brutal exploitation of thousands of serfs. These wars, which would continue over the course of much of Peter's reign, involved repeated clashes with Sweden, the Ottoman empire, and Ukrainian Cossack forces under Ivan Mazepa. Victories at Poltava, Riga, and Reval offset a major defeat at the River Prut and the loss of a Russian foothold on the Black Sea at Azov.

Aside from his attention to Peter's campaigns, Shestakov also made a careful survey of the tsar's reforms, which were tied to his plans for the expansion of the realm. Better state administration required the restructuring of the bureaucracy. Regional governorships were likewise redesigned and redistricted. The power of the landowning nobility was strengthened when Peter granted the landlords ownership of their estates. Peter's other reforms were designed to encourage the country's modernization. He supported Russia's nascent industrialization by aiding in the establishment of mills and factories and by allowing entrepreneurs to employ unpaid serf labor—something that allowed them to become very rich. He also granted merchants the right of self-government in urban areas. Finally, Peter supported efforts to enlighten the empire's elites through the founding a newspaper and schools staffed by English, Dutch, and Swedish teachers.

According to Shestakov, Peter's brutal exploitation of the population resulted in widespread discontent and a series of popular uprisings. Kondraty Bulavin, for instance, led a Cossack rebellion in 1707–1709. His uprising, like those that preceded it, was mercilessly crushed. Such factors led Shestakov to summarize Peter's accomplishments as a bitter victory but not a pyrrhic one:

> Under the reign of Peter I, Russia made great progress; nevertheless, it remained a country in which serf oppression and the tyranny of the tsar reigned supreme. The Russian Empire was enlarged and strengthened at the cost of hundreds of thousands of toilers and the impoverishment of the entire people. Peter I did a great deal to create and strengthen the land-lords' and merchants' national state.

Peter, in other words, brought the Russian empire into the historical stage of development that Marx referred to as feudal absolutism, although this status was complicated by the persistent power of his noble and economic elites. Perhaps for this reason, Shestakov used the expression "the land-lords' and merchants' national state" to describe the Russian empire for the remainder of the chapter. This led him to pay more attention to the post-Petrine economic elite than to Empress Elizabeth and her reign. Catherine the Great's reign was also neglected, aside from her extension of additional rights and privileges to the landed nobility. Such concessions, designed to increase the authority of the state among its economic elites, aggravated the conditions of serfdom and led to an array of Cossack and peasant re-bellions, most notably under Emelian Pugachev in 1773. As in previous chapters, Shestakov and his brigade stressed the multiethnic nature of this ultimately unsuccessful uprising.

Chapter 7 concluded with a survey of the Russian empire's conquests during the Catherinian period. In the south, Russia annexed Crimea and Azov after buying off the local Crimean Tatar elite with noble titles and bribes. Wars then followed against the Ottoman empire under the leader-ship of Alexander Suvorov. At the same time, freebooting Cossack hosts were broken up and coopted into the empire. In the west, more wars were fought with Sweden, while Catherine colluded with Austria and Prussia to partition Poland, first in 1773 and then again in 1793 and 1795 in the wake of the Kosciuszko rebellion. In the east, Russian forces conquered what is present-day Kazakhstan, signaling a long new period of interethnic tension and popular rebellion against the Russian state.

When Stalin turned to the textbook's chapter on the eighteenth century, he approved of its characterization of Peter the Great as a western-izing reformer. This is clear from his editing that stressed that the Streltsy were members of the "old army" who had "demanded the restoration of the old customs." They were a "reactionary rebellion," according to Stalin, and opposed what the general secretary identified in Marxist terms as Peter's progressive modernization program. It is interesting in this connection to note that Stalin did not object to Shestakov's depiction of Peter as reliant on foreign advisors, technology, and administrative practices.[123] Indeed, when the text turned to Peter's establishment of public schools, Stalin even added Germans to the list of European instructors hired to staff the new institutions. Such foreign specialists apparently helped Peter win wars and modernize the country—something that Stalin saw as progressive in a Marxist sense.

Stalin's assessment of Peter as an important historical figure did not lead him to suppress Shestakov's discussion of the peasantry's deepen-ing impoverishment during his reign. In Marxist terms, these two aspects of the period were closely linked, after all. Perhaps unsurprisingly, when Stalin turned to the textbook's treatment of the Bulavin and Pugachev re-bellions, he explicitly connected the lessons of these failed peasant upris-ings to those detailed in earlier chapters. Although Shestakov was more explicit about the futility of Pugachev's rebellion than he had been about peasant uprisings earlier in the textbook, here too Stalin insistently reit-erated his position that all such movements were crippled by the lack of working class and party leadership.

Stalin's other corrections in regard to this period focused on terminol-ogy and style. Most notable is Stalin's transformation of Shestakov's de-scription of the post-Petrine years from "the landlords' and merchants' national state" to "the landlords' and merchants' state." Similar to a cor-rection he made in chapter 6, this editing was also related to the subtitle of chapter 7, "The Empire of the Landlords and Merchants," and stressed two major historical shifts: the ruling class's transformation from a feudal elite to a more protocapitalist one and Russia's evolution from a national state to an imperial one.

Stalin made few changes to the second part of the chapter, seemingly content to essentially ignore Elizabeth and Catherine. Pausing briefly on the latter's cooption of Crimea, he drew attention to how the "traitorous" khan and his nobles had been induced to betray their common-born kin in exchange for favorable terms. This editing evoked Stalin's and Zhdanov's stress on unity in earlier chapters and suggests that they believed the Crimean Tatars' internal discord to have left them vulnerable to Russian imperialism. (Zhdanov would make two further corrections in this regard elsewhere in the chapter, noting that a lack of unity had also undermined Pugachev's movement and independent Poland.)

This is not to say, of course, that Stalin assumed an entirely apologetic position in regard to eighteenth-century tsarist imperialism. As previously noted, Stalin did not alter Shestakov's broad condemnation of the violence and exploitation inherent within the system. That said, if Shestakov concluded his chapter by listing the peoples that Russia had colonized over the course of the eighteenth century, Stalin now took objection to this formulation. According to the general secretary, it was the Russian tsar, not the Russian people, who indulged in this imperialism. This distinction between the ruling elite and the rest of the society would become increasingly important to Stalin in the following several chapters.

Chapter 8: Tsarist Russia—The Gendarme of Europe

Chapter 8 examined the period between the late eighteenth century and the mid-nineteenth century—a time of revolution and conservative reaction. Shestakov and his brigade began by surveying the French Revolution of 1789. A popular rebellion of urban and rural commoners, it was co-opted by the bourgeoisie, who executed King Louis XVI and consolidated power within the new republic. According to Shestakov, as the revolution became more radical, power was seized by the Jacobins, an alliance of petty bourgeois artisans and peasants. Opposition at home and abroad led the Jacobins to retaliate with a campaign of terror against perceived enemies of the people.[124] Large landholdings were liquidated and turned over to the newly emancipated peasantry. In time, this period of revolution shifted toward reaction and the Jacobins were overthrown by the bourgeoisie. Such a counterrevolution was possible, according to Shestakov, because the French working class was weak and disorganized and because the peasants were willing to support the bourgeoisie in exchange for land.

Catherine the Great found the events of 1789 threatening and offered Louis XVI and his court refuge in Russia. She suppressed domestic sympathy for the revolution, supported Austria and Prussia in their campaigns against republican France and even considered going to war herself. These plans were realized by her heir, Paul I, who dispatched an army under Suvorov to crush the revolution. Although Suvorov's campaign proved inconclusive, an opportunity for change appeared when Napoleon Bonaparte seized supreme power for himself. According to Shestakov, Paul encouraged Napoleon to declare himself emperor and offered him an alliance when he broke off relations with Great Britain. This led to Paul's assassination at the hands of his nobles, who plotted against him with the aid of the British ambassador.

Paul's heir, Alexander I, began his reign with a series of regional and European conflicts. Renewing ties with Britain, he clashed with Napoleon in an unsuccessful war that forced him to recognize French primacy on the continent. Alexander then shifted to expand his imperial domain at the expense of Sweden and the Ottoman empire. According to Shestakov, Alexander's modus vivendi with Napoleon faltered as his nobility expressed their distaste for revolutionary France and his merchants sought closer ties with Britain. Hostilities with France resumed in 1812, when Napoleon invaded Russia. Immediately, the textbook averred, the whole country rose to repulse the French invaders. Despite massive losses, the Russian army held its ground in engagements such as the Battle of Borodino. And although the Russian commander, Mikhail Kutuzov, subsequently ceded first the battlefield and then Moscow to the French, the latter were forced to retreat that winter after a fire destroyed much of the city. Russian forces then counterattacked and drove Napoleon's Grande Armée out of Russia and back across Europe to Paris. Alexander and his allies then restored monarchical rule where Napoleon had toppled it and formed the Holy Alliance to defend the new status quo.

In the wake of this war, highborn Russian officers took note of how well their European peers lived. Progressive elements recognized the Russian system to be despotic and oppressive, particularly in its maintenance of serfdom. Dissident groups formed in St. Petersburg and Ukraine; according to Shestakov, they hesitated to call for a mass uprising to overturn the system and instead planned to use the military to implement reform. These groups mutinied in December 1825 during a brief interregnum that followed Alexander's death. Although the militants in St. Petersburg enjoyed the support of the urban population, they failed to take advantage it and were quickly suppressed. The militants in the south fared no better. According to Shestakov, the failure of the Decembrists to coordinate their uprising with the common people explained their defeat. That said, their example proved important to subsequent generations of revolutionaries.

Nicholas I, Alexander I's heir, responded to the Decembrist revolt with police repression. His regime's treatment of the peasantry was particularly brutal. According to Shestakov, over the following twenty-five years, this oppression would trigger over a thousand peasant uprisings and the murders of hundreds of landlords. Tsarist repression would also affect elites, such as the poets Alexander Pushkin and Mikhail Lermontov, the writers Nikolai Gogol and Vissarion Belinsky, and the composer Mikhail Glinka. Glinka and the Ukrainian writer Taras Shevchenko were especially known for their celebration of the common people in ways that that did not meet with the approval of the tsar or his inner circle.[125]

Nicholas's repression at home was matched by his brutality in the Caucasus. There, he was challenged by Shamil, a leader of the region's Muslim highlander peoples, who formed an independent state and army to resist Russian colonization. According to Shestakov, the peasants of the Caucasus provided Shamil with dogged support, whether in the Gury region and among the Cherkess, or further south, in present-day Armenia and Azerbaidzhan. After some twenty-five years, however, Russian forces managed to defeat Shamil by occupying the Caucasus and buying off his supporters among the highlander elders.

Shestakov and his brigade then shifted focus back to France to describe how the country's industrialization catalyzed social unrest in 1848. Popular protest turned into street fighting between workers and the forces deployed by the bourgeoisie. Turmoil spread across Europe, forcing Nicholas to send troops into Austro-Hungary to prop up the Habsburg monarchy. This unrest laid the groundwork for an extended discussion devoted to Karl Marx and Friedrich Engels, who were formulating a new approach to revolution. According to these thinkers, it was the working class that could form a revolutionary force educated and organized enough to overthrow the bourgeoisie, establish a dictatorship of the proletariat, and build a new communist society.

The chapter concluded with a discussion of imperial Russia at the end of Nicholas's reign. Halting industrialization, impeded by the persistence of serfdom, left the country vulnerable when Nicholas attempted to expand his empire south into the lands of the Ottoman empire. Britain and France, eager to put Russia in its place, came to the Ottomans' aid and dealt Russia an embarrassing defeat in what became known as the Crimean War. Despite the heroic action of Russia's armies, the empire was forced to sue for peace. According to Shestakov, this "revealed to the whole world the extreme backwardness of serf Russia."

Inasmuch as Nicholas died at the end of the Crimean War, resolution of this domestic crisis fell to his son, Alexander II, who proposed that the landowners emancipate their serfs themselves rather than wait for a social explosion that might threaten the entire system. In this, Alexander was responding to pressure not only from the impoverished peasantry but also from a new generation of revolutionaries such as Herzen, who agitated on behalf of the serfs.

When Stalin turned to Shestakov's eighth chapter, his editing reflected continuing concerns from earlier sections. A stickler for terminology, he stressed the distinction between the propertied elites who led the first stages of the French Revolution and the Jacobins who ended up in power—the "bourgeois revolutionaries" and the "petty bourgeois democrats," respectively. According to Stalin, the Jacobins, while radical,

> were not consistent revolutionaries. As petty-bourgeois democrats, they were in favor of the private ownership of the land, factories and mines. They prohibited the workers from going on strike and fighting against the capitalists.

In Stalin's mind, the Jacobins' shortcomings, along with the disorganization of the working class, ultimately allowed the bourgeoisie to defeat them both.

Stalin was more satisfied with Shestakov's treatment of the War of 1812. He cut a few elements of hyperbole in the text, explained why Kutuzov had abandoned Moscow, and clarified the reactionary nature of Alexander's Holy Alliance after the war's conclusion. Similar concerns over hyperbole governed Stalin's editing of the chapter's discussion of the Decembrists and Nicholas's establishment of a well-ordered police state. Here, the general secretary also deleted Shestakov's quantification of the peasant unrest, perhaps being unimpressed by the number of uprisings that took place over the course of a quarter century.

In Shestakov's description of Nicholas's campaign against Shamil in the Caucasus, Stalin deleted an extended discussion of the popular support that the rebel imam enjoyed in Gury, among the Cherkess, and in Azerbaidzhan and Armenia. Curiously, Stalin did not interpolate into the discussion any Marxist-Leninist explanation for the eventual defeat of this twenty-five-year insurgency that might have focused either on poor organization or a lack of working-class leadership. This suggests that Stalin saw this episode as an example of anticolonial resistance to Russian imperialism rather than a more modern, revolutionary movement.

True to form, when Stalin turned to the Parisian unrest of 1848, he resumed his Marxist-Leninist stress on the constituent elements of modern revolutions. Accordingly, he clarified that the uprising had failed both because the workers had been poorly organized and armed and because "the peasants had failed to come to their aid." Stressing the breadth of the unrest in Europe, he deleted personal information about Marx's family life to keep the spotlight on his ideological work.

Stalin's last revisions to the chapter continued to focus on the sobriety of the narrative. In regard to Shestakov's discussion of Herzen, for instance, Stalin clarified that he was a "bourgeois democratic" revolutionary interested in the plight of the peasantry rather than a Marxist focusing on the working class. Zhdanov followed up on Stalin's editing with the same sort of pedantic concerns, presumably aided by his professional consultants. According to Zhdanov, Paul had not actually urged Napoleon to declare himself emperor, the Russian army had not stood its ground at Borodino, and there was no need for the hyperbolic claim that the Crimean War had demonstrated the country's backwardness "to the whole world." Such editorial restraint did not, however, stop Zhdanov from making sure that the textbook explicitly stated that Nicholas I's reactionary politics earned Russia the moniker "the gendarme of Europe."[126]

Chapter 9: The Growth of Capitalism in Tsarist Russia

Shestakov began chapter 9 with tsar Alexander II's decision in 1861 to emancipate the serfs. He quickly clarified that although this imperial edict freed the peasantry from bondage, it also stripped them of much of the land that they had traditionally farmed, leaving them even more impoverished than before. The peasants found this unfair and rose in protest, forcing the government to deploy troops to suppress the uprisings. Shestakov illustrated his point by describing the revolt of a peasant named Anton Petrov, who led his village into rebellion near Kazan—an event that ultimately cost Petrov and about three hundred of his neighbors their lives. Other Russian revolutionaries followed Herzen in condemning this state of affairs—Nikolai Chernyshevsky, Nikolai Nekrasov, and others. Chernyshevsky endured nineteen years in prison and exile for his efforts to inspire the peasantry to protest their lot in life.[127]

Shestakov then turned to detail the postemancipation period of the so-called Great Reforms. Although the Zemstvo initiative of 1864 ostensibly opened up municipal governance to popular democratic participation, the textbook noted that the voting franchise was weighted to guarantee de facto control to the landlords. The military reforms of 1874 lightened the burden of army service somewhat but did not alter the fact that virtually all the country's soldiers were drawn from the peasantry. In other words, little changed as a result of the Great Reforms, according to Shestakov, aside from the fact that emancipation freed up laborers to work in the country's growing industrial economy.

Alexander's liberalism was likewise called into question by his reaction to the Polish rebellion of 1863, when Poles from across the socioeconomic spectrum attempted to throw off Russian rule. Alexander suppressed the rebels harshly, hanging their leaders and exiling more than a hundred thousand people to Siberia. Once the uprising was defeated, the tsar attempted to divide Polish society against itself, according to Shestakov, by allowing the peasantry to buy land from their former masters at advantageous prices.

At the same time that Alexander was suppressing the Poles, he was also setting his sights on Central Asia. Over the course of thirty years, Russian troops colonized the territory of present-day Kazakhstan, Turkmenistan, Uzbekistan, Tadzhikistan, and Kyrgyzstan. Less successful wars were waged against the Ottoman empire for still more territory. Alexander treated these new possessions as colonies and dispatched officials and merchants to collect taxes, establish a cotton-growing monoculture and swamp local markets with cheap Russian goods. Local uprisings against this imperialism were suppressed by force.

Shestakov then shifted focus back to Marx and Engels, introduced in the preceding chapter. According to the textbook, these communist ideologists understood that a revolutionary workers' uprising would require a party to coordinate the struggle. This led them to convene the First International. Shestakov noted that Marx and Engels denounced those revolutionaries who believed that socialism could be achieved without the violent overthrow of the bourgeoisie or that such a revolution did not have to be worker led. Such beliefs, according to Marx and Engels, merely reinforced the capitalist system.

Even as Marx and Engels refined this analysis, Parisian workers rose in rebellion at the conclusion of the Franco-Prussian War in 1871. Although the bourgeoisie tried to co-opt this revolution as they had in 1789, the radicals retained the initiative and set up a government called the Commune that turned the factories over to the workers and transformed churches into community centers. From London, Marx and Engels called upon the Commune to seize Versailles, where the bourgeoisie had taken shelter. Delays in the transmission of this message allowed Paris to be encircled, however, by the forces of the bourgeoisie and their Prussian allies. In the ensuing battle, tens of thousands of Communards were killed and many more imprisoned. Shestakov concluded that, although the Commune had been a failure, it marked the first international revolutionary workers' association and provided a model for further activism.

Turning their focus back to Russia, Shestakov and his brigade outlined the growth of the empire's capitalist economy after 1861. In rural regions, poor and middling peasants found themselves exploited both by the landlords and an emergent group of prosperous peasants known as kulaks. Those ruined by this economy migrated to the cities to work in factories or to the Siberian steppe to eke out an existence in agriculture. Obliquely invoking Marx and Engels, Shestakov noted that those in industry began organizing against their oppressors faster than those who remained on the land. Mainstream Russian society learned about the dignified poverty of the peasantry from elite writers, artists, and composers such as Lev Tolstoi, Ilya Repin, Modest Mussorgsky, and Nikolai Rimsky-Korsakov.[128]

According to Shestakov, as Russia's impoverished masses became restless, a group of revolutionaries known as the Narodniki emerged. Dismissing the workers' potential to contribute to a successful uprising, they concentrated their agitational work on the peasant village. When the peasantry failed to respond to the Narodniki's calls for revolution, the radicals changed tactics and launched a campaign of terrorism targeting imperial officials. Although they eventually succeeded in assassinating Alexander II in 1881, their tactics, according to Shestakov, made conditions in Russia worse. A follow-up attempt to kill the new tsar, Alexander III, in 1887—a plot involving Vladimir Lenin's older brother, among others—also ended in failure. Shestakov concluded that the Narodniki had undermined the cause of revolution in three ways: by underestimating the workers' revolutionary potential, by impeding the formation of a mass party, and by focusing their wrath on individual exploiters rather than the exploitative class as a whole.

Vladimir Lenin was only seventeen at the time of his brother's conviction and execution. Learning from his brother's error, he concluded that only an organized working-class movement might be able to lead the peasantry to overthrow tsarism. At this time, Marxist discussion circles had formed in major Russian cities, inspired by the exiled revolutionary Georgy Plekhanov and his Emancipation of Labor group. First Lenin and then Stalin joined this nascent party during the 1890s and concentrated on organizing workers, peasants, and the non-Russian peoples. According to Shestakov, Lenin worked in St. Petersburg to help found what would later become the Bolshevik party, while at the same time denouncing the Narodniki and others who failed to understand Marx's teachings on revolutionary struggle. After being arrested, Lenin spent time in internal exile before moving abroad to found the party newspaper ISKRA. In the meantime, Stalin worked to organize workers in the Caucasus. According to Shestakov, Stalin behaved heroically during a police massacre of striking workers in 1902; surviving arrest, prison, and exile, he then returned to Transcaucasia to help Lenin lead the Revolution of 1905.

When Stalin turned to chapter 9, he rejected Shestakov's title for the chapter—"Tsarist Russia. A Capitalist Country"— to stress that the empire was merely transitioning toward a modern economy. He then toned down Shestakov's already-sober appraisal of the 1861 emancipation of the serfs to stress that Alexander II made his proclamation only in order to forestall the imminent threat of a full-scale peasant rebellion. Commenting on the unrest that followed, he clarified that the risings were provoked by a long-standing desire for land rather than disappointment over the proclamation itself.

When the narrative shifted to a discussion of the revolutionaries of the 1860s and 1870s, Stalin felt it important to clarify that Chernyshevsky and Nekrasov had been "revolutionary democrats"—by which he meant Narodniki—and not true revolutionaries in the Marxist sense. Later in the chapter, the general secretary would launch an all-out assault on the Narodniki, following a line of attack initiated by Lenin some forty years earlier. Criticizing the revolutionaries for their initial focus on the village, Stalin questioned whether any peasant revolution would have been possible without an alliance with the working class. Even worse was Narodniki's willingness to resort to political terror when the peasantry proved unwilling to rise up on its own. Elaborating on Shestakov's point about the ineffectiveness of terrorism, Stalin argued that this tactic "led to no improvement what[so]ever. The place of the assassinated tsar or minister was taken by another, more cruel than the first." Aside from this, Stalin strengthened the textbook's assessment of the damage that the Narodniki had done to the revolutionary cause. They had diverted popular attention away from the oppressors responsible for society's suffering, impeded the formation of a Marxist workers party and stymied work on a worker-peasant alliance.

Stalin then turned to the textbook's section on the 1863 Polish rebellion. Here, he stressed that it was the Polish nobility that had led the uprising and that it assumed significant proportions only near Warsaw. Equally notable were Stalin's revisions to the textbook's description of the reprisals that followed, which deemphasized official efforts to pit the Polish peasantry against their "social betters" and exile former rebels to Siberia.

When Stalin turned to the textbook's account of the Paris Commune, he stressed the degree to which the revolution had been initiated by the petty bourgeoisie rather than by the more affluent bourgeoisie. He then seconded Shestakov's positive assessment of the petty bourgeoisie's establishment of the Commune and socialization of the means of production. That said, Stalin blamed the petty bourgeoisie for their failure to challenge the bourgeoisie at Versailles—they were apparently "wavering revolutionaries" who naively "believed in the 'good intentions'" of their social betters. This lack of revolutionary class consciousness played a major role in the downfall of the Commune, as did its members' failure to ally with the peasantry.

Equally important, according to Stalin, was the collective's lack of organized leadership: "The Paris Commune was crushed because the workers still lacked a Marxian revolutionary party of their own capable of leading them unwaveringly against the bourgeoisie."

Turning back to the subject of worker unrest in Russia on the eve of Lenin's appearance in St. Petersburg, Stalin took note of a major strike in 1885. This action had been dramatic enough, according to the general secretary, to frighten the tsarist government into passing legislation designed to afford workers some protection on the shop floor. This apparently stimulated interest among the workers in collective struggle, setting the stage for the organizational initiatives of the 1890s.

Lenin, in Stalin's mind, deserved credit for transforming Plekhanov's Emancipation of Labor group from a debate club into a mass revolutionary movement. In this vein, he stressed Lenin's work among the workers and peasants of St. Petersburg but also deleted apparently exaggerated mention of his appeals to non-Russians suffering from colonial oppression. More dramatically, Stalin almost completely eliminated the textbook's discussion of his own early tenure in the party. Denying that he had served as Lenin's lieutenant during the earliest days of the Bolshevik movement, Stalin also deleted a picture of his childhood home and nearly a page of biographical detail on his role in the prerevolutionary Caucasian underground. Replacing this entire subsection with a modest statement about labor militancy in the region, the general secretary then noted laconically that it was here in 1898 that "Comrade Stalin, Lenin's pupil, carried on his revolutionary work."

Zhdanov also played a significant role in editing chapter 9, probably in consultation with his historical consultants. He clarified in an early passage, for instance, that the 1864 Zemstvo reforms had given disproportionate power not only to the rural gentry but to urban merchants and industrialists as well. In the textbook's discussion of the tsarist state's attempt to drive a wedge between Polish peasants and their noble landlords, Zhdanov scaled back the terms under which the former serfs were allowed to buy land from their former masters. He similarly nuanced Shestakov's treatment of the tsar's wars of conquest against the Ottoman empire during the latter half of the nineteenth century, noting that Russian underdevelopment made them needlessly costly. Zhdanov also proposed that Borodin and Tchaikovsky needed to be included in the textbook's list of composers who celebrated peasant and folkloric traditions.

Elsewhere, Zhdanov showed a different sort of concern over Shesta- kov's text, particularly in regard to its harsh characterization of tsarist colonial policy in Central Asia. Leaving the textbook's discussion of the establishment of a cotton-based economy in place, he deleted mention of how the Uzbeks, Tadzhiks, and others had been coerced into abandoning their cultivation of cereal crops. He likewise struck out detail on how Rus- sian manufacturing had been allowed to crowd out locally produced goods in cities like Bukhara and Samarkand. These corrections are eye-catching, insofar as neither Stalin nor Zhdanov denied or downplayed the oppres- sive nature of tsarist imperialism. Instead, it would appear that Zhdanov was uncomfortable with the degree to which the Russian colonial focus on cotton anticipated the USSR's pursuit of a similarly monocultural economy in Central Asia.

Chapter 10: The First Bourgeois Revolution in Russia

Shestakov's tenth chapter on the 1905 revolution began with a survey of strike activity at the turn of the twentieth century. The textbook noted that Lenin used ISKRA to call for the peasants to unite in a common strug- gle with the workers. This agitation was opposed by another party, the Socialist-Revolutionaries, who, apparently supported the interests of the prosperous kulaks and pursued a program like that of the Narodniki.

At the same time, Lenin was also struggling to reorganize the Rus- sian Social-Democratic Labor Party (RSDLP), out of which the Bolsheviks would later emerge. According to Shestakov, Lenin's program, approved by the RSDLP's second congress, called for socialism to be built by overthrow- ing the tsar, guaranteeing the workers an eight-hour day, and abolishing the vestiges of serfdom in the countryside. This required the creation of a van- guard party, staffed by committed revolutionaries. In this, Lenin faced op- position from other RSDLP delegates, who felt that the party should admit a wider array of people—something that Lenin believed would undermine the movement. Lenin's demand that the revolutionary workers ally with the peasantry was also challenged by RSDLP delegates like Lev Trotsky and Yuly Martov, who contended that the workers should ally instead with the bourgeoisie. Lenin won the debates, allowing his majority to claim the sobriquet "Bolsheviks." His RSDLP opponents, in the minority, became known as the "Mensheviks." Stalin, Shestakov noted, was unable to take part in the congress, insofar as he spent 1903 in prison.

The 1905 revolution itself was triggered by the disastrous Russo-Japanese War. This fiasco was then compounded in early January 1905, when workers at the Putilov plant in St. Petersburg went on strike. At the urging of Father Georgy Gapon—a police provocateur, according to Shestakov—they marched on the Winter Palace to present their demands to the tsar. The Bolsheviks regarded this action as too mild but accompanied the strikers anyway. A massacre followed, which provoked a general strike and the erection of barricades in major cities.

As the standoff mounted that spring, workers in Ivanovo-Voznesensk formed a local council, or soviet, to coordinate their activism. Although this strike crumbled after the regional governor threatened to execute the protestors, Shestakov claimed that other soviets quickly formed elsewhere with Bolsheviks at the helm. This urban activism was matched by risings in the countryside, where peasants threatened to seize land and estates.

Lenin, who was living abroad at the time, called upon the workers to rise up. Shestakov illustrated Lenin's determination to arm the workers by noting that he even attempted to send a shipload of rifles to the rebels. Later, when the crew of the battleship Potemkin mutinied on the Black Sea, Lenin again tried to aid the insurrectionists by dispatching Bolsheviks to lead them. At the RSDLP's third congress in London in April 1905, Lenin rallied the party around his calls for an armed uprising and instructed party activists to forge an alliance between the workers and peasants to take power.

That fall, Russia was brought to a standstill by another general strike. Soviets coordinated the construction of barricades in a variety of cities under Bolshevik leadership. That said, the workers lacked the numbers or the arms necessary to overthrow the tsar. Nicholas too lacked the troops needed to suppress the rebels. This led the tsar to issue a manifesto promising civil rights and popular representation to divide the ranks of the opposition.

Unfooled by the tsar's promises, the Bolsheviks continued to agitate for an armed uprising. Lenin and Stalin met for the first time in December 1905 as the party planned its seizure of power. In Moscow, a number of worker districts went into open rebellion, assisted by local peasants, women, and even children. Lenin called upon the workers of St. Petersburg to rebel as well, only to see his call undermined there by Mensheviks under Trotsky and the Socialists-Revolutionaries (SRs), who advocated for an alliance with the bourgeoisie instead. This was a foolish decision, according to Shestakov, as the bourgeoisie had already conspired with the tsar to suppress the workers' and peasants' rebellions. This treachery in St. Petersburg doomed the Moscow uprising, which the tsar crushed in a bloody massacre that left many dead and many others sentenced to hang.

In the countryside, the peasants continued to rise, clashing with the authorities and landlords more than seven thousand times between 1905 and 1907. In time, however, Nicholas was able to regain control over rural Russia by the use of punitive military raids. According to Shestakov, much the same happened among the non-Russian peoples in Ukraine, Finland, and the Caucasus, where local workers rebelled under the leadership of their Russian compatriots. As in the central Russian regions, the provincial non-Russian bourgeoisie sided with the tsar and enabled Nicholas to eventually divide and conquer the opposition. Elements of the tsarist navy mutinied in 1906 but were unable to catalyze a mass uprising elsewhere in the Baltic fleet. As these rebellions faltered, the tsar and his prime minister Petr Stolypin hunted down those who had sided with the revolution.

At the same time that Nicholas was suppressing these revolutionaries by force, he was also convening a series of Dumas that allowed him to reinforce the tsarist system instead of reforming it. In urban areas, according to Shestakov, the domestic and foreign bourgeoisie profited from their support of the tsar; in rural areas, the landlords and their kulak allies consolidated their hold on the land. As a result, the economy boomed after 1907, although Russia remained underdeveloped and dependent on foreign capital.

After the failure of the revolution, Lenin escaped abroad, almost drowning as he fled to the ship that was to carry him back into exile. Stalin, for his part, was arrested and exiled to Siberia multiple times during these years, each time escaping to return to St. Petersburg. Together, Lenin and Stalin rebuilt the Bolshevik party organization as they waited for another revolutionary opportunity. That moment came in 1912, when British capitalists ordered the shooting of striking workers in the Lena goldfields. This triggered a renewed wave of strikes and peasant uprisings.

Amid this unrest, Lenin gathered his Bolshevik followers in Prague to confront the Mensheviks and others in the RSDRP who were not committed to the idea of revolution. Forming an independent party, Lenin's Bolsheviks proposed to lead the workers in conjunction with the peasantry to overthrow the tsar, improve industrial conditions and transfer agricultural land to those who worked it. This new militant party campaigned both underground and legally in party newspapers to educate the workers and develop their sense of class consciousness. Lenin's efforts abroad were matched by that of a half dozen prominent Bolsheviks on the ground in Russia. According to Shestakov, by 1914 a new revolutionary scenario was in the process of catalyzing—something that the tsarist government managed to supress only with the storm of patriotic jingoism that accompanied its entrance into World War I.

Stalin expressed considerable concern about Shestakov's tenth chapter when he turned to edit the SHORT HISTORY in July 1937. He began with its title—"The First Russian Revolution"—and revised it into "The First Bourgeois Revolution in Russia" to stress that this social explosion, like those in France in 1789 and 1848, signaled a shift from the feudal period into capitalism rather than socialism. He also corrected the first section's chronological dating of the revolution to clarify that the unrest concerned more than just 1905. Stalin accepted Shestakov's prehistory of the crisis but stressed the early duplicity of the Bolsheviks' rivals, especially the SRs, who he alleged were only "pretending to champion the interests of the peasants" while actually supporting the rural kulak bourgeoisie.

Stalin also thoroughly revised Shestakov's account of Lenin's ambitions for the RSDLP at its second congress. Agreeing that the immediate goal was the overthrow of tsar, the general secretary clarified in line with Marxist-Leninist theory that Nicholas's regime was to be replaced by a democratic republic—a bourgeois parliamentary system that would industrialize the country in the context of capitalism before being overthrown by a socialist one. During this democratic phase, the party would guarantee its urban constituents an eight-hour workday, cede its peasant supporters confiscated land, and take advantage of the free press to raise these constituents' class consciousness. To accomplish this objective, Stalin also clarified Lenin's thoughts on RSDLP party norms. As the vanguard of the workers' movement, the party had to be made up of proven activists. This Stalin contrasted to a proposal he attributed to Trotsky and Martov, according to which party membership was to be open to all well-wishers—even those who did not intend to abide by the party's program or submit to its discipline. Stalin's discussion of Lenin's position improved upon Shestakov's, clarifying Lenin's objections to granting RSDLP membership to those who were unreliable or uncommitted to the cause of the revolution.

In Stalin's editing of the narrative on the 1904–1905 Russo-Japanese War, he made several alterations to the text in order to characterize the army and navy as representing the tsarist state rather than Russia per se—changes that blamed the government rather than the people for subsequent disasters at the front. Segueing to Bloody Sunday in January 1905, Stalin agreed with Shestakov that Gapon was a police informer, adding cynically that the priest's "secret intention was to cause bloodshed and so weaken the labour movement." He also deleted Shestakov's mention of Bolshevik participation in the march in order to distance the party from complicity in the fiasco.

Having objected to the text's treatment of Lenin at the Second Party Congress in 1903, Stalin raised fewer objections to Shestakov's description of the party leader during the revolution in 1905. Stalin did, however, delete discussion of Lenin's early demands from abroad for an uprising and his attempts to provide arms to the rebels and leadership to the mutinous sailors. Such editing should not be understood as questioning Lenin's commitment to revolution; instead, Stalin likely wanted to focus on Lenin's successes rather than his failures.

Stalin made few corrections to the textbook's factual accounting of 1905, aside from its treatment of the Moscow uprising. Improving the readability of this section, Stalin first deleted two instances of hyperbole—a description of the Bolshevik Mikhail Frunze as "fiery" and mention of children as taking part in the defense of working-class districts. Second, he cut mention of a lesser-known Bolshevik activist—Zinovy Litvin-Sedoi—in order to generalize about the party's leadership of the uprising.[129] Third, he added mention of Admiral Fedor Dubasov, the notorious tsarist officer who put down the Moscow uprising with such bloodshed. Fourth, Stalin sought to explain how the tsar had rallied his demoralized troops to crush the revolution by stressing that his hasty exit from the Russo-Japanese War had temporarily bolstered morale within the ranks. Stalin's final intervention in the textbook's discussion of popular unrest in 1905 concerned uprisings in the non-Russian regions. Shestakov, as already detailed, credited Russian workers with the leadership of these protest actions. Stalin reversed this and argued that the non-Russian restiveness was actually homegrown. At first glance, this decision would seem to suggest that Stalin wished to recognize these militants for their initiative in Ukraine, the Caucasus, and elsewhere. That said, Stalin's editing here should probably be read as less congratulatory. After all, the general secretary is known to have believed that the 1905 revolution failed in part because of the lack of coordination between rebellions in the non-Russian regions and those in more central areas of the empire. In other words, Stalin's crediting of non-Russian militants for their uprisings was a way of displacing blame more than it was a recognition of their service and sacrifice.[130]

Nearing the end of Shestakov's narration of the 1905 revolution, Stalin found the textbook to be utterly inadequate in its analysis of the reasons behind the Bolsheviks' defeat. This led him to insert a whole paragraph providing a detailed postmortem on the Revolution of 1905. According to the general secretary, the first reason for the failure of the revolution was the weakness of the worker-peasant alliance. Although the peasants were apparently willing to work with the workers, they remained monarchists at heart and hesitated to commit to the revolution. As a result, they lent their support to the SRs instead of the Bolsheviks. The second reason, Stalin continued, was confusion over leadership within the workers' ranks. Some workers followed the Bolsheviks, but others supported the Mensheviks and their treacherous bid to find common cause with the bourgeoisie. The third reason stemmed from the tsar's decisive action in concluding the Russo-Japanese War—something that cost Russia dearly on the international scene but allowed him to redeploy the army to strengthen his position at home.

Such findings clarified 1905 and set up the chapter's conclusion regarding the Bolshevik party's subsequent efforts to rebuild and break with the Mensheviks. For that reason, Stalin's editing in the rest of the chapter was generally quite superficial. First, he deleted the text's superfluous account of Lenin's brush with death while escaping into exile. Second, he struck a gratuitous description of himself as Lenin's "beloved friend." And third, he added the name of a female Old Bolshevik—Yelena Stassova—to the textbook's list of Bolshevik activists during the revolutionary period and deleted Nadezhda Krupskaia's appellation as "Lenin's wife."[131]

In his revisions that followed, Zhdanov did little aside from supporting Stalin's editorial interventions, whether in regard to the 1903 party congress, the tsarist army during 1905, or events during the First Russian Revolution such as peasant land seizures or poorly organized sailor mutinies. Toward the end of the chapter, he suppled several lines of text to explain why the Russian economy remained underdeveloped and dependent on foreign capital despite rapid growth between 1907 and 1913. Aside from that, Zhdanov's editorial work reflected prosaic writerly concerns stressing word economy and pacing. As in previous chapters, it was Stalin's interventions that determined how the chapter's thesis and internal argumentation was to be finalized.

Chapter 11: The Second Bourgeois Revolution in Russia

Shestakov began chapter 11 by describing the context within which World War I erupted in August 1914. According to the text, the largest capitalist powers found themselves locked in an increasingly aggressive, imperialistic competition for new territories and markets. Germany, a relative latecomer to the Great Game, looked to challenge Great Britain, France, and Russia for their colonial possessions. Soon, two blocks had developed—the Entente, consisting of Britain, France, and Russia, as well as Japan and the United States, and the Central Powers, consisting of Germany, Austro-Hungary, Bulgaria, and the Ottoman Empire. Eager for a predatory war of conquest, the governing elites of each country publicly represented the conflict that erupted in 1914 as defensive in order to avoid alienating those who were to do the fighting and dying. In Russia, the tsarist government was aided by the Mensheviks and SRs, whose betrayal of the masses was akin to that of the social democratic parties of the Second International elsewhere in Europe.

Shestakov spent considerable time outlining the devastating economic and social costs of the war. Part of the reason for these losses was chronic Russian underdevelopment. That said, the textbook made it clear that the defeats that the Russian army suffered were also due to treachery within the general staff, the government, and the imperial household.

The betrayal of the Mensheviks and SRs meant that in Russia only the

Bolsheviks opposed the war. Lenin and Stalin's party, according to Shestakov, called upon the workers and peasants to reject the "patriotic" calls of the Mensheviks and their capitalist paymasters and transform the world war into a revolutionary one. This was difficult, however, as Lenin was in foreign exile and Stalin, Molotov, Sverdlov, and many other Bolshevik leaders languished in Siberia. Nevertheless, Lenin and Stalin remained committed to the cause and rallied the Russian workers to revolution. Each year, more workers went on strike and more peasants rose in protest. Non-Russians toiling in the empire's colonies likewise rebelled. Even Russian soldiers at the front began to refuse to fight, choosing to fraternize with their German and Austrian opponents instead.

By early 1917, the tsarist state was overwhelmed by setbacks both at the front and at home. Some of Nicholas's advisers quietly recommended that he conclude a separate peace with the Germans and then use the army to crush restive Russian elements as he had in 1905. At the same time, the bourgeoisie and its leaders Pavel Miliukov and Alexander Guchkov, who had until that point supported Nicholas, began plotting to remove him in order to prevent a revolution and the loss of the war. According to Shestakov, both conspiracies were swept away that February when the workers and peasants rebelled under the leadership of the Bolsheviks to overthrow the monarchy themselves. Nicholas was arrested and exiled to Ekaterinburg, where he and his family were eventually executed after attempting to join anti-Bolshevik forces.

In the aftermath of the February Revolution, workers' and soldiers' soviets appeared everywhere. Peasants' soviets followed. But according to Shestakov, while the Bolsheviks were leading the workers and peasants in the streets, the Mensheviks and SRs took control of the soviets on behalf of the petty bourgeoisie. With the help of these traitorous parties, the bourgeoisie then co-opted the country's new Provisional Government. The ruling tandem of the soviets and the Provisional Government—known as "dual power"—then proceeded to stymie popular demands for peace, land, control of the means of production, and an end to colonial rule.

According to Shestakov, Lenin, who was still abroad, and Stalin, who had just returned to Petrograd, both denounced the Provisional Government and its Menshevik and SR supporters. Lenin managed to return to Russia in April, where he was met by Stalin and a handful of close comrades. While still at the Finland Train Station in Petrograd, Lenin addressed a waiting crowd, denouncing the Provisional Government and calling for a socialist revolution.

When Stalin turned to edit chapter 11, he revised its title from "The Second Russian Revolution" to one that more explicitly reflected the event's bourgeois nature. He also interpolated new information into the discussion of the origins of World War I by elaborating on the various combatants' imperialist designs. Russia, the general secretary averred, sought to seize Constantinople—Istanbul—from the Ottoman empire. In discussing the treachery of the Mensheviks and SRs at the start of the war, Stalin linked these parties more closely to the Second International and declared them to be petty bourgeois organizations that naturally sided with the bourgeoisie against the workers and peasants.

Stalin found Shestakov's description of the war itself satisfactory for the most part, deleting only sentimental detail about soldiers being separated from their families. He also recharacterized the Russian army as "tsarist" in order to blame its failures on the government rather than on society at large. Stalin also found Shestakov's discussion of revolutionary activism during the war to be acceptable, although here, as elsewhere, he deleted the text's description of the Bolshevik movement as "Lenin's and Stalin's party" and instead stressed Lenin's unchallenged primacy as party leader. In this vein, Stalin also cut mention of his own experience in Siberian exile, as well as that of Molotov, Sverdlov, "and many others," instead noting in more general terms that much of the party leadership had spent the war in confinement. Deleting several melodramatic lines about how he and Lenin had struggled to stay in contact with the Russian workers during this difficult time, Stalin refashioned another of Shestakov's statements to talk more generally about how the Bolshevik party remained active despite the arrest of its leadership. Other editing in this section focused mostly on technical and stylistic issues.

When Stalin turned to the overthrow of the tsar in February 1917, he clarified that it was the bourgeois Cadet party under Miliukov that was plotting against the tsar, striking out all mention of Guchkov and his more conservative Octoberists. Elsewhere, Stalin worked to improve the historical accuracy of Shestakov's overview of the events in question, adding mention of women to the discussion of popular unrest and noting that slogans calling for peace alternated with those for bread—editing that increased the diversity of the opposition to the regime. At the same time, he offered "uprising" as a synonym for "revolution" in places, hinting that not all militants were committed to systemic change. Deleting mention of the tsar's execution, Stalin used that space in the text to contend that the soviets that took shape in 1917 were fundamentally different than those in 1905. If the soviets during the first Russian revolution had comprised workers in urban areas, this time they consisted of both workers and soldiers, the latter of whom were basically peasants in uniform. For Stalin, this meant that the soviets in 1917 represented a much broader and more representative swath of society than ever before.

Stalin agreed with Shestakov that the "petty-bourgeois" Mensheviks and SRs had managed to co-opt the soviets in the aftermath of the February revolution. That said, the fact that the councils continued to exist alongside the Provisional Government meant that they could still be Bolshevized. When Lenin returned to Russia from abroad in April 1917, Stalin stressed the party leader's plans for doing just that in order to lead the workers, soldiers, and peasants against the Provisional Government and toward a truly working-class revolution. He even cut mention of his own April reunion with Lenin in order to double down on the point.

Chapter 12: The Great October Socialist Revolution in Russia

Chapter 12 of the SHORT HISTORY began with the party conference where Lenin presented his April theses that outlined how the party was to prepare for the coming revolution. According to Lenin, the party would take control of the soviets and expel the Mensheviks and SRs. This would allow the party to organize the workers and peasants to overthrow the bourgeoisie by ending the war, giving the landlords' property to the peasantry, and liberating the country's non-Russians from their colonial bondage.

In the face of Bolshevik-organized worker and soldier protests, the Provisional Government was forced to dismiss Miliukov and Guchkov. That said, it did not alter its policies to exit the war, redistribute land, or enfranchise the non-Russians. This, according to Shestakov, led the masses to gravitate more and more to the Bolsheviks. The Mensheviks and SRs responded to this by accusing Lenin of being a German agent.

At the start of the summer of 1917, the Mensheviks and SRs still controlled a majority at the First Congress of Soviets. There, they called for support for the Provisional Government and a new offensive at the front. When this offensive ended in disaster, soldiers increasingly abandoned the parties for the Bolsheviks. Workers, peasants, and the non-Russians also began to express their dissatisfaction in public with increasing frequency. On July 3, a major protest erupted in downtown Petrograd. The bourgeoisie and its Menshevik and SR collaborators attacked the protestors, firing upon them and breaking up their organizations. Many Bolsheviks were arrested, and PRAVDA was shut down. In spite of the fact that these actions forced Lenin and the Bolshevik leadership underground, the party continued to grow in popularity.

At the Sixth Party Congress that August, Stalin called for the Bolsheviks to prepare for an armed uprising. In the aftermath of the congress, party members fanned out across the country to ready the masses for revolution. According to Shestakov, when the bourgeoisie attempted to stage a coup d'état under General Lazar Kornilov, the Bolsheviks convinced his soldiers to defect to the side of the revolution. Soon, the masses were driving the Mensheviks and SRs out of the soviets and electing Bolsheviks in their place.

In October, the party under the leadership of Lenin and Stalin prepared to take power. According to Shestakov, the majority of the working class already backed the Bolsheviks, as did many of the soviets and trade unions. The party also assembled a militia called the Red Guard. In rural areas, the peasants began seizing landlord land; on the empire's periphery, the non-Russians rose up as well. At the front, the soldiers demanded peace and refused to fight.

On the eve of the Bolshevik insurrection, Grigory Zinoviev and Trotsky leaked the party's plans for the coming revolution. This led the Provisional Government to mobilize its remaining forces to suppress the uprising. According to Shestakov, the Bolsheviks responded by setting up a special committee called the Fighting Center under Stalin, Sverdlov, Felix Dzerzhinsky, Andrei Bubnov, and Moisey Uritsky to lead the seizure of power. The Red Guards responded to Lenin and Stalin's call to take over Petrograd and toppled the Provisional Government.

Lenin marked the victory of the revolution with a manifesto that proclaimed that power had passed into the hands of the workers. The Second Congress of Soviets then ratified the first three decrees of the Great Proletarian Revolution—on peace, land, and state power—and took steps to place the country's factories under worker control. According to Shestakov, a government was quickly organized under Lenin and anti-Bolshevik resistance was suppressed. Workers seized the factories and peasants took the land. On the periphery of the former empire, the non-Russian peoples liberated themselves from the bourgeoisie and landlords with the aid of Russian workers operating under Bolshevik leadership.

As Lenin and Stalin organized the new Soviet state, they structured it as a fraternal union of all the peoples of Russia. Their decrees on peace and land were followed by one ensuring workers' control over the means of production. The new state also abrogated the enormous debt that the tsar and Provisional Government owed to foreign creditors. According to Shestakov, the enemies of Soviet power—the landlords, capitalists, generals, and clergy—reacted to this victory by retreating to the periphery of the former empire to regroup. There, they set up rival governments and began to muster forces to fight the Bolsheviks. But the workers and peasants refused to support them, and the Red Guard and Cheka defeated the early counterrevolutionary revolts. With this, Shestakov triumphantly concluded, "a dictatorship of the proletariat was established on the territory of the former tsarist empire."

When Stalin turned to vet Shestakov's text during July 1937, he pursued many of the same editorial priorities in regard to chapter 12 that had preoccupied him elsewhere in the textbook. Obsessed with terminological precision, he brought the text into tight conformity with the party canon, stressing the fact that the October revolution was a "socialist" revolution rather than a "proletarian" one, that its goal was the establishment of Soviet power rather than working-class power, and so on. As in previous chapters, he also devoted considerable to time to revising instances of ambiguity and hyperbole.

Stalin also stressed balance in the narrative, noting the attention that the Bolsheviks paid to their various constituencies in the lead-up to the October seizure of power—the workers, peasants, soldiers, and non-Russian peoples. He also highlighted the initiatives that they took in order to realize these demands. This detail reinforced the textbook's claims about the Bolsheviks' distinctiveness and explained their dramatic rise in popularity over the course of 1917.

As in chapter 11, in chapter 12 Stalin stressed the conspiratorial nature of the Mensheviks and SRs. Deleting Shestakov's mention of how the parties had defamed the Bolsheviks as traitors and German spies, the general secretary interpolated detail on how they had supported the war and the Provisional Government, helped in the suppression of the July Days protests, sabotaged the October Revolution, and volunteered to help foreign imperialists wage a counterrevolutionary struggle against the new Soviet republic.[132]

When Stalin turned to Shestakov's narrative of the October seizure of power itself, he made a number of revisions that improved the overall accuracy of the account. At least twice, he replaced Shestakov's expression "the party of Lenin and Stalin" with the more institutional term "Bolsheviks." He also deleted the textbook's crediting of the Russian proletariat and the party with the revolution in non-Russian regions, suggesting instead that those areas had liberated themselves with the help of the nascent Soviet government.

Although generally satisfied with Shestakov's narration of the October Revolution, Stalin found it seriously undertheorized. For that reason, he added a series of explanations for the Bolsheviks' victory based on what he had written about the revolution some thirteen years earlier in 1924.[133] First, the Provisional Government undermined its popular support by refusing to listen to the people, whether in regard to the war, land reform, or worker control over the means of production. Second, the soviets, in contrast, proved willing to listen to popular demands and used them to form an alliance of workers, peasants, and soldiers. Third, this broad alliance then broke with the petty bourgeois Mensheviks and SRs and sought out truly revolutionary leadership from the Bolsheviks. In other words, the Bolsheviks' victory in October stemmed from their uncompromising commitment to the people's revolutionary demands. Interestingly, although this set of explanations matched the general secretary's views of the revolution expressed elsewhere between 1937 and 1938, they reveal him to have lost interest in an array of international factors that he had originally identified as having contributed to the revolution in 1924.[134]

After interpolating this analysis into the text, Stalin then returned to more technical revisions to the narrative, adding and deleting content in the name of accuracy and word economy. That said, he also made several more critical revisions to the chapter's conclusions, which reduced the triumphalism with which Shestakov and his brigade ended their discussion of the establishment of Soviet power. First, Stalin struck out the claim that the Bolsheviks had succeeded in establishing a fully functioning dictatorship of the proletariat in only a few months. Second, he cut commentary in the text that suggested that the nascent Red Guard and Cheka immediately succeeded in defeating all the counterrevolutionaries who opposed the new republic. Third, he underscored his argument about the inconclusive nature of the revolution in late 1917 by interpolating a rather uncongratulatory warning into the very end of the chapter. "Later on," Stalin wrote,

> it became much more difficult for the Soviet Government to combat counterrevolutionary plots, for the Cadet and Socialist-Revolutionary and Menshevik plotters began to obtain the direct military assistance of foreign capitalist governments. This was a military intervention of the capitalist governments against the Soviet Government and the Soviet system. This fight of the soviets against intervention lasted three years.

In other words, for Stalin, the 1918–1921 civil war would be almost as important to understanding the history of the Bolshevik revolution as October 1917 itself.

Chapter 13: Military Intervention. The Civil War

Shestakov opened his thirteenth chapter by outlining the circumstances surrounding the Bolsheviks' negotiation of a separate peace with imperial Germany at Brest-Litovsk. According to Shestakov, Lenin and Stalin justified their decision to agree to the Germans' unfavorable terms by saying that their concessions would only remain in force until Germany was consumed by revolution. Lenin and Stalin then sent Trotsky to Brest Litovsk to conclude the armistice; there, the latter's delaying tactics cost the Soviet republic dearly until Lenin secured the needed peace himself.

Imperial Germany then quickly moved to annex still more territory and colonize the region in spite of its treaty obligations. According to Shestakov, the Germans installed a Ukrainian puppet government under Pavel Skoropadsky in Kiev and aided the Georgian Mensheviks in Tbilisi. In Donetsk, Voroshilov helped Ukrainian workers resist the Germans and their White Cossack allies. Elsewhere in Ukraine, working-class resistance was coordinated by Nikolai Shchors.

In the Russian republic, the Bolsheviks used Brest Litovsk as a breathing space to allow for the establishment of a socialist economy. According to Shestakov, in the cities, the former bourgeoisie rejected the idea of worker control of industry and engaged in sabotage, leading the Bolsheviks to nationalize their economic assets. In the countryside, the kulaks resisted grain collection efforts. This led the party to bolster its alliance with the peasantry to ensure the food supply.

According to Shestakov, the threat of world revolution led the Entente to intervene militarily in the Russian civil war in 1918, allying with the former bourgeoisie, the Mensheviks and the SRs. Entente support allowed the Mensheviks and SRs, in conjunction with Czechoslovak prisoners of war, to seize parts of the middle Volga region, the Urals, and Siberia. In time, these anti-Bolshevik forces raised rebellions in other areas and assassinated a number of leading Bolsheviks. They even attempted to kill Lenin in the fall of 1918, wounding him with poisoned bullets. Shortly thereafter, the Entente support spurred White Cossack groups to vie for control of Tsaritsyn and the North Caucasus. Stalin, Voroshilov, and Kirov coordinated the defense of these areas but were unable to prevent British aid from reaching the bourgeoisie in Azerbaidzhan, Armenia, and Turkmenistan.

The collapse of Germany and Austro-Hungary in November 1918 briefly raised hopes that pro-Bolshevik Spartacists might take control of what remained of the former Central Powers. Unfortunately, Shestakov averred, their revolution in Berlin and Bavaria was undermined from within by the German Social Democrats, who sided against them with the reactionary German White Guards. The leaders of the Spartacist uprising, Karl Liebknecht and Rosa Luxemburg, were then murdered in a savage act that the textbook claimed was roundly condemned by the world proletariat. Shortly thereafter, the new Hungarian Soviet republic was overthrown by the Entente. Such defeats led Lenin to form the Third Communist International—the Comintern—in Moscow in order to aid inexperienced communist movements abroad and better coordinate the world revolution.

Determined to destroy the nascent Soviet republic, the Entente increased its aid to the anti-Bolshevik White movement. The first campaign of the Entente under Alexander Kolchak in early 1919 was followed by a second campaign under Anton Denikin later that year. Stalin, Dzerzhinsky, and Frunze helped repulse Kolchak while Stalin, Ordzhonikidze, Kirov,

Semen Budenny, and Betal Kalmykov defeated Denikin. The Entente then launched a third campaign, a Polish invasion of Ukraine, in 1920, which was also successfully rebuffed by the Red Army, driving the invaders back to the gates of Warsaw.

During the last stages of the civil war, Red Army forces under Stalin and Voroshilov expelled Petr Wrangel, the Entente's last remaining White hireling, from his base in Crimea. According to Shestakov, the civil war then concluded in Central Asia and the Caucasus, where the Entente had helped the local bourgeoisie to take power. Lenin and Stalin sent Frunze and Valery Kuibyshev to help local workers and peasants liberate Central Asia; Ordzhonikidze, Kirov, and Anastas Mikoian were dispatched to do the same in the Caucasus. These victories, according to Shestakov, allowed the Soviet republic not only to preserve the gains of the revolution at home but also to set an example for the workers of the world abroad.

When Stalin turned to work on Shestakov's chapter on the civil war in July 1937, he retitled the chapter to underscore the role that foreign imperialists had played in the conflict. Expanding upon Shestakov's account of the context in which the embarrassing Brest-Litovsk treaty was signed, Stalin argued that the treaty was more a product of exigency than a wager on imminent German revolution. First, the Russian army had disintegrated and was no longer capable of resisting the German advance. Second, the Bolsheviks' negotiating position had been compromised by Trotsky and Nikolai Bukharin, who had deliberately played into the Germans' hands. Both of these factors left Lenin little choice aside from accepting the Germans' onerous demands. Although Shestakov had included Stalin in this struggle with Trotsky on equal terms with Lenin, the general secretary downplayed the role ascribed to him in the affair.

As the chapter progressed, Stalin emphasized again and again the degree to which domestic anti-Bolshevik forces were dependent on foreign imperialist support. Not only were Trotsky and Bukharin held to have served German interests at Brest Litovsk; Ukrainian nationalists and Georgian Mensheviks were also said to have spent much of 1918 on the Germans' payroll. The end result was the impression that these groups would have lacked the historical agency to rebel without foreign coordination. Indeed, in his discussion of the situation in Ukraine, Stalin was careful to differentiate the conduct of Ukrainian elites from the ordinary people, saying that the

"German soldiers found it very hard to contend against the rebel Ukrainian workers and peasants." Curiously, the general secretary spent much less time on such nuances in regard to his native Georgia, perhaps because of the genuine popularity of Menshevism in that republic at the time.

Stalin also expanded Shestakov's indictment of the Russian bourgeoisie and White generals for collaborating with the Entente. He strengthened accusations against the Cadets, Mensheviks, and SRs in a similar way. Bourgeois nationalists in the Caucasus such as the Azeri Mussavatists and Armenian Dashnaks were likewise cast as British pawns, while feudal hold-overs such as the Central Asian khan of Khiva and emir of Bukhara became the crown's satraps. Intriguingly, at the same time that the general secretary expanded the Entente's responsibility for starting the Russian civil war, he deleted moments of clear hyperbole from the textbook's account. Thus, the line about the SRs attempting to assassinate Lenin with poisoned bullets was cut, as was another shrill statement about how "the horde of the Turkish Sultan" had "strangled" Armenian workers in league with the local bourgeoisie.

Stalin's stress on the Entente's sponsorship of the anti-Bolshevik opposition should not be considered coincidental, whether in regard to the Russian bourgeoisie, the White Guards, and the non-Russian bourgeois nationalists or in regard to Trotsky, Bukharin, the Mensheviks, and the SRs. Nor should it be surprising that all these groups, in Stalin's telling, operated within a vast left-right alliance under international imperialism's leadership. Indeed, these revelations are best seen as a bid to historicize the pervasive conspiracies being uncovered in the USSR in 1937 as the Shestakov text was being prepared for release.[135]

If Stalin exaggerated the role of the Entente to foreshadow the looming threat of omnipresent conspiracy, other aspects of his editing also reflect the increasingly xenophobic context of the Great Purge. Shestakov had narrated the revolution and civil war in a way that prioritized domestic events by downplaying revolutionary unrest abroad.[136] The German Spartacist uprising was characterized as a brief bid for power, doomed by both the movement's own weakness and by the counterrevolutionary nature of the German Social Democrats. The Hungarian Soviet republic was likewise dealt with in a hasty, dismissive way. These defeats left the Moscow-based Comintern the "headquarters of the world revolution." Already an unenthusiastic evaluation of this revolutionary moment, Shestakov's account was further depreciated by Stalin, who cut down the SHORT HISTORY's treatment of the Spartacists and the Comintern even more.[137]

Further on in the chapter, Stalin made a variety of technical and stylistic changes. Perhaps most notable was his elimination of the traditional Soviet periodization of the civil war—a narrative approach that divided the conflict into the first, second, and third campaigns of the Entente. Stalin apparently objected to the schematic nature of this storytelling and renamed the campaigns after the White generals who had led them: first Kolchak, then Nikolai Yudenich and Denikin, and then the Polish "pans" and Wrangel. The general secretary also stripped the text of other literary devices that served to heighten its drama and suspense, presumably because he found them to pander too much to their audience.

At the same time that Stalin was eliminating elements of Shestakov's narrative strategy, he strengthened others. Soviet propagandists since the early 1930s had been attempting to enhance the accessibility of their writing by invoking the names of famous Bolsheviks in a way that would personify party history.[138] Shestakov's text attempted to maintain this approach, despite the degree to which it was complicated by the bloodletting of the Great Purge. Apparently aware of the risk of including protagonists in the narrative who might later be exposed as enemies of the people, Shestakov populated his storyline with only two sorts of heroes: those whose reputations were considered unimpeachable (e.g., Lenin, Stalin, Molotov, Voroshilov) and those who had already died in the line of duty (e.g., Vasily Chapaev, Shchors, Dzerzhinsky, Frunze, Kirov, Kuibyshev, Ordzhonikidze).[139] Stalin upheld this approach to propaganda in his editing, interpolating only the names of two well-known Red Army marshals—Alexander Egorov and Vasily Bliukher. At the same time, he deleted mention of Kalmykov from the text for no apparent reason other than that his was not a household name.[140] Fascinatingly, at the same time that Stalin was broadening the historical agency enjoyed by these heroes in the text, he was reducing the amount of commentary devoted to his own service to the party and state. Among other things, he ordered Shestakov to replace an illustration of him reviewing Budenny's Red Cavalry with a portrait of Egorov. This suggests that Stalin not only disliked the excesses of his personality cult but also was eager to diversify the text's Bolshevik pantheon of heroes.

At the end of chapter 13, Stalin left in place Shestakov's conclusion that the victorious Bolsheviks owed a debt to the workers of Britain, France, and Germany who had aided them in their struggle. That said, such internationalist sentiment should not distract from the overall impression conveyed in this chapter and those preceding it that Shestakov and especially Stalin were determined to characterize the Russian revolution as something fundamentally national and homegrown.

Chapter 14: The Turn to Peaceful Labour. Economic Restoration of the Country

When Shestakov and his brigade turned to their penultimate chapter on the period following the revolution and civil war, they hailed the Bolshevik "victors" and their intention to "build a joyous country of socialism." Surveying the results of seven years of war and intervention, the textbook noted that not only had industry ground to a standstill, but so too had agriculture and trade. Something had to be done to restart the economy—something that would liberate economic actors and allow them to begin producing again.

Traditionally, historians have thought of Lenin's New Economic Policy as a concession to peasant agriculturalists and small-scale entrepreneurs that would allow for a reopening of the market in order to revive the moribund economy. Shestakov's explanation for the policy differed markedly. According to the SHORT HISTORY, agriculturalists had played an essential role in the worker-peasant alliance during the civil war by supplying grain to the cities and the Red Army. Now, they would serve the state by selling their grain on the free market and paying taxes that would fund industrialization and social engineering. Put another way, private trade would pay for the building of socialism.

As much as the early 1920s was a time of transition from war to peace, security concerns remained paramount, especially in the Far East. There, Pavel Postyshev and Bliukher fought the last battles of the civil war against the Japanese and their White Guard allies. It was only in 1922 that the Red Army under Bliukher defeated these invaders and secured the Soviet republic's far eastern border. According to Shestakov, this victory allowed for the official formation of the USSR later that year—a "friendly and joyous family" that would grow from a handful of socialist republics in 1922 to eleven by 1937.

Shestakov then shifted to memorialize Lenin, who died after a long illness on January 21, 1924. Mourned by people across the USSR and throughout the world, he was commemorated by Stalin in a vow that was quoted at length in the textbook. According to Stalin's eulogy, the Soviet people understood that the founder of the Bolshevik movement had furnished them with a vanguard party capable of leading them into the communist future. This path would be determined by a dictatorship of the proletariat directing the efforts of the worker-peasant alliance—a collaborative effort that would harness the talents of all the peoples of the USSR. According to Shestakov, Stalin had spent his entire revolutionary career working alongside Lenin. With Lenin's passing, Stalin would assume the leadership of the effort to build of socialism in the USSR.

When Stalin turned to chapter 14, he made relatively few changes to what was a fairly simple narrative. As elsewhere, he reined in Shestakov's triumphalism about the construction of socialism and reorganized the chapter under the motif of a "turn to peaceful labour" and the "economic restoration of the country." Similarly, he deleted Shestakov's giddy claim that the USSR became a happy and joyous family immediately after its founding in 1922. Most of Stalin's other changes to the chapter reflected his interest in terminological precision and narrative detail. Perhaps the only exceptions to this rule were two eye-catching cuts: first, he deleted Postyshev from the discussion of the civil war in the Far East, insofar as this party veteran had fallen out of favor in early 1937.[141] Second, while sanctioning the text's lengthy citation of his eulogy to Lenin, he added the caveat that he had delivered it at the party's request. More importantly, he deleted the last paragraph of the chapter that codified his status as Lenin's heir. Stalin apparently felt that his position was clear enough that there was no need such gratuitous hallelujahs.

Chapter 15: The USSR is the Land of Victorious Socialism

Shestakov's textbook concluded with a long chapter that focused on Stalin's years in power at the head of the party and state. It began with an assessment of the Soviet economy, circa 1925. According to Shestakov, the economy was weak and its industrial base obsolete. Stalin therefore began within the context of the New Economic Policy to plan for the construction of a socialist economy in the USSR. Industrialization was necessary to modernize the economy and provide the machinery and equipment necessary to overhaul agriculture. Inspired by these plans, Soviet society began to transform the economy with the same intensity with which it had just fought the civil war.

Stalin's plans were opposed, however, by enemies of the party. According to Shestakov, traitors within the former left opposition—Trotsky, Zinoviev, Lev Kamenev, and their followers—attempted to undermine the economic transformation. These oppositionists soon joined forces with the USSR's bourgeois enemies abroad. Together, they attempted to sabotage the economy by engaging in wrecking and terrorism throughout the country.

According to Shestakov, it was within the context of this open conflict with the opposition that Stalin decided to embark on a more centralized, unified approach to economic transformation, oriented around central planning and administrative command. Known as the "Great Break," this transition to a mass, coordinated approach to industrial development would not only produce results in the fastest time possible, but it would also mobilize the entire Soviet population to assist in its realization. Shestakov then outlined many of the accomplishments of the first Five-Year Plan, focusing on the construction of major factories, dams, power stations, and railways.

Turning to agriculture, Shestakov observed that the rural economy in the USSR was obsolete and unable to take advantage of up-to-date scientific knowledge. For this reason, the party began to agitate among the peasantry for the collectivization of small-scale farms into mechanized agricultural collectives. According to the text, the state was able to convince the peasants of the advantages of this new mode of production in both word and deed. The kulaks, however, realized that there was no place for them within this new economy and attempted to resist collectivization through terrorism and wrecking. They found support and aid with the former right opposition—Bukharin, Alexei Rykov, and their supporters—who also objected to the Five-Year Plan. As with the left opposition, the party was able to defeat the kulaks and their rightists allies. This allowed for the transformation of Soviet agriculture as Stalin outlined.

Capitalizing on these victories in industrialization and collectivization, the USSR completed the first Five-Year Plan ahead of schedule. By 1932, averred Shestakov, it already enjoyed a fully functioning socialist economy. Such successes led to the emergence of new hostility among the enemies of the revolution—whether the White generals and Chinese warlords abroad or the former Mensheviks and SRs at home. This forced the USSR to shift from the task of building socialism to that of defending it.

The USSR's attainment of socialism, according to Shestakov, allowed for increased productivity and newfound prosperity. It also led to the emergence of a new kind of worker who routinely overfulfilled his or her production norms—people like Alexei Stakhanov in coal mining, Alexander Busygin in metalworking, Dusia and Maria Vinogradova in textile weaving, Maria Demchenko in sugar-beet harvesting, Pasha Angelina in tractor driving, and so on. Their labor heroism led to the expansion of transport networks, the modernization of urban spaces, and breakthroughs in science, education, and culture. Aviators conquered the skies while agriculturalists revolutionized crop yields. All this was a sign of the success of Soviet socialism.

Shestakov noted amid this triumphalism that the rise of socialism in the USSR was matched by the growth of hostility among the USSR's enemies. Most dangerous were the fascists, the "hireling dogs of the bourgeoisie," who ruled Germany and Italy. Along with the fascist militarists in Japan, they sought control over their working classes and knew this would be impossible to achieve without first destroying the USSR. For that reason, the Japanese had taken Manchuria and were threatening the Soviet Union from the east. Meanwhile, Italy and Germany were helping fascist generals in Spain make war on their own people. And all the while, these fascists were working to undermine the USSR, infiltrating spies into the country and recruiting Trotskyite holdovers to engage in wrecking activities. Together, they murdered Kirov and planned the assassinations of Stalin, Voroshilov, Ordzhonikidze, Kaganovich, and Molotov. According to Shestakov, their goal was to weaken the USSR and undermine its ability to defend itself in the event of war.

Such a set of foreign and domestic threats, averred Shestakov, required Soviet border guards and the rest of Soviet society—even children—to keep a watchful eye out for intruders. The Red Army, in turn, was proclaimed to be ready to defend the USSR. Abroad, foreign workers also prepared to defend the USSR within the context of the Comintern's antifascist Popular Front, looking upon the Soviet republic as their only true fatherland. Here, Shestakov went into considerable detail about pro-Soviet movements in

Spain, France, China, and elsewhere, operating under the Comintern and its leader, Georgy Dimitrov.

Summarizing the transformation of Soviet society under Lenin and Stalin since 1917—specifically the liberation of the workers, peasants, and non-Russian nationalities—Shestakov noted that many of these changes had been codified within the 1936 Stalin Constitution. This document, which had apparently been drawn up by Stalin himself, proclaimed that socialism had been attained and that the USSR was a worker-peasant state. This had been possible, according to Shestakov, thanks to the elimination of capitalism, exploitation, and private property. As would befit a socialist society, the new constitution also provided for an array of social entitlements for all toilers in the society: work, rest, education, and retirement.

According to the Stalin constitution, the country was ruled by the Supreme Soviet and a government headed by the Council of People's Commissars. Municipal administration was provided by local soviets. All these bodies, according to the textbook, were run by elected officials; all Soviet citizens above the age of eighteen were entitled to vote and hold office.

Shestakov then noted that it was the "All-Union Communist Party (Bolsheviks) [that] leads the government"—a statement that echoed Lenin's belief in party vanguardism. According to the textbook, the party comprised the most active and conscious members of the USSR's toiling classes, operating under the direction of the Central Committee and its Politburo. Shestakov noted that the party and its governing bodies enjoyed the faith of the Soviet populace. Aside from this popular mandate, the party also apparently benefited from the loyal support of trade unions and organizations such the All-Union Leninist Communist Youth League (the Komsomol) and the young pioneers.

Shestakov concluded the chapter with several final paragraphs about Stalin, who was described as "our beloved chief, father, and teacher" and "the continuer of Lenin's cause." Stalin was described as tirelessly devoted to the liberation of workers and peasants, not just in the USSR but throughout the whole world. Unattributed paeans to the general secretary followed from Kaganovich and the Comintern official Dmitry Manuilsky, describing Stalin as brave and unwavering—the personification of the Bolshevik party vanguard.

When Stalin turned to editing chapter 15, he objected to the way that

Shestakov characterized socialism as already having been fully realized. Socialist construction, according to the general secretary, was proceeding apace and the socialist fundamentals of the economy were already in place, but socialism itself was still a work in progress. Stalin took particular exception to the way the textbook described much of the planning for the "Great Break" during the late 1920s, perhaps viewing it as overly triumphalist. More importantly, the general secretary removed the routine citation of his personal authority in connection with industrialization efforts under the New Economic Policy and during the first Five-Year Plan, in one place forbidding the publishers from flanking the discussion with a full-page portrait of him on glossy paper. Instead, according to Stalin, it was the party leadership that had devised the plans for industrialization in the 1920s and then decided to curtail NEP and centralize economic planning.

When Stalin turned to the struggle with the left opposition, he attempted to provide an explanation for the nature of this resistance to the party leadership. Instead of merely writing off the former leftists as "traitors" as Shestakov had, Stalin clarified that Trotsky, Zinoviev, Kamenev, and others doubted whether socialism could be built in a single country like the USSR. According to the general secretary, they believed that Soviet workers and peasants were too backward to be able to run an economy without capitalists and kulaks behind the scenes. Eager to restore a capitalist economy within the USSR, the left oppositionists apparently combined forces with like-minded former Mensheviks, SRs, and enemies of the USSR abroad to defeat the Bolsheviks.

This discussion of the opposition's lack of faith allowed Stalin to repeatedly stress that the results of the "Great Break" demonstrated Soviet workers to be fully capable of industrializing without the aid of capitalist elements. Similarly, Soviet peasants had proven themselves able to modernize the country's agricultural economy without the kulaks or right oppositionists like Bukharin and Rykov. According to Stalin, a new system of socialist economic relations had proven possible to build in one country after all. He then added detail to bolster this conclusion—more examples of economic productivity, more sites of industrial transformation, more names of Soviet heroes, and so on.

As noted earlier, at the same time that Stalin stressed the accomplishments of Soviet workers and peasants under the party's leadership, he reined in Shestakov's declaration of victory in 1932. Deleting the textbook's claim that the country had "entered into the socialist period" at the end of the first Five-Year Plan, Stalin instead argued that the accomplishments of the period should be regarded only as ensuring the future realization of socialism. Such concerns led Stalin to strike more instances of hyperbole from the text—claims such as "the power of the Soviet Union became invincible." He likewise downgraded other discussions that waxed rhapsodic about "socialist riches," total mobilization, technological supremacy, and creative genius. Particularly hard hit was the subject of Soviet aviation, which lost three portraits, a photograph, and map to Stalin's red pencil.

When Stalin turned to the section of the chapter on foreign enemies, he deleted much of Shestakov's commentary on fascism abroad, whether in Germany, Italy, Spain or Japanese-occupied China. This had the overall effect of reducing the sense of imminent threat and claustrophobic tension that pervaded the later chapters of Shestakov's galleys. He also toned down the interconnectedness between the embattled workers' movement abroad and Soviet society at home. Particularly eye-catching was Stalin's alteration of the textbook's discussion of the Popular Front. Affirming the text's contention that the Popular Front demonstrated foreign workers' support for the USSR, Stalin detached the alliance from the Comintern and then struck out all remaining references to Dimitrov's organization—a deletion that almost certainly stemmed from Stalin's loss of confidence in this internationalist project.[142]

Stalin's commentary on domestic enemies was equally interesting. If Shestakov had described the foreign-sponsored domestic opposition as consisting largely of Trotskyites, Stalin added Bukharinites and Rykovites to this traitorous group. This hint about the existence of an omnipresent left-right conspiracy anticipated Bukharin and Rykov's show trial and executions on charges of treason in early 1938 after the publication of the SHORT HISTORY.[143]

As elsewhere in the chapter, Stalin objected to elements of the personality cult that Shestakov interpolated into the final section on the 1936 Constitution. This led him to cross out several references to the constitution as a "Stalinist" document that he had supposedly had a hand in writing. He also rejected Shestakov's explicit celebration of his role as the personification of the party vanguard and then deleted the last three paragraphs of the chapter, including its evocative quotations from Manuilsky and Kaganovich. Stalin's annoyance with all such references was confirmed pages later when he struck his birthdate out of a chronological table in the appendixes, angrily writing "Bastards!" into the margins.

Aside from these alterations to the textbook's discussion of the constitution, Stalin was also careful to maximize the accuracy of Shestakov's account. Agreeing with the textbook's claim that the USSR had eliminated exploitation, the general secretary was more critical of the implausible boast that it had completely eliminated private property as well. Similarly, Stalin agreed that the constitution guaranteed both the right to work and rest, but he disputed the contention that everyone who worked was entitled to an annual vacation. This, he clarified, applied only to "workers and office employees"—a formula that denied this entitlement to millions of the country's collective farmers.

Perhaps the most interesting of Stalin's revisions to the section on the 1936 Constitution were those that focused on the leadership of Soviet society. He began by sanctioning Shestakov's stress on elections to municipal councils and the all-union Supreme Soviet. He then went to considerable lengths to rewrite the textbook's discussion of the voting franchise in order to add more detail about this constitutional guarantee. Even more curiously, he then struck out all mention of the primacy of the communist party from the text, as well as full page illustrations featuring portraits of prominent Politburo and Central Committee members. The importance of this editing is hard to exaggerate, as it removed from the Shestakov text its most important endorsement of the vanguard role that the party played in Soviet society.

Assuming the unlikely mantel of a democrat, Stalin suggested through this editing that power in the USSR lay with the people and their elected representatives in the government—something that contradicted Lenin's advocacy of party leadership that the textbook had been advancing since its chapter 9. One way to understand this editing is to view it as marking the culmination of Shestakov's thousand-year narrative of Russo-Soviet state building. What is more, it coincides with recent revelations that Stalin and the party leadership were planning to force regional bosses in mid-1937 to stand for competitive elections in Soviet state administration in order to make them more accountable to public opinion.[144] And while this idea was quietly abandoned later that year after the SHORT HISTORY had gone to press, this stress on elections was preserved in later editions of the textbook. It seems likely that the editors at the State Instructional-Pedagogical Publishing House retained this fiction to conceal the absolute monopoly that the party leadership enjoyed over Soviet decision making during these years.

Stalin's overall vision of the "usable past" promoted by the SHORT HISTORY was summarized in the chronological table printed on the last pages of the textbook. At first glance just a list of key dates, this table outlined a profoundly etatist, russocentric vision of the prerevolutionary, revolutionary, and postrevolutionary history of the Soviet Union. A thousand-year story of state building that collapsed much of the prehistory of the USSR into a single, linear, russocentric arc, this narrative then shifted left in the nineteenth century to trace the trajectory of the Russian revolutionary movement and its Bolshevik vanguard through 1917. After that, it promptly resumed its etatist course. Stalin's revisions to this chronology during the summer of 1937 reinforced its implicit statism by cutting almost all mention of popular protest and the personality cult. Hailed upon its release as a "major victory on the historical front," the SHORT HISTORY marked the triumph of state power over the revolutionary tradition.

––––––

As is clear from the preceding analysis of Stalin's editorial transformation of the SHORT HISTORY, this new narrative represented a major sea change in the way that Soviet society was to make sense of the past. Reversing earlier tendencies that condemned the prerevolutionary elite as backward, tyrannical and cruel, Stalin's usable past stressed the progressive aspects of state building and centralized leadership. Breaking with the idea that the October 1917 revolution marked the beginning of a new era, the SHORT HISTORY highlighted a thousand years of continuity as it traced the USSR's prerevolutionary lineage back though imperial Russia and Muscovy to medieval Kiev Rus. This new stress on the importance of centralization, the state, and national unity was complemented by an explicitly uncongratulatory treatment of premodern peasant uprisings and sparce attention to grassroots activism in more modern periods. The end result was a vanguardist "great men of history" approach to progress and change that governed the preceding millennium.

At the same time, the SHORT HISTORY endorsed an explicitly russocentric narrative. True, the first two chapters of the textbook concerned regional and eastern Slavic history predating the Muscovite past, but many of these developments were teleologically cast as precursors to subsequent Russian ones. What's more, the construction of the narrative pivoted not only on Russia-centered events, but on Russian historical agents and Russian historical agency as well. Although non-Russian historical developments and personalities did appear frequently in the text, the timing of their appearance and their role in the narrative was governed by an exclusively Russian point of view. Put another way, despite the fact that the non-Russian peoples would seem to have had much to offer any definitive account of the prerevolutionary history of the USSR, the SHORT HISTORY allowed them only an oblique role in the storyline that was too disjointed and disconnected to allow for the creation of independent narratives of their own.

Reorganizing history in this linear, statist way, Stalin's usable past played a central role in the promotion of a stoic, autarchic, russocentric sense of patriotism in the USSR during the late 1930s. And evidence suggests that this reading of history and national identity proved catalytic in the decades that followed, at least among Russian speakers.[145] Of course, this historical revisionism came at the expense of many of the original values of 1917—internationalist revolution, radical political transformation, grassroots activism, and liberation from the traditional strictures of class, ethnicity, and gender. For that reason, Stalin's usable past is best seen as a profoundly conservative and pragmatic "victory on the historical front."

A SHORT HISTORY
OF THE U.S.S.R.

Edited by Professor
A. V. SHESTAKOV

CO-OPERATIVE PUBLISHING SOCIETY OF FOREIGN
WORKERS IN THE U.S.S.R.   MOSCOW 1938

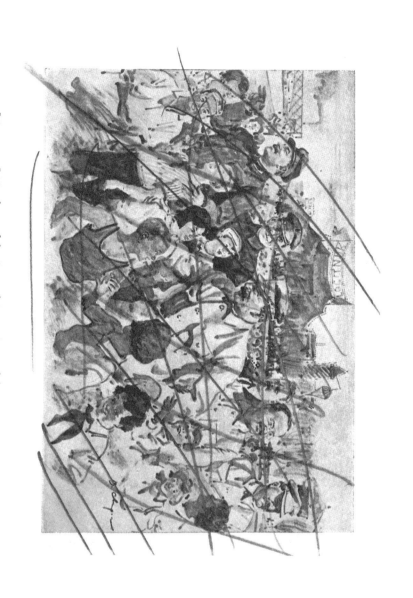

[FIGURE 4:] Members of the Central Committee of the Communist Party of the Soviet Union (Bolsheviks) surrounded by children. [Cut by Stalin: RGASPI, f. 558, op. 11, d. 1584, l. 3. Also Zhdanov: f. 77, op. 1, d. 854, l. 00b.]

AN ~~ELEMENTARY~~

SHORT HISTORY OF

THE U.S.S.R.

~~WITH~~

~~SHORT ACCOUNTS OF WORLD~~

~~HISTORY~~[1]

Textbook for 3rd & 4th classes

~~Compiled by the Department of U.S.S.R. History~~
~~at the Moscow State A. S. Bubnov Pedagogical Institute~~
~~under the direction of~~ *Edited by*[2] Professor
A. V. SHESTAKOV

Indorsed by the All-Union Government Commission[3]

CO-OPERATIVE PUBLISHING SOCIETY OF FOREIGN
WORKERS IN THE U.S.S.R.   MOSCOW 1938

In order to realize the resolutions of the C.P.S.U.(B.) Central Committee and the U.S.S.R. Council of People's Commissars, and at the directive of the administration of the Moscow State A. S. Bubnov Pedagogical Institute, this textbook was compiled by responsible workers within the U.S.S.R. History Department including: Professor A. V. Shestakov (the director), Professor N. G. Tarasov and Lecturers I. D. Kuznetsov, D. N. Nikiforov, A. S. Nifontov and N. D. Firsov. Others taking part in the work include B. A. Gardanov, Yu. V. Gote, Z. G. Grinberg, D. Ya. Kin, A. I. Kazachenko and S. A. Nikitin. Final revisions to the text were performed by Professors A. V. Shestakov, A. Z. Ionisiani and N. G. Tarasov and Lecturers N. D. Kuznetsov and A. S. Nifontov.[4]

Contents

IV. THE RISE OF THE RUSSIAN NATIONAL STATE

V. THE EXPANSION OF THE RUSSIAN STATE

VI. THE PEASANT WARS AND REVOLTS OF THE OPPRESSED PEOPLES IN THE 17TH CENTURY

VII. RUSSIA IN THE 18TH CENTURY: THE EMPIRE OF LANDLORDS AND MERCHANTS

VIII. TSARIST RUSSIA—THE GENDARME OF EUROPE

IX. *THE GROWTH OF CAPITALISM IN* TSARIST RUSSIA. A CAPITALIST COUNTRY[7]

X. THE FIRST RUSSIAN *BOURGEOIS REVOLUTION IN RUSSIA*[10]

Maps

Introduction

1. Our ~~Happy~~[1] Country

The U.S.S.R.—the Land of Socialism. There is only one ~~such~~ *Socialist*[2] country in the world. That country is our country.

Our country is the largest country in the world. To the north, it is bounded by eternal ice; and in the south it is so hot in the summer that oranges and lemons ripen, and tea and cotton grow.

Our country is the richest in the world in natural resources. Everything needed for existence is found in our country.

Year after year, there is more of grain and other wealth in this country.

Year after year, the number of factories, schools, theatres and cinemas increases.

Its old cities are growing at an unusually rapid pace, and new cities are being built.

The working people of the U.S.S.R. are becoming ~~richer~~ *more prosperous*[3] all the time, and their life is becoming better and happier.

In no other country in the world is there such friendship among the various peoples as in the U.S.S.R. In the 11 ~~Socialist~~ *Constituent*[4] Republics of the Soviet Union there are ~~120~~ 50[5] different nationalities, making a total of 170,000,000 inhabitants. All are united in one fraternal union, which we call the Union of Soviet Socialist Republics, or U.S.S.R., for short. All the peoples of the U.S.S.R. work for the common good. In the U.S.S.R. there are no parasites, capitalists and landlords, as there are in other countries. *In the U.S.S.R. there is no exploitation of man by man.*[6] All of us work for ourselves, and not for parasites.

In the past, our country was a backward country; now it has become the most advanced and mighty country in the world.

That is why we love our country so much; that is why we are so proud of our U.S.S.R.—the Land of Socialism.

The road to Socialism was mapped out for us by the great Party of the Communists, the Bolsheviks. This Party led the struggle of our fathers and mothers, *the struggle of the workers and peasants,*[7] when they overthrew the rule of the tsar, of the landlords and capitalists. Under the leadership of the Communist Party we *created a workers' and peasants' government, and*[8] built Socialism.

What this book teaches. It tells you how people lived in the past; how the peoples of the U.S.S.R. fought their oppressors and enemies; how they succeeded in making our country the Land of Socialism. From this book you will also learn about the life and struggle of the people in other countries.

All this is called HISTORY.

We love our country and we must know its wonderful history. Those who know history understand present-day life better, are better able to fight the enemies of our country, and make Socialism stronger.

I

Our Country in the Distant Past

2. How People Lived in the Distant Past

How we know how people lived long ago. One day some children were digging a pit on the bank of a stream. In the ground they found some curious bones and a stone. They took them to school and showed them to their teacher.

"Children," said the teacher, "you have found some very interesting things. These are the bones of ancient monsters. ~~In these parts~~ *Once upon a time,*[1] very long ago, those animals lived ~~in these parts~~[2]. They are now extinct. And the stone is a tool with which the people, who lived very long ago ~~in our country~~[3], killed wild animals."

The teacher tied the stone to a stick and it then looked like a heavy hammer.

The teacher told the children that all over the U.S.S.R. scientists were making excavations, and from the things they found they learned how people lived in the remotest times.

The life of primitive man. ~~Scientists have established that about~~ *About*[4] five hundred thousand years ago, nearly the whole of our country was covered with a thick layer of ice.

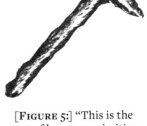

[**FIGURE 5:**] "This is the sort of hammer primitive peoples used," said the teacher. [A SHORT HISTORY (hereafter SH), 9]

Centuries passed, and the ice gradually melted. It began melting in the south. And it was in the south that the first human beings appeared.

Their life was very hard. Around them roamed wild animals: huge mammoths and bears. They hid from these animals in caves and dugouts. They fed on roots ~~and,~~ berries *and the flesh of animals which they killed;*[5]

[**FIGURE 6:**] ~~Prehistoric people killing a mammoth that they had driven into a pit.~~ [Cut by Zhdanov: RGASPI, f. 77, op. 1, d. 854, l. 2ob.]

and they clothed themselves with the skins of these animals. People went hunting together and sometimes they managed to kill *even*[6] so strong an animal as a mammoth. What they caught they ~~combined together~~ *shared in common*[7].

More centuries passed. People learned to produce fire, and to make tools out of stones, wood and bones. They invented the bow and arrow. ~~They tamed dogs, cattle and horses. They began to practice agriculture and animal husbandry.~~ *Gradually they learned how to tame wild animals, and began to rear cattle. Thousands of years later they learned to cultivate useful plants, and began to engage in agriculture. They built themselves huts, or tents, and made clothes from the skins of animals and from coarse linen.*[8]

For a long time people used stone and bone implements.[9] Many thousands of years passed before they learned to obtain ore, and to smelt copper and other metals. ~~They built themselves huts, or tents, from the hides of cattle and from coarse linen.~~[10]

In *those* distant times ~~people lived in such a way that~~[11] all things—tools, and the food obtained by hunting or tilling the soil—were held in common. All equally shared the life of arduous toil.

3. From the Clan to the State

Clans and tribes. ~~In distant times, people lived in clans. In clans, they nomadically roamed the steppe with herds of camels, sheep and horses. In clans, they lived in villages on rivers and lakes and practiced agriculture. They held everything in common and defended their fields, meadows, woods and fishing grounds from other clans.~~

~~Group affairs were decided at meetings of all the adult members of the clan. The work of the clan was directed by elected elders.~~ *It was impossible for one man to hunt big animals, catch fish with nets, or clear forests for cultivation all by himself. That is why, in olden times, relations did not separate, but lived together, in clans, sometimes numbering several hundred people. The clan held all things in common. Tools were used in common. The members of the clan went hunting and fishing together, and cultivated the land by their common efforts. The spoils of the hunt and the fruits of the harvest were shared among the clan. The cattle was held in common. The work of the clan was directed by elected elders. The affairs of the clan were discussed and settled at meetings of the whole clan. The clan protected its members. If a member of the clan was killed by a member of another clan, the relations of the killed man avenged his death. There were frequent wars between the different clans over arable land, pastures, forests and fishing.*[12]

Several neighbouring clans formed a TRIBE. A tribe consisted of several thousand people. All the people of the tribe spoke the same language and followed the same customs. Each tribe had an elected chief.

~~For many centuries, people lived in clans and tribes but gradually inequality arose among them. In the place of the COMMON OWNERSHIP of food and implements there emerged PRIVATE PROPERTY.~~

~~Some members of the clan came to have more property than others. Rich and poor emerged among them.~~

People lived in clans and tribes for many centuries. Gradually, the clans began to break up into families. The larger and stronger families began to take possession of parts of the land and part of the cattle and live for themselves. They ceased to share things with the others. They took possession of the captives of war and compelled them to work for them. In this way inequality arose in the tribes. Instead of the common ownership of food and implements, there was now private property. Some members of the clan began to own more property than the others. There arose among them the rich and the poor.[13]

The rich men and the war chiefs of the warlike and strong tribes made raids upon their neighbours, took captives and forced them to become SLAVES. The tribal chiefs and the rich men of the tribe procured more slaves than the other warriors. ~~They forced their slaves to work for them on their own property.~~[14]

Those who obtained many slaves became richer than others. The rich chiefs gathered warriors around themselves, fed and clothed them, and provided them with arms. With the help of these warriors the chiefs made fresh raids. The booty and captives obtained from these raids were kept by the chiefs and their warriors.

The chiefs and rich men of the tribe compelled not only the slaves to work for them, but their fellow tribesmen as well, and despoiled them of part of the fruits of their labour. In this way there arose in the tribes oppressors—the rich, and oppressed—the poor.[15]

The state. A small group of rich people began to live at the expense of the large majority of the toilers; they oppressed and robbed them. ~~In the place of equality there appeared inequality; the oppressors and the oppressed also appeared. Some had power over others: the rich men ruled over their slaves and fellow tribesmen. These rich men's chiefs were called princes, khans, tsars and kings. They became the rulers of their tribes and the other tribes that they conquered.~~ *The chiefs, with the help of their warriors, compelled the slaves and their own fellow tribesmen to obey them. They became the rulers of their tribes. These tribal chiefs were called princes, kings, tsars or khans.*[16] To keep the people in subjection the princes, khans and tsars increased the numbers of their warriors, established their own courts, and introduced various punishments. ~~In this war, STATES were formed of various tribes.~~[17]

These chiefs were not content to rule over their own tribes, but subjugated weaker neighbouring tribes. In this way states were formed.[18]

4. The Most Ancient States in Our Country

The first states in Trans-Caucasia and Central Asia. The most ancient states in our country arose in the south ~~among the tribes~~[19] of Trans-Caucasia. This was about 3,000 years ago. The first state in Trans-Caucasia was known as URARTU, *and was situated in the region of Mount Ararat, near Lake Van*[20]. Its kings ruled over the ~~Armenian and~~[21] Georgian tribes. They had many slaves who built ~~luxurious~~[22] palaces for them and dug canals to irrigate the kings' fields and orchards.

This was the state of the forerunners of present-day Georgia.[23]

The kings of Urartu were constantly at war with the neighbouring states. The wars were very cruel. This can be seen from ~~one~~ *the*[24] inscription which one of the kings of Urartu ordered his slaves to cut on a rock. This inscription reads as follows:

"Sixty-four thousand; part I put to the sword, and part I carried away alive."[25]

Similar states existed in Central Asia. *These were the states of the forerunners of the present-day Uzbeks, Tadjiks and Turkmens.*[26] Their rulers were also constantly at war with their neighbours. ~~There were times when the states of Central Asia and the Trans-Caucasus fell under the power of their neighbours for a long time.~~[27]

In the ancient states of Trans-Caucasia and Central Asia there were many towns. To protect the towns from enemies, high stone walls were built around them. Skilful craftsmen and slaves built houses for the rich, and also warehouses and shops. ~~People lived in the towns in a way that was completely different than when they lived in clans and tribes.~~ *Many handicraftsmen lived in the towns and a brisk trade was carried on.*[28]

The ~~urban~~ inhabitants *of the towns*[29] invented the alphabet and learned to read and write. In Georgia, for example, ~~under the tsar Farnavaz,~~[30] the alphabet was invented more than 2,000 years ago. ~~Inhabitants of the cities began to study the sciences of the time as well.~~ *The first learned men appeared in the towns; science and art began to develop.*[31]

~~The first states in Siberia and on the Black Sea.~~ ~~Long ago, rulers, khans and tsars appeared among the nomadic peoples of southern Siberia, the Kazakh steppe and along the Black Sea.~~ ***The peoples inhabiting ancient Siberia and Eastern Europe.*** *In ancient times, South Siberia and the Black Sea* *coast were inhabited by numerous tribes of nomad herdsmen. Under the command of their tsars, they wandered from place to place over the steppes with their herds of cattle and horses in search of good pastures.*[32] About 2,500 years ago the nomad tribe known as the SCYTHIANS was particularly distinguished for its power. The Scythian ~~rulers~~ *tsars*[33] ruled over numerous nomad and settled agricultural tribes and ~~these rulers had many~~ slaves.

More than ~~2,000~~ 2,500[34] years ago settlers from Greece landed on the north coast of the Black Sea. Here they built several cities and carried on a big trade with the Scythians. They bought cattle, grain and fish from the Scythians, and sent them across the sea to Greece. Gradually the Greek cities grew and ~~at one time formed~~ *united to form*[35] a whole state.

The rich Greek rulers and merchants did no work. All the work was performed for them by slaves, mostly Scythian captives of war. Two thousand years ago, the Scythian slaves, under the leadership of a slave named SAVMAK, rose in rebellion against their oppressors and took power into their own hands. But the slave revolt was crushed by Greek troops that came from over the sea.

In the 4th century *of our era*[36], the Greek cities were overrun and ravaged by a powerful nomad people, the Huns. In the 5th century, ATTILA, the fierce ruler of the Huns, marched from the steppes of the Black Sea region against the peoples of Western Europe and subdued many of them. But after the death of Attila his kingdom fell to pieces as a result of the attacks of other nomad tribes who came from Asia. In the 6th century the nomad Khazars built a state on the Volga where the Huns had formerly ruled; and further up the Volga the BULGAR state was formed.

[**FIGURE 7:**] A slave in chains. [SH, 14]

For many years the Khazars and Bulgars had to contend against the neighbouring SLAVONIC TRIBES.

5. The Slavs

The Slavs and their neighbours. Fifteen centuries ago the Slavonic tribes inhabited the lands on the shores of the Baltic Sea, *along the rivers Dniepr and Danube,*[37] and the upper reaches of the rivers Oka and Volga. ~~The Slavs—the forefathers of the Russian people—lived at that time as clans and tribes.~~ *Later on, the Slavs inhabiting Eastern Europe formed three big nations—the Russians, Ukrainians and Byelorussians.*[38]

In the east, their neighbours were the Volga tribes, the forefathers of the present-day MARIS, MORDOVIANS and other nationalities, and *also*[39] the Bulgar and Khazar states. In the south, the Slavs waged war against the nomads of the *Black Sea*[40] steppes. They also waged war against the rich *and, for that time, civilized*[41] Greek state of Byzantium (the country which is now Turkey). The *Greek* craftsmen ~~of Byzantium~~[42] built splendid buildings, palaces and churches. The Greeks had their writers, musicians and painters. They manufactured beautiful silk fabrics, pottery, and articles of gold and silver. ~~Byzantium had a great number of well-equipped soldiers.~~[43]

Byzantium had a great number of well-equipped soldiers.[44] But the brave Slavs, in spite of their backwardness, frequently defeated the Greek troops. In the middle of the 9th century ~~the Slavic Russ tribe~~ *they*[45] waged a successful war against the Greeks. ~~This Russ tribe~~, *and*[46] even attacked Tsargrad (Constantinople), the capital of Byzantium.

In the west, the Slavs were obliged to wage war against the German tribes and ~~raiding~~[47] Varangians.

The occupations of the Slavs. ~~The main occupation of the Slavs was agriculture. In the forest lands, they did not plow the land, but merely scattered seeds in the soil that was mixed with ash that came from burned trees.~~ *The ancient Slavs engaged in hunting and collecting wild honey. Later, agriculture became their chief occupation. They burned down sections of the forest and scattered seeds on the soil mixed with ashes.*[48] In this way they obtained good harvests; but the soil was exhausted within three or four years and it was necessary to burn down another section of the forest. In the steppes the land was broken up with the aid of mattocks and then seeds were sown; but even by this method the land became sterile within four or five years. The old fields had to be abandoned and new ground broken. This work was very, laborious, particularly with the primitive implements

MAP SHOWING ANCIENT PEOPLES AND STATES ON THE TERRITORY OF THE U.S.S.R.

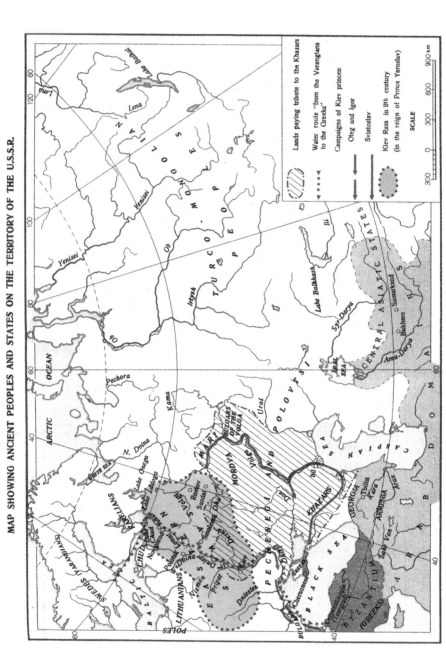

[MAP 1:] Map Showing Ancient Peoples and States on the Territory of the U.S.S.R. [SH, 12–13. Stalin corrected the map in the 1937 Russian edition to read "Nomadic *Turco-Mongolian* Peoples of the Kazakh Steppe." RGASPI, f. 558, op. 11, d. 1584, l. 8]

[**FIGURE 8:**] ~~A Slavic village.~~ [Cut by Zhdanov: RGASPI, f. 77, op. 1, d. 854, l. 5.]

used, and could not be performed by a single family. For this reason, the work was performed jointly by the whole clan. When the ~~PLUG~~ SOKHA[49], or wooden plough with an iron tip, was invented, horses were harnessed to the ploughs. Cattle manure was used to fertilize the soil. A small plot of land cultivated by a single family could now provide ~~a rich harvest~~ *food for many years running*[50]. It was no longer necessary to cultivate the land in common, and this system began to disappear. A plot of cultivated and manured land began to be regarded as the property of the family cultivating it. The clan and tribal chiefs *seized large plots of land and*[51] compelled their slaves to cultivate ~~their large plots of land~~ *them*[52]. On these plots also worked free, but impoverished, people from the various clans. The owners of ploughs and horses hired them out to those who did not own any in return for ~~some~~ *a*[53] part of the latter's harvest and thus became rich. ~~It was in this way that the~~

~~clans disappeared and gave way to~~ *The equality which existed formerly disap-peared; the clan was divided into*[54] oppressors and oppressed; into rich land-owners and poor tillers. In the ~~8th~~ *9th*[55] century the Slavs already had ~~their own~~[56] BOYARS, who were the landowners and rich men, and also ~~their own~~[57] PRINCES, the tribal rulers. The princes and boyars traded with the Greeks and other neighbours in grain, honey and bees-wax; but mostly they traded in slaves, captured in war by the DRUZHINAS, or retinues, of the princes and boyars. The trade was carried on in ~~especially~~[58] fortified places along the ~~busy~~[59] trade routes, mostly ~~on~~ *along*[60] the banks of the big rivers. In the 9th century the Slavs had ~~15~~ *a few*[61] towns. The most important of these were Kiev and Novgorod.

II

The Kiev State

6. The ~~Founding~~ *Rise*[1] of the Principality of Kiev

The Varangian conquests. In the 9th century the North Slavs were subjugated by robber bands of Varangians, who came from over the Baltic Sea. The Varangian chief settled in Novgorod and from that city his warriors raided the neighbouring tribes, robbed them of their ~~grain and~~ furs, *honey and wax,*[2] and carried away captives. The Varangians took the ~~fur~~ *booty*[3] and ~~prisoners~~ *captives*[4] to Byzantium where they sold them to the Greeks. They went in boats along the rivers and lakes, then they dragged their boats over dry land to the River Dniepr. *Navigation on the Dniepr was obstructed by the rapids where big rocks blocked the river. At this spot boats had to be taken out of the water and dragged with their cargoes along the banks. The warlike tribe of Pechenegs, who tended their herds in this neighbourhood, took advantage of this and often attacked the passing merchants.*[5] From the Dniepr travellers passed into the Black Sea and from there, ~~went~~ *keeping close to the coast, sailed*[6] to Byzantium. This passage was known as "the passage from the Varangians to the Greeks."

The Slavs who lived around Novgorod often rebelled against the Varangians and sometimes succeeded in driving them across the sea. But not for long. The Varangians would return in larger numbers and again establish their rule over the Slavs.

Rurik and Oleg. It is related in ancient records, that at the end of the 9th century, Novgorod was ruled by the Varangian prince, Rurik. The Slavs whom he had subjugated paid him tribute. After Rurik's death, the warlike Oleg became prince. He did not remain in Novgorod, but went down the Dniepr and reached Kiev, which he conquered and made his capital.

From the beginning of the 10th century the Slav ~~state~~ *principality*[7] of Kiev was known as Kiev Russ.

Oleg united many Slavonic tribes under his rule and imposed heavy tribute upon them. A number of Slavonic princes were exterminated; the rest ~~accepted Oleg's invitation~~ *submitted to Oleg*[8] and joined him in plundering

[**FIGURE 9:**] Prince Oleg. [SH, 18]

and conquering[9] the Slavonic population. The Varangian conquerors soon combined together merged[10] with the Slavic princes and boyars Slavs[11] and adopted their language and together with them ruled the Kievan state[12].

Prince Oleg was a very energetic man. Under his rule Kiev was strongly fortified. Forts were built along the frontiers to protect the state from nomad peoples[13]. In 907 According to ancient tradition[14], Oleg, with a huge army, partly in boats and partly on horseback, went to war against Byzantium. He laid waste to the country around Tsargrad (Constantinople) and besieged that city. The Greek Emperor (as the chief ruler of the Greeks was known) paid Oleg a huge ransom: much gold, costly fabrics, wines and slaves. In the year 911, the[15] Greeks concluded a commercial treaty with Oleg.

Oleg greatly strengthened Kiev Russ. He gathered the scattered Slavonic tribes and principalities under his rule. Kiev Russ began to be respected by Byzantium, and by the neighbouring western states.

Prince Igor. After the death of Oleg in 857[16], Rurik's son, Igor, became prince. Under his rule the integration expansion[17] of Kiev Russ continued. Like Oleg, Igor was constantly at war. Under his reign two[18] campaigns were conducted against the Caucasus and two campaigns against[19] Byzantium. The Greeks paid Igor a large and costly ransom. He concluded a treaty with the Greeks in which he[20] pledged himself to protect Byzantium from nomad raiders.

Every autumn Igor collected tribute from the population. To collect this tribute he went among the people, and so this tribute was known as the "people's tribute." When the prince and his warriors came to a village, the inhabitants brought him furs, honey, wax and grain. The people's tribute was a heavy burden upon the population.

One year Prince Igor collected tribute from the Drevlyans, a Slavonic tribe which lived on the right bank of the Dniepr[21]. The Drevlyans gave him all he demanded. Igor departed. But then it seemed to him that he had collected too little. He returned and demanded an additional tribute. The Drevlyans then said to themselves: "If a wolf gets into the habit of visiting a herd he will devour it all. Let us kill him." They defeated the prince's druzhina, took the prince prisoner and put him to death by tying his legs to the tops of bent trees on either side of him; when the trees were released and straightened, he was torn in half.

[**FIGURE 10:**] The people's tribute. The prince and his men collecting
tribute from the people. The people have brought skins of animals,
wax and honey. The prince's servant checks the tribute and enters on
a tablet the amount of tribute that has been brought. [SH, 20]

7. Princess Olga and Prince Svyatoslav

Princess Olga. When Igor died, his wife, Olga, ruled the country. She
took cruel vengeance on the Drevlyans for killing her husband. Her warriors besieged the capital of the Drevlyans. They were encamped outside
the walls of the city for a whole year, but could not take it. *According to tradition,*[22] Olga then resorted to a stratagem. She called upon the Drevlyans
to pay a very light tribute—three pigeons and three sparrows from each
household. The Drevlyans agreed to pay this tribute. Olga ordered bits of
touchwood to be tied to the les of the pigeons and sparrows; the touchwood
was set alight and the birds released. The pigeons and sparrows flew back
to their nests in the city, and soon the whole city was on fire. Olga's forces
rushed into the burning city and killed many of its defenders. Olga then
imposed a heavy tribute upon the Drevlyans. Later on, however, she fixed
a definite amount of tribute for all the tribes, and so introduced order in

the levying of this tribute. Olga travelled to Byzantium to learn from the Greeks how to govern her country. ~~Olga was very pleased when she heard the Greek priests preaching that tsars ruled by divine right. She realized that the Greek religion would be an excellent means of strengthening the prince's power and of gathering the scattered Slavonic tribes into one state~~ *and there she became familiar with the religion of the Greeks*[23].

At that time the Slavs still adhered to their old beliefs. They did not understand the forces of nature and feared them. Their habitations were blown away by storms. Houses and trees were struck by lightning and burned. The sun burned up their crops. They ~~thought of~~ *believed that*[24] the sun, the wind and the thunder storm ~~as~~ *were*[25] gods. They made images of them in wood and stone, and sacrificed animals and sometimes children and captives, to them. In this way they hoped to placate the terrible gods they had themselves invented.

~~Olga understood that while the Slavs adhered to this old faith, they would stubbornly resist the prince's power.~~ *Olga was very pleased when she heard the Greek priests preaching that tsars ruled by divine right. She realized that the Greek religion would be an excellent means of strengthening the prince's*

[**FIGURE 11:**] The prince with a troop of horsemen.
From an ancient drawing. [SH, 21]

power and of gathering the scattered Slavonic tribes into one state.[26] She therefore adopted the Greek religion—Christianity—and tried to persuade her son, Svyatoslav, to do the same. But Svyatoslav refused. He believed that the Slavs could be united and a powerful state formed only by force of arms.

Prince Svyatoslav. After Olga, Svyatoslav became Prince of Kiev ~~in~~ 957. Svyatoslav spent all his life at war. *During his campaigns he*[27] slept on the ground in the open air, near the camp fire, using his saddle as a pillow. He ate whatever food was available—horseflesh, or the flesh of wild animals, roasted on burning coals. He was quite fearless and usually would warn his foes that he was going to attack them. He would send a messenger to say: "I am going against you."

Svyatoslav subjugated many tribes on the banks of the River Oka, plundered the cities of the Bulgars on the Volga and of the Circassians on the River Kuban, and laid waste to the kingdom of the Khazars. From that time the kingdom of the Khazars ceased to exist. The principality of Kiev, however, became stronger than ever. All the country on the shores of the Black Sea ~~ended up~~ *came*[28] under the rule of the Prince of Kiev.

Later on, Svyatoslav went to war against the Bulgars *who lived*[29] on the banks of the Danube. He captured many cities from them and wanted to transfer his capital from Kiev to the Danube. The cunning Byzantian emperor, fearing to have such a strong and warlike neighbour, urged the nomad Pechenegs, who then lived in the steppes on the shores of the Black Sea, to attack Kiev. While Svyatoslav was driving the Pechenegs from Kiev, the Bulgars on the Danube conspired with the Greeks to make war on him. ~~Having started this new~~ *In this*[30] war against the Bulgars and Greeks, Svyatoslav was defeated ~~and~~. *While*[31] returning to Kiev *he*[32] fell into an ambush set for him by the Pechenegs near the Dniepr Rapids, and was vanquished. Svyatoslav himself was killed[33] in battle. The Prince of the Pechenegs made his skull into a wine cup and drank from it at his feasts.

8. The Princes of Kiev Introduce a New Religion and Laws

The wars of Prince Vladimir. After a prolonged struggle against his brothers, Vladimir, Svyatoslav's son, became ruler of the principality of Kiev, and, like his father, went to war against his disobedient subjects. He crushed the rebellion of the tribes in the north, and plundered the cities of the Bulgars on the Volga. Then he marched his warriors against Poland and captured several of their[34] cities. He subjugated the Slavonic principality of Polotsk and the lands of several Lithuanian tribes, the western neighbours of the Slavs on the shores of the Baltic Sea. This is how the power of the principality of Kiev grew under Vladimir. Byzantium began to respect it more than ever. Vladimir helped Byzantium to crush a mutiny *of the Greek soldiers*[35]. As a reward for this the Byzantian emperor gave Vladimir his sister for wife. Vladimir decided to adopt the Christian religion. He thought that the adoption of the Greek faith and his kinship with the Emperor of Byzantium would make it easier for him to handle the rebellious people and raise his status *strengthen his rule*[36].

The introduction of Christianity. In the year **988**, Vladimir destroyed all the images of the ancient Slavonic *heathen*[37] gods in Kiev. The inhabitants of Kiev were forced to immerse themselves in the River Dniepr. The Greek priests, who had been brought over from Tsargrad (Constantinople), read prayers over the people as they stood in the water. This was called baptism.

Again and again the people rose up *rebelled*[38] against this new religion; but all the uprisings *rebellions*[39] were crushed by the prince's warriors.

Compared with idolatry, the introduction of Christianity marked a step forward in the development of Russia.[40] It was accompanied by the spread of Greek *culture and*[41] education among the Slavs. Byzantian craftsmen taught the Slavs to build and decorate houses and churches. Learned Greek monks invented the Slavonic alphabet, and this began to be used in the Kiev state. The prince gave the Greek priests and monks money and land. The monks wrote religious books in the Slavonic language, translating them from the Greek. They also wrote about what happened in *recorded the important events of*[42] their time. These records were kept "from annum to annum" (from year to year) and were called "annals." From these annals a great deal can be "learned about the history of our motherland *the Eastern Slavs*[43] and of the neighbouring countries. We also learn about those times from the folksongs and the legends called BYLINAS. The bylinas contain many stories about the brave deeds of the Slavonic heroes, or BOGATYRS, and about their struggles against the nomads who attacked the Kiev state.

Prince Yaroslav the Wise. After the death of Vladimir Yaroslav, who was later called the Wise, became Prince of Kiev.

Under Yaroslav, the first code of laws of the principality of Kiev, known as "Russkaya Pravda," or Russian Right, was compiled. "Russkaya Pravda" contained the laws protecting the rights of the slaveowners, landowners and merchants.

~~He made war with the Poles, who for a time captured Kiev and other cities. But the people rose up and defeated all the Poles. Their leader the king barely managed to escape and ran away to Poland, stealing the Kievan principality's treasury.~~[44]

9. ~~Popular~~ *Spontaneous*[45] Rebellions of the People in the Principality of Kiev

How the princes and boyars ruled the principality of Kiev. The princes of Kiev had a large number of warriors in their druzhinas consisting of boyars and serving men. The kinsmen of the prince and the boyars governed the cities and the lands in the name of the prince. Some of the boyars owned large estates, and in their wealth they rivalled the prince.

The prince, his army, the boyars, the priests and monks, all lived on the labour of the slaves and the husbandmen, the SMERDS, as they were called. The smerds owned *small plots of*[46] land and *small*[47] farms, and they were free men, *that is, they were not serfs*[48]. Under the first princes of Kiev they only paid a tribute, to collect which the princes went among the people.

In Kiev and other cities there lived handicraftsmen, merchants and the ~~oppressed~~ townfolk *poor*[49]. The merchants traded with the smerds and handicraftsmen and supplied goods to the princes, boyars and their troops. The merchants held the handicraftsmen in debt. The richer merchants carried on trade with other countries.

The free handicraftsmen built houses, churches and bridges, made clothes, pottery and arms. In furnaces blown with bellows they smelted ore and obtained iron. Blacksmiths worked in the cities and villages.

The inhabitants of the cities were governed by assemblies of the citizens known as the VECHE. The Veche elected the city chiefs from among the rich and prominent citizens. *The prince could not recruit soldiers or go to war without the consent of the Veche. Therefore he had to heed the Veche in many things.*[50] The princes tried to take the rule over the cities into their own hands, and tyrannized the smerds in the villages with impunity.

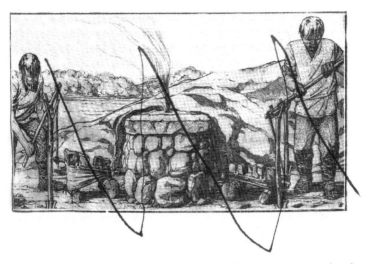

[**FIGURE 12:**] ~~A Catalan Forge, within a stone furnace. In it is coal and~~ ~~iron ore. People fan the furnace with bellows in order to melt the iron~~ ~~out of the ore.~~ [Cut by Zhdanov: RGASPI, f. 77, op. 1, d. 854, l. 9.]

The smerds turned into serfs by the princes and boyars. In the 11th century the princes and boyars greatly increased their oppression of the people. They established their own laws, acted as judges, and ill-treated the people. For example, under Yaroslav the Wise, the penalty for murdering a boyar was a fine of 80 grivnas (or 36 pounds of silver); but the penalty for murdering a smerd was only 5 grivnas.

The princes and boyars seized the land and declared it to be their own property. The smerds living on these seized lands were compelled to work in the fields of the princes and boyars, build bridges and fortifications. Gradually, the free husbandmen were turned into bonded peasants, that is to say, into serfs. The smerds retaliated by fresh revolts against the princes and boyars.

Spontaneous rebellions[51] **against the princes and boyars in the cities.** During the 11th and 12th centuries, there were many revolts in Kiev, Novgorod, and other cities. The princes and boyars brought out their druzhinas to crush these rebellions, and did so without much difficulty, *for the rebellions were spontaneous and unorganized*[52]. In 1113, the oppressed common people[53] of Kiev rose in rebellion against the rule of the prince, the merchant usurers and the rich Kiev-Pechersk Monastery. This rebellion was supported by the smerds. The boyars and merchants, *frightened by the rebellion*, ~~locked themselves in the prince's chapel and elected~~ *hastened to call*[54] Prince Vladimir Monomach to become Prince of Kiev. Vladimir crushed the rebellion. Fearing fresh outbreaks, he slightly reduced the debts to the usurers and introduced a slight improvements[55] in the conditions of a section of the husbandmen.

Vladimir Monomach was well known in Byzantium and Europe. *For the period in which he lived he*[56] was an educated man ~~and knew several foreign languages~~[57]. His mother was the daughter of the Emperor of Byzantium, and his sister was the wife of the German Emperor. His own wife was the daughter of the King of England. Vladimir Monomach was the last strong prince of Kiev.

10. The Land of Novgorod

The break-up of the principality of Kiev. In the 12th century, the principality of Kiev was ~~broken~~ *divided*[58] up among the sons, grandsons and kinsmen of ~~the prince~~ *Vladimir Monomach*[59]. They were constantly at war with one another over principalities and cities. During these wars the princes mercilessly plundered the smerds and city people, and forcibly pressed them into military service. The princes also treated one another cruelly. The vanquished princes had their eyes put out, and were starved to death in dungeons. Some of the princes ~~barricaded themselves off from each other,~~[60] became rich and declared their independence of the chief prince, the Grand Prince of Kiev. Thus, in the 12th century, the principality of GALICH VOLYNIA, west of Kiev, that of SUZDAL-ROSTOV in the north, and the land of NOVGOROD became rich and strong. The principality of Kiev was sacked by *nomad raiders*,[61] the Polovtsi, *from the south*[62]. The story of the struggle against these raiders, in the 12th century, has come down to us in the ancient "Lay of Igor's War."

The land of Kiev was laid waste still more by the plunder of the princes and boyars. The peasants could no longer bear their violence and deserted the Dniepr, to go as far away as they could, to the Oka and the Volga. Trade in Kiev began to decline. ~~Very few merchants began to travel by this inconvenient route "from the Varangians to the Greeks." Trade between Europe and the Asian~~

~~states now was now conducted~~ *The merchants began to travel from Europe to Asia*[63] by other routes, avoiding Kiev. The city of Kiev began to lose its importance as a ~~state~~[64] capital. By the ~~12th~~ *13th*[65] century Kiev became a desolate city. Novgorod became the principal city for trade with foreign countries.

The government of the land of Novgorod. ~~Already in the 11th century Kiev began to gradually lose control over the rich Novgorod lands, with its huge holdings in the north and the east. The main city in this land was Novgorod, which possessed several thousand households.~~ *Novgorod was situated on the route to the Baltic Sea, on the shores of which there were rich German and Swedish cities. The Novgorod merchants and boyars carried on a big trade with their neighbours, the Germans and Swedes. From them they bought cloth, weapons and other articles they could not manufacture themselves, and in exchange they sold furs and the products of agriculture. To obtain furs for their foreign trade, the Novgorod boyars and merchants conquered lands in the north and east and forced the hunters inhabiting those lands to surrender the spoils of the hunt to them. Thus Novgorod became the principal city of a very*

[**FIGURE 13:**] A Veche in Novgorod. The town handicraftsmen are airing their grievances against the boyars and rich merchants. [SH, 28]

big country. There were several thousand houses in this city. While Kiev was de-
clining, the Novgorod boyars and merchants were becoming rich by plundering
subjugated peoples and by trading with foreigners.[66]

All the affairs of the land of Novgorod were administered by the boyars,
rich merchants and priests. They assembled the inhabitants of Novgorod
in the Veche, or general assembly, but all matters were decided as the rich
and strong boyars wanted them to be. The mayor of Novgorod, known as
the POSADNIK, was elected by the Veche; but it was always a rich boyar who
was elected. The powers of the prince of Novgorod were limited. This was
definitely[67] established after the great rebellion in Novgorod in **1136**. At that
time, the people of Novgorod rose against the boyars and merchants, The
prince and the boyars fled; the people confiscated the lands of the prince and
his retinue and deprived them of the right to own land ~~forever~~[68]. They decreed that the prince must always have. beside him a posadnik who must be
elected by the Veche. The prince could neither go to war, sit in judgment or
dismiss or appoint officials without the consent of the posadnik. But ~~again~~[69]
the fruits of the people's victory over the prince were *again*[70] usurped by the
all-powerful Novgorod boyars. The inhabitants of Novgorod, the smerds of
the surrounding villages, and the subjugated tribes rebelled against their
rule many times. A rebellion broke out in 1209, the people in Novgorod
accusing the boyars of imposing excessive taxation and of oppressing the
smerds. The houses of many of the boyars and merchants were sacked, and
many of the oppressors were banished from the land of Novgorod. *But these*
were no more than spontaneous revolts.[71] The people were unable to break the
power of the boyars and merchants *owing to their lack of political conscious-*
ness and organization[72].

Novgorod's wars against the Swedes and Germans. In the beginning of the 13th century the Swedes attacked the land of Novgorod. They
marched from the Baltic Sea and the River Neva, where Leningrad is situated today. Novgorod defeated the Swedes on the Neva. In commemoration
of this victory, Prince Alexander, who was in command of the Novgorod
forces, was afterwards known as Alexander Nevsky (Alexander of Neva).

In **1242**, German knights tried to seize the land of Novgorod. They first
appeared on the shores of the Baltic Sea in the 12th century and mercilessly plundered and exterminated the Slavs, *Lithuanians and other tribes*[73]
inhabiting the Baltic country. Here they built their castles and towns and

still further increased their cruelties. They imposed their religion upon the inhabitants, deprived them of their freedom, and converted them into serfs.

The German knights, at the head of a strong army, fell upon the land of Novgorod, laid waste to its towns and threatened to destroy the city of Novgorod. Prince Alexander Nevsky collected his forces and gave battle to the Germans on the ice of Lake Chud. The battle was a very stubborn one; the ice became red with blood. In this Battle on the Ice the Germans failed to withstand the onslaught of the brave Novgorod warriors and were put to flight. Alexander Nevsky pursued the enemy to the very frontiers of his land. Thus the Novgorodians resolutely repelled the enemy and saved their land from the German invaders.

11. Suzdal Russ

The land of Rostov-Suzdal. ~~From the earliest times, troops from Kiev and Novgorod had raided the tribes that lived between the Volga and Oka. These invaders met stubborn resistance from the inhabitants of these regions: the Mordovians, Merias, Vess and other tribes.~~ *From the earliest times the land between the Volga and the Oka was inhabited by the Mordovians, Merias, Vess, and other tribes. It was also inhabited by Slavs.*[74] By the 10th century the Slavonic towns of Rostov and Suzdal had sprung up in this region. ~~The princes and boyars built other towns as well and fortified them. In an array of regions they proclaimed the land to be their own property and compelled the population to give them a portion of their harvest.~~[75]

Slav agriculturalists ~~and handicraftsmen~~[76] from the southern districts ~~and towns~~[77] of the principality of Kiev, which had been laid waste by the nomads, came here to settle ~~among the local tribes~~ *to escape from the violence of the princes and boyars. But here, too, the princes and boyars seized the land and compelled the inhabitants to work for them.*[78]

~~In the middle of the 12th century, the Rostov-Suzdal principality began to attract the attention of the princes of the Kievan state. This principality was on the far border of the Kievan state and was considered a part of it, but formerly had had little of interest to offer.~~ *At first the land of Rostov-Suzdal did not attract the attention of the princes of Kiev. But things changed in the 12th century, when this remote country became settled.*[79] Prince Yuri Dolgoruky, *son of Vladimir Monomach,*[80] came here from Kiev with a strong force of warriors and established his power, subordinating the domains of a number of boyars and minor princes to his rule. Among the estates he thus seized was the village of Moscow.

But the prince who most strongly established his rule in Rostov-Suzdal Russ was Andrei Bogolyubsky, Yuri Dolgoruky's son. He fought against Novgorod, against the Bulgars on the Volga, and against the Mordovian tribes. Then he captured Kiev and became the Grand Prince over extensive lands, covering nearly the whole of the principality of Kiev.

The principality of Vladimir-Suzdal. Andrei Bogolyubsky established his capital in the city of Vladimir, on the banks of the River Klyazma. ~~By that time the~~ *From that time on his*[81] principality ~~had become~~ *became*[82] known as Vladimir-Suzdal. Andrei Bogolyubsky tried to subjugate all the local princes and boyars.

Dissatisfied with Andrei Bogolyubsky's autocratic rule, the boyars conspired against him and killed him ~~in his own palace~~[83]. His place was taken by Prince Vsevolod. He confiscated the villages and lands belonging to the ~~resistant~~ *disobedient*[84] boyars and sternly punished ~~the boyars~~ *those*[85] who tried to establish themselves as independent princes.

Vsevolod organized several campaigns against Novgorod. He always managed to get his adherents chosen for elective positions in Novgorod.

Vsevolod extended his rule even ~~over~~ *to*[86] Kiev. He waged war on the Bulgars and Mordovians on the Volga. Several years later the city of Nizhni Novgorod (now the city of Gorky) was founded in that district on the Volga. Vsevolod failed to establish his power firmly over the other minor princes and boyars. After his death the principality of Vladimir-Suzdal ~~divided~~ *broke*[87] up into small domains. Every ~~owner~~ *prince and boyar*[88] tried to be independent and refused to obey the Grand Prince. The various small principalities fought one another.

~~At the beginning of the 13th century, Mongol invaders attacked these fragmented principalities that had been weakened by their wars against one another and conquered them.~~ *There was no united, strong state. Every rich landowner tried to secure more land and power. The princes were constantly at war with each other. The continuous wars ruined the peasant population. When later, in the 13th century, the Mongol conquerors attacked the Russian principalities they met with no real, united resistance. The land of Vladimir-Suzdal was broken up into small parts and could not defend its independence.*[89]

III

Eastern Europe under the Rule of the Mongol Conquerors

12. The Mongol Conquerors *and the Tatar-Mongol Yoke*[1]

The Mongols in the 12th century. The Mongols were nomad herdsmen. They inhabited the country that is now the Mongolian People's Republic.

In the 12th century the Mongols ~~had~~ *were divided into*[2] large warlike tribes, each headed by a khan. The khans owned many cattle and extensive pastures. The tribes under the khans' rule paid them tribute. The khans waged war against each other and against their neighbours over tribute and pastures.

In the beginning of the 13th century a gifted military leader named Genghiz Khan rose above the rest of the Mongol khans. He gathered an enormous army of various tribes and subjugated the ~~Turkish state~~ *Eastern Turco-Mongolian peoples.*[3]

[**FIGURE 14:**] A charge of Mongol horsemen. [SH, 32]

Genzhiz [SIC] Khan's horsemen swept down upon the enemy like a hurricane. They burned the wooden walls of fortresses with lighted grenades made of day and oil. Stone walls were broken down with huge engines. Nothing could withstand their onslaught.

Genghiz Khan's conquests in Central Asia and the Caucasus. After subjugating North China, Genghiz Khan marched his forces to Central Asia and conquered it. From Central Asia, rounding the southern coast of the Caspian Sea, his forces marched to the Caucasus and conquered Armenia and Georgia. In Georgia the Mongols met with strong resistance. At that time Georgia was a stronger state than Armenia. The Georgians fought bravely, but the Mongols defeated them and imposed heavy tribute upon Georgia *and Armenia*.[4] For hundreds of years Central Asia and the Trans-Caucasian peoples ~~were~~ *remained*[5] under the rule of the Mongols.

Khan Batu and his Russian conquests. After subjugating all the peoples of the Caucasus, the Mongolian army, in 1224, defeated the combined forces of the Slavonic princes and the Polovtsi in a battle on the River Kalka. Carrying rich booty with them, the Mongols returned to Asia.

Fourteen years later the Mongols again appeared on the Volga. At their head was Khan Batu, the grandson of Genghiz Khan, who by that time had died. *This time the Mongols attacked the Russians from the east.*[6] ~~He~~ Batu[7] destroyed the kingdom of the Volga Bulgars and vanquished the Mordovians, then defeated the armies of the Russian princes one by one, captured Kiev in **1240**, and marched on to Western Europe. Meeting with the resistance of the Czechs, Batu turned back and established in the lower reaches of the Volga a state known as the Golden Horde, with Sarai as the capital. This was a rich city, with stone palaces, ~~mosques,~~[8] orchards and a mint. The Khan of the Golden Horde began

[**FIGURE 15:**] Khan Batu. [SH, 33]

to rule the conquered lands[9]. The princes remained in their domains, but they were subjects of the khan.

The Tatar-*Mongols*[10] collected tribute from the people for the benefit of the khan. Viceroys were appointed to every city at the head of military forces for the purpose of collecting the tribute. No mercy was shown to anyone. In the words of an old ballad: ". . . from those who have no money their children are taken; from those who have no children, their wives are taken; from those who have no wives, their heads are taken" (that is to say, they are taken captive and sold into slavery). The priests and monks paid no tribute; the khan exempted them. In return for this exemption, the priests and monks read prayers in the churches on behalf of the rule of the khan, and urged the people to submit to him.

There were continuous revolts against the Tatar tribute collectors. The khans of the Golden Horde then charged the Russian princes themselves with the collection of the tribute. After subjugating the Russian principalities, Batu also laid waste to many Ukrainian and Byelorussian lands.

Thus was the Tatar, or rather, the Tatar-Mongolian yoke imposed.[11]

13. Moscow and the First Moscow Princes

Moscow. On the hill on which the Kremlin now stands, there was in the beginning of the 12th century the village of Moscow. In ancient documents Moscow is first mentioned in **1147**. In 1156, Moscow was surrounded by a wooden stockade.

The Tatar-*Mongols of Khan*[12] Batu burned down Moscow and the wooden stockade that protected it. Part of its inhabitants perished, and part fled to the surrounding forests. But gradually the inhabitants returned and began to till the land.

Towards the 14th century Moscow became the capital of a small principality. Moscow was centrally located among the Russian principalities, which helped the princes of Moscow to unite all the other principalities around it. Moscow was surrounded by forests, and this helped to protect it against enemies, and particularly, against the Tatars. Since Moscow was situated on convenient river routes, the princes were able to collect large sums in the form of duties imposed on all goods carried on the Moscow River.

RUSSIAN PRINCIPALITIES AND THE GOLDEN HORDE IN THE 13TH AND 14TH CENTURIES

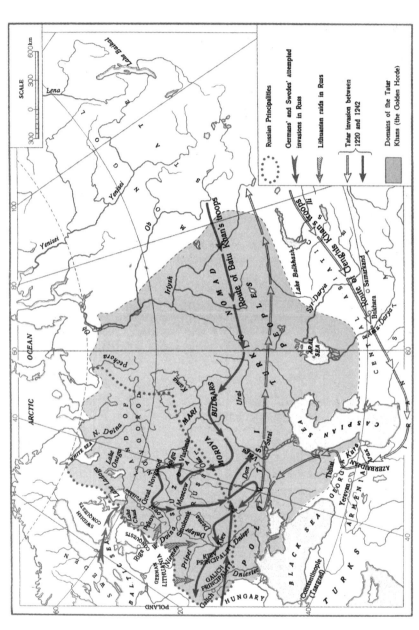

[MAP 2:] Russian Principalities and the Golden Horde in the 13th and 14th Centuries. [SH, 34–35. Stalin corrected the map in the 1937 Russian edition to read "Nomad *Turco-Mongolian* Peoples of the Kazakh-Steppe" and "Mongol *Empire State*." For the 1938 English edition, the mapmakers rendered "Nomadic *Turco-Mongolian* Peoples" as "*Turkic Nomad Peoples*" and "Genghiz" as "Genghis." Compare RGASPI, f. 558, op. 11, d. 1584, l. 18 and KRATKII KURS ISTORII SSSR (hereafter KKISSSR), 26–27, SH, 34–35]

Ivan Kalita. Moscow ~~grew and~~[13] became particularly strong under Prince Ivan (**1328–1341**), who was nicknamed Kalita, or Money-Bag. By means of gifts and flattery, Kalita got into the good favour of his overlord, the Khan of the Golden Horde, and obtained from him the right to collect the tribute for him in all the lands of Russia. Part of this tribute he kept for himself *and his principality*[14]. With the money thus hoarded he bought villages, counties, and even whole principalities. He also denounced his neighbour princes to the Tatars and incited the Tatar khan against them. Because of his denunciations, the Tatars killed the princes and laid waste to their principalities. Kalita annexed these ruined principalities to his principality of Moscow. The khan elevated Kalita over all the other Russian princes, *and gave him the title of Grand Prince*[15]. At the beginning of his reign Kalita had only four towns in his possession; at his death he bequeathed to his children 97 villages and towns.

Thus, resorting to every means, Kalita gathered the disunited Russian principalities into a single state with Moscow its centre.[16]

Kalita's descendants were also "gatherers" of the lands of Russia. At the end of the 14th century the principality of Moscow had become ~~such a strong state among the Russian principalities~~ *so strong*[17] that Kalita's grandson, Dmitry, decided to rise in open revolt against the Tatar yoke. In **1380**,

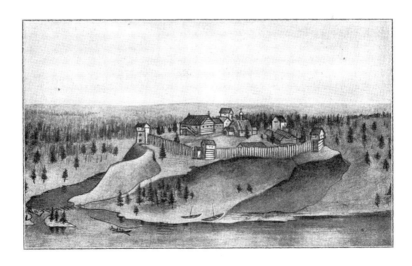

[**FIGURE 16:**] Moscow in the 12th century. [SH, 36]

on Kulikovo Field, on the River Don, he defeated the Tatar army *headed by Khan Mamai*[18]. Two years later, *however,*[19] the Tatars collected their forces again, attacked Moscow, captured it, and compelled it to pay tribute, but a smaller amount than before.

The young principality of Moscow grew strong, *nevertheless*[20]. The strength of the old enemy, the Golden Horde, was declining. But a new and strong enemy appeared on the western frontiers of the principality of Moscow. This was the Lithuanian state which had united with Poland.

Lithuania and Poland, the enemies of the Moscow state. ~~Uniting under the rule of a single prince,~~ The[21] Lithuanian tribes were neighbours of the Slavs, *and lived in the west*, on the shores of the Baltic Sea. *Towards the 13th century they united under the rule of a single prince,*[22] and in the 13th and 14th centuries they conquered the lands of the Byelorussians and part of the lands of Ukraine and Russia. Lithuania became a large state. At the end of the 14th century its frontiers nearly reached those of the Grand Principality of Moscow and included the city of Smolensk. The Lithuanian prince, Yagailo, who had married the Queen of Poland, became the King of Poland and Lithuania. The alliance between Lithuania and Poland strengthened both states. They now began to press upon the Grand Principality of Moscow more strongly than ever.

The Ukrainians, Byelorussians and Russians had lived a hard life under the rule of their princes and boyars. But their lot became worse under the rule of the Polish and Lithuanian conquerors, who reduced all the peasants to serfdom.

The PANS, as the Polish landlords were called, compelled the peasants to change their Greek Orthodox religion for the Roman Catholic religion which they themselves professed. The Polish pans in the Ukraine were particularly insistent on this change. In the towns the pans prohibited Ukrainians and Byelorussians from engaging in trade and handicrafts. The administration of the towns was entirely in the hands of the pans. The latter dreamed of subjugating the whole of the principality of Moscow; but they were attacked by the German knights who had settled on the shores of the Baltic Sea. The Germans sacked the Lithuanian and Polish towns and laid waste to the land. The Poles and Lithuanians were not strong enough to fight the Germans and wage war against Moscow at the same time; but when their united forces had defeated the Germans they resumed their attacks upon the Moscow state with greater energy. In order to subdue Moscow the pans concluded an alliance with the Tatars.

14. Tamerlane and the Decline of the Golden Horde

Tamerlane. While the young principality of Moscow, having united under the rule of a single prince, grew and became strong, the old empire[23] of Genghiz Khan gradually became enfeebled. China threw off the yoke of the Mongols. The Mongol Empire itself gradually broke up into separate parts. Only from time to time now great conquerors arose among the Mongol khans. One of these conquerors was Tamerlane.

Tamerlane was born in Central Asia, in 1336. When he was a young man he became the leader of a band of daring warriors and placed his forces at the service, first of one ruler, and then of another. Tamerlane first came to the forefront during the suppression of a popular rebellion in the city of Samarkand, in Central Asia. After cruelly suppressing the rebels, Tamerlane proclaimed himself the ruling khan, and made Samarkand his capital.

Tamerlane conquered a number of neighbouring states. In 1395 he defeated Tokhtamysh, the Khan of the Golden Horde, and thus helped Moscow to free itself more quickly from the Tatar yoke. ~~This allowed Moscow to struggle more successfully~~ *The princes of Moscow took advantage of the declining strength of the Golden Horde and turned their forces*[24] against Lithuania and Poland. At the end of the 14th century, Tamerlane destroyed Tbilisi, the capital of Georgia, and took the Georgian king captive.

Tamerlane was fierce and cruel. Once, after capturing a town, he buried alive 4,000 of the inhabitants. After capturing another town he ordered his warriors to cut off the heads of 70,000 inhabitants, collect them and heap them up tower-high.

In every country he subjugated, Tamerlane chose the best craftsmen and sent them to Central Asia. To his capital, Samarkand, which he wanted to convert into a beautiful city, he sent 150,000 craftsmen. He built many palaces in the city and outside the city. The walls of these palaces were decorated with paintings depicting his campaigns. Tamerlane's Mosque in Samarkand is to this day an edifice of striking grandeur and beauty.

The Uzbeks in Central Asia. After Tamerlane's death in 1405, the states he conquered gradually became independent again.

In the 15th century, Central Asia was conquered by the nomad Uzbeks, who ~~until~~ *before*[25] then had inhabited the country of what is now Kazakhstan. The Uzbeks firmly established themselves in Central Asia. The Uzbek khans became the rulers of the ~~modest but hardy~~[26] Horezm and Bokhara states.

IV

The Rise of the Russian National State

15. The Expansion of the Moscow State under Ivan III, *and the End of the Tatar-Mongol Yoke*[1]

The annexation of Novgorod and the release of the Moscow state from the yoke of the Tatar khans. In order to fight the Tatars and the Lithuanian and Polish pans, the princes of Moscow strove to enlarge their domains and to establish their rule over all the lands of Russia. This was achieved by Ivan III. He became Grand Prince ~~after~~ *in*[2] **1462**. But he was still subjected to the Khan of the Golden Horde, although the latter was now weakened. Ivan deceived the khan by assuring him of his loyalty, but secretly he strove to ~~collect~~ *gather*[3] forces and emancipate himself from subjugation to the Tatars. Ivan. III united under his rule a number of neighbouring principalities. The princes did not want to be united under the rule of one ~~ruler~~ *prince*[4], and had concluded alliances with the Tatars and Lithuania, against Moscow. Nevertheless, Ivan III succeeded during his reign in making Muscovy a strong and united Russian national state. The land of Novgorod alone remained ~~outside of the union~~ *a separate state*[5].

At the end of the 15th century, Ivan III went to war against Novgorod, ~~which was heavily involved in foreign trade~~[6]. The boyars of Novgorod concluded an alliance with Lithuania, but this did not save them. Ivan III defeated the Novgorod army, and Novgorod ~~from that moment~~[7] also became a part of the united Russian state. By this time the Golden Horde had broken up into three khanates: Kazan, Astrakhan and Crimea. The Realm of Siberia, on the River Irtysh, seceded from it. The break-up of the Golden Horde gave an ~~enormous~~[8] advantage to the princes of Moscow. The Golden Horde was no longer terrible for the Russian state, which had now become strong.

Choosing a favourable moment, Ivan III declared to the Khan of the

[**Figure 17:**] Foreign merchants unloading their
wares at the wharf in Novgorod. [SH, 41]

Golden Horde that he no longer recognized his overlordship over Moscow.
The khan then went to war against Ivan III. The opposing armies met on the
River Ugra, but neither of them dared to go into battle. They stood facing
each other for several months. The winter frosts set in. The khan lacked
fodder for his horses, and, moreover, news was received of revolts in the
Horde. The khan decided to turn back, *and Ivan III thus became the "victor"*.
This was in the year **1480**. *The yoke of the Tatar-Mongols, which Russia had
borne for over two hundred years, was thrown off.*[10]

The Golden Horde had become quite feeble, and soon after it fell to
pieces.

Ivan III's war against Lithuania and Poland. In 1500 a stubborn war
broke out between Ivan III and the King of Poland and Lithuania. The Polish
and Lithuanian armies were utterly defeated and their chief commander
was taken prisoner. The King of Poland and Lithuania then concluded an alliance with the German knights of the Baltic. At first, the Germans inflicted

defeat on the forces of Ivan III; but soon after, his armies took the offensive, defeated the Germans, and laid waste to their lands.

The war ended with the conclusion of an armistice for six years. Ivan III retained possession of the Russian and Byelorussian lands he had captured from the pans.

Under the reign of Ivan III the possessions of the Russian state increased threefold.

[**FIGURE 18:**] The emblem of the principality of Moscow in the reign of Ivan III. [SH, 42]

"Ivan III, Ruler of all the Russias." After the conquest of Byzantium by the Turks in 1453, Ivan III married the Greek princess, Sophia Palaeologue. Ivan III now declared ~~everywhere~~[11] that he was the successor to the Byzantian emperors. He adopted the ancient emblem of Byzantium, the Double Eagle, as the emblem of the Moscow state, and he began to call himself Tsar and "Ruler of all the Russias."

Ivan now made great efforts to beautify Moscow. For this purpose he invited Italian craftsmen, technicians and painters to Moscow. He reconstructed the small Moscow Kremlin, and converted it into a huge stone and brick castle, with buildings of a kind hitherto unseen in Moscow. To this day the walls and towers of the Kremlin built by the Italians serve as a striking monument of the times of Ivan III.

In the Kremlin Palace Ivan introduced the pomp and customs of the court of the Greek emperors.

The increase in the power of the Prince of Moscow, *however*,[12] led to an increase in the boyars' oppression of the masses of the peasantry.

16. How the Peasants in the Moscow State Were Oppressed in the 15th Century

Forced labour (barshchina and obrok). In all parts of the principality of Moscow there were the estates of the prince, boyars arid the monasteries. The landlords lived with their families, servants and guards in manors which were shut off by high fences. The villages in which the peasants

[**FIGURE 19:**] A ~~boyar's~~ *prince's* manor house. [Edited by
Zhdanov: RGASPI, f. 77, op. 1, d. 854, l. 17; SH, 44]

lived were scattered all around the manor. ~~In each village there were a few~~
~~households.~~[13] The peasants lived in low huts without windows or chimneys,
and with an earthen floor. They tilled the land with the sokha, or wooden
plough.

~~The peasants did everything for the landowners in exchange for the~~
~~plots which that cultivated and which no longer belonged to them.~~ *The plots*
of land which the peasants cultivated for their sustenance no longer belonged to
them, but to the prince, the boyars and the monasteries. In return for the right
to use the land the peasants were compelled to do all that the landlord demanded
of them.[14]

~~They built his manor house, his outhouses, his bridges, dug ponds and~~
~~trenches, threshed and ground his grain, and mowed his hay and stacked it~~
~~on the manor grounds.~~ *They tilled the landlord's land, threshed and ground his*
grain, mowed his hay and stacked it in the manor grounds, built his manor house,
his outhouses, constructed bridges, and dug ponds and roadside trenches.[15]

But this was not enough for the princes, the boyars and the monasteries.

They still thought that the peasants were tilling too much for themselves and too little for their masters. They therefore began to take part of the plots of land which the peasants cultivated *for themselves*[16]. They compelled the peasants to do more work on the master's land. This forced labour was known as BARSHCHINA.

In addition to barshchina, the peasants were compelled to give their masters a part of the produce of their farms, such as grain, cattle, chickens, eggs, milk, butter and so on. This payment in kind was called OBROK. Those peasants who failed to perform barshchina or pay obrok were severely punished. They were beaten with sticks almost to death and flung into prison.

The peasants become bound to the soil. The peasants were allowed to leave their masters if they desired to do so but were compelled to leave their farms and farm buildings and pay up all their debts to their masters, which debts were considerable. On leaving one master the peasant had to seek another who would allow him to settle on his land. The conditions for tilling the land were the same in the new place as they were in the old. The peasant could not escape from bondage except by fleeing to lands where there were no masters. *But s*uch[17] free land became more and more scarce.

The landlords found it unprofitable to allow the peasants to leave whenever they desired. The boyars and the monasteries began to allow peasants to go to another master only after the harvest work was over. In 1497 Ivan III passed a law which permitted peasants to pass from one master to another only *on St. George's Day,*[18] in the late autumn, at the end of November[19].

In this way the peasants were tied to their masters' land to an ever greater extent. The master had the right to sit in judgment over his peasants, and to beat them with sticks if they disobeyed him. In addition to the boyars and the monasteries, a new type of landlord arose during the reign of Ivan III. These were the POMESHCHIKS, or gentry who had been in military service, or in the service of the princes and boyars. As a reward for their services in war, or for protecting the frontiers, they received from the prince grants of land with the peasants who lived on it. From this land, which was tilled by the peasants and was entirely under the rule of the pomeshchik, the latter had to maintain himself and his family, acquire military equipment and a horse, and in case of war, to provide a certain number of men.

The prince "placed" his serving men on parts of the new lands which they conquered. These estates were therefore called "POMESTYA" (from the word "pomestit"—to place) and the landlords were known as POMESH-CHIKS. The boyars, however, owned their land by right of inheritance; the land passed from father to son and these estates were therefore called VOTCHINAS, or patrimonies.

V

The Expansion of the Russian State

17. Ivan IV and the Defeat of the Volga Tatars

The autocrat. Tsar Ivan III's grandson, the future ~~terrible tsar~~[1] Ivan IV, *known as Ivan the Terrible,*[2] lost his father at an early age. The boyars poisoned his mother and ruled the country for ten years. The young Ivan grew up among the arrogant boyars, who treated him with contempt and imbued him with all the bad habits imaginable.

In **1547**, Ivan, then only seventeen years of age, proclaimed himself to be the autocratic tsar, the first of the rulers of Moscow to claim this title, and began to govern the country by himself, ignoring the boyars.

Ivan IV considered it very important for the purpose of strengthening his rule that people in his kingdom should acquire education by reading books which glorified the reign of the tsar. For this purpose he made use of the art of printing books which had been invented abroad, and established a printing office in Moscow. Here books were printed under his strict supervision. The first Russian printer to work in this printing

[**FIGURE 20:**] Tsar Ivan the Terrible (1530–1584). From a painting by V. Vasnetsov. [Zhdanov reversed Figures 20 and 22. See RGASPI, f. 77, op. 1, d. 854, l. 18; f. 17, op. 120, d. 373, ll. 143, 1440b, 628. Also SH, 46]

office was Ivan Fedorov.[3]

The conquest of Kazan and Astrakhan. In order to strengthen his power, Ivan IV pursued the same policy of conquest as was pursued by his grandfather, Ivan III, and by his father, Vasili III, who had captured Smolensk from Lithuania. Ivan IV decided first to capture the Tatar khanates on the Volga. With a large army and many cannon, he laid siege to Kazan, the capital of the khanate of Kazan, in the autumn of 1552.

The siege lasted the whole autumn. The Tatars fought with desperate courage and stubbornness. The tsar blew up the secret tunnel from Kazan to the river, and the inhabitants of Kazan were compelled to drink contaminated water from puddles and wells. Still the people of Kazan continued to defend their city, repelling the attackers day and night.

The tsar ordered the walls of the city to be undermined and blown up with gunpowder. Fierce fighting took place at the city gates and in the breaches of the walls. Even the Tatar women and children took part in the fighting, defending their city from the enemy. But the strength of the de-

[**FIGURE 21:**] The Church of Vasili the Blessed, built by
Ivan IV after the capture of Kazan. [SH, 48]

fenders of Kazan became exhausted. Ivan IV's troops, numbering 150,000, overcame the Tatars. ~~By his order, they killed all the residents of Kazan.~~[4] Kazan was sacked and burned to the ground.

~~In honor of the victory over the Tatars, Russian masters built the nota-~~ble Church of ~~Vasili the Blessed In Moscow during Ivan's reign.~~[5]

A large number of Moscow serving men and merchants were transferred to Kazan; the Tatars, however, were permitted to live only in a suburb. The lands of Kazan were distributed among Russian serving men. In many parts of the Kazan khanate fortresses were built, in which Muscovite troops were stationed. These fortresses were built by the forced labour of the inhabitants of the khanate of Kazan: Tatars, Mordovians, Maris, Chuvash and Bashkirs. With the subjugation of Kazan they all came under the rule of Ivan IV.

In 1556, the armies of Ivan IV captured the city of Astrakhan on the Volga, the capital of the Nogai Tatars. Thus, the whole of the Volga route fell into the hands of the Russian tsar.

After this, Ivan IV seized the northeastern part of the Caucasus and built several fortresses on the River Terek. The

[**FIGURE 22:**] Ivan Fedorov at his printing press. [Zhdanov reversed Figures 22 and 20. See RGASPI, f. 77, op. 1, d. 854, l. 18; f. 17, op. 120, d. 373, ll. 143, 1440b, 628. Also SH, 49]

Circassian and Kabardin princes began to enter his service.

From a national state, the Russian state began to grow into multinational state, that is to say, a state ~~assembled from~~ *consisting of*[6] different nationalities.

18. Reprisals against the Boyars and Ivan IV's Wars

The oprichniks. After conquering the lands of the Tatars on the Volga and entrenching himself in the North Caucasus, Ivan IV went to war against the Baltic Germans, Poland, Lithuania and the Swedes. His object was to reach the shores of the Baltic Sea and establish intercourse with the

~~educated western~~ *West European*[7] nations. The Swedes and Germans barred the way of foreign craftsmen travelling to Moscow, and did all they could to hinder Russian trade.

After the first defeats in the war, Ivan discovered that he was being betrayed by ~~an array of~~[8] the big patrimonial boyars. These traitors went into the service of the Poles and Lithuanians. Tsar Ivan hated the boyars, who lived in their patrimonies like little tsars and tried to limit his autocratic power. He began to banish and execute the rich and strong boyars. He thought it necessary to fight the boyars in order to crush these little tsars and to strengthen his position as sole ruler. To fight the boyars he recruited from among the pomeshchiks a special force, several thousand strong. This force he called the OPRICHNIKS.

The oprichniks wore a special uniform. ~~The oprichnik, dressed from head to two in black, rode on a dark horse with a black saddle.~~[9] Attached to his saddle each oprichnik had a dog's head and a broom. This was the emblem of their office: to hunt and track the enemies of the tsar, and to sweep away the treacherous boyars.

Ivan IV and his oprichniks exterminated many boyars. The lands of the executed boyars were distributed among the oprichniks and other pomeshchiks. In this way, Ivan the Terrible strengthened autocratic power in the Russian state and destroyed the privileges of the boyars.

[**FIGURE 23:**] An oprichnik with a broom in his hand and a dog's head fastened to his saddle. From an ancient drawing. [SH, 50]

He thus, as it were, completed the work, started by Ivan Kalita, of gathering together the scattered appanage principalities into one strong state.[10]

Peasants and Cossacks. *During the reign of Ivan IV, the conditions of the peasants became much worse. Towards the end of his reign peasants were forbidden to leave their masters even in the late autumn, on St. George's Day.*[11]

To escape the plunder and violence of the landlords and oprichniks, the peasants fled from Central Russia to the steppes in the southern regions of the country and settled there. Many of these fugitive peasants settled on the banks of the rivers Don and Dniepr. Soon settlements sprang up here, the inhabitants of which called themselves Cossacks.

The war for the Baltic lands. For twenty-four years Ivan the Terrible waged war for the purpose of conquering the lands of the Baltic; but in the end he failed. The Poles and the Lithuanians captured the Baltic region, ~~gaining the submission of the Germans there,~~[12] and reconquered the Byelorussian lands which Ivan the Terrible had captured at the beginning of the war. The Swedes drove him from the coast of the Gulf of Finland. A convenient sea route for trade with foreign countries was thus lost.

Ivan the Terrible was therefore obliged to carry on trade with foreign countries only through the White Sea, which was an inconvenient route, and, moreover, was frozen for several months in the year. It was an English sea captain who discovered this route by chance. He was trying to reach the Indian Ocean VIA the Arctic Ocean, but a storm drove his vessel to the mouth of the Yermak North Dvina, where, later, the Port of Archangel was built. ~~At the end of the 16th century the lands of Western Siberia were joined to the kingdom of Moscow.~~[13]

The conquest of the Siberian kingdom. *At the end of the 16th century the lands of Western Siberia were joined to the kingdom of Moscow.*[14] The kingdom of Siberia was inhabited by Tatars and other Siberian peoples. They were ruled over by Khan Kuchum. In **1581**, the Stroganovs, a family of rich merchants, owners of land in the Urals, sent a small detachment of mercenary troops consisting of Cossacks, well armed with firearms, against Kuchum. This detachment, under the command of Yermak, defeated the much more numerous army of Khan Kuchum which was armed with bows and arrows.

Ivan the Terrible rewarded Yermak with a suit of armour and his own fur coat, and also gave the Cossacks in his detachment rich rewards. Later on, however, Kuchum succeeded in defeating Yermak's detachment. Yermak himself perished in the River Irtysh during a night attack by Kuchum's warriors. ~~Yermak wore iron chainmail. Fleeing from those attacking him on the riverbank, he leapt onto a boat but stumbled, fell into the water, and drowned.~~[15] Kuchum once again established his rule in the kingdom of Siberia, but not for long. A few years later an army was sent against him from Moscow, which finally subjugated the kingdom of Siberia.

Under the reign of Ivan IV, Russia's possessions were enlarged many-fold. His kingdom became one of the biggest states in the world.[16]

[**FIGURE 24:**] Yermak. [SH, 51]

EXPANSION OF THE RUSSIAN STATE IN THE XIV–XVII CENTURIES

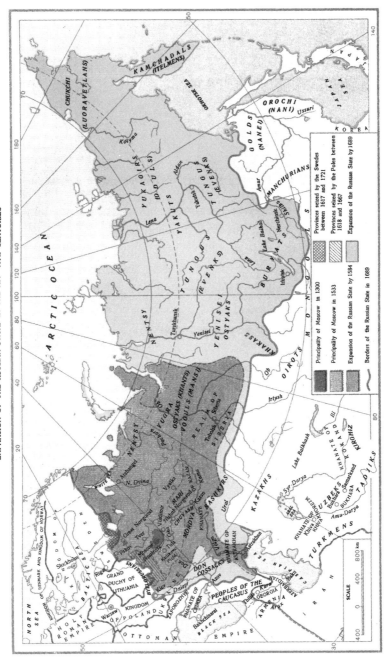

[MAP 3:] A Map of the Expansion of the Borders of the Russian *Russian* State in the XIV–XVII Centuries. [SH, 52–53. In the 1937 edition, Stalin shortened the title and replaced the adjectival ethnonym "Russian" (Russkoe) with the more general adjective "*Russian*" (Rossiiskoe). Compare RGASPI, f. 558, op. 11, d. 1584, l. 27 and KKISSSR, 42–43]

VI

The Peasant Wars and Revolts of the Oppressed Peoples in the 17th Century

19. The First Peasant War in the Russian State

Tsar Boris Godunov and the beginning of the peasant revolts. Ivan IV died in **1584**. Shortly before his death he killed his eldest son, ~~also named~~[1] Ivan, in a fit of anger, by striking him on the temple with his staff. Two other sons remained, Fedor, who was an imbecile, and Dmitry, who was still a child. The imbecile Fedor became tsar. Under his reign the country was governed by his brother-in-law, Boris Godunov, who was formerly one of Ivan the Terrible's oprichniks. Little Dmitry, who had lived with his mother in the town of Uglich, died, *or was done to death by Godunov's adherents.*[2]

After the death of Fedor in 1598, Boris Godunov became tsar.

Under Godunov's reign the conditions of the peasantry became much worse. The peasants fled from the landlords to the Ukraine and to the Don. For three years running the harvest had failed. A severe famine set in. The peasants ate chaff, cats and dogs, and were even reduced to cannibalism. A plague broke out; corpses were strewn along the roads, but there was no one to bury them. In a number of places the peasants rose in revolt and wrecked the mansions of their oppressors, the boyars and the pomeshchiks. Popular unrest also broke out in the towns.

The first attempts of the Polish pans to subjugate the Russian ~~king-dom~~ *state*.[3] The old enemies of the Russian state, the Polish pans, decided to take advantage of the favourable situation created for them by the unrest, to attempt to subjugate Russia. For this purpose they spread die rumor that Dmitry, the son of Ivan the Terrible, did not die in Uglich, but had fled from Boris Godunov to Poland. The Poles found a man to suit their purpose, proclaimed that he was the TSAREVICH, or Crown Prince, Dmitry, and sent him with their army against Moscow. This false Dmitry was to dethrone

Boris Godunov and take his place as tsar. In the Ukraine, False Dmitry, as he is known, was joined by the Cossacks of the Don and the Dniepr, who were discontented with the boyars.

At this time Tsar Boris Godunov died, and the tsar's troops made no resistance to False Dmitry. False Dmitry reached Moscow without hindrance, and entered the city with great pomp as the real tsar. The mother of the dead Tsarevich Dmitry had been bribed by the boyars and publicly recognized the pretender as her son. False Dmitry became tsar.

The Poles rejoiced; their plan had succeeded. Their henchman was tsar in Moscow. False Dmitry married a Polish woman named Marina Mnishek and he granted her father large tracts of land. The Poles who came to Moscow were given the best positions in the state and began to oppress and rob the people. False Dmitry openly treated the ancient Russian customs with contempt.

Unrest broke out among the people against the Poles and against the new tsar.

The people began to attack the Poles. The boyars, taking advantage of the unrest, conspired against False Dmitry and killed him. The pretender's corpse was burned on a bonfire and his ashes were rammed into a cannon and shot out in the direction from which he had come.

False Dmitry was succeeded on the throne by Vasili Shuisky, a rich patrimonial landowner and boyar of ancient family. He was chosen as tsar on Red Square in Moscow. This election was arranged by the boyars and the rich merchants during the popular revolt against the Poles.

The peasant Ivan Bolotnikov, the peasants' leader. The peasant revolt continued under the reign of Shuisky. At this time, an energetic leader named Bolotnikov rose among the peasants. Bolotnikov had formerly been a serf to one of the boyars and had fled from him. He had been to ~~other countries~~ *Turkey and Italy*[4], and had seen a great deal. He was a gifted military leader, and the peasants, minor serving men and Cossacks rallied to him in large numbers. He collected an army in the south, and in **1606** marched on Moscow to overthrow the boyar tsar, Vasili Shuisky, *and to put a "good" tsar in his place*[5].

In the towns and villages along the line of march the rebels captured the tsar's officials, exterminated the boyars and pomeshchiks, laid waste to their estates and destroyed the houses of rich merchants. ~~On the Volga,~~

[**FIGURE 25:**] Peasants going to join Bolotnikov's army. [SH, 55]

~~there was an uprising underway of the oppressed peoples—the Mordvins and the Tatars. In Siberia, the enslaved Ostyaki and Vorguls also rose up.~~[6] Detachments of small landowners, who here discontented with the tyranny of the boyars and with the boyar tsar, Shuisky, also joined Bolotnikov's army.

Bolotnikov laid siege to Moscow. The small landowners who had joined Bolotnikov soon realized that his victory would ~~cost them their estates and serfs~~ *weaken the power of the landlords*[7]. During a battle outside of Moscow these landlord detachments betrayed Bolotnikov and deserted to the side of the boyars and Tsar Shuisky. Bolotnikov's army was defeated.

Bolotnikov retreated, first to Kaluga and then to Tula, in order to prepare for another attack on Moscow. Shuisky with a large army besieged Bolotnikov in Tula. The rebel army defended itself heroically. ~~The siege of Tula lasted three months. Only Shuisky's craftiness allowed him to take Tula. He built a dam, flooded the city and forced the besieged to surrender. Many of those surrendering sat on barrels of gunpowder, lit the fuses and~~

~~blew themselves up in order to avoid falling into captivity. Shuisky cruelly exacted revenge on the rebels. People by the thousands were drowned in the river or had their heads cut off,~~ *but suffered defeat. This is not surprising. The peasants at that time had no such ally and leader as the working class. Besides, the peasants themselves lacked political consciousness. They did not fight against tsarism and landlordism, but against the bad tsar and the bad landlords. They wanted a "good" tsar and "good" landlords.*[8]

In the winter of **1607** Ivan Bolotnikov was taken prisoner by the boyars. They put out his eyes and then took him to the river and drowned him in a hole in the ice. ~~Along with the Tatar and Mordvin landlords, Shuisky crushed the uprising of the Volga and Siberian peoples.~~[9] The conditions of the ~~enserfed~~ *defeated*[10] peasantry became still worse. Shuisky issued new decrees increasing the state of bondage of the serfs. These decrees gave the landlords the right to search for and bring back fugitive peasants for a period of fifteen years from the time of their escape. The peasant revolts continued. ~~After the failure of their first attempt to subjugate Russia, the Polish pans made another attempt.~~[11]

20. The Struggle against the Polish Usurpers

The Polish usurpers and their expulsion from Moscow. *After the failure of their first attempt to subjugate Russia, the Polish pans made another attempt.*[12] They put forward another pretender. The rumour was spread that it was not False Dmitry who was killed in Moscow, but another man and that Dmitry had escaped. This new False Dmitry marched at head of a Polish army 10,000 strong. He encamped with his army in the village of Tushino, near Moscow, and called upon Shuisky to abdicate the throne in his favour. Shuisky appealed to the Swedes for help. The Swedes, taking advantage of the weakness of the Moscow government, captured Novgorod. ~~Worried about a Swedish power in Russia,~~ *At the same time*[13] the Polish king, Sigizmund, reached Smolensk at the head of an army, defeated the Moscow troops and captured the city. Russia's enemies were tearing her to pieces.

The Moscow nobles drove Shuisky from the throne and compelled him to enter a monastery. At this time the second False Dmitry was killed. *Meanwhile, popular unrest continued. The Moscow boyars were unable to cope with the rebels.*[14] To save themselves they chose the Polish Crown Prince,

Wladislaw, son of King Sigizmund, tsar in place of Shuisky. "It is better to serve the Crown Prince than be beaten by our own serfs," they said. In the autumn of 1610, the Polish forces entered Moscow *with the help of the boyars*[15] and occupied the Kremlin. The Polish pans plundered the Treasury of the Moscow tsars. The usurpers seized the landed estates and distributed them among their adherents, and oppressed and robbed the Russian people.

Six months later, in the spring of 1611, the people of Moscow rose in rebellion against the Polish oppressors. Barricades of tables, boxes and logs were built in the streets of Moscow. Behind these the people of Moscow fired at the Poles. From the roofs of the houses a rain of bullets and stones poured down upon them. The Poles set fire to Moscow, and the greater part of the city was burned. The Poles fortified themselves behind the walls of the Kremlin. In the autumn of 1611 the whole[16] people of Russia rose in rebellion against the Polish usurpers.

[**FIGURE 26:**] Minin calling upon the people to fight the Poles. [SH, 58]

The march against the Poles entrenched in Moscow was organized and led by a Nizhni Novgorod meat merchant, Kozma Minin. He appealed to the people in the towns to collect money; with this money he equipped a large host and[17] army. The choice of commander of his army fell upon Prince Pozharsky, an experienced military leader. A number of the peasant detachments who were fighting the landlords joined his army. This decided the issue. The people's army marched to Moscow and besieged the Poles in the Kremlin. In 1612 the Kremlin was captured and the Poles fled from Moscow. They were also compelled to leave the lands they had seized; but Smolensk remained in their hands. It was only five years after the war that the Swedes restored Novgorod to Russia; but the whole coast of the Gulf of Finland, with the Russian towns on it, remained in the possession of Sweden. In 1613 an assembly of representatives of the landlords, merchants and Cossacks was held in Moscow. This assembly elected Michael, of the boyar family of Romanov, tsar.

The suppression of the peasant movement. The new tsar waged a fierce struggle against the popular movement, which had not yet subsided. Numerous armed detachment of fugitive peasants and Cossacks roamed around Moscow and all over the country. The tsar sent troops to crush these detachments and those who had taken part in the rebellion. In Moscow the tsar's chancellories, with their scriveners and under-scriveners, got busy again; and again the people groaned under the tyranny of the VOYEVODAS, or governors of provinces, and officials.

With a generous hand Tsar Michael distributed estates and high salaries to the landlords.

Tsar Michael carefully protected the interests of the landlords who had elected him.

21. The Revolts of the Townspeople and of the Oppressed Nationalities in the 17th Century

Revolts in the towns. After the death of Tsar Michael Romanov, his son Alexei became tsar of Muscovy. By his order a heavy salt tax was introduced in 1646. This tax roused the anger of the people. Fearing a rebellion, Tsar Alexei repealed the tax. But the tax was not the only trouble. Even after it was repealed the people of Moscow rose against their oppressors. In 1648

[**FIGURE 27:**] The Zemsky Sobor in 1649. [SH, 60]

the people of Moscow caused a "riot," as popular rebellions were called at that time. The people well remembered the wrongs inflicted upon them by the tsar's servants and officials. They demanded that the chief of these officials be surrendered to them for punishment.

The tsar promised to fulfil the demands of the rebels, but he sent his horsemen against them, who beat them with whips and trampled upon them with their horses. Then the crowds of people wrecked the houses of the most hated of the boyars and tsarist officials. They *and*[18] killed a number of them. The rebellion was crushed by the tsar's troops. In that year, 1648, a rebellion in Kursk was *rebellions in other towns were*[19] also crushed. After this, the tsar assembled[20] the representatives of the boyars, landlords and merchants in what was known as the ZEMSKY SOBOR. In **1649** they passed a law granting the landlords the right to search for and bring back fugitive peasants no matter how long since they had escaped. The peasants were made complete serfs. A census was taken of all villages and peasant households. It became very difficult for a fugitive peasant to hide anywhere. At that time, also, handicraftsmen and small traders were forbidden to move from one town to another without permission.

In the towns the handicraftsmen lived in special districts called SLO-BODAS, according to their occupations. For example, there was a Tanners' Sloboda, Potters' Sloboda, Gunsmiths' Sloboda, etc. There were many such slobodas in Moscow which was the largest city in the country. The narrow crooked streets of these slobodas in Moscow were lined with small houses with two or three tiny windows.

The handicraftsmen earned little. Their lives were very hard; they were robbed by the voyevodas and merchants.

The revolts of the handicraftsmen and town poor continued. These revolts assumed particularly large dimensions in Pskov arid Novgorod in 1650. They were joined by the peasants. Tsar Alexei had to send a large army to suppress the revolts.

The town poor rose in rebellion also in subsequent years. For example, a great revolt broke out in Moscow in 1662.[21] In suppressing this revolt the tsar's soldiers killed and drowned in the River Moscow several thousand rebels.

[**FIGURE 28:**] Handicraftsmen in the market square selling their wares. [SH, 61]

The Bashkir rebellion. In the same year, in the Urals, the Bashkir people, who had been conquered by Ivan IV soon after he had captured Kazan, rose in rebellion. The Bashkirs were joined by the Tatars ~~and Kalmyks~~[22]. The rebels captured a transport containing weapons and obtained gunpowder. They fought against the Moscow soldiers for three years. They laid siege to the tsar's fortresses; but in the end they were ~~repulsed~~ *defeated*[23].

22. Ukraine's Struggle against Polish Domination. Ukraine Joins Russia

Bogdan Khmelnitsky and the Ukrainian peasant war against the Polish pans. Beginning with the 13th century the Ukraine gradually passed under the yoke of the Polish and Lithuanian pans ~~(see lesson 13)~~[24]. The latter transformed all the peasants into serfs. Even slight offenses by their serfs they punished with death. In some of the Polish manors permanent gallows were erected. The Poles forcibly compelled the Ukrainian people to adopt their religion.

In Poland, and in Byelorussia, too, the peasants groaned under the tyranny of the pans. The serfs fled from the pans to the Dniepr, where they built small fortifications below the Rapids and called the place ZAPOROZHSKAYA SECH, or the Camp below the Rapids; and they called themselves Zaporozhye Cossacks. In other places, in the Ukrainian towns and villages, ~~there were~~ *lived the*[25] town Cossacks. The town Cossacks as well as the Zaporozhye Cossacks were divided into rich and poor. The Cossacks were organized in regiments. Their chiefs were elected by the Cossacks. These chiefs were called hetmans.

The peasants and Cossacks frequently rose in rebellion against the Polish rulers. Even the rich Cossacks were discontented with the Poles because they robbed the land, and because of their oppression.

In **1648** a great rebellion of Cossacks and peasants broke out against the Poles. This rebellion was led by a rich town Cossack named Bogdan Khmelnitsky.

Bogdan Khmelnitsky sent his people disguised as beggars and monks to the villages of the Ukraine to rouse the peasants for the struggle against the pans. Soon the peasants rose in rebellion in all parts of the Ukraine and Byelorussia. The rebels began to wreck the mansions of the pans. The latter were compelled to split up their forces in order to fight Khmelnitsky and the rebel peasants. Khmelnitsky succeeded in defeating the Polish troops and in capturing their chief leaders.

The news of Khmelnitsky's victories rapidly spread throughout the Ukraine, Byelorussia and Poland. The peasants rallied to Khmelnitsky's standard in large masses. *One of the most outstanding of the peasant leaders was Maxim Krivonos.*[26] Khmelnitsky, however, did not want to give the peasants freedom. He ~~was~~ himself *was*[27] a landlord and owned serfs. He started negotiations with the Poles and concluded a treaty with them which granted many concessions to the Cossacks. The Poles promised to pay the Cossacks regular salaries, to supply them with arms, and not to deprive them of their liberties.

~~The peasants, having seen Khmelnitsky's treachery, began to struggle with the pans without him, under the leadership of their chief Maxim Krivonos.~~[28]

[**FIGURE 29:**] ~~Zaporozhian Cossacks join the campaign under Khmelnitsky's leadership.~~ [Cut by Zhdanov: RGASPI, f. 77, op. 1, d. 854, l. 250b.]

The Polish pans deceived Khmelnitsky, however, and failed to carry out their promises. Then Khmelnitsky went to war against the Poles again.

The Ukraine joins Russia. There seemed to be no prospect of the war coming to an end. The Poles were devastating the country. In order to extricate himself from his difficult position, Khmelnitsky, in **1654**, concluded a treaty with Tsar Alexei of Moscow, who professed the same religion as he. In accordance with this treaty Ukraine became subject to Russia. The Cossack elders received the rights which formerly they had tried to obtain from Poland. The peasants of the Ukraine were released from the oppression of the pans. No one was now forcing an alien religion upon them. But the fact that the Ukraine was joined to Russia did not free the toilers of the Ukraine from the oppression of their elders and hetmans. To assist Khmelnitsky, the tsar made war upon Poland. The war ended with the annexation by Russia of all the lands on the left bank of the Dniepr and of the city of Kiev.

23. Stepan Razin's War against the Boyars and Landlords

The Cossacks of the Don. The peasants who fled to the south, to the banks of the River Don and its tributaries, formed large Cossack settlements which were called STANITSAS.

There was no equality among the Cossacks of the Don in the middle of the 17th century. Some of the Cossacks had seized the best lands, accumulated property, began to trade, and became rich. Others remained poor. The poor Cossacks either had to go into bondage to the rich Cossacks, or to obtain their livelihood by robbery. The tsar's voyevodas hunted down the fugitives and returned them to the landlords. The poor Cossacks hated the Moscow landlords bitterly. They were roused to rebellion by the Cossack Stepan Razin.

Stepan Razin and his struggle against the boyars and landlords. A foreign traveller, who was in Muscovy at that time, described Razin as follows: "He is of majestic appearance and noble bearing; proud of feature, tall in stature, his face slightly pock-marked. He possessed the ability to inspire fear and love."

Stepan Razin rallied large masses of poor people to his standard. He was elected ataman, or chief. Many Cossacks and other people who were enraged against the tsar's voyevodas and the landlords joined him.

In the spring of **1670**, Razin, at the head of an army of 7,000 men, attacked Tsaritsin on the Volga (now called Stalingrad) and captured that town. Here the tsar's soldiers, the STRELTSI, came over to his side. Then he marched on Astrakhan and captured that town after a siege of two days. The rich merchants, boyars and the tsar's officials were put to death by the Cossacks. Razin threw the voyevoda of Astrakhan from the belfry of the church. In Astrakhan Razin's followers elected administrators from among the Cossacks.

With the munitions captured in Astrakhan, Razin moved up the Volga. He captured cities and wreaked vengeance on the tsar's voyevodas and officials. He sent messengers among the peasants to call upon them to join his ranks.

In response to Razin's call, the peasants rose in rebellion, killed their landlords, burned down the manors, and joined Razin's army in whole detachments. The peoples of the Volga, the Chuvash, Tatars, Mordovians and Maris, marched with the Russian peasants. The fact that they spoke different languages did not hinder them. Their hatred for the tsar and the landlords united them into one common family.

Suppression of the peasant movement and execution of Razin. The tsar and the landlords gathered ~~all~~[29] their army and regiments of mercenary foreign soldiers and marched against Razin. Razin found it hard to contend against these well-armed forces. He gave them battle near Simbirsk. Razin was wounded. His army was defeated. With a small detachment he managed to retire to the Don. But the ~~elite~~ *rich*[30] Cossacks of the Don captured him and surrendered him to the tsar. The tsar pronounced the following sentence on him: "Put him to a cruel death."

Razin was ~~brutally~~[31] executed in Moscow in **1671**.

Tsar Alexei dealt cruelly with the rebel peasants. Thousands of the rebels were hacked to pieces, whipped to death and hanged on gallows. The peasant ~~revolution~~ *revolt*[32] was crushed.

During the Razin rebellion, as was the case during Bolotnikov's rebellion, the peasants did not have an organized working class for their reliable ally. Nor did they understand the aim of the rebellion; they could wreck the landlords' mansions and kill the landlords, but they did not know what to do further, what new order to introduce. This was the cause of their weakness.[33]

[**FIGURE 30:**] The execution of Stepan Razin. [SH, 65]

24. The Subjugation of the Peoples of Eastern Siberia

The subjugation of *Eastern*[34] Siberia. Detachments of Cossacks penetrated Siberia along the rivers, travelling in boats; often they had to cross
overland from one river to another and dragged the boats across. A Cossack, Semen Dezhnev, at the head of a small detachment, was the first to
reach by sea the narrow straits between Asia and America. Cape Dezhnev,
the most eastern promontory of Asia, is named after him.

The Cossacks were followed by Moscow voyevodas who settled in the
newly built towns, and there issued their orders to the Cossack detachments. The Cossacks were able to subjugate the native inhabitants by

means of their firearms, the use of which many of the peoples of Siberia did not know. The subjugation of the peoples of Eastern Siberia to the Russian tsar took a hundred years. At the end of the 17th century nearly the whole of Siberia was subjugated. The Hakassi, Oirots, Buryat-Mongolians, Evenkis and Yakuts now paid tribute, or YASAK, as it was called, to the Russian tsar.

[**FIGURE 31:**] The fortress Yakutskaya built by the Russians
in the 17th century, in Siberia, on the River Lena (on the
site [of] the capital of the Yakut A.S.S.R). [SH, 67]

The oppression of the Siberian peoples. All over Siberia small wooden fortresses were built in which the voyevodas and soldiers were stationed. From them the voyevodas went forth among the native population to collect the tribute.

The voyevodas compelled the local population to till the land around the fortresses and used the harvested grain to maintain the soldiers. Russian peasants were forced to settle in Siberia, or were induced to do so by the offer of various privileges.

The voyevodas bribed the native princes in order to obtain their assistance in robbing the native population. Sometimes the voyevodas sold the natives into slavery in Central Asia. They also sent the Cossacks to conquer other peoples. In 1651 the Cossack, Khabarov, with a detachment of men, reached the River Amur. On his way he burned all the villages that resisted him. The inhabitants of these villages fled to the forests.

In the wake of the tsar's voyevodas and soldiers came Russian merchants, priests and monks. The merchants sold vodka to the native people and traded with them when they were intoxicated, buying valuable furs from them for next to nothing. The priests and the monks seized the land from the native population, built churches and monasteries, and robbed the people by forcing them to be baptized and to bring gifts to the church.

[**FIGURE 32:**] ~~The sale of people into slavery in Siberia.~~ [Cut by Stalin: RGASPI, f. 558, op. 11, d. 1584, l. 340b. Also Zhdanov: f. 77, op. 1, d. 854, l. 270b.]

The yoke of the tsarist government lay very heavily upon the subjugated peoples of Siberia. Many times they rebelled, killed their oppressors and burned the fortresses and towns. But the voyevodas and merchants gathered fresh military forces and wreaked cruel vengeance on the rebels.

25. The Economic System and the Administration of the State in Russia at the End of the 17th Century

Landlordism. After suppressing the peasant revolts, the landlords increased their oppression of the serf peasants. They compelled the peasants to pay their obrok in money. In addition, they took larger and larger quantities of grain, flour, butter, eggs, poultry, sheep, cloth and linen from the peasants. The landlords consumed a large amount of these things themselves, but they also sold a large amount *on the side*[35]. Hundreds of cartloads of grain, flax, lard and hides were sent to market by the landlords. Part of these goods were sold in the country and part were sent abroad. The landlords were keen on making agriculture as profitable as possible. Thus they became rich by robbing the peasants.

[**FIGURE 33:**] An iron smelting shop with water-driven
bellows and wooden hammer. [SH, 69]

Industry and commerce. There were very few mills and factories in Russia at the end of the 17th century. At that time they were only beginning to appear. During the reign of Tsar Alexei. The foundry in which canon and church bells were cast, was enlarged. In the towns of Kashira and Tula there were iron works and armouries; there were also small iron mines and workshops in which free craftsmen and serf peasants were employed. Skilled craftsmen were brought from abroad. In the iron works the hammers and small blast furnaces in which the ore was smelted were worked by water power. The water was made to run in a groove and turn a wheel like in a water mill. By means of various devices the wheel was made to work the bellows for the furnace and raise and drop the hammer.

The premises of these works were built of wood. In addition to the cannon foundry in Moscow, there was only one factory built of brick—a weaving mill where serf weavers wove cloth by hand for the tsar's household.

There were also potash works in the Volga district and salt works in the north and in the Urals.

With the annexation of the Ukraine and the conquest of Siberia trade in Russia greatly increased. Trade was carried on all over the country. Goods were carried over long distances by means of barges along the rivers in the summer, and by means of sledges in the winter.

Scores of English and Dutch ships brought *foreign*[36] goods from abroad and carried from Russia, via Archangel, *lumber*,[37] furs, hides, potash, tar, grain, wax, honey and caviar. Every year Russia exported goods to an amount exceeding 15,000,000 gold rubles. The Dutch and English merchants tried to keep the trade with Russia entirely in their own hands. To be able to trade independently Russia had to have her own ships, and ports more convenient than Archangel which was frozen for many months in the year. Such ports existed on the Black Sea and Baltic Sea; but the Black Sea was then in the hands of the Crimean Tatars and the Turks, while the shores of the Baltic Sea were in the possession of the Swedes.

The administration of the state. In Russia all affairs of state were administered by the tsar, the autocratic ruler. He lived in the Kremlin, in Moscow. The tsar had his counsellors, the boyars, whom he assembled ~~two times a day~~ *from time to time*[38]. The council of the boyars was called the Boyars' Duma. The tsar decided all questions as he thought fit, but in important matters he took counsel with the boyars ~~without fail~~[39].

[**FIGURE 34:**] Foreign mercenaries in Russia armed with muskets. [SH, 71]

The tsar governed the country through the medium of his chancelleries, known as PRIKAZI. The chiefs of the chancelleries were boyars appointed by the tsar. There were over fifty chancelleries, but there was no order in their work. The officials in the chancelleries were called DYAKS and PODYACHIS, that is, scriveners and under-scriveners. They wrote documents and received petitions; but it was impossible to obtain access to these officials without paying a bribe. Every petitioner had to being a gift, such as fish, cake or poultry.

The country was divided into a number of large UYEZDS, or counties. The uyezds were governed by voyevodas. The voyevodas were appointed from among the boyars and nobility. They, too, like the officials in Moscow forced the people to give them bribes.

In addition to the standing army of Streltsi and warriors, Tsar Alexei had a mercenary army of well-armed foreigner; but this army was a small one.

The Boyars' Duma and the chancellories functioned very badly. The whole administration of the state needed thorough reform.

26. Culture in Russia in the 17th Century

Culture. The whole system of life in Russia at that time was backward, but the state of education of the people was worst of all. The population of this enormous country was almost entirely illiterate. Even in Moscow, the capital, there were very few schools, and very few people who could read and write.

In Moscow, a few educated men, landlords who had been abroad, appeared. Their manner of life was the same as that of wealthy people in Western Europe. They knew foreign languages and loved to read learned books. But there were very few people of this kind. The boyars and the tsar's officials scowled upon their connections with foreigners.

Only the tsar, and the boyars who were close to him, had doctors to tend them when they were sick. These doctors were foreigners. There were no Russian doctors at that time. The common people went to sorcerers when they were sick. The sorcerers pretended to heal the sick by means of incantations, charms, and various mixtures from which more patients died than were healed.

There were no theatres in those days. The first theatre was built by Tsar Alexei for himself. In this theatre plays were staged which sometimes lasted the whole day. At night, after attending the theatre, the tsar would take a bath to wash away the "sin," for to attend theatrical performances was regarded as a sin.

The priests taught the people to be obedient to the tsar, the boyars and the landlords. "All power comes from God," said the priests. "God suffered in patience and commanded you to do the same." Whoever denied the doctrines of the church or read forbidden books was burned at the stake.

Habits and customs. The boyars and merchants wore long beards and long KAFTANS, or robes. The wives and daughters of the boyars, nobles and rich merchants covered their faces with thick veils. They were forbidden to meet and talk to other men. The common people ignored the customs of their oppressors. The women of the townspeople, handicrafts men and peasant serfs were much freer.

With the assistance of the church and the priests, the[40] tsar and the landlords kept the ~~Russian people~~ *people of Russia*[41] in ignorance. They encouraged them to go to the taverns and get drunk with vodka so as to obscure the ~~people's~~ *their*[42] minds more easily.

Russia was in need of thorough reform; if this reform had not been brought about she would have remained a backward and ignorant country. The reformer who strengthened the landlords' and merchants' ~~national~~ *Russian*[43] state was Tsar Peter I.

[**FIGURE 35:**] Peter I (1672–1725). [Zhdanov reversed Figures 35 and 36: RGASPI, f. 77, op. 1, d. 854, ll. 30–300b; SH, 74]

VII

Russia in the 18th Century. The Empire of Landlords and Merchants

27. The Wars of Peter I and Popular Rebellions

The war against the Turks and Peter I's travels abroad. At the very end of the 17th century Peter, the son of Alexei, became tsar, and was known as Peter I, Soon after his accession to the throne the clever and active young tsar began to introduce certain innovations. He ignored the Boyars' Duma and struck up a great friendship with the foreigners living in Moscow. He took them into his service and formed a new army after the fashion of foreign armies, while *the old army, known as*[1] the Streltsi, was being discarded.

In 1695 Peter went to war against Turkey ~~for land on~~ *in order to secure an outlet to*[2] the Black Sea. He built a fleet of 29 ships on the River Don, and with his army, which was trained by foreign officers, he attacked the Turkish fortress at Azov and captured it.

During this war Peter became still more convinced that it was necessary to reorganize the whole life of the country and to adopt the military and naval methods of the Europeans.

Peter travelled abroad. The most advanced countries in Western Europe at that time were Holland and England. In Holland, Peter worked as a shipwright in the Dutch shipyards. In England he perfected his knowledge of shipbuilding. He spent about two years abroad and learned a great deal. In Russia, the Streltsi, who were dicontented [sic, discontented] with the innovations which Peter introduced, mutinied *and demanded the restoration of the old customs. This was a reactionary rebellion.*[3] Peter returned from abroad and personally led the suppression of the Streltsi rebellion which, if successful, would have dragged Russia back to the past. The rebellion was crushed and the Streltsi regiments ~~destroyed~~ *dissolved*[4].

[**FIGURE 36:**] Soldiers of Peter I's regular army. [Zhdanov reversed Figures 36 and 35: RGASPI, f. 77, op. 1, d. 854, ll. 30–300b; SH, 75]

The beginning of the war against the Swedes. In 1700 Peter I went to war against the Swedes in order to obtain possession of the Baltic coast. At that time the Swedes possessed the best army in the world and a fine navy. The King of the Swedes at that time was Charles XII. Charles attacked Peter's army, which was besieging the Swedish fortress of Narva, routed it, and captured all his artillery and many prisoners.

Peter, however, was not dismayed. He ordered the bells to be removed from the churches to be cast into cannon. He chose 250 young men and made them learn to read and write and the elements of mathematics in order to become artillery men and craftsmen. A new army consisting of serf peasants was formed and trained on modern lines.

To maintain this army large sums of money were required.[5] Peter imposed taxes on public baths, flour mills, inns, and even on oak coffins, and the price of salt was doubled. He increased the penalties for serfs who escaped from their masters, and ordered all the colonies of fugitive peasants in the upper reaches of the Don to be destroyed. From the Bashkirs he confiscated large numbers of horses for his cavalry.

In **1703** Peter captured from the Swedes the marshy estuary of the Neva and there built a fortress and the town of Petersburg (now Leningrad), which became the capital of the country under Peter. To build this fortress and town Peter conscripted vast numbers of serf peasants from all over Russia. These serfs died in thousands from starvation and disease. The people retaliated against these tortures by rising in rebellion.

Popular rebellions. During the reign of Peter I the Bashkirs rose in rebellion, and unrest broke out among the Kalmyks. In **1707** a rebellion broke out among the Cossacks and peasants of the Don. This rebellion was led by the Cossack, Kondrati Bulavin. The rebels captured a number of towns. Peter sent a whole army against Bulavin. At this time the rich Cossacks conspired against Bulavin and attacked the farm in which he lived. Bulavin kept his foes at bay until all his bullets were spent. Not desiring to fall into the hands of his enemies, he used his last bullet to take his own life.

[**FIGURE 37:**] The last moments of Bulavin's life. [SH, 77]

The rebels continued their struggle against Peter's troops for two years. ~~All the~~ The rebel[6] villages on the Don were burned to the ground. Almost without exception, all the rebels who were taken prisoner were executed. Thousands of fugitive serfs were restored to their masters.

The reasons for Bulavin's defeat were the same as those for the defeat of previous rebellions of peasants and Cossacks.[7]

After crushing the popular rebellions, Peter concentrated all his forces on the struggle against the Swedes.

28. The Wars against the Swedes and the Eastern Countries

The rout of the Swedes. Taking advantage of the treachery of the Ukrainian hetman, Mazeppa, Charles XII, the Swedish king, invaded the Ukraine, VIA Poland. In **1709** the Swedish and Russian armies met at Poltava in Ukraine[8].

The Swedish troops were defeated, Charles XII and Mazeppa fled to Turkey, Charles persuaded the Turks to declare war on Russia. The war against Turkey was resumed.

Peter sent an army 40,000 strong against the Turks. Turkey, however, mustered an army five times as large. Peter's army was surrounded on the River Prut, and he was compelled to sign a peace treaty. According to that treaty, Azov again was Turkish. *in accordance with which the fortress of Azov was restored to the Turks.*[9]

After his failure in the war against the Turks, Peter resolved to crush the Swedes and to get a tight hold of the Baltic coast. He captured Riga and Reval from the Swedes and built a strong navy. A naval battle took place in which the Swedish fleet was defeated.

The war against the Swedes lasted twenty-one years. At last the[10] Swedes were compelled to sign a peace treaty which ceded to Russia the lands on the coasts of the Gulf of Riga and the Gulf of Finland.

Peter now decided to entrench himself on the Caspian coast, through which lay the routes to the east, to Central Asia, India and Iran.[11]

Peter's fight for the Caspian coast. *Peter now decided to entrench himself on the Caspian coast, through which lay the routes to the east, to Central Asia, India and Iran.*[12]

Peter mustered an army of 80,000 men and, starting out from Astrakhan, marched against the dominions of Iran. He had beforehand come to an agreement with the Georgian princes, who were then the vassals of Iran, and with the Armenian merchants, to help him in his war against the Shah of Iran.

The first military engagement took place in Dagestan. The peoples inhabiting this country stubbornly resisted Peter's army. Peter was compelled to return to Astrakhan.

But in addition to the army which he sent overland, Peter also dispatched troops by sea. These forces landed in the towns on the shores of the Caspian Sea and captured them. In this way Peter captured the towns of Derbent and Baku.

The towns of Azerbaidjan, which Peter captured, were inhabited by peoples who had been subjugated to the shahs of Iran (they had been built[13] two or three hundred years before Peter had started his campaign)[14]. All this time the Azerbaidjan people were at constant war with the Iran conquerors and fought for their independence and against oppression. This is why the native population of Azerbaidjan did not seriously resist Peter's forces.

The lands of Azerbaidjan reverted back to Iran shortly after Peter's death.[15]

Peter I achieved his object. The Baltic coast fell into the hands of Russia. Russia came nearer to Europe. Peter waged unceasing war against the backwardness of Russia and reformed the country on European lines.

29. Peter I's Reforms

Reforms in the administration of the state. In place of the Boyars' Duma, Peter established the Senate, which consisted of persons appointed by him. In place of the fifty chancellories, he established twelve Ministries, which had charge of the army, the navy, relations with foreign countries, economic affairs and the Courts of Justice. In the Senate and the Ministries, all affairs were administered by nobles.

Peter divided the whole of Russia into eight GUBERNIAS, or provinces. At the head of each gubernia he appointed a governor, who administered the country in that area and was in charge of recruiting soldiers and collecting taxes.

In order to increase the power of the nobility, Peter declared all *their*[16] estates to be their private property. In **1721**, after his victory over the Swedes, Peter adopted the title of Emperor. From that time on Russia was known as the Russian Empire.

Economic reforms. In order to increase the revenues of the state Peter introduced a poll tax, and all male peasants, young and old, were compelled to pay this tax. During Peter's reign, a number of *factories (or[17] MANUFACTURES, as they were called)*[18] and mills were opened. In these factories serf labourers worked on hand looms. Merchants were given money for building new factories and mills.

[**FIGURE 38:**] Interior of silk weaving factory in the reign of Peter I. [SH, 80]

In England, at that time, many free wage workers were already working in such mills. Peter, however, in order to ensure that the merchants obtained a sufficient number of workers, attached whole villages of serf peasants to each mill. Under his reign over 200 factories and mills were established. The arms factories in Tula were greatly enlarged. In the Urals, new iron works and cloth mills sprang up.

The merchants and the factory owners quickly grew rich. Peter granted the merchants self-government in the towns.

Education. Peter devoted a great deal of attention to education and even tried to introduce it by force. He sent the sons of the nobility abroad to learn shipbuilding and foreign languages. Schools were opened in which navigation, engineering, medicine and other arts and sciences were taught. The teachers *in these schools*[19] were Englishmen, Dutchmen, Swedes, *Germans*[20] and men of other nationalities, whom Peter had invited to serve him in Russia.

Peter ordered grammar schools to be opened in all the gubernias, which the children of the nobility were compelled to attend to learn reading, writing, arithmetic and geometry. He even forbade nobles to marry if they could not read and write.

Peter introduced the first newspaper on the European model. This newspaper bore the title of "Vedomosti," and in order to make it easier to read he simplified the Russian alphabet.

Before Peter's reign the year was counted from September 1; he introduced the new calendar which counted the year from January, as was done abroad.

The new calendar was introduced on January 1, 1700 and is in use to this day.

Peter ordered the nobles to cut off their beards and to wear wigs and short coats, as was the fashion in Western Europe. He allowed only priests and peasants to wear long robes and beards.

He also ordered his courtiers to arrange ~~dinner parties~~ *what were called* "assemblies,"[21] with European dancing and games—~~assemblies—in their houses~~.[22]

Under the reign of Peter I, Russia made great progress; nevertheless, it remained a country in which serf oppression and the tyranny of the tsar reigned supreme. The Russian Empire was enlarged and strengthened at the cost of the lives of hundreds of thousands of toilers and the impoverishment of the ~~entire~~[23] people. Peter I did a great deal to create and strengthen the landlords' and merchants' ~~national~~[24] state.

30. The Empire of the Nobility in the 18th Century

The rule of the nobility. Peter I died in 1725. After his death the nobility at court, relying on the aristocratic regiments of the Guards, organized plots, dethroned emperors and empresses who displeased them, banished them, imprisoned them, and even killed some of them. The longest to reign were the empresses Anne and Elizabeth.

During their reigns there were several wars against Turkey, Sweden and other countries. On the conquered territory new estates were formed which were granted to the nobles with the peasants living on them.

In Petersburg, the nobility built themselves magnificent palaces and arranged sumptuous feasts and balls. The imperial court and the nobles of Russia now copied the customs of the French kings and their courtiers.

The nobles learned to speak French; the men adopted the French fashion in clothes and wore velvet coats, knee breeches and long silk stockings. Their high-heeled shoes were embellished with costly buckles, and on their

[**FIGURE 39:**] Empress Elizabeth taking the air,
surrounded by her courtiers. [SH, 82]

heads they wore powdered curled wigs. The women wore costly clothes of the finest silk and lace. Their hair was dressed in the elaborate French style of that time.

The nobles learned to speak French; the men adopted the French fashion in clothes and wore velvet coats, knee breeches and long silk stockings. Their high-heeled shoes were embellished with costly buckles, and on their heads they wore powdered curled wigs. The women wore costly clothes of the finest silk and lace. Their hair was dressed in the elaborate French style of that time.

The magnificently dressed nobles in their powdered wigs could not, nor would they work. But to run the factories and build palaces the nobles needed learned men and experts. They were invited from abroad, and this entailed great expense.

~~An Academy of Sciences, devised by Peter I, was opened just before he died.~~ *The idea of establishing an Academy of Sciences had occurred to Peter I, and actually this Academy was opened in the year of his death.*[25] All the members of the Academy were foreigners. The ~~university~~ *Academy*[26] took in students; but the nobles would not study, and peasants were not admitted.

M. Lomonosov. The first Russian scientist was not a noble, but a peasant from the village of Denisovka, near the town of Archangel. His name was Michael Lomonosov. Lomonosov made his way from the Far North to Moscow, and in order to enter a school he had to pretend to be the son of a noble, for otherwise he would not have been admitted. He was very poor and often went hungry, but thanks to his perseverance he passed an eight year course of study in five years. His abilities were recognized, and he was granted a scholarship to enable him to continue his studies abroad. On his return to Russia he was appointed a member of the Academy of Sciences.

[**FIGURE 40:**] Academician M. Lomonosov, the first Russian scientist (1711–1765). [SH, 83]

Lomonosov was an outstanding scientist in the fields of physics, chemistry and other sciences. He made many great scientific discoveries. He laid the foundations of Russian science and was the first to write books in pure Russian, purging the language of many obsolete Slavonic words.

On Lomonosov's proposal the first university was established in Moscow, in 1755. A statue of Lomonosov still stands on the grounds of the Moscow University. Lomonosov died in 1765, in the reign of Catherine II.

Empress Catherine II. In 1762 the nobles placed Catherine II on the Russian throne, having first, with her assistance, killed her husband, Peter III.

Under the reign of Catherine II the rights of the nobles were still further extended. She distributed among them over a million peasants as serfs. In order to obtain the means for living their luxurious lives the nobles began to oppress the peasants more than ever.

[**FIGURE 41:**] ~~A landowner's estate.~~ [Cut by Zhdanov: RGASPI, f. 77, op. 1, d. 854, l. 34ob.]

Forced labour, or barschina, as it was called, reached such dimensions that the peasants were obliged to spend nearly all their time working for the landlords. The serfs did everything for their masters; they tilled their land, they served as blacksmiths and cooks, domestic servants and huntsmen, and even as actors for their private theatricals. The only time the peasants had left to work for themselves was on church holidays and at night. Under Catherine's reign, obrok, or the tax in kind, increased almost five-fold.

The nobles sold and bought peasants as if they were slaves. The price of a woman serf ranged from twenty to thirty roubles; the price of a handicraftsman or a serf who could read and write ranged from one hundred to two hundred rubles. A small child could be purchased for ten to twenty kopecks. The landlords priced their dogs more highly than their serfs.

The landlords tormented their peasants to the utmost. The story is told of the woman landowner, Saltychikha, who beat her serfs to death, poured boiling water over them, and set their hair alight. She murdered over a hundred serfs.

These horrible conditions caused the peasants to rise in rebellion.

31. The Peasant War under the Leadership of Pugachov

The beginning and progress of the peasant war. The first to rise in rebellion were the Cossacks on the River Yaik (now the River Ural). *The tsar's government had deprived the Ural Cossacks of their liberties and imposed heavy taxes upon them in the effort to convert them into serfs like the peasants of Central Russia.*[27] The Cossack elders compelled the rank-and-file Cossacks to pay extra taxes which they put in their own pockets, and they also kept for themselves the pay that was intended for the Cossacks.

In **1773** the poor Cossacks rose against their oppressors.

At the head of the rebellion stood the Don Cossack, Emelian Pugachov, a strong, wise and brave man.

The Cossacks captured a number of fortresses and besieged Orenburg.

The serf workers in the Ural iron mines and iron works rallied to Pugachov's standard. Tied to these works like slaves, the peasants hated their laborious toil. Already at the beginning of Catherine's reign, 50,000 out of the 200,000 serfs employed at the works ~~were~~ *took part* in rebellions[28].

[**FIGURE 42:**] Emelian Pugachov. [SH, 85]

The workers readily joined Pugachov's army. They supplied his army with guns, cannon and cannon balls. Famous captains of Pugachov's army, like Khlopusha and Beloborodov, were factory workers.

The Bashkirs also joined the Pugachov rebellion. The nobles had driven the Bashkirs from their land and established iron works on it. The Bashkirs rose in rebellion against this robbery more than once, but they were crushed. In the year 1740 alone, about 30,000 rebel Bashkirs were tortured to death or distributed among the nobles as their property. Four hundred Bashkir villages were plundered, wrecked and burned to the ground, But the Bashkirs refused to submit. Fifteen years later, under their leader Batyrsha, they rose again and fought the tsar's armies for two years. But they were crushed once again. Batyrsha was taken prisoner and murdered while in prison in Petersburg.

[**FIGURE 43:**] Pugachov sitting in judgment on the
landlords. From a painting by V. Perov. [SH, 86]

The Bashkirs now rose again and with their horsemen joined Pugachov's army. One of their leaders was Salavat Yulayev. He was a brave young rebel who with his army rendered Pugachov great assistance.

At the same time, the Russian, Tatar, Chuvash, Mordovian and Mari serf peasants on the Volga also rose. Pugachov gave himself out as the emperor,

Peter III. He announced that his wife, the wicked Catherine II, and the nobles had failed to kill him as they had intended, and that he had escaped. He signed orders in the name of Peter III and sent manifestoes all over the country *calling for the extermination of the nobility and* declaring in them[29] that he would free the peasants from the power of the landlords, from compulsory military service, and from taxes.

The whole of the Volga district, the Urals, and also part of Siberia were swept by the rebellion. The estates and mansions of the nobles were wrecked, their granaries were ransacked and the grain taken to supply Pugachov's army. The peasants seized the landlords' land.

Pugachov and his army reached Kazan and captured it.

Soon, however, Catherine's troops began to press upon Pugachov's army. Pugachov was compelled to retreat south, down the Volga. The Volga towns along his line of march surrendered to him without a fight, but he could not hold them.

Suppression of the peasant rebellion. In the second half of[30] August 1774 Pugachov reached Tsaritsin (now Stalingrad), A few days later he suffered a decisive[31] defeat in battle against the empress' soldiers and fled to the steppes with the remnants of his army. Here traitors *the treacherous rich Cossacks*[32] betrayed him to the authorities.

Pugachov was chained, put into a large wooden cage and taken to Moscow. On January 10, **1775**, the brave leader of the peasant war, Emelian Pugachov, was executed in Bolotnaya Square.

Salavat Yulayev was also captured. His captors slit his nostrils and with a red hot iron branded on his forehead the words, "thief and murderer." After this he was taken to Bashkiria, and in every village in which he had led the rebellion he was fiogged [SIC, flogged] with a whip. His tortures were so unbearable that he committed suicide.

The peasants fought bravely and staunchly, but being ignorant, they did not clearly understand the object of their struggle. Being disunited, they were unable to establish the firm organization and strong army needed for the struggle. The working class, which could have led the peasants and oppressed peoples in the struggle, did not yet exist. *The alliance between the working class and the peasantry was lacking.*[33]

This is the reason why the peasants and the oppressed peoples were defeated.

32. Catherine II Conquers *New* Lands and *Subjugates New* Peoples[34]

The conquest of the Crimea and subjugation of the Ukraine. Peter I waged war against the Turks in order to capture the Black Sea coast (see lessons 27–28),[35] but he failed. It was only in the reign of Catherine II that Azov was recaptured from the Turks, and the Crimea conquered. At that time the Crimea was governed by Tatar khans who were subjects of Turkey. The *traitorous*[36] khans and their Murzi, the nobility, sold themselves to Catherine and helped her to establish her rule over the Crimea.

Russian landlords appeared in the Crimea and robbed the Crimean peasants of their best lands, especially on the southern Crimean coast.[37] Large numbers of Tatar peasants fled to Turkey and the Russian nobles took possession of the*ir* lands of those who fled to Turkey[38]. On the Black Sea coast Catherine founded the fortress of Sevastopol, where warships were built.

In this war against Turkey, the celebrated Russian general, Alexander Suvorov, became famous.

Suvorov started his military career as a common soldier. He lived a strict mode of life, ate coarse soldiers' food, slept in hay stacks and thus hardened his body. At the head of an army of 25,300 men he defeated the Turkish army, which was 100,000 strong.

Simultaneously with the conquest of the Crimea all the territory of the Ukraine stretching from the left bank of the Dniepr was definitely annexed to Russia. The hetman system was abolished. Russian troops were brought to the Zapozhskaya Sech and the Sech was destroyed forever. Its lands were seized by the tsarist generals. Part of the Zaporozhye Cossacks were transferred to Kuban, in the North Caucasus; others went to Turkey, while the poor Cossacks and peasants were compelled to work as serfs. Catherine granted the Ukrainian elders the same rights as those enjoyed by the Russian nobility.

The partition of Poland. During the 18th century Poland was greatly enfeebled. Poland was governed by the biggest landlords who were *constantly*[39] quarrelling among themselves. The king's power was slight. When the Ukrainian peasants (GAIDAMAKI)[40] under the rule of Poland rose in rebellion, the Polish pans were able to subdue them only with the aid of Russian soldiers.

Polish lands were also conquered during Catherine's reign. Catherine made an agreement with the neighbouring states of Austria and Prussia by which the three countries divided parts of the territory of Poland among themselves. Russia obtained the ancient Byelorussian and Ukrainian lands on the right bank of the Dniepr.

[**FIGURE 44:**] A. V. Suvorov—the famous Russian military commander (1729–1800). [Cut by Stalin: RGASPI, f. 558, op. 11, d. 1584, l. 43ob. Also Zhdanov: f. 77, op. 1, d. 854, l. 36ob. This portrait was restored to later editions.]

In 1794, a rebellion *of the Poles*[41] against tsarist Russia, led by Kosciuszko, broke out in Poland with the object of restoring Poland's independence. Catherine sent a large army led by Suvorov to Poland to crush the rebellion.

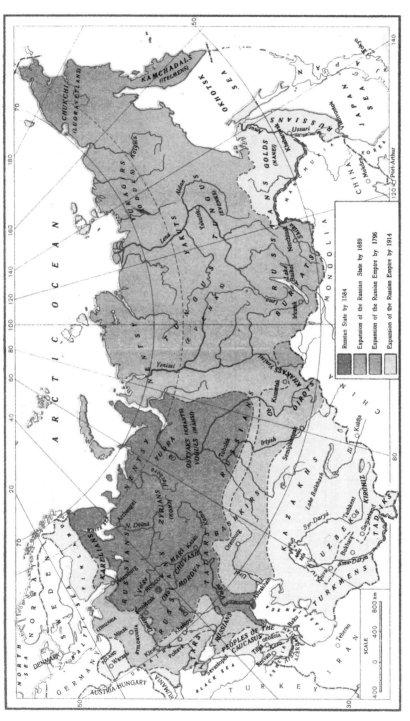

EXPANSION OF THE RUSSIAN STATE FROM THE XVI CENTURY TO 1914

Russian State by 1584

Expansion of the Russian State by 1689

Expansion of the Russian Empire by 1796

Expansion of the Russian Empire by 1914

[MAP 4:] Expansion of the Russian *Russian* State (from the XVI Century until the XX Century 1914). [SH, 90–91. In the 1937 Russian edition, Stalin replaced the adjectival ethnonym "Russian" (RUSSKOE) with the more generic adjective "Russian" (ROSSIISKOE), corrected the time frame to 1917 and replaced the term "Tsardom" in the legend with "*State*" twice. Later editing replaced 1917 with 1914. Compare RGASPI, f. 558, op. 11, d. 1584, l. 45 and KKISSSR, 74–75; SH, 90–91]

Kosciuszko was defeated; he himself was severely wounded in battle and taken prisoner. Catherine annexed Lithuania from Poland.

For many years after[42] Poland ceased to exist as an independent state.

Conquests in Kazakhstan and ~~of the people~~[43] in the Far North. In the 18th century the Kazakh herdsmen were divided into three states known as the Small Horde, the Medium Horde and the Great Horde. These hordes were governed by khans and sultans. The Kazakh nobility and merchants carried on trade with Russia and with neighbouring states in Central Asia such as Kokand and Bokhara, and also with China. All, these countries tried to subject the Kazakhs to their rule.

But the most persistent in these efforts was Russia. During the reign of Catherine II a large part of the Small Horde adjacent to Russia was annexed. The khans of the Small Horde betrayed their people and helped the tsarist rulers to seize the Kazakh lands.

More than once the Kazakh people rose in rebellion against the traitorous khans and against their subjection to ~~Russia~~ *the Russian tsar*[44].

In 1783, ~~the~~ brave ~~Kazakh~~[45] Sarim Datov headed the rebellion of the Kazakh people. For fourteen years they fought against their enemies under this fearless leader who became a national hero. Sarim was killed by his enemies and the rebellion was suppressed. Catherine's troops marched far into the Kazakh steppe and built fortresses there. The tsarist generals established their rule over the whole of the Small Horde. In the first half of the 19th century the whole of Kazakhstan was conquered.

At the end of the 18th century the last remaining lands of the northern peoples of Siberia were subjugated to the rule of Russia[46], The tsar's soldiers crossed the Bering Strait, into the far north of America, and established Russia's rule over Alaska. In the 19th century the Russian tsar sold Alaska to the American government for next to nothing, not knowing that much gold was to be found there.

~~The Siberian people heroically struggled with the tsar's soldiers.~~[47]

Towards the end of Catherine's reign the ~~new~~ *final*[48] conquest of Azerbaidjan began ~~(see lesson 37)~~[49].

To the numerous peoples groaning under the rule of tsarism new peoples were added: the Poles, Crimean Tatars, Azerbaidjanians and the Kazakhs.

VIII

Tsarist Russia—The Gendarme
of Europe

33. The Bourgeois Revolution in France and the Struggle Waged against It by Catherine II and Paul I

The overthrow of the royal power in France. On July 14, **1789**, the people of Paris rose in rebellion and stormed and captured the prison known as the Bastille. The prisoners were released. The flag of the revolution was raised over its towers.

[**Figure 45:**] The insurgent people of Paris storming the Bastille. [SH, 93]

The revolution quickly spread over the whole country. In all towns the handicraftsmen, small traders and the few factory workers *of that day*[1] rose in rebellion. Everywhere the peasants attacked the manors of the nobility, seized their land and demanded the total abolition of serfdom. Many nobles fled abroad.

Relying on the help of the revolutionary people, the bourgeoisie seized power. It was the bourgeois revolution that was victorious in France.

King Louis XVI tried to escape from France. Catherine II ordered her ambassador in Paris to issue a Russian passport to the king to enable him to enter Russia. On the way, however, the king was caught and brought back to Paris in disgrace.

The feudal states of Austria and Prussia, with the help of the French nobles who had fled from the revolution, started war against ~~bourgeois~~ *bourgeois-revolutionary*[2] France, The king knew about the counter-revolutionary designs of the invaders and secretly helped them.

The revolutionary government *of France*[3] organized the defence of the country, France was proclaimed a republic, and Louis XVI was beheaded as a traitor to the people.

After the execution of the king the revolutionary Jacobins, who were the representatives of the ~~petty bourgeoisie~~ *petty-bourgeois democracy*[4] (the peasants and artisans), came into power. The leaders of the Jacobins were Robespierre and Marat. Marat was known as the "Friend of the People." Under the rule of the Jacobins, the peasants were completely liberated from serfdom. The revolutionary government confiscated the land from the landlords and sold it to all those who wished to buy. Much of the landlords' land was bought by the peasants, but a large part of it passed into the hands of the bourgeoisie.

The Jacobins, however, were not consistent revolutionaries. As petty-bourgeois democrats they were in favour of the private ownership of the land, factories and mines. They prohibited the workers from going on strike and fighting against the capitalists.[5]

The revolutionary people rose in defence of their country. The republican army routed the armies of the invaders and drove them out of France. Then the armies of France began to fight beyond their own borders to liberate other peoples from the rule of kings and feudal nobles.

Fearing that bourgeois-*democratic*[6] France would become strong, England, which was a strong industrial country, started war against her.

The counter-revolutionaries *inside and outside the country*[7] fought the revolution by every means in their power. They sent assassins to kill the

[**FIGURE 46:**] Marat (1744–1793). [SH, 94]

leaders of the revolution, and actually did kil! Marat. The Jacobins retaliated with ruthless terror against the enemies of the people.

Soon, however, the big bourgeoisie *of France*[8] succeeded in seizing power again. The Jacobin leaders were executed. General Napoleon Bonoparte [SIC, Bonaparte] became the leader of bourgeois France.

The bourgeois revolution liberated the French people from the rule of kings and landlords ~~and,~~ *but*[9] in its place it established the rule of the bourgeoisie. The bourgeoisie was victorious because the working class in France was weak and unorganized, while the peasants, who with the aid of the bourgeoisie had liberated themselves from the power of the landlords, supported ~~them~~ *the bourgeoisie*[10]. The French revolution abolished the oppression of the landlords, but increased the oppression of the bourgeoisie, the capitalists.

The struggle waged by Catherine II and Paul I against the bourgeois revolution. Catherine II was afraid that the revolution would spread to her empire. There were people in Russia who sympathized with the revolution. An educated[11] nobleman named Radishchev, *one of the most enlightened and progressive men in Russia at that time*,[12] wrote a book *entitled A Journey From Petersburg To Moscow*[13] in which he openly opposed serfdom and autocracy, and expressed sympathy towards the peasant revolts against the landlords. Catherine banished Radischev [sic, Radishchev] to Siberia and ordered his book to be burned.

[**Figure 47:**] A. Radishchev (1749–1802). [SH, 96]

Catherine II thought it her principal mission to combat the bourgeois revolution *in France*[14]. She readily allowed the French nobility who fled from France to take refuge in Russia, and ordered all Russian subjects in Paris to leave ~~from there~~ *France*[15]. She gave her assistance to all the countries that were waging war against France. She granted money to Austria, ceded part of Poland to Prussia, promised both the assistance of Russian troops, and prepared her army for war. Only her sudden death in 1796 prevented her from starting war against bourgeois France.

After Catherine's death, her son, Paul I, ascended the throne. Paul continued the struggle against the bourgeois revolution. He ordered all private printing shops in Russia to be shut down and prohibited the reading of French books or any discussion of the French revolution.

Paul I declared war on France and sent an army against her under the command of Suvorov. Suvorov won several victories, but Russia's allies, Austria and Prussia, failed to help him. The Russian army could obtain no food supplies. Paul recalled Suvorov's army and concluded peace with France. At this time Napoleon Bonaparte overthrew the government *set up by the revolution*[16] in France and declared himself supreme ruler over the country. When he saw that Napoleon was fighting the revolution, Paul I ~~convinced him to become the French emperor~~ *concluded an alliance with him*.[17]

Paul's negotiations with Napoleon led to a rupture between Russia and

England. From being England's ally, Paul became her enemy. The Russian nobility, displeased with Paul's alliance with France, plotted against him with the aid of the English ambassador in Petersburg and assassinated him. ~~Alexander I, Paul's son and successor, had taken part in the plot against his father. Alexander I also continued his struggle with bourgeois France.~~[18]

34. Tsar Alexander I. The War of 1812

The annexation of Georgia. Alexander I, *Paul's son and successor, who had taken part in the plot against his father,*[19] continued the conquest of the Black Sea coast and the rich lands of the Caucasus which Peter I and Catherine II had started. First of all he entrenched himself in Georgia.

In Georgia, as in Russia at that time, the landlords were in power. The peasants toiled for the landlords from daybreak to dark. The peasants lived in huts of stone and clay, *or* in dugouts~~, or in caves dug in the mountains~~[20]. The greater part of the harvests. of their fields and orchards was taken from them by their masters, the landlords. The rulers of the countries adjacent to Georgia—Turkey and Iran;—made devastating raids upon the rich lands of Georgia and reduced the Georgian peasants to even greater poverty.

After one of these raids, when the Iranese captured over 10,000 Georgians, the Georgian king appealed to Paul I for aid. Tsarist troops were sent to Tbilisi, the capital of Georgia. In **1801**, Georgia was finally annexed by Russia. The devastating raids of the shahs of Iran upon Georgia ceased.

Georgia became a dominion of tsarist Russia. Russian officials were appointed as judges and to *other*[21] administrative posts. They insisted on conducting all official business in the country in Russian, which the Georgian people did not understand, Serfdom continued in Georgia. Greatly oppressed, the Georgian peasants frequently rebelled against their own landlords and the tsarist officials, but they were ruthlessly crushed by the tsar's soldiers, who were assisted by the Georgian princes and nobles. With the aid of the Georgian feudal nobility, Alexander I firmly established his power in Trans-Caucasia,

The conquest of Finland and Bessarabia. In 1805, *after resuming his military alliance with England,*[22] Alexander I declared war on Napoleon I, who had proclaimed himself Emperor of France.

Napoleon defeated Alexander I's troops and demanded that Russia cease trading with England, France's principal enemy. Vanquished, Alexander I was obliged to agree to this. In compensation Napoleon promised not to hinder the Russian emperor in his wars against Sweden and Turkey. Napoleon had by this time subjected nearly all the peoples of Western Europe to the rule of France.

Soon after, Alexander I declared war on Sweden and his troops quickly occupied Finland, which then belonged to Sweden. In the winter the Russian army crossed the ice in the Gulf of Bothnia and threatened the capital of Sweden. In 1809 the Swedish king was compelled to conclude peace and agree to cede Finland to Russia.

Three years later Alexander I succeeded in wresting from Turkey the land of Bessarabia, lying between the rivers Dniester and Prut, which Turkey had previously seized.

The war against Napoleon in 1812. The alliance between Russia and France was not maintained for long. The Russian landlords and merchants keenly desired free commercial intercourse with England and demanded that the tsar should break his alliance with Napoleon. The nobility were also afraid that the influence of bourgeois France, *where serfdom had been abolished*,[23] would weaken their power in Russia. They presented a petition to the tsar in which they demanded that the power of the serf-owning landlords be increased and that the war against bourgeois France be resumed. Alexander I yielded. Trade with England was resumed; preparations were started for another war.

[**FIGURE 48:**] Napoleon Bonaparte (1769–1821). [SH, 98]

In the summer of **1812** Napoleon invaded Russia with an enormous army of over 500,000 men. The Russian army numbered only 200,000. The Russian army retreated, destroying all the stocks of food and equipment on the way. Soon Napoleon captured Lithuania and Byelorussia and marched on Moscow. Napoleon's invasion of Russia roused the ~~entire~~[24] Russian people for the fight against the invaders. The peasants began to wage guerilla warfare against Napoleon.

At the end of August the biggest battle of the war was fought at the village of Borodino, near Moscow. The Russian soldiers fought stubbornly against the enemy who was devastating the country. More than 50,000 Russians fell in this sanguinary battle, but *in spite of that the strength of*[25] the Russian army ~~held its ground~~ *remained unbroken*.[26]

The French losses were enormous, but they still retained their ~~strength~~ *superiority in numbers*[27]. General Kutuzov, the commander of the Russian army, decided to surrender Moscow to Napoleon *without a fight and to retreat in order to save his army*[28].

The French occupied Moscow. A great fire broke out in the city and ~~very~~[29] many houses were destroyed. The French could obtain no food ~~or shelter~~[30] in Moscow.

Winter set in. It was impossible for the French to hold Moscow under such conditions. Napoleon and his army retreated along the road through country that had been devastated during his march on Moscow. His attempts to retreat by another road failed, for the other routes were occupied by Russian troops.

[**FIGURE 49:**] The French in burning Moscow. [SH, 99]

The frost came early that year. Napoleon's troops suffered from the cold and disease broke out in their ranks. The Russian guerilla fighters, or irregular troops, attacked and exterminated the French stragglers. Of Napoleon's vast army only 30,000 men survived and returned from Russia.

Napoleon mustered a new army and continued the war. This time, however, he had to face the alliance of Russia, Prussia, Austria, England and Sweden. Napoleon was defeated near Leipzig. The Allies crossed the frontiers of France and occupied Paris.

The victors restored the rule of the old French kings *and princes*[31]. The brother of the king who had been executed during the revolution was placed on the throne. Napoleon was banished to a remote island in the Atlantic Ocean. All the countries in Europe which Napoleon had conquered were again ruled by their kings or princes whom Napoleon had deposed.

As a reward for the part he had taken in the fight against Napoleon, the Allies ceded to Alexander I a part of Poland, with its capital, Warsaw.

In order to combat ~~the revolutions~~ *revolution in Europe*[32], the Tsar of Russia, the King of Prussia and the Emperor of Austria concluded a *reactionary*[33] alliance known as the "Holy Alliance." These monarchs pledged themselves to help each other to suppress popular rebellions. At the head of this *reactionary*[34] alliance was the Russian tsar, Alexander I. *Tsarist Russia became the gendarme of Europe.*[35]

35. The Decembrists

The secret societies of the *revolutinary* [sic, *revolutionary*] nobles. Alexander I kept a huge army under arms. The troops near the European frontier weve [sic, were] stationed in special military settlements where, while performing their military duties, they tilled the land and thus provided their own food. The commander of these military settlements was General Arakcheyev, a cruel and brutal man.

The hard life of the soldiers, who had to serve in the army for twenty-five years, was worse than penal servitudes. They spent the whole day either at work in the fields or at military drill. Even their wives were chosen for them by the officers. For the slightest offense the soldiers were cruelly flogged, often to death.

The tyranny of the tsar and the serf system disgusted the more progressive people among the nobility. Many of them were army officers. During the campaigns in France they had seen that the peasants were much happier after the abolition of serfdom and that wage labour in farm and factory was more productive than serf labour. They had seen that in the cities of Western Europe people were more prosperous and educated than in the cities of Russia.

These noblemen longed to introduce such conditions in their own country. They organized secret revolutionary societies: the Northern Society and Southern Society.

The members of the Northern Society wanted to abolish serfdom, that is to say, the power of the landlords over the peasants, but they wanted the landlords to retain possession of nearly all the land. They thought that a tsar ~~should remain~~ *was needed*[36], but that it was necessary to limit his power. The ~~members~~ *leaders*[37] of this society were Ryleyev, a poet and friend of the poet Pushkin, and the army officers Trubetskoy and Kakhovsky. The Southern Society was formed in the tsar's army in the Ukraine. It was led by Colonel Pestel, an educated and brave man. He thought that it was necessary to give the peasants not only liberty, but also land. He ~~thought that~~ *wanted*[38] Russia ~~should~~ *to*[39] be a republic. He proposed that the tsar and his family be exterminated.

But the members of these secret societies were nobles and were afraid of calling upon the people to revolt. They remembered the peasants' revolt against the nobles during the reign of Catherine II. They wanted to bring about revolution only with the aid of the soldiers whom they commanded.

The Decembrist rebellion. In 1825 Alexander I died. He left no children. His brother Nicholas was to ascend the throne.

On the morning of December 14, **1825**, the army officers who were members of the Northern Society in St. Petersburg brought their men out to the Senate Square and refused to take the oath of allegiance to Nicholas I. They were joined by the naval guards. The rebels waited for the orders of their chief leader, Prince Trubetskoy, but he quailed at the last moment and failed to appear on the square. The rebellion was thus left without a leader. Nicholas called out troops that were loyal to him and surrounded the ~~square and its mutineers~~ *mutinous regiments*[40].

A large crowd of serfs, artisans and building labourers gathered near the rebel troops. They pelted the soldiers who remained loyal to the tsar

[**FIGURE 50:**] December 14, 1825 in Petersburg. The rebels [were]
shot down with cannon on Nicholas I's orders. [SH, 102]

with firewood and stones. But the aristocratic revolutionaries were afraid
to ~~summon them for help~~ *take advantage of their help*[41].

Nicholas sent the Governor of St. Petersburg to negotiate with the
rebels. Kakhovsky killed the governor. Nicholas was not sure of the loyalty
of his troops and for a long time did not dare to resort to force. ~~It was only
toward evening when~~ *Towards the evening, however,*[42] cannon were brought
up ~~that~~ *and*[43] he ordered the gunners to fire point blank at the rebels. The
cannon roared. The rebels and the people scattered. Hundreds of killed and
wounded were left lying on the square.

Two weeks later, near Kiev, in the Ukraine, the army officers in the
Southern Society rose in rebellion at the head of the Chernigov Regiment.
They led their regiment out to join other troops who belonged to the organization, but they were defeated by troops whom Nicholas I had sent to
crush the rebellion.

After crushing the rebellion Nicholas I ordered the rebels to be arrested
and cruelly punished. Five of the principal leaders, Pestel, Ryleyev, Kakhovsky, Muravyov-Apostol and Bestuzhev-Ryumin, were hanged. Over one

hundred officers were banished to Siberia. Hundreds of soldier were forced to "run the gauntlet," that is to say, they were forced to run between ranks of soldiers armed with sticks who beat them as they ran ~~(each was hit hundreds and even thousands of times)~~[44].

Many of the soldiers were sent to penal servitude or for active military service in the Caucasus.

[**FIGURE 51:**] P. Pestel, K. Ryleyev, M. Bestuzhev-Ryumin, S. Muravyov-Apostol and P. Kakhovsky—the five Decembrists executed by order of Nicholas I. [SH, 103]

The revolutionary nobles who rebelled in December 1825 became known as the Decembrists. Their numbers were small and they lacked contact with the people. But the Decembrists were the first to come out in open, organized, armed rebellion against the autocracy in the very capital of the tsar. Their cause was not crushed. It was continued by the generations of revolutionaries that followed them.

On ascending the throne Nicholas I thought it was his principal mission to combat revolution, and he did all he could to preserve the old, serf system.

36. The Kingdom of Gendarmes and Officials

Nicholas I. Nicolas I's teacher, speaking of him as a boy: said: "I never saw him with a book; his only occupation was drill and soldiers." This is the sort of man who became Emperor of Russia.

Nicholas I was very much frightened by the rebellion of December 14, 1825. For the purpose of combating revolution he established a special police force called the GENDARMERIE. The Chief of the Gendarmes was subordinate only to the tsar.

Strict surveillance was established over the whole population. The gendarmes and the secret agents of the police scoured the whole country; they listened to the talk that went on among the people and even to private conversations. People were arrested on the slightest suspicion and on the basis of unverified reports.

Nicholas I governed Russia through the medium of the nobility and officials among whom were many who took bribes and robbed the Treasury. The government officials and the judges compelled the people to give them bribes; they insulted and tormented the people.

Nicholas I established the stern discipline of the stick in Russia. Under his reign soldiers, peasants, persons under arrest, in fact all who opposed the landlords and the tsar were flogged. They were flogged with birches, knouts, whips and sticks.

The peasants were compelled to work harder than ever for the landlords. All their land was taken from them and the barshchina and obrok were increased.

The peasants could not bear this life of slavery and rose against the tyranny of the serf owners. They killed the cruellest of the landlords, wrecked and burned their mansions and refused to perform the barshchina or pay obrok. Peasant disturbances continued ~~without interruption, amounting to about a thousand over the course of Nicholas I's 30-year rule.~~[45]

The tsar's soldiers and police ruthlessly suppressed the discontented peasants and sternly punished them. ~~416 peasants were exiled to Siberia for the murder of landlords in just a 9-year period.~~[46]

Life in tsarist Russia became unbearable.

The great Russian writers. *The great Ukrainian poet Shevchenko.*[47] In the reign of Nicholas I there lived the Russian genius and poet, Alexander Pushkin. He wrote fine poems, plays, novels, etc., such as EUGENE ONEGIN, BORIS GODUNOV, THE CAPTAIN'S DAUGHTER, and many others of which we are so proud today. Pushkin was the creator of Russian literature.

Pushkin was born in Moscow, in 1799, in a noble's family. He began to write poetry when he was still a boy. He was educated at the school for the nobility, called the Lycee, in Tsarskoye Selo (now called Pushkin), near Leningrad. After leaving the Lycee he became a famous poet and associated with the Decembrists. In his poems he strongly condemned serfdom and autocracy. At that time such poems could not be published, and so they were copied by hand and widely distributed and read in secret.

Tsar Alexander I heard of these poems and banished Pushkin, first to the south, and later to his estate in the country for a period of two years. To the very end of his life Pushkin was under the constant surveillance of the gendarmes. Nicholas I, under whose reign Pushkin's lot was particularly hard, knew of the poet's connection with the Decembrists and persecuted him for it. Pushkin's poems could be published only with the consent of the tsar himself.

The tsar hated Pushkin. The courtiers persecuted and insulted the great poet. Nicholas I was well aware of this persecution, but took no measures to stop it, not even when Pushkin was deliberately provoked into fighting a duel. He fought this duel in the beginning of 1837 with a man who had insulted him, and was killed.

Free thought was crushed in this kingdom of gendarmes. Nicholas I exiled the other celebrated poet, Michael Lermontov, to the Caucasus, there to serve in the army. The tsar sent him there, where he was always in danger of being hit by the bullets of the mountaineers, because he had written a poem in which he branded the court parasites as the murderers of Pushkin. In the Caucasus, Lermontov was killed in a duel with a ne'er-do-well army officer. When Nicholas I heard of this he said: "Serves the dog right."

The third great writer of that day, Nicholas Gogol, described in his

[**FIGURE 52:**] Alexander Pushkin (1799–1837). [SH, 106]

works the rule and tyranny of Nicholas I's officials. In his celebrated DEAD SOULS and THE INSPECTOR GENERAL, Gogol presents a vivid and truthful picture of the hard life of the people in serf Russia.

It was during the reign of Nicholas I that Vissarion Belinsky, the celebrated Russian literary critic and revolutionary, died. Sick with consumption, he was hounded to death by the gendarmes.

The great Russian composer, Michael Glinka, also led a hard life under the reign of Nicholas. Glinka composed the first Russian national opera, RUSLAN AND LUDMILA, in which he reproduced the music not only of the Russian folk songs, but also of those of other nationalities inhabiting Russia. The aristocracy failed to appreciate the beauty of this remarkable opera and it ceased to be shown soon after it was produced. Indignant at this, Glinka left Russia. He died in a foreign country.

Nicholas I also treated cruelly the Ukrainian revolutionary poet and artist, Taras Shevchenko. Shevchenko was a serf who later was able to purchase his freedom.

In his poems Shevchenko described the oppression of the Ukrainian and other peoples in tsarist Russia, the hard lives of the serfs, the tyranny of the tsars and pans who trampled on the rights of the people.

[**FIGURE 53:**] Vissarion Belinsky (1811–1848). [SH, 107]

[**FIGURE 54:**] Taras Shevchenko (1814–1861). [SH, 108]

Nicholas I conscripted Shevchenko for the army, banished him to Kazakhstan and even forbade him to write and paint. For ten years Shevchenko was tormented in the soldiers' barracks, but his spirit remained unbroken. He continued to write his poems in secret. His complete works were published in the Ukraine for the first time under the Soviet Government in a collection of his poems entitled Kobzar.

37. The Conquest of the Caucasus

The conquest of Armenia. The annexation of Azerbaidjan was commenced in the reign of Catherine II. Many small principalities in Azerbaidjan were snatched from the rule of Iran and annexed to Russia. In the reign of Alexander I large forces of Russian soldiers were sent to Azerbaidjan and Georgia.

The Shah of Iran tried to win back his dominions. In the reign of Nicholas I the Russian troops defeated the shah's troops and annexed ~~the ancient state of~~[48] Armenia, the peoples of which had been suffering under the yoke of the Iran rulers for hundreds of years. Thus, tsarist Russia strengthened its rule in Trans-Caucasia.

The new dominions were separated from Russia by the lofty Caucasian mountains. In these mountains the warlike mountaineers lived. No one could ~~subordinate~~ *subdue*[49] them. Nor could Nicholas I subdue them for a long time.

His troops set fire to the mountaineers' AULS, or villages, and killed all those who fell into their hands. In the foothills near these mountains forts were built from which the Russian soldiers raided the mountaineers' villages and forced them further and further into the mountains.

Hiding in the mountain gorges and forests, knowing every inch of their native mountains, the freedom-loving mountaineers fought stubbornly for their independence and defended their land inch by inch.

But success in this struggle was prevented by ~~their division into~~ *the lack of unity among*[50] the tribes and nationalities, of which there were ~~more than thirty~~ *nearly a score*[51] in the North Caucasus at that time. Often there were feuds between the various tribes, and the Russian generals incited them against each other and defeated them one by one.

The mountaineers' fight for independence under the leadership of Shamil. The mountaineers were united by the gifted and energetic leader Shamil. Shamil was born in Daghestan, and even in his childhood he was distinguished for his courage and determination.

He was strong, bold, agile, a splendid horseman, an excellent marksman, a tireless swimmer and runner. He was brave, experienced ~~and educated,~~[52] and exercised great influence among the mountaineers. He became an able ruler and gifted military leader.

He created a large mountaineers' state. At the head of the various regions he appointed chiefs from among the ablest and bravest mountaineers. Every mountaineer was obliged to learn to shoot, to handle a sword, and to ride a horse in order to be able to defend his country from its enemies.

[**FIGURE 55:**] Shamil (1798–1871). [SH, 110]

Shamil mustered a*n* ~~strong~~[53] army of over 30,000 men. He also had artillery. He lured detachments of Russian soldiers deep into the mountains and blocked their line of retreat with rocks and felled trees. Caught in this ambush, the Russian soldiers were exterminated by the mountaineers.

~~The peasants of the Caucasus provided Shamil with great help in his struggle with Nicholas I. They rose up against their landlords at the tsar's troops. Especially powerful was the uprising in Gury.~~

~~The peasants of Gury overran many landlord estates and laid siege to the main city of Gury. Georgian landlords had fled to Gury from their estates. They led Russian troops through impassible mountain trail and with them attacked the peasants. The uprising was mercilessly suppressed and the peasants were forced to rebuild the roads, forts, and estates that they had destroyed.~~

~~The peasants of Azerbaidjan and Armenia equally bravely fought with~~

[**Figure 56:**] Mountaineers going to war against the tsarist troops. [SH, 111]

~~their landlords and tsarist invaders during these years, preventing them from putting further pressure on Shamil.~~[54]

The final conquest of the Caucasus. For twenty-five years the mountaineers of North Caucasus fought heroically under Shamil's leadership, but they were unable to defeat Nicholas I's huge army. Nicholas dispatched troops to the Caucasus in ever increasing numbers. Forests were cut down, *villages were destroyed,*[55] mountain roads were laid, and slowly but surely the Russian army advanced.

Shamil's army was melting away. Large numbers of his warriors were killed or taken prisoner. The Russian generals succeeded in buying over the elders of some of the *mountain*[56] tribes. With several hundred mountaineers Shamil hid in the Aul of Gunib, on a high mountain in Daghestan. Surrounded on all sides by the Russian army, Shamil and his comrades bravely defended themselves, but at last were compelled to surrender. This happened after the death of Nicholas I, in the reign of Alexander II.

~~The mountaineers of the North Caucasus, the Cherkess, defended their land and freedom with similar heroism. They fought with the Russian tsar's troops for over 70 years. Their flowering region was destroyed.~~[57]

38. The Revolution in Europe in 1848.
Karl Marx and Frederick Engels

Nicholas I and the revolution of 1848. In the middle of the 19th century industry in Europe had already made great progress. In a number of countries large industrial centres had sprung up. Factories and mills employing modern machinery had increased in number, and railways were being rapidly built. The factory owners were making huge profits. Millionaires arose. They became ~~all-powerful~~ *a power*[58] and controlled the state.

Growing industry created a great demand for workers. A numerous working class, which had not existed before, came into being, the class we call the proletariat. The proletariat began openly to fight for its rights against the capitalists. The proletariat of Paris, in particular, covered itself with glory in the revolution of 1848.

On February 22, 1848, a revolution broke out in Paris and quickly spread to ~~all~~[59] other towns in France. The king fled to a foreign country. France was proclaimed a republic.

But it was a bourgeois republic. The revolution brought no relief for the workers. At the end of June 1848 the proletariat of Paris rose in revolt against their capitalist masters and the bourgeois *republican*[60] government.

[**Figure 57:**] Rebellion of the workers of Paris, June 1848. [SH, 112]

The workers fought heroically for three days. Their wives and children made bullets out of lead, helped to build barricades, and amidst the hail of soldiers' bullets brought food for the fighters. The bourgeoisie sent well-armed troops against the workers. They fought the workers ruthlessly. The workers were badly organized and insufficiently armed *and the peasants failed to come to their aid*[61]. The rebellion was suppressed. The bourgeoisie took severe reprisals against the vanquished workers; thousands were shot, thrown into prison or sent to penal servitude. The bourgeoisie triumphed.

As soon as the first news of the revolution in Paris *and of the unrest in Prussia and Austria*[62] reached him, Nicholas I moved his ~~300,000-man~~[63] army to the frontiers of Prussia and Austria. He waited for a convenient moment to send his troops to crush the revolutionary movement, which he hated so much.

After France, the revolution broke out ~~immediately~~[64] in many other countries in Europe. In Vienna, the capital of Austria, the workers, university students and other citizens rose and overthrew the rule of the aristocracy. The emperor fled from Vienna.

In Berlin, the revolutionary workers fought on the barricades for eighteen hours and forced the king to yield. A new government was set up in Prussia, and serfdom was abolished.

The workers and townspeople rose against their kings, nobles and *partly against*[65] the ~~big~~[66] capitalists in other ~~cities~~ *countries*[67] of Europe.

The revolution spread to Hungary, which was part of the Austrian Empire[68]. At the request of the Emperor of Austria, Nicholas I sent an army to Hungary and crushed the revolution.

This is how Tsar Nicholas I, the gendarme of Europe, fought against revolution.

But no power on earth could suppress the young class, the proletariat, which rose in revolt in 1848.

Karl Marx and Frederick Engels. The teachers and leaders of the proletariat were those men of genius, Karl Marx and Frederick Engels.

In 1848, Karl Marx and Frederick Engels came forth as the leaders of the revolutionary workers in Germany. Marx was then 30 years of age, and his friend Engels was 28 years of age. They were the first revolutionary Communists. Before the revolution they had founded, the Communist League and had written their celebrated COMMUNIST MANIFESTO. In this manifesto they called upon the workers of the world to fight their enemies, the capitalists. Since then the slogan, "Proletarians of all countries unite!" has been inscribed on the standards of the workers all over the world.

After the revolution in Germany was crushed, Marx and Engels were compelled to leave Germany and to emigrate to England. There they lived and worked under very difficult conditions. Marx's family was often in want. ~~Marx and his children frequently suffered from malnutrition. Frequently, there wasn't enough to be able to afford a doctor for the sick children.~~[69] Engels helped his friend as much as he could and shared all his joys and sorrows, his successes and failures.

The hard conditions of life, however, did not break the spirit of these great revolutionaries. They tirelessly continued the great work they had started in the cause of emancipating the toilers from the oppression of the capitalists.

They wrote many books from which the workers learned how to fight the capitalists and to vanquish them. Marx and Engels taught the workers that there has always been a fierce struggle between the oppressed and the oppressors. Under capitalism this struggle was waged between the bourgeoisie and the workers; it was inevitable and would end in the victory of the working class. The working class would overthrow the bourgeoisie and establish its own revolutionary rule, the dictatorship of the proletariat. The victorious proletariat would build a new, Communist, society in which there would be neither classes nor oppressed. This is what Marx and Engels taught.

Marx and Engels called upon the workers of all countries to unite and form a single, powerful Communist Party.

39. Tsarist Russia on the Eve of the Reform of 1861

The development of industry. ~~Toward~~ Until[70] the middle of the 19th century industry in serf Russia had developed slowly. Only one-tenth of the population of Russia lived in towns. The ~~total number of factories and mills numbered less than ten thousand and the~~[71] total number of workers employed in factories and mills was not more than 500,000. Among them were many serfs whom their masters had sent to the factories to earn money to pay their obrok. Machines, and steam engines to drive the machines, were only just being introduced in the factories. Steamships were just beginning to appear on the Volga and Dniepr. Only one large railway had been built, between Moscow and Petersburg.

The manufacturers could not build many factories because there were not enough free people to become *wage*[72] workers. Moreover, it was difficult to sell goods in Russia because the serf peasants bought very little.

The increase in the town population and in the number of factories caused an increase in the grain trade in Russia. In addition, the landlords exported large quantities of grain, particularly to industrial England. They wanted more grain to sell, and so began to oppress their serfs more than ever.

Many landlords began to understand that serfdom was a hindrance to the development of commercial farming and that free wage workers tilled the land better and actually cost less than serfs. They began to talk about abolishing serfdom.

The Crimean War. In order to become complete master of the Black Sea coast, to drive the Turks entirely out of the Caucasus, and to be able to export the landlords' grain to Europe VIA the Bosporus and Dardanelle Straits, Nicholas I, in **1853**, again declared war on Turkey, which by that time had become enfeebled. But England and France did not want Russia to become strong and crush Turkey. They *concluded an alliance with each other and*[73] declared war on Nicholas I.

The *allied*[74] fleets ~~of England and France~~[75] entered the Black Sea. Their warships were driven by steam engines and equipped with heavy guns. Nicholas I ~~possessed~~ *had*[76] only a fleet of sailing ships. The enemy landed a large army in the Crimea and besieged Sevastopol. The range of the enemy's guns and rifles was twice that of the Russians'. The tsar's generals did not even have good maps of the Crimea. Military supplies were in the hands of corrupt government officials and contractors. Such was the military technique of backward, serf Russia.

The naval fort at Sevastopol lacked land fortifications. In a short space of time the people and the soldiers built earthworks and on them placed batteries of guns. Nicholas I's sailing ships dared not go into battle against the enemy's fleet. The Russians therefore sunk their ships at the entrance of Sevastopol harbour, and thus barred the way to the enemy's fleet.

The siege of Sevastopol lasted eleven months. The Russian soldiers died in hundreds every day, stubbornly defending the town. Finally, the principal fortification, Malakhov Kurgan, which was known as the Gate of Sevastopol, was captured by the French after a heavy bombardment.

Sevastopol lay in ruins. It was impossible to hold it any longer. The ~~heroic~~[77] garrison retreated from the ruined fort. The defeat of Nicholas' Russia was complete. Nicholas I died suddenly during the siege of Sevastopol. Alexander II became tsar.

In **1856** peace was signed in Paris. Russia was forbidden to maintain a navy or forts in the Black Sea; but Sevastopol remained in Russia's possession.

The defeat in the Crimean War revealed ~~to the whole world~~[78] the extreme backwardness of serf Russia.

After the war, peasant disturbances broke out over the whole country and, at an assembly of nobles. Tsar Alexander II declared that it would be better for the nobles to liberate the peasants ~~themselves,~~ *"from above,"*[79] than wait until the peasants revolted and liberated themselves *"from below"*[80].

A. I. Herzen. Prominent among those who came out strongly against serfdom and tsarist tyranny was the *bourgeois democratic*[81] revolutionary and author, Alexander Herzen.

Nicholas I had banished Herzen from the capital. On his return from exile Herzen went abroad. In London he and his friend Ogarev began to publish the journal KOLOKOL (THE BELL) in the first Russian printing office that was free from the tsarist censorship. This journal strongly advocated the ~~interests of the enserfed~~ *liberation of the*[82] peasants and the oppressed peoples. It was secretly transported to Russia. By this time Alexander II was on the throne. Those who were caught reading KOLOKOL were arrested and banished to Siberia.

[**FIGURE 58:**] Alexander Herzen (1812–1870). [SH, 117]

The Growth of Capitalism in Tsarist Russia. ~~A Capitalist Country~~[1]

40. The Abolition of Serfdom in Russia

Alexander II's Manifesto of February 19, 1861. *Fearing that the peasants would rise in revolt and break up the serf system themselves,*[2] Alexander II, on February 19, 1861, issued a manifesto liberating the peasants. The peasants became free; they could no longer be bought and sold; they ceased to be the property of the nobility.

But the peasants were granted little land, in fact they had less than before the Reform, as the emancipation of the serfs was called. The land that was left to them was inferior land, for the landlords took the best lands for themselves. *Moreover, the landlords deprived the peasants of the free use of the forests, meadows and pastures.*[3] The landlords divided the land in such a way that the peasants' lands were cut off from the watering places for cattle, the forests and pastures. The peasants were therefore obliged to beg the landlords to permit them to use sections of the latters' [SIC] land on any terms the landlords cared to impose.

For their land and liberation the peasants were compelled to pay the landlords compensation, and the price they had to pay for the land was twice and three times that of its actual value. This compensation was paid in installments, and for a period of over forty years the peasants paid the landlords for their emancipation a total of over two billion rubles.

The tsar and the landlords robbed the peasants in the Crimea, the Ukraine and the Caucasus even more. In the Crimea they took for themselves the best lands on the Black Sea coast. Here were the palaces and estates of the tsar, the tsar's family and his court aristocracy, who appropriated all the land. ~~Very few~~ *The*[4] peasants in the Ukraine also received *very little*[5] land. The landlords did not want to give them the fertile black soil. In

[**FIGURE 59:**] ~~Anton Petrov calls upon the peasants to demand complete liberty.~~ [Zhdanov: RGASPI, f. 77, op. 1, d. 854, l. 50.]

Georgia, in addition to paying enormous sums in compensation, the peasants were obliged to continue working for the landlords for many years and to pay them one-third of the harvest of their vineyards and fields.

This sort of liberation from serfdom roused great discontent among the peasants all over the country. The peasants demanded complete liberty and all the land *they required*[6] without compensation. Troops were sent out to subdue the peasants and sanguinary battles were fought[7] in which hundreds were killed and wounded.

~~Especially savagely suppressed was the uprising of peasants in the village of Bezdna in the gubernia of Kazan. The peasant Anton Petrov called upon the peasants to reject the tsarist manifesto and demand land from the landlords without compensation. Attempts were made to arrest him, but the peasants prevented it. Soldiers were sent in who fired into the crowd. The first volley was followed by others. About 300 peasants were killed or wounded. Anton Petrov was executed.~~[8]

N. Chernyshevsky. The most enlightened people of those days championed the interests of the peasants. One of these was Nicholas Chernyshevsky, a great man of learning and a revolutionary *democrat*[9]. Even as a child, living in Saratov, the hard lives led by the serfs and the Volga bargemen impressed him. While the introduction of the Reform was in preparation he wrote many magazine articles in which he demanded that the peasants be granted complete liberty and all[10] the landlords' land without compensation.

After the Manifesto of February 19 was proclaimed, ~~he~~ *Chernyshevsky*[11], with a number of other ~~revolutionaries~~ *revolutionary democrats*[12], resolved to rouse the peasants to revolt against the tsar and the landlords. For this purpose Chernyshevsky wrote a manifesto entitled "To the Serf Peasants." This manifesto was intercepted by the tsar's gendarmes.

Alexander II ordered Chernyshevsky to be imprisoned in the Fortress of Peter and Paul ~~for two years~~[13] and afterwards sent him to penal servitude. The staunch revolutionary never renounced his convictions, and for fully nineteen years he was either kept in prison in Siberia or he remained in exile. Marx, Engels and Lenin thought very highly of Chernyshevsky as an outstanding man of learning and as a staunch and brave revolutionary *democrat*[14].

[**FIGURE 60:**] Nicholas Nekrasov (1821–1877). [SH, 120]

[**FIGURE 61:**] Nicholas Chernishevsky [SIC!] (1828–1889). [SH, 119]

The poet N. Nekrasov. It was ~~then~~ *during these years*[15] that the gifted Russian poet, Nicholas Nekrasov, wrote his poems. In his simple verses he vividly depicted the hard lot of the peasants in tsarist Russia. He wrote about the manner in which human beings were tormented under serfdom and how mercilessly the peasants were exploited by the landlords and the capitalists even after the Reform. "In place of the chains of serfdom many others were forged," wrote Nekrasov.

Nekrasov's poems became the favourite songs of the revolutionaries of that time. They are sung by the Russian people to this day.

Reform of the administration. Under serfdom the serfs were completely in the power of the landlords who acted as judges over them.

After the Peasant Reform a village STAROSTA[16], or elder, was appointed in every village to govern the peasants. Several villages were combined to form a VOLOST, which was governed by a volost elder[17]. The volost and village elders were elected from among the rich peasants. They were subordinate to the tsar's officials. They squeezed the taxes out of the peasants and helped the police to keep them in subjection. Peasants involved in minor cases were tried in volost courts by judges elected in each volost. The volost judges could sentence peasants to be flogged, fined or imprisoned. Corporal punishment was retained for peasants and criminals.

In the gubernias and uyezds Zemstvo, or local, Administrations were set up which managed the schools and hospitals and supervised the repair of bridges and roads. The money for these purposes was taken from the peasants. The peasants also had the right to vote in the elections and to be elected to these Zemstvo Administrations, but the electoral system was such that the peasants could elect only one representative for every 3,000 households, and there was therefore a small number of them in the administrations. The peasant representatives in the Zemstvo Administrations were mostly kulaks, or village usurers and exploiting farmers. All the work of the Zemstvo Administrations was directed by the landlords. *City* DUMAS, *or councils, were set up to take charge of municipal affairs, but only manufacturers, merchants and rich houseowners had the right to take part in the elections to these dumas.*[18]

The conditions of military service were *also*[19] changed. All males reaching the age of 21 became liable for military service. The period of military service was reduced to six years. As before, however, the peasants served as common soldiers, while the officers were chosen only from the nobility.

After the Reform all power still remained in the hands of the tsar and the landlords; they owned enormous tracts of the best land and kept the peasants under the strict surveillance of the police and government officials.

After the abolition of serfdom, however, more factories began to spring up in Russia, railways began to be built faster, and trade began to develop more widely. Serf Russia was becoming a capitalist country.

41. The Struggle of the Poles for Independence. The Wars of Alexander II

The Polish rebellion of 1863. For many years the ~~Polish people~~ *Poles, headed by the Polish nobility,*[20] had been preparing to liberate Poland from the rule of the Russian tsar. In Warsaw, the revolutionaries formed what was known as the National Committee, which made preparations for a rebellion.

In 1863, this National Committee, *headed by the nobility,*[21] raised a rebellion and proclaimed itself the government of Poland.

The rebellion affected Poland, *part of*[22] Lithuania and *part of*[23] Byelorussia. Everywhere detachments of rebels were formed. The rebels were armed with pistols, hunting rifles, pikes and swords. Avoiding pitched battles with strong forces of Russian troops, they began to carry on guerilla warfare. The rebel detachments hid in the forests from which they made sorties upon the tsarist troops. In the course of eighteen months over a thousand such sorties were made.

The rebellion was particularly strong in Byelorussia. Here, under the leadership of Kastus Kalinovsky, the peasants, armed with scythes and axes, attacked and burned the landlords' manors, exterminated small detachments of Russian troops, and killed landlords, tsarist officials and army officers.

Alexander II sent a whole army to crush the rebellion. Eighteen months passed before the tsarist generals succeeded in crushing the valorous rebels. In Byelorussia and Lithuania the suppression of the rebels was led by the cruel General Muravyov. He mercilessly hanged the prisoners he captured. Brave Kastus Kalinovsky was also captured and hanged.

After the rebellion was crushed the tsar's government exiled ~~more than 100 thousand~~ *tens of thousands of*[24] Poles to Siberia.

During the rebellion, Tsar Alexander II hastened to pass a law abolishing serfdom in Poland and Lithuania on terms ~~more advantageous~~ *less onerous*[25] for the peasants than those in the other gubernias in Russia. The various services which the peasants were required to render were abolished. In Lithuania the peasants were allowed ~~to buy landlord land~~ *to retain their plots of land*[26] for a lower price than that paid by the peasants in the other gubernias, and in Poland they obtained them gratis. The tsar did this in order to win the peasants to his side *in opposition to the Polish landlords*[27].

The conquest of Central Asia. Meanwhile, Tsar Alexander II resolutely set out to conquer Central Asia.

After entrenching herself in Kazakhstan ~~(see lesson 32)~~[28], tsarist Russia in the course of ten years conquered Kirghizia. The Kirghiz stubbornly resisted the Russian troops, but their resistance was broken.

Following the course of the River Syr-Darya, the Russian forces attacked the Uzbek city of Tashkent. The ~~Tashkent residents~~ *Uzbeks*[29] fiercely defended their territory and once recaptured Tashkent from the Russians. It was only in 1865 that the Russians were able at last to establish themselves firmly in that city.

Three years after the capture of Tashkent the Russian forces captured Samarkand, an ancient city in Bokhara, once the Tamerlane capital. The Emir of Bokhara accepted the overlordship of the Russian tsar and was compelled to yield to him the most fertile lands of ~~theirs~~ *Bokhara*[30].

The next to be subjugated were the dominions of the Khan of Khiva. The khan also accepted the supremacy of the Russian tsar. After this the khanate of Kokand was conquered.

For twelve years the warlike tribes of Turkmenia fought the tsarist troops to protect their independence. They repulsed strong Russian forces from Geok-Tepe, their principal fortress, and yielded only after the Russians had subjected it to heavy artillery bombardment. Following this the tsar's troops captured Ashkhabad.

At the end of the 19th century Russia conquered the Pamirs, the "Roof of the World."

Thus, in the course of thirty years of stubborn war, *landlord*[31] Russia conquered the peoples of Central Asia.

Tsarist officials and Russian merchants came to Central Asia in the wake of the Russian armies.

They imposed heavy taxes upon the population, robbed them of their lands and property and cheated them in trade. The khans, elders and mullahs, or Mohammedan priests, helped the Russian tsar to rob the subjugated peoples.

On the lands fit for the purpose ~~the population was forced to grow~~[32]American cotton *began to be sown* ~~in the place of cereal crops~~[33]. Cotton was needed for the growing textile industry in Russia. ~~The native rich and Russian manufacturers lived off of the labor of the enslaved Uzbek, Turkmen and Tadjik poor~~ *All the profits from cotton growing were pocketed by the native rich and Russian manufacturers, who exploited the poor Uzbeks, Turkmens and Tadjiks.* ~~Urban markets were flooded with products from Russian mills and factories, leading to a decline of local artisanal handicraft and trade.~~[34]

The peoples of Central Asia were entirely at the mercy of the tsar's generals, *the nobles*[35] and capitalists. More than once the oppressed masses rose in rebellion, but the Russian ~~troops~~ *nobles*[36], assisted by the wealthy section of the native population, obtained the upper hand.

Central Asia became a colony of tsarist Russia.

The war against Turkey. Towards the close of the reign of Alexander II Russia once again went to war with Turkey. Once again the Russian tsar failed to capture the Straits, the gateway from the Black Sea to the Mediterranean. In accordance with the peace treaty, Turkey ceded to Russia the important commercial port of Batumi on the Black Sea. *The Russian forces far outnumbered those of Turkey, but owing to Russia's backwardness the war entailed enormous losses. Hundreds of thousands of badly armed soldiers needlessly sacrificed their lives.*[37]

42. The First International and the Paris Commune

The First International. Marx and Engels regarded the revolutionary ~~uprising~~ *movement*[38] of the European workers of 1848 merely as the beginning of the proletariat's struggle for its emancipation. They realized that this struggle would be a stern one and that the bourgeoisie would fight hard to retain its rule. The great leaders of the proletariat were of the opinion that in order to fight the bourgeoisie successfully the proletariat must form an *international*[39] party. This is why they formed the first international proletarian association.

In **1864**, at a congress of workers' representatives held in London, Marx and Engels proposed that the International Workingmen's Association be formed. This proposal was adopted and the First International was thus founded. The leader of the First International was Karl Marx. The First International united the working class movement in different countries. Marx drew up a program for this movement. For nearly ten years Marx led the First International and was busy organizing the masses of the workers. His faithful assistant in this was Frederick Engels.

Marx and Engels staunchly and persistently defended the interests of the working class, and constantly fought all those who tried to lead the proletariat along wrong and harmful roads. Marx and Engels unceasingly exposed those who tried to persuade the workers to believe that Socialism could be built peacefully, without overthrowing the rule of the bourgeoisie. These people called themselves Socialists *but in fact they supported the capitalists and betrayed the workers*[40]. Marx and Engels also constantly explained what enormous harm was done by those who regarded themselves as revolutionaries, but who opposed the establishment of the rule of the workers, opposed the dictatorship of the proletariat.

Marx and Engels said that such opinions benefited only the enemies of the working class, the capitalists. Such opinions were harmful because they tended to reconcile the workers to capitalist exploitation, weaken the proletariat and help the capitalists to crush the workers.

The Paris Commune. In 1870 war broke out between Prussia and France. In this war Prussia was victorious. The French armies were defeated. The *French*[41] emperor, *Napoleon III*[42], was captured with his army. In Paris *the revolutionary workers and the petty-bourgeois masses made*[43] a revolution began[44], but it was the bourgeoisie that assumed power. The Prussian army marched on Paris. A *citizen army, known as the*[45] National Guard, was then formed in Paris. Many workers joined this army.

The Germans reached Paris and besieged it. The workers' battalions rose to defend their city and vowed that they would rather die than surrender Paris to the enemy. Surrounded by the enemy troops the population of Paris bravely held out for four and a half months. The workers and their families starved. The bourgeois government, fearing that the workers would rise in revolt *against the bourgeoisie, resorted to downright treachery and*[46] came to an agreement with the Germans behind the backs of the people to surrender

[**FIGURE 62:**] Karl Marx. [SH, 126–127]

[**FIGURE 63:**] Friedrich Engels. [SH, 126–127]

Paris. But the workers retained their arms. The German troops, seeing that the Paris workers represented a menacing force, dared not enter the city.

The bourgeois Prime Minister, the contemptible traitor and enemy of the people, Thiers, then sent soldiers to surprise the workers and take the artillery away from them. But working women saw the soldiers approaching and raised the alarm. The National Guard saved the guns. Many soldiers went over to the side of the people and shot two of their generals on the spot. Thiers, the Ministers, the generals, the bourgeoisie, the profiteers, government officials and priests then ~~ran away~~ *fled*[47] from Paris to Versailles.

[**Figure 64:**] Battle between Communards and Thiers'
soldiers in one of the squares of Paris. [SH, 128]

On **March 18, 1871**, power in Paris passed into the hands of the working class. The working class set up its own government known as the Paris Commune. ~~Many~~ *Some*[48] of the members of the Paris Commune were Socialists, members of the First International that was founded by Marx and Engels.

Marx and Engels called upon the Commune to advance on Versailles, where the *bourgeois*[49] government of Thiers had taken refuge. But ~~they lived in London and their instructions reached besieged Paris late—Thiers's soldiers had seized the revolutionary city in a tight encirclement~~ *the Commune lacked the determination to take this step. This lack of determination was due to the fact that there were many petty-bourgeois, wavering revolutionaries in the Commune who believed in the "good intentions" of the bourgeoisie. Marx severely criticized them for their lack of determination. Meanwhile, Thiers' troops were closing in upon Paris.*[50]

The Commune transferred the factories of the fugitive bourgeoisie to the workers. Churches and monasteries were transformed into clubs for the people. Everything was done to improve the conditions of the toilers. An order was issued to move the workers from their dark and damp cellar dwellings to the houses of the rich.

The whole world tensely watched the great struggle of the Paris proletarians. But the Communards were besieged, cut off from the rest of France. They *failed to establish an alliance between the workers and peasants against the bourgeoisie; they*[51] failed to win the peasantry to their side.

The Communards fought heroically against the numerous and ~~extremely~~[52] well-armed forces of the Versailles *bourgeois*[53] government. Women and children fought shoulder to shoulder with the men. On May 21, Thiers' troops forced their way into Paris. *The German army assisted them.*[54] The bourgeoisie wreaked cruel vengeance on the Communards. In the course of one week tens of thousands of men, women and children were shot. Still larger numbers of workers were imprisoned or deported to remote islands to serve terms of penal servitude.

The Paris Commune was crushed. It lasted 71 days, but the proletariat will remember it forever. Every year the workers put wreaths on the graves of the Communards who lie buried in one of the cemeteries of Paris, at the wall of which the heroic Communards were shot.

The Paris Commune was crushed because the workers still lacked a Marxian-revolutionary party of their own capable of leading them unwaveringly against the bourgeoisie. Another reason was that the workers lacked the support of the peasants; they failed to understand the importance of an alliance between the workers and peasants.[55]

In **1876**, the First International ceased to exist.[56]

The importance of the First International was enormous. It was the first international association of workers and served as the model for the Communist International that was founded by Lenin.

Marx died in **1883** and Engels in **1895**. Their teachings directed the struggle of the workers for Communism along the right road and served as the basis of the activities of ~~our great leaders~~[57] V. I. Lenin and ~~J. V. Stalin~~ *of our Communist Party*[58].

43. ~~Capitalist~~ *Capitalism in*[59] Russia

How the workers and peasants lived under capitalism. After the Reform of 1861, tens of millions of peasants *continued to*[60] live in horrible poverty and under oppression. They had little land. In order to maintain themselves and their families and to pay the taxes they had to rent land from the landlords or borrow money from them. In return for this the peasants were compelled to till the landlords' land with their own horses and implements. Thus, the peasants still remained in ~~the worst~~[61] bondage to the landlords.

The landlords were like vampires, sucking all they could out of the peasants. Towards the end of the 19th century, half the peasants in Russia became poor peasants, having no horses at all or only one wretched nag. The middle peasants still managed to make ends meet; but if the harvest failed they were pauperized, fell into greater bondage to the landlords and ~~somewhat prosperous~~[62] peasant kulaks and were forced to work for them as labourers.

The peasants were not only robbed and oppressed by the landlords but also by the kulaks.

The ruined peasants deserted the countryside and went into the towns. The towns were growing rapidly because of the development of industry. At the end of the 19th century there were already more than two million industrial workers in Russia. Large industrial centres sprang up; engineering works in Petersburg and Nizhni Novgorod (*now the city of Gorky*)[63]; iron and steel works in Tula, the Urals and the Donetz Basin, and textile mills in the Moscow, Vladimir, Kostroma and Yaroslavl gubernias.

The ruined peasants drifted to these places. There was also a great demand for labour for the construction of railways. Towards the end of the 19th century there were already over 30,000 kilometres of railways in Russia, and the building of the Siberian Railway had been started.

To the spacious lands of Siberia came hundreds of thousands of peasant families. Notwithstanding the severe climate, they toiled stubbornly and perserveringly to cultivate this rich country. The peasants penetrated deep into the TAIGA, as the Siberian forests are called. The ancient dominions of Russia began to be populated by masses of ruined ~~Russian~~[64] peasants.

[**FIGURE 65:**] Workers demanding an increase of
wages from their employer. [SH, 130]

The lot of the workers was no better than that of the peasants. The factory owners compelled the workers, not only men, but also women and children, to work thirteen and fourteen hours a day. Often they had to work seventeen and eighteen hours a day. The workers were compelled to work on holidays; there was no such thing as vacations.

The wages paid for this hard labour were miserable indeed, for masses of starving peoples stood at the factory gates begging for work.

The workers were fined, that is, part of their wages was deducted, on the slightest pretext. The factories were filthy, damp and gloomy, and there was hardly any ventilation.

The workers lived in filthy and congested barracks. The beds on which they slept were never empty; when the workers on the day shift rose to go to work the workers from the night shift came to sleep in them.

Both the workers and peasants were equally oppressed in tsarist Russia. But the factory workers began to organize earlier than the peasants and to fight their oppressors. Later on they were followed by the peasants.

The Narodniki. The Russian revolutionaries of that time, *known as Narodniki*,[65] did not appreciate the leading role of the working class. They mistakenly thought that the peasantry was the main force and that liberation from the rule of the tsar and the landlords could be obtained *merely*[66] by means of a peasant revolt. They did not understand that the peasants alone, without ~~the leadership of~~ *an alliance*[67] with the working class, could not vanquish tsarism *and the landlords*[68].

Soon after the Peasant Reform of 1861 these revolutionaries began to organize secret revolutionary circles of young people, mostly students. At the meetings of these circles the question of how to help the peasants was heatedly discussed. Finally it was decided that it was necessary to go into the villages, "among the people," as they said, and call upon the peasants to rise in revolt against the tsar and the landlords. This is why these revolutionaries were called Narodniki, from the word "narod," meaning the people. But the peasants did not follow the Narodniki.

Then the Narodniki decided to continue the struggle by their own efforts without the people. They resolved to start the struggle by assassinating the tsar and organized a secret society called Narodnaya Volya, or Will of the People. They spent much time and effort in preparing for the assassination of the tsar. Only on March 1, 1881 did they succeed in assassinating Alexander II[69] by hurling a bomb at him.

Assassinations, however, ~~changed nothing~~ *led to no improvement whatever. The place of the assassinated tsar or Minister was taken by another, more cruel than the first.*[70] Alexander II was succeeded by his son, Alexander III, in whose reign the conditions of the workers and peasants became even worse. The tsar's gendarmes tracked down and arrested nearly all the revolutionaries of the Narodnaya Volya. Alexander III ordered five of them to be hanged, and the rest were sentenced to life-long imprisonment in a fortress, or to penal servitude.

It was not just by chance that the Narodniki failed. The method they chose of fighting tsarism *by means of terrorism*[71] was a wrong one, and harmful for the revolution.

The activities of the Narodniki were harmful because they made it difficult for the working class to understand that it must play the leading part in the revolution, and because they hindered the formation of a ~~mass~~ *Marxian workers'*[72] party. They diverted the attention of the toilers from the fight against the ~~exploiter~~ *oppressor*[73] class as a whole to the futile assassination of individual representatives of this class, and hindered the ~~formation of a mass revolutionary party~~ *alliance between the workers and the peasants*[74].

In 1887 a small group of revolutionaries made another attempt to assassinate the tsar (Alexander III), but failed. The organizers of this attempt, Lenin's elder brother, Alexander Ulyanov, and his comrades, were captured by the gendarmes and hanged. *The old mistake was repeated with the same bad consequences.*[75]

[**FIGURE 66:**] Leo Tolstoy
(1828–1910). [SH, 133]

[**FIGURE 67:**] Ilya Repin
(1844–1930). [SH, 133]

At that time Vladimir Ilyich Ulyanov (Lenin) was already seventeen years of age. On learning of his brother's execution he said: "No, we will not take this road. This is not the road to follow." Lenin was right. Only the organized working class *in alliance with the peasantry, and*[76] leading the peasantry, could achieve complete victory over the rule of the tsar and the landlords.

The writer Leo Tolstoy and the painter I. Repin. In the second half of the 19th century there were many gifted writers, painters and composers in Russia.

One of these was Leo Tolstoy. He began writing[77] when he was still a young man, when he was taking part in the wars against the Caucasian mountaineers, and in the defence of Sevastopol during the Crimean War. He wrote his most important works after he had retired from the army and went to live on his estate, Yasnaya Polyana, near the town of Tula. In his principal novel, War and Peace, a great work of art, he *vividly*[78] tells the ~~detailed~~[79] story of Russia's war against Napoleon in 1812. In his works Tolstoy ~~wonderfully~~[80] depicted the life of the landlords under serfdom and under the capitalist system. Towards the end of his life he began to depict the awful conditions of the peasants after the Reform of 1861. Tolstoy did not believe in revolution, but he saw how hard was the lot of the peasants and sternly condemned the tyranny of the tsarist officials, landlords and capitalists.

In that period also there lived the great Russian painter, Ilya Repin. He

[**Figure 68:**] "Volga Bargemen." From a painting by I. Repin. [SH, 134]

was born in the Ukraine, in a soldier's family, and from childhood loved to draw. He became a celebrated painter. Repin knew the hard lot of the Russian peasants, for he himself had come from the people. His pictures are famous throughout the world.

In the second half of the 19th century there lived the great Russian composers, Moussorgsky, Rimsky-Korsakov, Borodin and Tschaikovsky.[81]

~~It was then that the composer~~[82] Moussorgsky composed the opera BORIS GODUNOV, and Rimsky-Korsakov the operas THE SNOW MAIDEN and SADKO. In their operas these composers made extensive use of the folk songs of the peoples inhabiting Russia. We often hear these beautiful compositions ~~of Russian music~~[83] today.

44. The Labour Movement from 1870 to 1900. V. I. Lenin ~~and J. V. Stalin~~[84]

The first workers' unions. The workers began their struggle against the capitalists during the reign of Alexander II.

The workers of a factory would come together and submit demands to their employers for improvements in their conditions and refuse to go on with their work until the employer had satisfied these demands. This ~~was~~ *is*[85] called a strike.

In order to be able to fight the capitalists more successfully the workers began to organize in unions.

The first union was formed in Odessa in 1875 and was called the South Russian League. This union made preparations to fight the autocracy and called upon the workers to unite in order to carry on the struggle for a revolution. Soon, however, the members of this union were arrested. Its leader, Zaslavsky, was sent to penal servitude, during which he died.

Three years later a union was formed in Petersburg known as the Northern League of Russian Workers, at the head of which were Khalturin, a carpenter, and Obnorsky, a mechanic. This union began to organize and lead strikes. But the tsarist government broke up this union too.

The labour movement, however, spread to new districts. The conditions of the workers were becoming worse, the capitalists robbed them more than ever.

Morozov, the cotton mill owner, for example, fined his workers unmer-

[**FIGURE 69:**] A conference of workers on the eve of the Morozov strike. [SH, 137]

cifully; by imposing fines on the workers he usually took back one-third of their wages. The workers could stand this open robbery no longer and in **1885**, 8,000 mill hands employed in the Morozov mills in the town of Orekhovo-Zuyevo came out on strike. The mills were brought to a standstill.

This strike had been organized beforehand. It was led by an advanced worker named Moiseyenko, who formerly had been a member of the Northern League of Russian Workers. With a group of fellow weavers he drew up a list of demands to be submitted to the mill owner, and these demands were confirmed by the workers at a secret conference.

Morozov rejected the demands and secured the arrest of one of the workers' leaders. A crowd of weavers forcibly released their arrested comrade, but the troops which had been sent for by Morozov defeated the workers. Six hundred strikers were arrested and scores were put on trial.

Strikes like this broke out in many factories in Russia. In the following year, the *tsarist*[86] government, *frightened by the growth of the labour movement and the strikes,*[87] ~~passed~~ *was obliged to pass*[88] a law prohibiting the mill owners from robbing the workers so brazenly.

The workers realized that they could achieve a great deal by means of organized struggle.

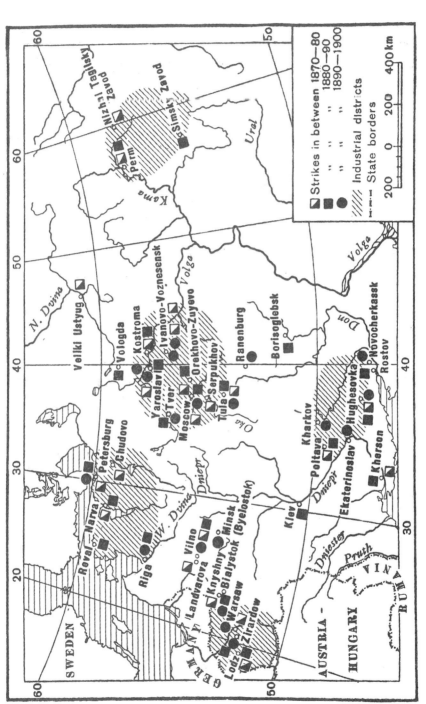

[MAP 5:] Map showing the spread of the strike movement in the second half of the 19th century. [SH, 13€]

The advanced workers of Russia first became acquainted with the teachings of Marx and Engels in workers' circles and in the unions.

The Emancipation of Labour Group. At that time *proletarian*[89] revolutionaries appeared in Russia who subscribed to the teachings of Marx, and were of the opinion that the proletariat must become the leader or the revolutionary movement.

One of these revolutionaries was George Plekhanov, the first propagandist of Marxism in Russia.

In 1883[90] Plekhanov went abroad and organized a revolutionary *Marxist*[91] group which was called the Emancipation of Labour Group. This group translated the works of Marx and Engels into Russian and distributed them in Russia. It also exposed the enormous harm that was being done to the labour movement by the teachings of the Narodniki and their methods of struggle.

In Russia numerous circles were formed for the study of the works of Marx. But neither the Emancipation of Labour Group nor these circles were connected with the labour movement.

This connection was established by Lenin ~~and Stalin~~,[92] who organized the Bolshevik Party and led the working class, *and* the peasantry ~~and the oppressed peoples~~[93] in the struggle against the tsarist government, the landlords and the bourgeoisie.

[**FIGURE 70:**] George Plekhanov (1856–1918). [SH, 138]

V. I. Lenin ~~and J. V. Stalin~~,[94] **the leaders**[95] **of the working class *and the founder of Bolshevism*[96].** Vladimir Ilyich Lenin (Ulyanov) was born in 1870, in the town of Simbirsk (now called Ulyanovsk). At school he was a very good pupil.

At the age of seventeen Lenin entered the Kazan University, but was soon expelled for taking part in the revolutionary students' movement. He then began to prepare for examination in all the subjects in the university curriculum. This examination he passed.

While still living in Kazan Lenin joined a Marxist circle and studied the works of Marx and Engels. He astonished everybody by his profound knowledge.

In 1893 Lenin went to Petersburg and there he began to teach in workers' circles.

In Petersburg Lenin amalgamated all the workers' circles into the League of Struggle for the Emancipation of the Working Class, and thus he paved the way for the creation of a genuinely revolutionary workers' party. On his proposal, similar leagues were formed in other towns.

[**FIGURE 71:**] Lenin at school. [SH, 139]

[**FIGURE 72:**] Lenin leading a workers' circle in Petersburg (in the 90's). [SH, 140]

Lenin ruthlessly fought against the Narodniki and against all those who misinterpreted the teachings of Marx.

Lenin studied every detail of the lives of the workers, wrote leaflets and books for them to read, and called for a persistent struggle against the capitalists.

The tsarist detectives succeeded in arresting Lenin. He was kept in prison for a long time and then exiled to Siberia for three years.

The Leagues of Struggle, which Lenin had organized, made an attempt to unite into a party. With this object the first congress of the Russian Social-Democratic Labour Party (R.S.D.L.P.) was convened in 1898, in the city of Minsk. The attempt to form a party at this congress failed, however.

On returning from exile Lenin went abroad and there started the first Marxist newspaper. It was called ISKRA, or THE SPARK.

ISKRA was printed on tissue paper so as to make it more convenient to smuggle it secretly into Russia.

[FIGURE 73:] Vladimir Lenin in the 90's. [SH, 141]

In ISKRA Lenin wrote articles calling upon the workers to unite in a revolutionary political party for the purpose of fighting the autocracy and the capitalists.

Lenin's ISKRA paved the way for the formation of the Bolshevik Party. ~~Lenin was helped in this by Comrade Stalin.~~[97]

The workers' struggle flared up and soon spread to the outlying districts of Russia, including Trans-Caucasia, *where, since 1898, Comrade Stalin, Lenin's pupil, carried on his revolutionary work*[98].

~~Joseph Vissarionovich Stalin was born in the small Georgian town of Gori in 1879. Stalin's father was a bootmaker and worked in a shoe factory.~~

~~While still a boy at the age of 15, Stalin became acquainted with an underground group of Russian Marxians. For reading revolutionary books, the young Stalin was expelled from school, where he had been an excellent student.~~

~~In 1898, Stalin joined a social-democratic organization. From that moment on, he worked only for the revolution.~~

~~Stalin, like Lenin, was loved by the workers, with whom he worked in study circles.~~

~~Persecuted by the tsar's police agents, the young Stalin moved from city to city and worked without rest or comfort.~~

[**FIGURE 74:**] ~~Hut in Gori, where J. V. Stalin was born.~~ [Cut by Stalin: RGASPI, f. 558, op. 11, d. 1584, ll. 690b-70. Also Zhdanov: f. 77, op. 1, d. 854, l. 60.]

~~In Batum, Stalin formed a large worker's organization. When the Batum police arrested several hundred workers, three thousand Batum workers surrounded the prison in order to aid their arrested comrades. Stalin headed up the demonstration. Soldiers and police started to fire into the protestors, killing 14 and wounding 30. Comrade Stalin survived unscathed. Risking his own life, Stalin saved a wounded comrade. In 1902, the police finally managed to capture Comrade Stalin and put him in prison. Then, they exiled him to Siberia. But Stalin escaped from there and one again appeared in his motherland. Here, Stalin took charge of the Caucasian revolution when it began in 1905 as a staunch Marxian revolutionary and as a follower and comrade-in-arms of Lenin.~~[99]

X

The First ~~Russian~~ *Bourgeois* Revolution *in Russia*[1]

45. The Eve of the ~~1905~~[2] Revolution

The Obukhov Defence and the Rostov strike. In *the beginning of*[3] the 20th century the revolutionary struggle of the workers increased in intensity. The workers organized strikes and demonstrations and mustered their forces for the struggle against the capitalists and the tsarist government.

At that time Nicholas II was tsar. His reign began in 1894.

In 1901, on the first of May, the day celebrated by the workers all over the world, the workers in the Obukhov Ordnance Works in Petersburg came out on strike and submitted a number of demands to the management. The

[**FIGURE 75:**] Strikers dispersed by Cossacks. [SH, 143]

officials were so astonished at this that they did not know what to do. They said to the workers: "At this rate you will not only demand our dismissal, but also the dismissal of the tsar's Ministers, won't you?" "Not only of the Ministers, but of the tsar himself," the strikers retorted.

The officials sent for the police and the military to crush the strikers. The strikers built barricades inside the works and around it, and the police and soldiers who arrived were met with a hail of stones and lumps of iron. The police and soldiers opened fire on the strikers. The workers fought the troops for several hours. A number of workers were killed and severely wounded. This battle was afterwards known as the Obukhov Defence. About 800 participants in this battle were arrested; many of them were sentenced to long terms of imprisonment and penal servitude.

The news about the heroic Obukhov workers quickly spread throughout the country. In all parts of boundless Russia the workers rose for the fight.

In 1902 a big railway strike broke out in Rostov on the Don. Many factory workers joined the railwaymen. The strike and meetings of workers were led by the Rostov Committee of the Russian Social-Democratic Labour Party. The members of this committee came out openly to speak at meetings and call upon the workers to fight resolutely and staunchly until complete victory over the tsar's government had been achieved. For several days mass meetings of workers were held on the outskirts of the town. ~~These meetings gathered~~ As[4] many as 30,000 Rostov workers *gathered at these meetings*[5]. The Rostov police and the local garrison could do nothing against the strikers.

To suppress the strike the Rostov authorities sent for the Cossacks in the ~~nearby~~ *adjacent*[6] towns. Only when the Cossacks arrived was the strike stopped.

The Rostov strike showed that the working class of Russia had already risen for the open political struggle against tsarism.

The peasant movement. The rising of the workers was followed by peasant risings. In the spring and summer of 1902 the struggles of the peasants in the Ukraine and the Volga districts affected over 300 villages. The peasants wrecked the landlords' manors, seized *their*[7] grain and distributed it among the starving, and seized their lands.

Soldiers were sent against the peasants. The peasants were shot down and flogged to death. Thousands of peasants were arrested and imprisoned. The peasant movement was crushed. The peasants did not yet understand that in order to achieve victory over the landlords it was first necessary to abolish tsarism.

In his newspaper ISKRA, Lenin called upon the peasants to fight against tsarism jointly with the workers. The work in the rural districts carried on by the Social-Democrats who supported ISKRA was hindered by the Socialist-Revolutionary Party, the S.R.'s, as they were called for short, which arose in the beginning of the 20th century. *While pretending to champion the interests of the peasants,* this[8] party really championed the interests of the kulaks and tried to carry out the mistaken program of the Narodniki.

Lenin persistently fought the Socialist-Revolutionaries.

The formation of the ~~R.S.D.L.P.~~ *Russian Social-Democratic Labour Party.*[9] Lenin's ISKRA rallied around itself the scattered Social-Democratic organizations which existed in Russia. Efforts were again made to form a revolutionary proletarian party, and this time they were successful.

In **1903** the Second Congress of the Russian Social-Democratic Labour Party was held secretly abroad. At this congress forty-three delegates from different parts of Russia gathered. A program drawn up by V. I. Lenin was adopted. This program dealt with the main object of the party of the working class, which is, to organize the Socialist Revolution, to establish the dictatorship of the proletariat, to ~~build~~ *achieve the victory of*[10] Socialism. But the program went on to say that in order to achieve this main object the party must *first of all*[11] achieve its immediate object, which is, to overthrow the *tsarist*[12] autocracy in Russia, *to establish a democratic republic,*[13] to introduce an eight-hour day for the workers, to abolish all the remnants of serfdom in the countryside ~~among the peasants~~ *and to give the peasants land*[14].

In order that these great objects might be achieved, Lenin insisted that only staunch fighters in the workers' cause, *tried friends of the working class,*[15] be allowed to become members of the Party. The Party, said Lenin, must be the vanguard of the working class, and the members of the Party must be devoted heart and soul to the revolution. *Lenin insisted that only those who accepted the Party's program and actually took part in the work of one of its organizations should be allowed to become members of the Party.*[16] This demand was opposed by ~~an array of~~ *Martov, Trotsky and several*[17] other delegates.

They proposed that the Party should admit as members all who expressed a desire to join or *promised to*[18] help the Party in some way without pledging themselves to participate in the work of any of the Party's organizations *or to submit to Party discipline*[19]. This proposal meant weakening the Party as the leader of the working class, for it enabled people who *belonged to the bourgeoisie and*[20] were unreliable and hostile to the Party to join.

Lenin's opponents at the congress, who were led by Martov and Trotsky, then proposed that in their fight against tsarism the workers should conclude an alliance not with the toiling peasantry, but with the bourgeoisie. Lenin showed how harmful this proposal of Martov and Trotsky was and argued that the working class must under no circumstances enter into an agreement with the bourgeoisie, for the latter would betray the workers. The workers must not unite with the bourgeoisie, said Lenin, but with the revolutionary peasants, and march together with them in the fight against the tsar and the landlords. Lenin and his supporters urged that immediately after the overthrow of tsarism *and the landlords*[21][,] the fight against the capitalists, the fight for Socialism, must be started.

The congress elected a Central Committee and the Editorial Board of the ISKRA and entrusted them with the guidance of the Party's work. To these bodies Lenin's supporters were elected. They obtained the majority of votes at the congress. The Russian word for "majority" is "bolshinstvo"; that is why Lenin's supporters came to be known as BOLSHEVIKS. His opponents, who were in the minority, came to be known as MENSHEVIKS, from the Russian word "menshinstvo," which means "minority." After the congress the majority of the Social-Democratic organizations in Russia supported the Bolsheviks.

Comrade Stalin did not attend the Second Congress of the Party because he was then in prison. In 1904 he escaped *from Siberia*[22], went to Trans-Caucasia and won the workers there to the side of the Bolsheviks.

The advanced workers had great faith in Lenin and Stalin. At that time their numbers could be counted in thousands.

In the summer of 1903 the first general strikes broke out in the big cities of the Ukraine and the Caucasus under the leadership of the Russian Social-Democratic Labour Party. All the factories were brought to a standstill. The workers gathered in the streets and squares in thousands. Speakers addressed the workers and spoke to them about revolution. The workers marched in processions carrying red flags, the banner of the proletarian struggle for Socialism. The tsarist government sent troops to these cities and suppressed the strikes.

But these strikes did not take place in vain; they hastened and brought nearer the revolution.

46. The Beginning of the Revolution

War against Japan. Tsar Nicholas II tried to crush the revolution by all the means in his power. His courtiers advised him to start war against Japan, for which preparations had been going on for a long time. They thought that the war would put off the revolution. "War rather than revolution!" said these courtiers.

But it was the Japanese who started the war first. In January 1904, the Japanese, without declaring war, attacked Port Arthur, a fort built by Russia on the shores of the Yellow Sea, where Russian warships were stationed. The best of these warships were blown up by the Japanese.

The Japanese transported troops across the sea from their islands to Manchuria. Well armed and trained, the Japanese army began to defeat the backward tsarist army, which was *badly armed and*[23] led by incompetent and corrupt generals.

The Japanese captured Port Arthur and defeated[24] the tsar's army at Mukden. In the narrow straits of Tsushima the Japanese fleet destroyed the last warships of the Russian navy[25] which had been sent from the Baltic Sea.

Defeated in the war, the tsarist government was compelled to sign a humiliating peace treaty with Japan. Japan annexed half of the Island of Sakhalin and Port Arthur, and entrenched herself in Korea.

Bloody Sunday and the first Soviet of Workers' Deputies. The defeats suffered in the war with Japan still further increased the hatred of the people towards the tsar's government. The war did not put off the revolution, it hastened it.

In the beginning of January 1905 the workers in the huge Putilov Works (now known as the *Kirov*[26] Works ~~Named in Honor of S. M. Kirov~~[27]) in Petersburg went on strike.

Soon the strike grew into a general strike of the workers in Petersburg. In the factories stormy meetings of workers were held. The workers sought a way of escape from their conditions of poverty and oppression. They put forward the demand for an eight-hour day, for the right to organize in unions, for freedom of the press and free speech. The workers also demanded that the landlords' land be transferred to the peasants and that a Constituent Assembly be called to change the system of government in Russia.

A few months before the strike the tsar's government had formed a society, known as the ~~workers' association~~ *Workers' Association*[28], for the purpose of combating the labour movement. This, society was led by the priest Gapon. Gapon was a provocateur, or agent of the police. When the strike started, Gapon, at meetings of his society, urged the workers to organize a procession to the tsar's palace and to submit a petition to the tsar. In this petition the workers included all their demands. The Bolsheviks urged the workers not to listen to Gapon. "You will not achieve liberty and land by means of petitions to the tsar," they said. "These must be won by armed force." Gapon, however, succeeded in persuading the workers to march to the palace to submit their petition. ~~The Bolsheviks went alongside the workers.~~ *Gapon's secret intention was to cause bloodshed and so weaken the labour movement.*[29]

On **January 9, 1905**, a cold and frosty morning, crowds of workers, with their wives and children, marched to the Winter Palace. Over 140,000 people marched in the procession.

The tsar's soldiers, lined up outside the Winter Palace, met the unarmed people with volleys of rifle fire. Over a thousand people were killed; many were cut down by the sabres of the Cossacks and trampled upon by their horses. The streets of Petersburg flowed with workers' blood.

The workers learned a severe lesson that day. It became clear to everybody that no faith could be put in the tsar and his servants. In the evening of that day the workers put up barricades in the working class districts. Over the barricades floated red flags. The workers attacked army officers and the police and disarmed them. In their struggle the workers were led by the Bolsheviks.

The news of the tsar's wicked deed caused an outburst of anger throughout the country. The workers stopped work and came out into the streets

[**FIGURE 76:**] January 9, 1905. The Square in front of the Winter Palace, where hundreds of workers were shot. [SH, 149]

singing revolutionary songs and shouting: "Down with the tsarist autocracy." Soon the revolution spread over the whole country.

Mass strikes and workers' demonstrations continued throughout the spring.

In **May 1905** a particularly stubborn strike began in the cotton mill town of Ivanovo-Voznesensk. This strike was led by the Bolsheviks.

The workers gathered in thousands on the banks of the river Talka, on the outskirts of the town. To lead their struggle against the tsar's government and the mill owners the workers elected deputies who formed a Soviet, or Council.

This was *one of*[30] the first Soviets of Workers' Deputies to be formed in Russia. This Soviet met every day, surrounded by thousands of workers. Meetings of workers were addressed by the Bolsheviks, who were at the head of the Soviet. The crowd listened eagerly to their revolutionary speeches. This heroic struggle of the workers lasted for over two months. The workers and their families starved, but they would not surrender. The governor of the gubernia ordered the soldiers to ~~execute~~ *shoot at*[31] the workers. At last the workers were exhausted. At a meeting of 40,000 workers the Soviet recommended that the strike cease. This strike steeled the workers and trained them for their future, more stubborn, struggles.

[**Figure 77:**] Peasants seizing a landlord's estate. [SH, 151]

The peasant movement. In the spring of 1905 unrest broke out among the peasantry. In Central Russia as well as on the Volga the peasants seized the land and cut timber and took the grain from the landlords' granaries and distributed it among the starving. They set fire to the landlords' manors, ~~and~~ demanded the distribution of the land, and *in a number of places seized*[32] the landlords' estates. The frightened landlords fled from their estates to seek the protection of the soldiers and police. The tsarist government sent soldiers and Cossacks against the peasants. The soldiers shot down the peasants and imprisoned and flogged many of them. But the peasants, supported by the workers in the towns, continued their struggle. The peasant movement grew wider and wider every day.

In Georgia the peasants stopped paying their tribute to the landlords. In a number of places they seized the land, pastures and woods, and refused to recognize the tsarist authorities. The government was carried on by the peasants themselves.

In Latvia and Esthonia ~~all~~[33] the agricultural labourers ~~to a man~~[34] rose in revolt in the spring and summer of 1905. They armed themselves and formed revolutionary peasant committees. Led by these organizations they drove the German barons, who were all[35] the landlords in those parts, out of their villages.

In the Ukraine and Byelorussia the peasants also rose against the tsar's government and landlords.[36]

The Third Congress of the R.S.D.L.P. ~~When the revolution in Russia began, Vladimir Ilych Lenin was living abroad, in Switzerland. When he learned of the shooting of the workers on January 9, Vladimir Ilych called upon the workers to rise up against the tsar in articles and letters. Lenin did everything possible to arm the workers with weapons. He send an entire ship to Russia from abroad full of rifles. But the ship ran aground not far from St. Petersburg and had to be scuttled, so that the weapons did not fall into the hands of the tsarist government.[37]~~

On Lenin's insistence the third congress of the Russian Social-Democratic Labour Party was convened in London in April 1905. At that time the Party had a membership of about 8,500. Delegates from twenty Bolshevik Committees gathered at this congress. The Mensheviks refused to take part in the congress and did not appear.

At the congress Lenin said that in order to achieve the victory of the revolution the Party must bring about an alliance between the workers and peasants and strengthen this alliance; with the combined forces of the workers and peasants start an armed insurrection to overthrow the tsar and to establish a revolutionary government of workers and peasants. The peasants must set up their revolutionary committees and seize all the landlords' land without compensation. The workers must lead and assist this struggle of the peasants.

Lenin went on to say that after the tsar and the landlords were overthrown the Bolsheviks would have to lead the workers and the poor peasants in the struggle against the capitalists and the kulaks, in the struggle for the Socialist revolution.

The Third Congress adopted all of Lenin's proposals.

The delegates returned to Russia and began very energetically to put into effect the proposals adopted at the congress.

Lenin was assisted in the work of leading the struggle for the victory of the revolution by Comrade Stalin, who was then working in Trans-Caucasia. Here Comrade Stalin worked to strengthen the Bolshevik Committees, made preparations for the Bolshevik congress, organized secret printing presses, wrote leaflets addressed to the workers, taught and organized the revolutionary workers and peasants and directed the preparations for an armed insurrection. Comrade Stalin worked very hard to unite the workers and toiling peoples of Trans-Caucasia and all the other parts of Russia into one family.

47. Preparations for an Armed Insurrection

The mutiny on the battleship Potemkin. The revolution spread to the army and navy. In June 1905, a mutiny broke out on the battleship Potemkin, then stationed in the Black Sea.

The battleship was at anchor off Odessa, where the workers were on strike. The sailors had heard about the events in Odessa, and were very excited and eager to respond to the call of the workers to join the struggle.

One day, while the sailors were at their mid-day meal, one of the sailors shouted:

"Boys, there's maggots in the soup!"

The ship's officers fed the men with cheap rotten meat and pocketed the difference in the price.

Discontent had been rife among the men for some time. The incident of the maggots hastened the outbreak. The men protested. The commander of the ship appeared and ordered the men to disperse. The men refused to obey. The commander then ordered thirty of the men to be arrested and shot. The men were fuming with anger and a sense of wrong. In response to the call of one of the sailors, Matyushenko, they took to arms and shouting, "Kill the monsters!" they hurled themselves upon the hated officers, killed them and threw them overboard.

The red flag was raised on the Potemkin.

The tsar sent warships to suppress the mutiny on the Potemkin, but the sailors on these vessels refused to fire at the rebel ship. The Potemkin, however, could not hold out without fuel and food. It also lacked sufficiently experienced Bolshevik leaders. ~~Upon learning of the mutiny on the Potemkin, Lenin sent from abroad representatives of the Bolshevik Central Committee. But the Potemkin had already been~~ *The Potemkin was*[38] compelled to make for Rumania and surrender to the authorities there.

In spite of failure, the Potemkin mutiny served to encourage the work-

[**FIGURE 78:**] The mutiny on the battleship Potemkin, June 1905. [SH, 154]

ers. It proved to them that the navy and army were beginning to come over to the side of the revolution.

The October General Strike. By the autumn of 1905 the revolutionary movement had spread over the whole country. ~~In September, bread factories and printing plants in Moscow went on strike. The workers from the bread factories and printing plants beat off the soldiers attacking them with stones sticks of firewood.~~[39] Day after day the ranks of the strikers were reinforced by additional groups of workers from the mills and factories. The workers organized open air meetings and often fought the police and soldiers who were sent to disperse them.

In the beginning of October a strike broke out on the Moscow railways, which soon spread to all the railways in the country. The post and telegraph workers also ceased work.

Teachers, doctors, professors and students ~~were drawn by~~ *followed*[40] the workers ~~into~~[41] the struggle. In Kharkov and Ekaterinovslav (now Dniepropetrovsk) the workers began to put up barricades, ransacked the gunsmiths' shops and opened fire on the soldiers and police. ~~In isolated cases, bombs were thrown at the troops.~~[42]

In many towns trade unions were formed under the leadership of the Bolsheviks. In the big industrial centres Soviets of Workers' Deputies were formed. These Soviets were the beginnings of the new revolutionary power of the workers and peasants. Many of the Soviets of Workers' Deputies began to prepare for an insurrection; they obtained arms by various means and began to drill the workers. In nearly all the large factories in which the Bolsheviks had their party organizations, action groups were formed. The tsarist government issued the order to the troops to "spare no bullets," and to shoot down the strikers mercilessly.

The soldiers shot down workers in a number of towns and broke up their meetings. The workers could not yet rise in armed rebellion. The number of action groups was small, and they lacked arms. However, the tsar also lacked sufficient forces to suppress the revolutionary movement. There was considerable unrest in the army; the soldiers began openly to display their sympathy for the revolution. This was largely[43] due to the work of the Bolsheviks in the army, where they secretly distributed leaflets calling upon the soldiers to join the revolution. *It was also due to the tsar's defeat in the war against Japan.*[44]

Frightened by the growth of the revolution. Tsar Nicholas II, on October 17, issued a manifesto in which he promised to grant the people liberty, and to convene a State Duma, or Parliament, of representatives of the people to administer the affairs of Russia jointly with the tsar. The Manifesto of October 17 was a piece of deliberate deception. The tsarist government merely wanted to gain time to muster its forces and to drown the revolution in blood. Although the manifesto was supposed to have granted liberty, the police continued to break up meetings and to arrest and kill workers and their Bolshevik leaders. In Moscow the tsarist rowdies killed Nicholas Bauman, a fine Bolshevik and leader of the Moscow workers. At his funeral 100,000 Moscow workers, headed by the Moscow Committee of the Bolshevik Party, followed his coffin.

In November 1905 Lenin arrived in Russia from abroad and guided all[45] the work of the Party and the struggles of the toilers.

Meanwhile, Comrade Stalin was also firmly, and in the manner of Lenin, preparing the toilers in Trans-Caucasia for battle against the tsar and his servants. He denounced the Mensheviks who were opposed to the preparations for armed insurrection. Addressing the workers of Tbilisi, Comrade Stalin said: "What do we need to be really victorious? For this we need three things—understand and remember this: first, we need arms; second, we need arms; third, I say again, we need arms."

In December 1905 the question of armed insurrection was discussed at a conference of the Bolsheviks. At this conference Lenin and Stalin met for the first time. Before that they had been acquainted only through the medium of correspondence and messages sent with comrades.

48. The December Armed Insurrection

The armed insurrection of the Moscow workers. On December 7, 1905, a general strike broke out in Moscow which quickly grew into an armed insurrection. At the hour appointed by the Bolsheviks, the factories, mills and railways came to a standstill. The electricity was cut off. The newspapers ceased to appear. The workers began to arm and the ranks of the action groups grew. The police and soldiers broke up the workers' meetings and fired at the houses where the action groups gathered. The workers began to put up barricades in Bronnaya Street, Tverskaya Street (now Gorky Street), at the railway stations, and at the Goujon Works (now the Sickle and Hammer Works). Soon many streets in Moscow were bristling with barricades made of carts, overturned tramcars, barrels, boxes and lamp posts. All these were piled up across the street and fastened together with telegraph wire and the overhead wires of the tramways. The tsar's cavalry and mounted police were unable to break through these barriers. At many of the barricades the workers' action groups, armed with revolvers, fired at the soldiers. Firing went on continuously in the streets of Moscow for several days. Workers' action groups from other places hastened to Moscow's assistance. That brave, ~~fiery~~[46] Bolshevik, M. Frunze, arrived from Ivanovo-Voznesensk with his action group.

The peasants brought grain and potatoes for the workers in Moscow and many of them took their place in the ranks of the fighters at the barricades. The working-class district of Presnya became the centre of the struggle. The action groups were led by ~~a worker—the Bolshevik Litvin-Sedoi~~ *the Bolsheviks*[47]. Under ~~his~~ *their*[48] leadership Presnya held out against the tsar's soldiers for ten days. Presnya was a proletarian fortress in which the insurgent workers were in power. The Presnya workers heroically defended their district. Their wives helped in the struggle. They nursed the wounded and brought food for them. Tremendous courage was displayed by the ~~youth and children~~ *young people*[49]. They acted as scouts, helped to build barricades, lay in ambush, and fought the soldiers.

The workers on the Kazan Railway also put up a stubborn fight against the tsar's soldiers.

[**FIGURE 79:**] Workers fighting at the barricades
in Moscow, December 1905. [SH, 158]

There were not enough troops in Moscow to contend with the insurgents. To reinforce them the tsar sent two regiments to Moscow. Only with the aid of artillery and machine guns did they succeed in defeating the insurgents. *The tsar's forces were commanded by General Dubasov.*[50] On December 18 the workers' action groups were compelled to abandon the barricades and hide their weapons in secret hiding places. Over a thousand persons were killed. For several days fires caused by artillery shells raged in the city. The bodies of dead workers, men, women and children, were lying about the streets. Many of the fighters in the revolution were shot and hanged by the tsar's troops.

This is how the tsar's executioners punished insurgent Moscow.

At the time of the armed insurrection in Moscow Lenin was in Petersburg. The Central Committee of the Bolshevik Party did its utmost to rouse the workers of Petersburg to rebellion, but the Mensheviks, headed by Trotsky, who were in the majority in the Petersburg Soviet, were opposed to supporting the armed insurrection in Moscow. The Mensheviks and Socialist-Revolutionaries disrupted the workers' and peasants'[51] revolution. They supported the bourgeoisie who had conspired with the tsarist government to suppress the revolution. A strike broke out in Petersburg in December, but it did not lead to an armed insurrection.

The peasants' struggle against the landlords. During the revolution, as a result of the influence of the labour movement and the call of the Bolshevik Party, the peasants nearly everywhere in Russia rose against their landlord oppressors[52]. All gubernias in Russia were affected by the peasant movement. During the three years of the revolutionary struggle more than 7,000[53] revolutionary peasant actions were registered. The peasants seized the land of the landlords and the monasteries, cut down their timber, attacked the landlords' manors and set fire to them. In the Saratov gubernia alone the peasants in the autumn and winter of 1905 destroyed about three hundred manors. The peasants drove out the police, the volost elders and village elders and elected their own administration. The more advanced peasants united in peasant unions. In this they were assisted by the Bolsheviks. The tsar and the landlords sent out punitive expeditions and suppressed the peasant revolts.

Armed insurrections of the oppressed peoples in Russia. In Trans-Caucasia, under the leadership of Comrade Stalin, the workers and peasants fought bravely against the tsar's troops. The whole of Georgia was up in arms[54]. Reinforcements of tsarist troops were rushed into Georgia. The

Georgian workers and peasants fought many an unequal[55] battle with these troops.

In December 1905 many towns and villages in Georgia were in flames, having been set on fire by the tsarist troops.

In the Ukraine the first outbreaks of armed insurrection occurred during the general strike in October. The biggest revolts broke out in December 1905 in the Donetz Basin, in Gorlovka and Lugansk (now called Voroshilovgrad). The factory workers and miners fought the tsarist troops for several days. In Lugansk the workers were led by the mechanic Kliment Voroshilov.

In Finland the workers formed an armed Red Guard. The Red Guard disarmed the tsar's police. The gendarmes, the police and the Russian government officials deserted their posts and fled to Russia.

The Finnish people elected their own government. The Finnish bourgeoisie, frightened by the increase in the power of the workers, came to an agreement with the tsar and betrayed the workers. The labour movement was cruelly suppressed. The Red Guard was destroyed; the government was dispersed.

Everywhere the oppressed peoples fought under the leadership of the Russian workers[56] against the hated tsarist government; but, like the Russian bourgeoisie, the bourgeoisie among these peoples fought against the revolution in alliance with the tsarist authorities.

This time the workers and peasants were compelled to retreat. The tsar, the landlords and the bourgeoisie proved to be the stronger. But the blood of the workers and peasants of all these peoples of Russia shed during the revolution cemented the ties of friendship between them and united them in a close and great union for future struggles.

The revolution of 1905 had its repercussions all over the world. It was the greatest struggle the proletariat had waged since the Paris Commune of 1871.

The Russian revolution stimulated a mass strike movement in Western Europe. Owing to the influence of the Russian revolution the toilers in Turkey overthrew their sultan, the toilers in Iran overthrew their shah and the toilers in China overthrew their emperor. China became a republic.

49. The Defeat of the ~~First Russian~~[57] Revolution

The suppression of revolutionary actions[58]. Notwithstanding the bloody reprisals of the tsar's government against the people in revolt the revolution continued. In 1906 there was still a number of workers' strikes and revolutionary actions by peasants, soldiers and sailors. The mutinies of the sailors in Kronstadt and Sveaborg in July and August 1906 were of special portent. Thousands of sailors rose in revolt, killed their officers, and established their own government in a number of fortified places. ~~The fleet did not support the uprising and the sailors of Kronstadt and Sveaborg were defeated.~~ *The sailors were badly organized, however, and the tsarist officers succeeded in suppressing the revolt.*[59] The government arrested over 4,000 sailors.

[**FIGURE 80:**] A group of exiles being led to Siberia. [SH, 162]

The tsar's Minister Stolypin issued a law for the ruthless extermination of the revolutionaries. Under this law, from 1906 to 1909, over two thousand persons were hanged and 25,000 were sentenced to penal servitude, exile and imprisonment. *Tens of thousands of revolutionaries were shot and tortured to death without trial.*[60] Arrested revolutionaries were tormented and tortured in the tsar's dungeons: needles were forced under their finger nails, they were scorched with red-hot irons[61] and starved to death. Stolypin vented his wrath particularly upon the Bolsheviks. Thousands of revolutionaries devoted to the cause of the workers perished on the gallows or in penal servitude.

Many of the Bolshevik Party organizations were ~~driven off~~ wrecked,[62] the Soviets of Workers' Deputies were destroyed and the trade unions and all the peasant organizations were closed down.

The State Duma[63]. *With the same object of suppressing the revolutionary movement*[64] Nicholas II, ~~in order to slow the revolution,~~[65] in 1906, convened the State Duma. According to the electoral law then passed, a handful of landlords and capitalists had the right to elect a larger number of deputies to the Duma than tens of millions of workers and peasants. Women were not given the right to vote. Such was the tsar's Constitution.

But soon the tsar violated even this Constitution. He dissolved the First and Second State Dumas because they were not always obedient to him and his Ministers. The tsar particularly disliked the Second Duma. To this Duma a large number of peasants and workers had been elected, including sixty-five Social-Democratic deputies. In their speeches in the Duma these worker and peasant deputies exposed all the tricks and deception of the tsar's government. The tsar ordered this Duma dissolved.

The tsar's officials drew up a new electoral law. The workers and peasants were still further restricted in their right to vote. All the peoples of Siberia and Central Asia were deprived of representation in the Duma, and the rights of the peoples of the Caucasus and Poland were curtailed.

Thus, when the Third Duma met in the Taurida Palace in Petersburg in the autumn of 1907, nearly all the seats were occupied by landlords, merchants, manufacturers, priests, generals and tsarist dignitaries in gorgeous uniforms.

Only a very few seats were occupied by deputies representing the workers, peasants and oppressed peoples of Russia.

The State Duma made no change in the system prevailing in Russia. The nobility, headed by the tsar, continued to rule and rob Russia.

The Third Duma passed a land law introduced by the tsar's Minister Stolypin. This law left the land in the possession of the landlords. The peasants had to be content with the land they already occupied, but the conditions of their tenure were changed. Before the new law was passed the majority of the peasants owned their land in-common, in village communities, and from time to time they re-divided this land according to the number of working members in each family. The Stolypin law abolished the common ownership of the land. Each peasant could claim private possession of the land he occupied, quit the community and become an independent farmer.[66] The peasants who quit the village community in this way were called KHUTORIANIE, or homestead farmers.[67]

The poor peasants who had no draught animals, implements or money to pay taxes, sold their allotments to the kulaks, that is, the rich peasants. This is exactly what the tsarist government wanted. It wanted to transform the kulaks into small landlords who would stand by the tsarist government.

As a result of the operation of this law over a million poor peasants were deprived of their land and completely pauperized.

The government induced the discontented peasants to migrate to the territories of the peoples inhabiting the border regions of Russia. The people in these regions were forcibly driven from their native soil into the desert and mountains.

Industry after the revolution. In suppressing the revolution the tsarist government was also assisted by foreign capitalists. Before the revolution these foreign capitalists had bought land in Russia containing iron ore, oil and coal, and had built factories. The French and English bankers granted the tsarist government huge loans with which to build railways, to strengthen the army and to pay the salaries of government officials. The revolution threatened to deprive the foreign capitalists of the Capital they had invested in Russia and of the enormous profits they obtained from these investments.

Even before the revolution the capitalists began to unite for the purpose of raising prices and of crushing the workers more quickly. These capitalist organizations were called TRUSTS and SYNDICATES. After the revolution bourgeois[68] trusts and syndicates became ever more numerous.

For a number of years Russian industry had been in a state of stagnation, but a revival set in in 1910. The output of coal, metals and oil, and the production of sugar and textile goods increased. Grain exports also greatly increased.

Russian industry took a ~~big~~[69] step forward at that time, but Russia still

[**FIGURE 81:**] Interior of a steel works. [SH, 165]

remained a backward country compared with Western Europe, and was dependent upon foreign capitalists. *There was no engineering industry in Russia, the capitalists who needed machines were obliged to import them from abroad. Nor was there a chemical industry in Russia; mineral fertilizers were not manufactured, In the manufacture of armaments Russia also lagged behind all other capitalist countries.*[70]

Hence, there were quite enough reasons why the first bourgeois revolution in Russia was defeated. The most important of these reasons was the absence of an alliance between the workers and peasants. Although the peasants felt that it was impossible to fight the landlords successfully without an alliance with the workers, they totally failed to understand that the landlords could not be defeated unless tsarism was overthrown. The peasants still believed in the good intentions of the "little father," the tsar. This is why the peasants would not enter into an alliance with the workers for the purpose of overthrowing tsarism, and why the peasants' sons in soldiers' uniforms helped the tsar to suppress the workers' strikes and insurrections. The peasants had more faith in the Socialist-Revolutionary com-promisers than in the Bolshevik revolutionaries.

There were also shortcomings among the workers. The working class, of course, was the leading force of the revolution, but it was not yet united and solid, for its Party, the Social-Democratic Party, was split up into two groups, Mensheviks and Bolsheviks. The former were compromisers and did not want to carry the revolution out to the end. The latter, the Bolsheviks, were consistent revolutionary Leninists and called upon the workers to overthrow tsarism. Owing to this split, the workers were not always united in their actions and the working class was unable to become the real leader (or hegemon) of the revolution.

The hasty conclusion of peace with Japan also helped the tsar to suppress the revolution. As long as the war continued and the tsar's army suffered defeat, the tsar remained weak and was compelled to yield to the pressure of the workers. After peace was concluded the situation changed and the tsar was able to muster his forces for the purpose of combating the revolution.[71]

50. Revival of the Revolution

Lenin goes abroad. Stalin's underground work in Russia. In spite of the numerous arrests and executions of revolutionaries, the Bolsheviks continued the revolutionary struggle. They printed and distributed leaflets, newspapers and pamphlets. They took advantage of the opportunities presented by the State Duma elections and the meetings of the Duma itself openly to present their revolutionary demands and to express the people's hatred for the existing system.

The whole of the tsar's police force was mobilized for the purpose of catching the elusive Lenin. To escape from the police the Party urged Lenin to go to Finland and then to Switzerland. While abroad, he continued to guide the workers' struggle. ~~As Vladimir Ilych was departing from Russia, he almost perished in the waters of the Baltic Sea. Hiding from persecution, he was to board his ship not in a major Finnish port, but on an island at one of the first ports of call in the Gulf of Finland. To do this, Vladimir Ilych, along with his peasant guides, had to cross the ice of the gulf. Not far from the island, Lenin fell through the thinning ice and was rescued only coincidentally.~~[72]

Comrade Stalin, Lenin's ~~beloved friend,~~[73] associate and comrade-in-arms, remained in Russia. His seething energy inspired the Bolsheviks in their hard and persistent labours. In 1908 Comrade Stalin was again arrested and exiled to Siberia; but neither prison nor exile could break Stalin's iron will, and a year later he escaped from Siberia and returned to Baku. A year after that Comrade Stalin was again arrested and again exiled to Siberia, but once again he escaped. Soon after, however, he was tracked down by the tsar's spies and arrested, and the government exiled him to the sparsely populated region of Narym. But this staunch revolutionary would not yield. In the summer of 1912 he secretly returned to Petersburg.

Lenin abroad, and Stalin working underground, or secretly, in Russia, continued the great struggle for Socialism, ready to give all their blood, drop by drop, for the cause of the working class.

The heroic Bolsheviks helped the working class to live through the hard times that followed the defeat of the revolution and to rise for the revolutionary struggle once again.

The Lena shootings. In the remote Siberian taiga, or forest, on the River Lena, there were gold fields belonging to English capitalists. The conditions of life of the workers employed in these gold fields were hardly to be distinguished from those of convicts. The English capitalists, however, made profits out of these gold fields amounting to 7,000,000 rubles a year.

In the spring of **1912** the workers in the Lena gold fields went on strike.

The English capitalists appealed to the tsar's government for troops, and a unit was sent under the command of an officer of the gendarmes. This officer immediately arrested all the workers' leaders, among whom were a number of exiled Bolsheviks. The workers demanded the release of their leaders. They marched to the offices of the company to present their demand, following a narrow path, three or four abreast. Suddenly a bugle call was heard. At the command of the officer the soldiers lined up along this path. Then the order was given—"Fire!"

Shots rang out, followed by many more. The soldiers were shooting down the workers. In the snow, in pools of blood, 250 dead and 270 wounded workers were lying.

The news of the shooting on the River Lena spread like wildfire throughout Russia. Hundreds of thousands of workers threw down their tools and poured into the streets to protest against this new massacre.

On May 1, 1912, 500,000 workers went on strike. In the rural districts the peasants again took up their axes, scythes and pitchforks and wrecked

[**FIGURE 82:**] The shooting of the workers in the Lena gold fields, April 4, 1912. [SH, 168. Zhdanov wrote into the margins the Russian abbreviation "*D. S. P.*" for unclear reasons. See RGASPI, f. 77, op. 1, d. 854, l. 71ob.]

the landlords' manors. From 1910 to 1914 there were over 13,000 cases of revolutionary peasant disturbances.

The Russian people were rising for another struggle and marching out to meet the new revolution.

The Bolsheviks form an independent Russian Social-Democratic Labour Party. In 1912, in the city of Prague, in Czechoslovakia [SIC], representatives of the Bolshevik Committees in Russia gathered at a conference. This conference decided to expel all the Mensheviks and all waverers from the Party.

Thus, the united, militant, Leninist Party of Bolsheviks was formed. This Party led the working class and the peasantry towards a new revolution for the overthrow of tsarism and the establishment of the rule of the workers and peasants, for an eight-hour day for the workers, and the transfer of all the land to the peasants without compensation.

In Russia the Bolsheviks strengthened their secret Party organizations as well as the trade unions, the workers' clubs and other legal workers' organizations which were under their leadership.

In Petersburg, Bolshevik newspapers, ZVEZDA (THE STAR) and later PRAVDA (TRUTH), were published[74]. The Bolshevik PRAVDA was written in simple language which all the workers could understand. It helped the workers to learn the principles of the Bolshevik Party. The police continuously persecuted the paper, prohibited it from being sold, and arrested and imprisoned its editors. V. I. Lenin wrote articles for PRAVDA and guided[75] it while he was abroad. Comrades Stalin, Molotov and other leading Bolsheviks also worked on the paper.

By this time the Party had trained many staunch and brave revolutionary Bolsheviks. Among them was J. Sverdlov. He began to take part in the revolutionary struggle when he was 17 years of age. He spent many years in prison, had been in exile from which he escaped several times[76], and finally made his way to Petersburg, where he carried on a fearless struggle against tsarism. Another of these fearless Bolsheviks was S. Kirov, who began his revolutionary career as far back as 1905 and did not cease his revolutionary activities for a single moment. Prison and exile alone tore this ardent revolutionary from his work for a time. Others in this noble band were M. Frunze, G. Ordjonikidze, V. Kuibyshev and F. Dzerzhinsky—all brave champions of labour's cause. Among the tireless and self-sacrificing Party workers were M. Kalinin, K. Voroshilov, L. Kaganovich, E. *Stassova*,[77] ~~V. I.~~ ~~Lenin's wife~~[78] N. Krupskaya and many others. This was the Iron Guard of the Party, indefatigable and staunch pupils and comrades- in-arms of Lenin and Stalin.

Lenin left Paris, where he was then living, to go to Austria so as to be nearer to the Russian frontier and more easily direct the work of the Bolsheviks in Russia.

At this time strike after strike broke out in Russia. In Baku, where Comrade Stalin had built up a strong Bolshevik organization, the oil field workers declared a general strike. The workers continued their struggle for about a month, but the employers proved to be the stronger. ~~The strike was suppressed.~~[79]

In the summer of 1914 the workers of Petrograd once again brought the factories to a standstill. They marched through the streets carrying red flags. They were attacked by the soldiers and police, but they built barricades and put up stern resistance. The country was on the verge of revolution.

The ~~wave~~ *revival*[80] of the revolution, however, was checked by the outbreak of the World War. Once again the tsarist government hoped to escape revolution by means of war.

[**FIGURE 83:**] Barricades in Petersburg in July 1914. [SH, 170]

XI

The Second ~~Russian~~ *Bourgeois* Revolution *in Russia*[1]

51. The World *Imperialist*[2] War

Defeat of Russia[3]. In the summer of 1914 ~~an unprecedented war~~ *the World War*[4] broke out. Preparations for this war had been going on for a long time. The big capitalist states were in rivalry with each other. At the beginning of the 20th century there was not a scrap of territory that had not been seized by some state. The capitalists of the various countries tried to seize from each other rich lands with large populations. Germany, particularly, looked with envy upon the lands ~~of~~ *which had been seized by*[5] England, France and Russia. She longed to take ~~them from them~~ *several African colonies from England, and the Ukraine, Poland and the Baltic regions from Russia. Russia longed to capture Constantinople from Turkey. England wanted to gain possession of Mesopotamia and Palestine. France wanted to seize Alsace-Lorraine from Germany.*[6] In preparing for this *robber*[7] war the capitalists separated into two camps. One camp consisted of England and France, and also Russia, which was dependent upon them. This alliance was called the ENTENTE. In the other camp were Germany, Austria-Hungary, Turkey and Bulgaria. The Entente was supported by nearly all the states of Europe. Japan and the United States of America were in alliance with it.

The bourgeoisie of the belligerent countries prepared for this predatory war in secret. The people knew nothing about it. When the war began the bourgeoisie of all belligerent countries deceived the people by saying that they were fighting to save their countries from enemy invasion. The Russian bourgeoisie were assisted in deceiving the people by *the petty-bourgeois, compromising parties,*[8] the Mensheviks and the Socialist-Revolutionaries. The *Social-Democrats who belonged to the*[9] Second International~~, which was organized in 1889,~~[10] also betrayed the cause of the workers and incited the workers and peasants in the different belligerent countries against each other.

[**FIGURE 84:**] A Russian soldier behind barbed wire entanglements cursing the tsarist government. [SH, 173]

The World War lasted four years and cost the lives of over 30,000,000 people. The heaviest losses were suffered by the army of tsarist Russia.

While the Germans were pouring a hail of shot and shell at the Russian army, the tsar's Ministers and generals failed to provide the Russian army with sufficient arms and ammunition.

Tens of thousands of Russian soldiers died every day from the fire of German guns and machine guns, and also from disease. But the tsar's generals, obedient to the orders of Tsar Nicholas II and of the Entente, again and again commanded the soldiers to attack. The generals paid no heed to the losses; to them the soldiers were only cannon fodder. In the very first months of the war the incompetent tsarist generals lost a whole army of 200,000 men on the battlefields of Germany. In Russia, hundreds of thousands of new recruits were conscripted. At first only young men were conscripted, but later older men up to 40 years of age were taken. ~~Workers were torn from their families, from their fathers and their mothers, from their young children.~~[11] Russia conscripted a total of 9,000,000 men for the war; but this huge army did not save Russia from defeat. The defeat was caused by the Russian Ministers and generals themselves. Jointly with the Russian

Tsarina, they betrayed military secrets to the Germans. Bleeding to death, dying from gas attacks, freezing in the trenches, the ~~Russian~~ *tsar's*[12] army, betrayed by its generals, was compelled to retreat.

In 1916 the Germans had captured Poland, Lithuania and part of Latvia. But the end of the war was not in sight. The war greatly disturbed the economic life of Russia. There was a shortage of metals, of coal and oil. Factories were brought to a standstill. The railways could not even handle the transportation of troops. The army and the people were in rags. The people at home and the soldiers at the front starved. The amount of grain that was sown diminished, for there were few people left to work in the fields. Large numbers of horses and cattle were taken from the peasants for the needs of the army. This long drawn out war was a terrible burden upon the shoulders of the workers and peasants.

The Bolsheviks during the war. ~~Lenin and Stalin's~~ *The Bolshevik*[13] Party opposed the World War. Lenin and the Party called upon the workers and peasants to turn their weapons against their oppressors, and exposed the despicable conduct of the Mensheviks *and Socialist-Revolutionaries*[14] and of their masters the capitalists. In the very first days of the war the workers' organizations were suppressed. The Bolshevik newspaper PRAVDA, was suppressed even before the declaration of war. The Bolshevik deputies in the Fourth State Duma were exiled[15] to Siberia for calling upon the workers to oppose the war and to make a revolution.

It was very hard indeed for the Bolsheviks to carry on their work during the war. Lenin was cut off from Russia by frontiers and the fronts. ~~Stalin, Molotov, Sverdlov and many others were once again~~ *The other leaders of the Bolshevik Party were*[16] in exile. Many Bolsheviks were in prison.

But ~~they~~ *the Bolsheviks*[17] carried on their work nevertheless.

~~Lenin, from abroad, and Stalin, from his place of far-flung exile, inspired the Russian workers in their letters and rallied them to the struggle.~~[18]

The revolutionary movement during the war. In Russia mass strikes broke out under the leadership of the Bolsheviks.

In 1915 there were 928 strikes; in January and February of 1917 the number of strikes reached 1,330. The workers ~~demanded~~ *continued their struggle under the slogans*[19]: "Down with the war!" "Down with the *tsarist*[20] autocracy!"

The workers of Petrograd (this is what Petersburg was called from 1914 to r 1924) were in the front ranks of the struggle. In October 1916 they organized a huge political strike against the war and the *tsarist*[21] autocracy. They even succeeded in winning a regiment of soldiers to their side.

The workers were also supported by the peasants. In their villages they rose for the struggle against the war, *the landlords*[22] and the Stolypin land laws.

But the most advanced peasants were in the army. In the army discontent grew, and under the influence of the Bolsheviks whom the Party had sent into the army to carry on revolutionary work, the soldiers began to protest against the war.

At the front the soldiers of the ~~Russian~~ *tsar's*[23] armies began to fraternize with the German and Austrian soldiers. Similar fraternization between the soldiers of the various belligerent countries occurred on other fronts. The soldiers demanded that the butchery be stopped.

During the war the oppressed nationalities ~~of the colonies~~[24] also began to rise for the revolutionary struggle against the tsarist government. Heavy taxation, the requisition of cattle and the violence perpetrated against the toilers gave rise to great discontent. This discontent increased still more when the people were conscripted for labour in the rear of the army.

In 1916 the Kazakhs, Kirghiz, Uzbeks, Tadjiks and Turkmens rose in rebellion. They attacked the towns, fought pitched battles with the tsar's soldiers and police and killed their volost elders, who were the servants of the tsarist authorities.

The Kazakhs formed armed units. The leader of this rebellion was the brave hero of the Kazakh people, Amangeldi Imanov.

The Uzbek rebels tore up the railway lines to prevent the despatch of troops, burned down railway stations and cut the telegraph wires.

In Kirghizia the rebels secured arms by capturing a munition train. In the mountains they erected gunsmith shops and workshops for making gunpowder.

The tsarist authorities sent troops equipped with guns, machine guns and armoured cars against the rebels. They crushed the revolts m blood and in the smoke of burning villages.

But the struggle of the workers, peasants, soldiers and oppressed people against the war and against the tsarist government steadily increased in intensity.

52. The Overthrow of Tsarism in February 1917

Insurrection in Petrograd. Tsar Nicholas II and his Ministers were thrown into consternation by the defeat at the front and the advancing revolution. They rushed hither and thither, not knowing what to do. Even the ~~bourgeoisie~~ *bourgeois party known as the "Cadets"*[25], and its leaders Milyukov ~~and Guchkov~~[26], ceased to support the tsar *because of the defeats at the front*[27]; but this party also feared revolution. The bourgeoisie decided to depose Nicholas II, put his brother Michael on the throne, suppress the incipient revolutionary movement and continue the war.

The tsar's courtiers advised him to stop the war, conclude peace with the Germans separately from the Allies[28] and then take measures to crush the revolution.

The plans of the tsar and the bourgeoisie never materialized. They were forestalled by the ~~revolution~~ *uprising*[29] of the workers and ~~peasants~~ *soldiers*[30] which began in February 1917.

In the beginning of 1917, the workers of Petrograd, starved and exhausted by the war, went on strike. The Bolsheviks led the workers in their struggle. They also succeeded in penetrating the soldiers' barracks and called upon the soldiers to support the workers in the struggle against the tsar. The working men *and working women*[31] marched through the streets shouting:

"Down with war!" "Down with the tsarist government!"

"Bread!" *"Peace!"*[32]

Soon the workers began to realize that the tsarist government could not be vanquished by strikes alone, that armed insurrection was necessary. And they rose in arms.

The tsarist Ministers ordered the workers to be shot down: without mercy. On the roofs and attics in the centre of the city the police placed machine guns and shot at the demonstrators.

The heroic struggle of the *Petrograd*[33] workers drew the soldiers to the side of the revolution.

On **February 27** the soldiers *in Petrograd*[34] refused to shoot at the workers and began to go over to the side of the people.

The rebel workers and soldiers arrested the *tsar's*[35] Ministers and put them in jail. All the imprisoned revolutionaries were released. Crowds of people set fire to the police stations and the courts. The young workers and the working women took part in the insurrection side by side with their brothers and husbands.

Tsar Nicholas II, *who was out of Petrograd at the time,*[36] ordered soldiers from the front to be sent against the insurgent people. But the revolutionary workers and soldiers went out to meet these soldiers from the front, explained to them what they were fighting for and urged them to refuse to carry out the orders of the tsar and the generals. The soldiers obeyed the workers. The revolution triumphed *over tsarism*[37].

When the news of the victory of the revolution in Petrograd reached other towns and the front, the workers and soldiers there also overthrew the tsarist rule.

As was the case in the first revolution of 1905, Soviets were set up everywhere; *but these were Soviets not only of workers' deputies as was the case in 1905, but*[38] Soviets of workers' and soldiers' deputies. ~~Soon, Soviets of peasants' deputies were set up as well.~~[39]

~~Tsarism was abolished one and for all. Nicholas II, the last tsar, was exiled to the Urals where in 1918 he attempted to get into contact with enemies of the workers in order to struggle with Soviet power. For this, he was executed with his family by the Ekaterinburg (now Sverdlovsk) Soviet.~~[40] *This is what marked the difference between the revolution of February 1917 and the revolution of 1905. Actually, the soldiers' deputies' in the Soviets were peasant deputies who, because of the war, were wearing soldiers' uniforms. Consequently, the Soviets of Workers' and Soldiers' Deputies were really Soviets of Workers' and Peasants' deputies. This signified that the alliance between the workers and peasants against tsarism had been established, and the Soviets of Workers' and Soldiers' Deputies were the bodies which represented this alliance.*[41]

Without this alliance the people could not have overthrown the tsar, and the revolution could not have been victorious.[42]

Two powers. The Mensheviks and Socialist-Revolutionaries, however, had the majority in the Soviets. The ~~better organized~~[43] bourgeoisie succeeded in using these *petty-bourgeois*[44] politicians as its tools, and with their aid it took power. The traitors to the revolution, the Mensheviks and Socialist-Revolutionaries enabled the bourgeoisie to set up its *bourgeois*[45] Provisional Government.

But the Soviets continued to exist side by side with ~~it~~ *the Provisional Government*[46]. Thus, two powers were created.

The bourgeoisie and the Mensheviks and Socialist-Revolutionaries in the Soviets wanted to continue the war against Germany until victory had been achieved. The land continued to remain the property of the landlords. The capitalists continued to rob the workers. The oppression of the different nationalities in Russia went on as before.

Lenin, in letters he sent from abroad, and the Bolsheviks in Russia headed by Comrade Stalin[,] who had returned from exile, exposed to the people the real nature of the Provisional Government and the deception perpetrated by the Mensheviks and Socialist-Revolutionaries.

[**Figure 85:**] The arrival in Petersburg of the leader of the proletariat, V. I. Lenin, April 3, 1917. Revolutionary workers and soldiers welcoming Lenin. [SH, 179. Stalin underlined April 3, 1917.

On **April 3, 1917**, after encountering many difficulties, Lenin ~~made it back~~ *returned*[47] to Russia. ~~J. V. Stalin travelled by train with some comrades to meet Lenin. After a long period of separation, the two leaders of the party and working class met on the platform of a train station. Lenin's train~~

~~then took them on to Petrograd.~~[48] The whole of revolutionary Petrograd, the workers, sailors and soldiers, came out to welcome him. Lenin was cheered and cheered without end. He climbed to the top of an armoured car to address the people and amidst the tense silence of the crowd he issued the passionate call: "Long live the World[49] Socialist Revolution!" This was a call for the struggle against the bourgeois Provisional Government and for the establishment of the rule of the working class. It was the call for Socialism.

XII

The Great ~~Proletarian~~ *October Socialist* Revolution *in Russia*[1]

53. The Bolsheviks Prepare for the ~~Proletarian~~ *Socialist*[2] Revolution

The masses follow the Bolsheviks. On Lenin's arrival the Bolshevik Party called a conference in Petrograd. Delegates representing 80,000 members arrived from all parts of Russia. Among those present were Molotov, Voroshilov, Sverdlov, Kuibyshev, Dzerzhinsky, Kossior, ~~Bubnov~~[3] and many others. The work of the conference was guided by Lenin and Stalin. They showed that the working class had only performed its first task; it had overthrown the *tsarist*[4] autocracy in Russia. *It was now necessary, they said, to perform the second task: to bring about the Socialist revolution; and*[5] this meant that the Party still had a hard and stern struggle ahead of it, because the bourgeoisie, which had begun to rule the country, would not yield power without a bitter fight.

They called upon the Party to win the majority in the Soviets of Workers' and Soldiers' Deputies and Soviets of Peasants' Deputies, and rid them of the Mensheviks and Socialist-Revolutionaries.

Lenin and Stalin called upon the Bolsheviks to organize the masses for the fight for the Socialist revolution. In order to achieve the victory of the Socialist revolution ~~in Russia and the whole world~~[6], they said, the working class, in close alliance with the poor peasants, must overthrow the power of the bourgeoisie. It was necessary *to curb the bourgeoisie,*[7] to take the land from the landlords and place it at the disposal of the peasants, to liberate the million-man oppressed nationalities in ~~all of~~[8] Russia and immediately to stop the war.

The conference adopted Lenin's and Stalin's proposals. The Bolsheviks carried out extensive and vigorous work among the masses of the workers, soldiers and sailors. They also worked energetically among the peasants. They explained to the people the decisions adopted by the Party conference and called upon them to fight against the Provisional Government and for the establishment of the power of the Soviets, for the cessation of the war and for the immediate transfer of all the land to the peasants.

[**FIGURE 86:**] The peasants demanding land. A sailor, their fellow villager, is calling for the immediate organized seizure of the landlords' lands. [SH, 182]

In Petrograd, workers' and soldiers' demonstrations began to be held. *Such a demonstration was held in April.* ~~Workers and soldiers marched through the streets of the capital in strict formation, carrying in their hands~~ *The demonstrators carried*[9] placards and banners inscribed with the Bolshevik slogans:

"Down with the war!"

"Down with the capitalist Ministers!"[10]

"All power to the Soviets!"

The Provisional Government, jointly with the Mensheviks and Socialist-Revolutionaries, were compelled to dismiss Guchkov and Milyukov, the capitalist Ministers who were most hated by the people, and appointed several Mensheviks and Socialist-Revolutionaries to the government.

But the government's policy remained unchanged. The war continued the land remained in the possession of the landlords, ~~and~~[11] the oppressed nationalities remained disfranchised *and the workers were threatened with lockouts*[12].

The revolutionary temper of the masses rose still higher. They began more and more to heed the voice of the Bolsheviks. The Bolshevik Party was becoming stronger.

~~The Mensheviks and Socialist-Revolutionaries deceived the masses and slandered the Bolsheviks. They accused the Bolsheviks and Lenin of treachery and called them German spies. They needed to do this in order to continue the war and in order to retain power.~~[13]

In the beginning of June 1917, the First All-Russian Congress of Soviets of Workers' and Soldiers Deputies was held in Petrograd.

At this congress the Menshevik and Socialist-Revolutionaries *still*[14] had the majority. They succeeded in persuading the Congress of Soviets to support the bourgeois government and to agree to an offensive at the front ~~against the Germans~~[15].

The offensive at the front was started immediately. It ended in the defeat of the Russian army. The soldiers refused to go into battle. They did not want to fight for the interests of the bourgeoisie, they demanded that all power be transferred to the Soviets. In vain did the Socialist-Revolutionary Kerensky, the Minister of War, ~~who Lenin referred to as a blabbermouth,~~[16] and the Provisional Government, try to persuade the soldiers to shed their blood for a cause that was not their own. "The bourgeoisie want the war, let them go and fight," answered the soldiers. The Provisional Government ordered those soldiers who refused to go into battle to be shot.

The soldiers became more and more convinced that the Mensheviks and Socialist-Revolutionaries were betraying their interests, and went over to the side of the Bolsheviks. Again demonstrations of workers and soldiers were organized in the principal cities of Russia.

The July demonstration and General Kornilov's mutiny. The summer of 1917 arrived. The Provisional Government still refused to concede a single one of the demands of the workers, soldiers,~~and~~[17] peasants and the oppressed nationalities in Russia.

Meanwhile, the chaos in industry and on the railways had increased. Mills and factories came to a standstill, there were no raw materials and no fuel. *There was a shortage of bread and meat. Famine was approaching.*[18]

The struggle waged by the workers against the capitalists and their government became more intense. Strikes were breaking out continuously. The workers organized armed detachments, called the Red Guard. In the rural districts, peasant revolts broke out.

The soldiers left the front in thousands. The oppressed nationalities, not having been liberated by the Provisional Government, came forward with their just demands.

On **July 3, 1917** the masses of Petrograd workers, soldiers and sailors marched in a demonstration carrying Bolshevik slogans. The bourgeoisie, in agreement with the Mensheviks and Socialist-Revolutionaries, *summoned from the front picked units made up of Junkers, that is, students of military schools, and kulaks and these*[19] shot at the demonstrators and wrecked the workers' organizations.

[**FIGURE 87:**] The shooting at the demonstration
in Petrograd, July 3, 1917. [SH, 184]

The Junkers and army officers raided the editorial offices of PRAVDA. Bolsheviks were arrested and flung into prison. Once again the Bolsheviks had to go underground. The Provisional Government issued an order for the arrest of Lenin. On the Party's insistence Lenin went into hiding. Dressed as a workingman, ~~wearing a wig~~[20] and with a passport made out in the name of Ivanov, a workingman, he went to live in a shack in a field at Sestroretsk, near Petrograd; somewhat later he crossed into Finland. The bourgeois police hounds sought for Lenin in vain. The workers were carefully guarding their beloved leader.

The bourgeoisie gave vent to its fury at home and at the front. Even the most backward workers began to understand what the policy of the Mensheviks and Socialist-Revolutionaries, who were defending the interests of the bourgeoisie, was leading to. Larger and larger numbers of workers began to join the ranks of the Bolsheviks. The membership of the Bolshevik Party rose to 200,000.

At the end of July, the 6th Congress of the Bolshevik Party was held ~~in secret~~[21] in Petrograd.

Lenin was not present at the congress. He was in hiding. The work of the congress was guided by Comrade Stalin. He called upon the Party to prepare for armed insurrection.

The congress mapped out the path to the victory of the *Socialist*[22] revolution and drew up measures for combating the economic chaos in the country.

After the congress the delegates dispersed all over Russia and began to prepare the workers and poor peasants for rebellion against the Provisional Government, for the overthrow of its power and the establishment of the ~~working class's~~[23] power *of the Soviets, the power of the workers and peasants.*[24]

The bourgeoisie *and the landlords*[25] then organized a plot against the revolution. On their instructions, General Kornilov gathered a large force of army officers, Cossacks and backward units of the army and marched them on Petrograd to smash the ~~workers' organizations~~ *Soviets of Workers' and Soldiers' Deputies, to crush the workers and peasants*[26], and to proclaim himself the unrestricted ruler of Russia.

In response to the call of the Bolsheviks, ~~all~~[27] the workers of Petrograd and the Petrograd troops rose to resist Kornilov. Revolutionary agitators-workers and soldiers were sent out to meet Kornilov's forces and they explained to the soldiers the real designs of their general. The soldiers in Kornilov's regiments refused to fight against the revolution. The bourgeois plot failed. *Under pressure of the workers and peasants Kerensky was obliged to arrest Kornilov and put him in prison.*[28] The victory of the workers *and soldiers*[29] over Kornilov still further strengthened the ~~revolution~~ *influence of the Bolshevik Party*[30].

After the Kornilov mutiny the workers and soldiers began to rid the Soviets of the Mensheviks and Socialist-Revolutionaries and to elect Bolsheviks in their place. In the autumn of 1917, the Bolsheviks had the majority in the Petrograd and Moscow Soviets. The Soviets ~~under the leadership of Lenin and Stalin's party~~[31] became genuine centres of the proletarian revolution. They issued arms to the workers, organized a Red Guard and prepared for armed insurrection.

In the beginning of October Lenin secretly arrived in Petrograd to lead the insurrection. He said that now the victory of the workers was ensured and that it was necessary to start the armed: insurrection at once, to overthrow the government of the bourgeoisie, the Mensheviks and the Socialist-Revolutionaries, and to establish the rule of the Soviets.

54. The ~~Proletarian~~ *Socialist*[32] Revolution Is Victorious

The victorious insurrection of October 25 (November 7) 1917. The Bolshevik Party ~~under the leadership of Lenin and Stalin~~[33] prepared for the last decisive battle, for the overthrow of the rule of the bourgeoisie by armed force.

The moment for the insurrection was ~~very~~[34] happily chosen. The World War was still continuing. In Russia, the majority of the workers followed the lead of the Bolsheviks. *The compromising parties, the Mensheviks and Socialist-Revolutionaries, had lost the confidence of the toilers.*[35] Many of the Soviets of Workers' and Soldiers' Deputies were controlled by the Bolsheviks. The workers had strong trade unions and a Red Guard. *The peasants refused to wait until the Constituent Assembly was convened, as the compromising Socialist-Revolutionaries and Mensheviks advised them to do, and followed the lead of the Bolsheviks who demanded the immediate seizure of the landlords' land.*[36] The peasants drove the landlords out of their estates and took possession of their land. The soldiers did not want the war to continue. *They rejected Kerensky's order to continue the war until victory was achieved and demanded peace.*[37] Against ~~the~~ *Kerensky's*[38] Provisional Government rose, *not only the workers and peasants, but also*[39] the peoples of Trans-Caucasia, Ukraine, Byelorussia, Central Asia and Finland. The Bolsheviks made energetic preparations for the insurrection. The plan of the insurrection was carefully worked out.

During the most decisive days of preparation for the insurrection, however, Kamenev and Zinoviev *deliberately*[40], and Trotsky *by his boastful bragging*[41], betrayed the plan and the date of the insurrection to the bourgeoisie. On hearing from these traitors about the impending insurrection the Provisional Government mobilized all the forces which still remained loyal to it ~~for the struggle with the revolution~~ *for the purpose of crushing the insurrection*[42]. But the days of bourgeois rule were numbered. The Central Committee of the Bolshevik Party set up a fighting centre, a special committee, *headed by Stalin,*[43] to guide the insurrection. ~~It consisted of: Stalin, Sverdlov, Dzerzhinsky, Bubnov and Uritsky.~~[44] In accordance with Lenin's instructions, this committee started the insurrection on **October 24** (**November 6**), **1917**. Lenin took his place at the head of the insurrection.

The Red Guards, the revolutionary soldiers and the sailors of Kronstadt

[**FIGURE 88:**] ~~The Fighting Centre that guided the October 1917 Uprising.~~ [Figure 88 appeared in the 1937 Russian edition but was deleted from all subsequent editions after Bubnov's purge. Compare KRATKII KURS ISTORII SSSR, 157 and SH, 188.]

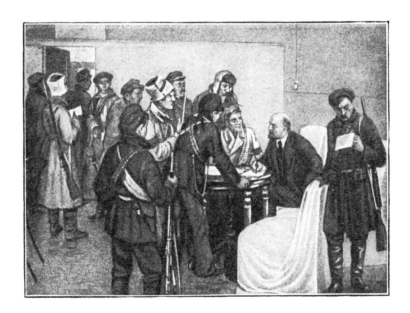

[**FIGURE 89:**] V. I. Lenin directing the insurrection in October 1917. [Figure 89 was shifted to replace Figure 88 in the 1938 English edition. See SH, 188]

[**FIGURE 90:**] *Lenin and Stalin among Red Guards.* [Figure 90 was added to the 1938 English edition to replace Figure 89 when it was shifted to replace Figure 88. See SH, 189]

rose to a man in rcsponse to the call of the *Bolshevik*[45] Party ~~of Lenin and Stalin~~[46]. The courage, revolutionary fervour and discipline of the soldiers of the revolution soon did their work. All the government offices and strategical points in Petrograd were captured by the Red Guards. The ministers of the Provisional Government together. with units of army officers and Junkers made a last stand m the Winter Palace.

On the morning of October 25 (November 7) the revolutionary forces closely surrounded the Palace. The revolutionary cruiser Aurora, with three torpedo boats, steamed up the Neva. The siege of the Palace lasted until evening. Darkness set in. The huge Winter Palace alone was illuminated. During the night the fight became hotter. Machine guns were rattling. Volleys of rifle fire rang out. Firing began between the forces in the Winter Palace and the attacking revolutionaries. The Red Guards began to storm the Palace.

[**FIGURE 91:**] Revolutionary sailors marching to storm
the Winter Palace in October 1917. [SH, 190]

The Bolsheviks who were guiding the attack on the Winter Palace called upon the besieged to surrender, but no reply was received. The signal was given. The guns of the Fortress of Peter and Paul opened fire on the Palace. The guns of the Aurora boomed. The bombardment had effect. The machine guns in the Palace were silenced. The revolutionary forces broke into the Palace. The officers and Junkers continued to fire, but they soon surrendered. Following a narrow corridor in the Palace, the Red Guards entered a round room. Sitting at tables were a few frightened men. This was the last bourgeois government of Russia. *Kerensky was not there; he had managed to escape.*[47]

The Ministers were arrested in the name of the Revolution and taken to the fortress.

The proletarian[48] **revolution is victorious all over the country.** The working class triumphed. On October 25 (*November 7*)[49], the inhabitants of Petrograd read with deep emotion the manifesto written by Lenin. In this manifesto Lenin wrote that the Provisional Government had fallen and that power had passed into the hands of the ~~workers~~ *Soviets of Workers' and Soldiers' Deputies*[50]. The cause for which the people had fought-the cessation of the war, the abolition of the landlords' ownership of the land and the creation of a Soviet Government—was now ensured. It was now possible to establish workers' control over the factories in order to combat the economic chaos.

On that very day the Second All-Russian Congress of Soviets of Workers' and Soldiers' Deputies was held. Lenin ~~announced~~ *introduced*[51] and the congress confirmed the first three decrees of the Great Proletarian Revolution: the decrees on peace, land and state power.

The decree on peace contained the proposal to all ~~peoples~~ *belligerent countries*[52] immediately to start negotiations for stopping the war and for ~~proclaiming all peoples equal~~ *concluding peace on the basis of equality*[53].

The decree on land abolished *the landlord class by abolishing*[54] the private ownership of the land and placed the land at the disposal of all the toilers. The peasants obtained from the Soviet Government *over*[55] 150,000,000 hectares of land.

The decree on state power transferred all power in the country to the Soviets.

Our country became ~~known as the Russian Soviet Federative Socialist Republic (for short, R.S.F.S.R.)~~ *a Soviet Republic*[56].

[**FIGURE 92:**] V. I. LENIN. [SH, 192–193]

The congress elected an All-Russian Central Executive Committee (~~VTsIK~~)[57] and a Council of People's Commissars (~~Sovnarkom~~)[58]. At the head of the Council of People's Commissars was Comrade Lenin. Comrade Stalin was elected People's Commissar of Nationalities.

Soon after the congress, Comrade Sverdlov was elected President of the ~~VTsIK~~ *All-Russian Central Executive Committee*[59]. ~~After his death in 1919, Mikhail Ivanovich Kalinin was elected President of VTsIK.~~[60]

The news of the victory of the proletariat in Petrograd quickly spread over the whole country. In a number of cities the workers had to fight fiercely to capture power.

[**FIGURE 93:**] Jacob Sverdlov (1885–1919). [SH, 192]

In Moscow the army officers and Junkers captured the Kremlin and a number of big buildings. The workers' Red Guards were obliged to dig trenches and conduct a real war against the counter-revolutionaries. Fighting in Moscow lasted a whole week. Only by means of artillery were the workers and soldiers able to compel the army officers and Junkers to surrender.

Telegrams came pouring in from all towns of Russia announcing the transfer of power to the Soviets. With the aid of the ~~Russian proletariat, under the leadership of the party of Lenin and Stalin~~ *Soviet Government*[61], the peoples of Siberia, Central Asia, Byelorussia, the Volga and the Ukraine east of the Dniepr, liberated themselves from the age-long yoke of the bourgeoisie and the landlords.

The victory of the Socialist Soviet Revolution was thus due to the following reasons:

1. The bourgeois government of the Socialist-Revolutionary Kerensky had become utterly discredited in the eyes of the workers and peasants. Kerensky wanted to continue the war until victory was achieved, but the workers, peasants and soldiers demanded that the war be stopped and peace concluded. Kerensky wanted to keep the land for the landlords, but the workers and peasants

[**FIGURE 94:**] Establishing workers' control over the factories. [SH, 195]

demanded the immediate seizure of the landlords' land for the benefit of the peasants. Kerensky wanted to curb the workers, but the workers and peasants demanded that the factory owners be curbed and placed under the control of the workers' organizations.

2. The second reason was that these demands served as the basis for a strong alliance between the workers and peasants in the form of Soviets of Workers' and Soldiers' Deputies against the bourgeois Provisional Government and its henchmen, the Socialist-Revolutionaries and Mensheviks, and in support of the Bolshevik Party.

3. The third reason was that the vast masses of the workers and peasants abandoned the compromising Socialist-Revolutionaries and Mensheviks, rallied around the Bolshevik Party, and recognized it as their leader and guide.

It was for these reasons that the October revolution was victorious.[62]

~~**Lenin and Stalin organize**~~ ***The Bolshevik Party organizes***[63] **the Soviet state.** In the very first days of victory of the Great Proletarian Revolution Lenin and Stalin set to work to organize the Soviet State in the form of a fraternal Socialist union of all the nationalities.

At the hands of the Soviet Government the nationalities of Russia obtained complete liberation, which no other people in the world has enjoyed.

[**FIGURE 95:**] Capture of the Kremlin by the insurgent workers
of Moscow in the October Days, 1917. [SH, 194]

The issue of the decrees on peace and land was followed by a decree on
workers' control. Workers' control was established over the capitalists in
the factories, over the production of goods, and over the warehousing, the
purchase and sale of all goods and raw materials.

The Council of People's Commissars also[64] announced the repudiation
of all debts to foreign countries, amounting to 9–10 billion gold rubles, that
were made by the tsarist and provisional governments[65].

But the enemies of the Soviet Government, the landlords, capitalists,
generals and priests, defeated in the capitals and in the central parts of the
country, fled to the border regions of Russia. The Mensheviks and Socialist-
Revolutionaries were in league with them.

They tried to entrench themselves on the Don, in the Ukraine west of
the Dniepr, in the Caucasus, and in the Orenburg steppe *in Siberia*[66], and
began to organize for war against the Soviet Government. But they had few
forces *of their own*[67]; the workers and peasants did not follow them. The revolts and plots organized by the Mensheviks and Socialist-Revolutionaries
failed. The Red Guard and the All-Russian Extraordinary Commission for
Combating Counter-Revolutionaries[68] (or Vecheka, for short), headed by
at the head of which stood[69] Felix Dzerzhinsky, defeated these treacherous

~~counterrevolutionaries. A dictatorship of the proletariat was established on the territory of the former tsarist empire~~ *proved sufficient to crush the plots of the Socialist-Revolutionaries, Mensheviks and their allies, the Cadets.*

[**FIGURE 96:**] Felix Dzerzhinsky (1877–1926). [SH, 196]

Later on it became much more difficult for the Soviet Government to combat counter-revolutionary plots, for the Cadet and Socialist-Revolutionary and Menshevik plotters began to obtain the direct military assistance of foreign capitalist governments. This was a military intervention of the capitalist governments against the Soviet Government and the Soviet system. The fight of the soviets against intervention lasted three years.[70]

XIII

Military Intervention. The Civil War[1]

55. The Soviets Fight for Peace. The Germans Seize the Ukraine

Peace with Germany. *Although the war continued,*[2] Russia's *old*[3] army *was no longer capable of fighting, and the soldiers*[4] dispersed ~~for~~ *to their* homes[5]. They crowded the trains and even swarmed on the roofs and buffers of the cars. Exhausted by the war, the country *and the army*[6] needed ~~at least a short~~ *a*[7] respite. In accordance with the decree adopted at the Second Congress of Soviets, the Council of People's Commissars addressed notes to all the belligerent countries proposing a general peace. The governments of England and France, which had been joined by that of the ~~USA~~ *United States of America*[8], did not reply to this proposal. Germany and her allies, however, more exhausted by the war than England and France, started peace negotiations with the Soviet Government~~, wishing to retain part of Soviet Russia's territory~~. *Germany wanted to retain part of the territory she had taken from Soviet Russia.*[9] The haughty German ~~generals and officers~~ *militarists*[10] were obliged to negotiate with the delegates of the workers and peasants of the Land of Soviets. The Germans submitted to the Soviet delegation exorbitant terms of peace.

As the old Russian army had disintegrated and there had been no time to create a new, regular Red Army, the Soviets were unable to continue the war.[11] For this reason, Lenin ~~and Stalin~~[12] instructed Trotsky, who was on the Peace Delegation, to ~~accept those terms~~ *sign the peace treaty*[13] with the Germans~~, as there was no other option~~[14]. But Trotsky ~~refused to sign the treaty with the Germans,~~ *obviously playing into the hands of the Germans and provoking them to start a fresh offensive against the unarmed Land of Soviets, broke off the peace negotiations.*[15] ~~Trotsky's violation of Lenin and Stalin's directive cost the Land of the Soviets dearly.~~[16] The Germans *took advantage of this*[17], started a new offensive and occupied Soviet territory. *The German troops were approaching Petrograd.*[18] On Lenin's insistence, a peace treaty was hastily concluded with the Germans *in the town of Brest. This was known as the Brest Peace.*[19] In addition to the loss of the Soviet territory that was captured by the Germans, the Soviet Government had to agree to other humiliating concessions to the German militarists. *These losses were due to the treachery of Trotsky and his helper Bukharin, who did all they possibly could to prevent the conclusion of peace.*[20] Lenin and Stalin were in favour of concluding peace on these unfavourable terms because they were convinced that the revolution would be victorious in Germany, that the Soviet Government in Russia would gain in strength, *succeed in creating a Red Army,*[21] and be able to regain what had been lost.

[**FIGURE 97:**] The Red Army in the first days of its organization. [SH, 198]

The Soviets had now gained a respite and set to work to build up the country's industry and create a strong Red Army. The Red Army was created in **1918.**

The Germans seize Soviet territory. ~~But the Germans quickly violated the agreement that they had signed and began a new offensive into Soviet territory.~~ *Although the Brest Peace that was concluded between the Soviet Government and the Germans applied to the whole territory of the Soviet State,*

including the Ukraine, several Ukrainian delegates, who had been bribed by the
Germans, refused to submit to the Soviet Government and concluded a separate
peace treaty with the Germans. In this treacherous treaty the Ukraine was de-
clared to be, not a ~~Soviet~~ Republic, but a bourgeois republic, and the Germans
pledged themselves, in the event of the Soviets resisting this, to render military
assistance to the Ukrainian bourgeois government, which was then called the
Ukrainian Rada. The rapacious German militarists took advantage of this treaty
to send their troops into the Ukraine.[22] *First they*[23] seized ~~Byelorussia,~~[24] the
Ukraine, *and then*[25] the Don region and Georgia. On their line of march the
Germans dispersed the Soviets and hanged the Bolsheviks and workers and
peasants who supported the Soviet Government.

The forces of the Red Army were then still weak, but they did not yield
Soviet territory to the Germans without a fight. At the head of the workers'
detachments which consisted of Donetz miners, poor peasants and revolutionary sailors, stood the beloved leader of the workers, the Lugansk mechanic, that brave and devoted Bolshevik one of the best pupils of Lenin
and Stalin, Kliment Voroshilov.

For six weeks Voroshilov's detachments held the Germans and White
Cossack units advancing on the Don at bay. In order to cut off Voroshilov's
detachments the Cossacks blew up a bridge across the Don. Under a hail of
shot and shell fired by the White Cossacks, the Red fighters built a tempo-
rary ~~sand and stone~~[26] bridge across the river. Part of the men worked on the
bridge while the others fought against the Cossacks. Comrade Voroshilov
cheered his men on, strengthening their determination by his own bravery, and succeeded in crossing the Don with his detachments and reaching
Tsaritsin *(now Stalingrad)*[27].

The German and Austrian troops quartered themselves all over the
Ukraine. The Germans set up as hetman of the Ukraine the big Ukrainian
landlord and tsarist general Skoropadsky. They restored the land to the
landlords and the factories to the capitalists.

The workers' organizations in the Ukraine were suppressed. Firing
squads, gallows and torments from the landlords, capitalists and German
militarists were now the lot of the working class and the peasants of the
Ukraine. The Germans confiscated the peasants' cattle and ransacked their
grain bins. Every day trainloads of Ukrainian grain, sugar, lard, meat, coal
and iron ore were dispatched to Germany and Austria. The plunder and

[**FIGURE 98:**] Nicholas Shchors,
Hero of the Civil War in
the Ukraine. [SH, 199]

violence of the German conquerors roused all[28] the Ukrainian workers and peasants to revolt. In this struggle against the Germans, Nicholas Shchors, son of a railwayman, acquired particular fame for his bravery. He fought as heroically against the enemies of the Ukrainian workers and peasants as that hero of the Russian people, Vasili Chapayev. The Germans did not keep the Ukraine for long. *The German soldiers found it very hard to contend against the rebel Ukrainian workers and peasants, and at*[29] the end of 1918, when revolution broke out in Germany, *the German soldiers fled back to Germany. The*[30] Ukraine once again became a Soviet country.

The predatory *Brest* Peace[31] was annulled by the Soviet Government.

56. The Soviet Republic in a Ring of Intervention and Counter-Revolution

The mills and factories become the property of the state. The fight for bread. Impoverished by the World War, Russia started the Socialist revolution at a time when the whole economic life of the country was in a state of extreme decline. The factory owners refused to submit to workers' control.

They spoiled their machines, refrained from repairing them when required, did not trouble to provide their factories with raw materials and fuel and often closed down their factories altogether. Their object was to strangle the revolution. The Soviet Government resolutely combated these enemies.

The banks, railways, and, *later on,* ~~many~~ *the*[32] factories were taken away from the capitalists. In 1918 ~~all~~[33] the factories which formerly had belonged to the capitalists became the property of the Soviet State, and workers and Soviet engineers were appointed as managers. Owing to the shortage of fuel and raw materials, however, many of these mills and factories could not be started immediately.

~~A famine grew~~ *There was a shortage of bread*[34] in the country. The kulaks, brutal enemies of the revolution, hid their grain in pits, allowed it to rot, or else they sold it to profiteers at tremendously high prices; they did all they could to prevent it from being used for the ~~workers~~ *Soviet*[35] Government and the Red Army. The working-class centres in Russia were cut off from the principal grain bearing districts by Russian counter-revolutionaries and foreign interventionists who were fighting the Soviet Government. Famine threatened to strangle the revolution.

In response to Lenin's appeal the workers formed what were known as Food Detachments to go into the villages to fight the kulaks and collect the surplus grain. On Lenin's proposal Committees of Poor Peasants were

[**FIGURE 99:**] A meeting of a Committee of the Rural Poor in 1918. [SH, 202]

formed in the villages. These committees helped the workers' Food Detachments to confiscate the grain from the kulaks and distributed among the poor peasants the horses and cattle taken from the kulaks.

The Party and the Committees of Poor Peasants won over the middle peasants as allies and friends of the working class and poor peasants. Seeing that the Soviet Government which had given them land was protecting them from the landlords and defeating the enemies of the country, the middle peasants began to fight for the Soviets side by side with the working class and poor peasants.

~~The Entente starts an invasion (an intervention)~~ *England, France and Japan start a military intervention*[36] **in the Land of Soviets.** The foreign bourgeoisie were afraid that sparks from the revolutionary conflagration in Russia would set the revolution ablaze all over the world. Nor could the foreign capitalists become reconciled to the idea that they could no longer rob the workers and peasants of Russia as they had done before the revolution. In alliance with the Russian landlords and bourgeoisie, the ~~foreign~~ bourgeoisie *governments of England, France and Japan*[37] started war against the Soviet Government. In the spring of 1918, the Czechoslovak prisoners of war captured *by the Russians*[38] during the World War, started a counter-revolutionary rebellion against Soviet Russia *with the aid of France*[39]. The Socialist-Revolutionaries and Mensheviks in conjunction with the Czechoslovaks ~~grabbed up~~ *seized*[40] part of the Volga Region, the Urals and Siberia. In the summer of 1918 the British government landed troops in Archangel, on the White Sea coast, and helped the Whiteguards there to overthrow the Soviets. The Japanese landed troops in Vladivostok.

The bourgeois governments which started war against the Soviet Government were then collectively called the Entente, which means an alliance, or the Allies.[41]

The Entente raised rebellions in different cities in Soviet Russia with the aid of the *Cadets*,[42] Mensheviks and Socialist-Revolutionaries. The bourgeoisie hired bandits to kill the leaders of the Revolution. In this way *the Bolshevik*[43] Uritsky and the favourite orator of the Petrograd workers, *the Bolshevik*[44] Volodarsky, were killed. In the autumn of 1918 the Socialist-Revolutionaries made an attempt to kill Lenin as he was leaving a meeting at a large factory in Moscow. ~~The bullets that were shot from the murderer's revolver were coated in poison.~~[45] Bleeding from his wound, Lenin was taken home and for many days he fought against death. All the toilers of the country were torn with anxiety about Lenin and breathed with relief and rejoiced when at last he recovered and returned to his work of administering the ~~workers'~~[46] State.

By this time the Entente ~~bourgeoisie~~ *governments*[47] had ~~grabbed up~~ *captured*[48] the White Sea coast, the Urals and Siberia. The White Cossacks tried to capture Tsaritsin, a large town on the Volga, and to cut off the grain supplies from Central Russia. The Central Committee of the Bolshevik Party sent Comrade Stalin to direct the defence of Tsaritsin. Here Stalin met Voroshilov, who, with his Red detachments, had arrived from the Donetz Basin. Knowing no rest, Stalin worked day and night strengthening the Tsaritsin front. He tracked down and exterminated the traitors who had managed to steal into *the rear of*[49] the Red Army, took measures to arm and equip the Soviet troops, and sent grain by the River Volga to the workers of Moscow, Petrograd and other cities. The Cossack Whites made repeated attempts to capture Tsaritsin, but in vain. Stalin and Voroshilov struck blow after blow at them and held this important city on the Volga.

While Tsaritsin was staunchly holding out against the Whites, Comrade Kirov was leading the Red Army against them in Astrakhan. Here, too, the efforts of the Whiteguards to capture the town failed.

~~**Revolution and**~~[50] **Civil war in Trans-Caucasia and Central Asia.** Germany helped the Georgian Mensheviks, the ~~traitors~~ *enemies*[51] of the *Georgian*[52] people, to entrench themselves in Georgia. The Mensheviks got into power by shedding rivers of blood. They shot large numbers of workers and peasants who were fighting for the rule of the Soviets.

The Armenian workers and peasants also failed to liberate themselves from the yoke of the bourgeoisie immediately. In Armenia, ~~the horde of the Turkish Sultan strangled the revolution with the Armenian bourgeoisie~~ *the Entente assisted the enemies of the Armenian people, the Dashnaks.*[53]

~~The Turkish Sultan~~ *Turkey*[54] wanted to seize Baku ~~(Azerbaidjan)~~ *in Azerbaidjan*[55], the important centre of the oil industry. In 1918 the rule of the Soviets was established in Baku. At the head of the Baku Soviet stood the Bolshevik Stepan Shaumian and other old Bolsheviks, friends and pupils of Comrade Stalin. In the summer of 1918 *the Mussavatists, enemies of the Azerbaidjan people cooperating with*[56] the Mensheviks and Socialist-Revolutionaries, appealed to the British government to send troops to Baku,

[**FIGURE 100:**] The shooting of the 26 Bolshevik
Commissars of Baku in 1918. [SH, 205]

ostensibly for the purpose of protecting the city from the Turks. After occupying the city the English had Comrades Shaumian, *Azibekov, Djapandze*[57] and other Baku Commissars, *twenty-six in all*[58], arrested on their way from Baku and taken into the desert in Turkmenia, where ~~the 26~~ *they* were shot.

At the same time the rapacious English capitalists sent their troops into Central Asia. In Turkmenia the English abolished the rule of the Soviets and in its place set up the rule of their obedient tools, the Whiteguard Socialist-Revolutionaries and Mensheviks.

In Khiva and Bokhara the English helped *the enemies of the Uzbek people*[59], the Khan of Khiva and the Emir of Bokhara, to retain their power.

57. Revolution in Western Europe

The November Revolution in Germany. The Great Proletarian Revolution in Russia divided the world into two camps. In Russia, comprising one-sixth of the globe, the rule of the proletariat, the builder of Socialism, was established. In the other five-sixths of the globe the bourgeoisie still reigned.

Soviet Russia shone out like a beacon lighting the path to the victory of Socialism for the workers in capitalist countries. The first of the West European workers to rise were the proletarians of Germany. Germany's defeat in the World War hastened the outburst of the anger of the masses. In **November 1918**, rebellion broke out in the cities, in the industrial centres, in the army and in the navy. Soon the rebellion spread to Austria.

The workers threw the emperors of Germany and Austria-Hungary from their thrones. With their generals and courtiers they fled to other countries to escape the anger of the people. Germany and Austria were proclaimed republics.

In Germany Soviets began to be set up, but the traitors to the revolution, the German Mensheviks who were known as Social-Democrats, secured the majority in them.

The bourgeoisie and their loyal servants, the Social-Democrats, formed armed units to fight the workers. These units shot down the workers who were fighting to transfer all power to the Soviets. The workers' rebellion which started in Berlin, the capital of Germany, in the beginning of 1919 was crushed by these Whiteguards. Large numbers of workers perished in the revolutionary battles, and thousands of the best fighters for the revolution were flung into jail.

~~At the same time,~~ The[60] leaders of the *German*[61] workers, Karl Liebknecht and Rosa Luxemburg, were arrested and killed. ~~The murderers wrapped Rosa's body in a blanket, weighted it down with heavy rocks, and threw it in a canal.~~[62]

~~The entirety of the world proletariat mourned the deaths of Karl and Rosa and hurled curses down on the butchers of the working class.~~[63]

The proletarian revolution was crushed. The bourgeoisie and their allies, the Social-Democrats, came into power. A few years later the bourgeoisie ~~expelled~~ *threw*[64] the Social-Democrats out of the government.

The Soviet Republics in Bavaria and Hungary. Only in one part of Germany were the workers in **1919** able to vanquish the bourgeoisie, establish their rule, and proclaim a Soviet Republic. That was in Bavaria.

The German bourgeoisie mobilized gangs of Whiteguards, spies and traitors to the revolution to fight the workers' government in Bavaria. For two weeks the Bavarian workers heroically kept their enemies at bay, but their forces were too weak. The workers were defeated.

Immediately afterwards a proletarian revolution began in Hungary, a country situated close to Germany. In **March 1919** Soviet rule was victorious in Hungary. A Soviet Republic was proclaimed and a workers' government was set up. A Hungarian Red Army was formed. The factories, mines banks and railways were proclaimed the property of the workers' state. The workers' families were removed from their dark and damp cellar dwellings to the well-lit and spacious houses of the rich. ~~The leaders of the world pro-letariat,~~ Comrades[65] Lenin and Stalin, and all the people of Soviet Russia, warmly greeted the Hungarian Soviet Republic. But soon troops of the ~~En-tente~~ *adjacent bourgeois countries*[66] were sent against little Soviet Hungary. Attacked from all sides, Soviet Hungary was crushed.

The Communist International. The proletarian revolution in West-ern Europe suffered defeat because there were no revolutionary Bolshevik parties there. The workers followed the treacherous leaders of the Second International. Lenin had fought these traitors even before the World War broke out. During the World War Lenin carried on a campaign for the cre-ation of a new, Third International, *the Communist International*[67].

During the revolutions in the west, in the course of workers' strikes and peasant movements, which increased after the World War, Communist Parties arose in a number of European countries. Their gaze was turned towards Red Moscow, towards the Bolsheviks and their leader Comrade Lenin.

On **March 2, 1919,** delegates from various countries: from Germany, England, France, Poland, Switzerland, Iran, Norway, the United States of America, China, Korea and other countries, at the risk of their lives and escaping from spies, made their way to Moscow to attend the first congress of representatives of the Communist Parties all over the world.

But these parties were still young; they lacked experience and were small in numbers. In Moscow, ~~under the leadership of Lenin and Stalin,~~[68] they, with the Bolsheviks of Soviet Russia, founded the Communist Inter-national, known for short as the Comintern, which is the ~~headquarters of the world revolution~~ *leader of the working class throughout the world*[69].

The congress elected the Executive Committee of the Comintern, and Soviet Moscow was chosen as its headquarters.

The foundation of the Comintern was a great victory for the cause of Lenin and Stalin, for the cause of Communism. Notwithstanding the first defeats of the proletarian revolutions in Western Europe, ~~and notwith-standing the barbarism of the fascists,~~[70] the Communist parties all over the world *grew and*[71] are still growing, ~~and~~[72] preparing the working class for the victory of the proletarian revolution.

58. The ~~First and Second Campaigns of the Entente~~ *Defeat of Kolchak, Denikin and Yudenich*[73]

~~The first campaign~~ *Kolchak, the tool*[74] **of the Entente.** The bourgeoisie of the Entente countries resolved to destroy the Soviets in Russia. They sent their troops to North Russia, Siberia, Central Asia, the Caucasus and the Ukraine. The Entente also organized the armies and campaigns of the counterrevolutionary Russian generals against Moscow.

In Siberia, in 1918, the Entente proclaimed the tsarist admiral Kolchak supreme ruler of Russia. They provided him with guns, shells, rifles and equipment for his soldiers.

Kolchak formed a White army. He ruthlessly shot the workers and flogged and killed the peasants. All over Siberia he restored the tsarist methods.

The tsarist officers, landlords, capitalists and priests hurried to Kolchak's standard from all parts of Russia, for they regarded him as the best protector of their interests.

Soon Kolchak started his attack upon Soviet Russia. He succeeded in capturing the town of Perm.

The Bolshevik Party mobilized its best forces and sent them to the front to defeat Kolchak. ~~Lenin dispatched Comrade Stalin and Dzerzhinsky against Kolchak.~~[75] ~~They~~ *The Bolshevik forces*[76] strengthened their line in the Urals ~~in a short period of time~~[77] and checked the advance of the White armies.

In the spring of 1919, Kolchak, on the orders of the Entente, resumed his attack on Soviet Russia. Serious danger threatened Soviet rule from the east. General Denikin was marching to Kolchak's assistance from the south, and, in the west, General Yudenich was marching against Petrograd. The Soviet people were now threatened by enemies on all sides. These enemies were equipped by the foreign capitalists.

But the principal enemy at that time was Kolchak. It was against him that the main forces of the Red Army were hurled. The soldiers of the Red

Army fought heroically against Kolchak's army. Wherever the fighting was hottest the Bolshevik Red Commanders and Political Commissars rushed forward in the front lines to attack the Kolchak troops, encouraging the Red Army men by their boldness courage and fearlessness.

The Red Army that was fighting against Kolchak was commanded by M. Frunze. Under his leadership the Red Army defeated Kolchak on the Volga and in the Urals in 1919. It was in Frunze's army that the popular hero Vasili Chapayev arose. Chapayev's division became the terror of the Whites. Kolchak repeatedly sent against Chapayev large forces, far superior in numbers to Chapayev's division, but Chapayev always emerged victorious. One day, however, Chapayev with a detachment of his troops were surrounded by a White army and they perished in the fight.

[**FIGURE 101:**] Vasili Chapayev, Hero of the Civil War. [SH, 209]

Notwithstanding various setbacks, however, the Red Army, in the autumn of **1919**, utterly routed Kolchak and drove the remnants of his army' across the Urals into Siberia.

At that time the workers and peasants in Siberia rose in rebellion against Kolchak and everywhere formed irregular troops known as Partisans.

In December 1919, the workers of Irkutsk rose in rebellion and captured Kolchak and his Ministers t̶h̶e̶m̶s̶e̶l̶v̶e̶s̶[78]. The Revolutionary Committee sentenced Kolchak to be shot.

The Red Army was victorious in Siberia.

The foreign interventionists and would-be annexationists were compelled to flee from Western and Eastern Siberia. The Red Army, assisted by the Siberian Partisan units which consisted of Russian workers and peasants, Buryat-Mongols, Yakuts, Evenks, Oirots and other nationalities inhabiting Siberia, drove them from our country.

[**FIGURE 102:**] Siberian Partisans with cannon of their
own make attacking Kolchak's forces. [SH, 210]

~~The second campaign~~ *Denikin and Yudenich, the henchmen*[79] **of the
Entente.** The defeat of Kolchak did not put a stop to the Entente's war
against the Soviet Republic. The foreign governments organized another,
~~second~~[80] campaign against the Land of Soviets. In the south, General Denikin achieved some success and captured a number of districts in the Don
Region and the Ukraine. The Entente gave him military assistance as it did
in the case of Kolchak. Denikin mustered a large White army consisting
of the conscripted local population and Cossack Whites commanded by
counter-revolutionary officers, and started his march on Moscow.

The Soviet Government, ~~under the leadership of the communist party,~~[81]
mustered all its forces against Denikin. Lenin addressed a letter to all the
Party organizations in which he issued the call: "All to the struggle against
Denikin." The Bolshevik Party sent its best members to the southern front.
Many thousands of workers and peasants joined the ranks of the Party and
went to the front. Many Young Communist League organizations went to
the front to a man. *In many cases n*otices[82] were put up on the office doors
of these organizations, saying: "Office closed; everybody has gone off to the
front." In the autumn of 1919 the Red Army had in its ranks two and a half
million workers and peasants.

The Central Committee of the Party commissioned Comrade Stalin to organize the defeat of Denikin. Stalin quickly grasped the seriousness of~the situation at the front ~~and together with the commander of the front Comrade A. Egorov~~[83] drew up a plan of campaign against the *Denikin*[84] Whiteguards.

At this time Denikin had seized all of the Ukraine and was approaching the very heart of the revolution, Moscow. This was the most dangerous period of the revolution. In every district he captured Denikin restored the rule of the landlords and capitalists. He restored the land to the landlords and the factories to the capitalists, imposed heavy taxes upon the people and shot the Communists and workers and peasants who fought on the side of the Soviet Government. Denikin's officers set fire to villages and organized pogroms, or massacres, of Jews.

The task of the Red Army was to smash the advancing Whiteguards. In **October 1919**, ~~on Stalin's orders,~~[85] the cavalry corps led by S. Budyonny struck at Denikin's forces. Like a hurricane Budyonny's invincible horsemen swept down on Voronezh and ~~destroyed~~ *inflicted a crushing defeat upon*[86] the White cavalry.

The Red Cavalry was followed up by the shock troops of the Red Army marching from the Orel district. *Here Comrade Ordjonikidze was in charge.*[87]

[**FIGURE 103:**] ~~J. Stalin in Budyonny's cavalry corps.~~ [Cut by Stalin, who wrote in the margins: "*In the place of this illustration add a portrait of Com[rade] A. Egorov.*" RGASPI, f. 558, op. 11, d. 1584, l. 1010b. Also Zhdanov: f. 77, op. 1, d. 854, l. 900b.]

[**FIGURE 104:**] ~~Alexander Egorov.~~ [Figure 104 was added at Stalin's request to the 1937 Russian edition but deleted from all subsequent editions after his purge in 1938. Compare KRATKII KURS ISTORII SSSR, 178 and SH, 212]

[**FIGURE 105:**] *Sergei Lazo—hero of the Civil War in the Far East. In 1920 Comrade Lazo was burned to death in the furnace of a locomotive by the Japanese interventionists* [Figure 105 replaced Figure 104 in the 1938 English edition. SH, 212]

Denikin's White army wavered under the crushing blow of the Red forces and hurriedly fled to the south.

Amidst winter's icy blasts, crossing frozen fields, the Red regiments under the command of A. Egorov[88] and Budyonny's cavalry continued, almost without stopping, to pursue the Whites further and further to the very shores of the Black Sea. Denikin's forces fled in panic, and in their rear Partisan rebellions broke out. This movement was particularly widespread in the North Caucasus. Under the leadership of *Comrade*[89] Kirov and Kalmykov *other Bolsheviks*[90] the workers and peasants of the mountain peoples made repeated raids upon Denikin's forces. The Partisans captured towns from the Whites and exterminated the landlords and army officers. The bigger Partisan units fought pitched battles with the White troops.

In order to help Denikin the Entente ordered General Yudenich once again[91] to march his army against Petrograd. In October 1919 Yudenich almost reached the gates of Petrograd.

The workers of Petrograd rose like a wall of steel in defence of the first city of the revolution. Day and night the workers, their wives and children dug trenches and put up barbed wire entanglements, and Petrograd was transformed into an impregnable fortress. Tens of thousands of workers and Young Communists poured into the ranks of the defenders of Petrograd. They marched out to the attack and at the end of 1919 struck Yudenich a crushing blow. The remnants of Yudenich's army were pursued right up to the frontiers of Esthonia.

Once again the[92] Entente's second[93] campaign against Soviet Russia ended in the utter defeat of the White generals. Denikin and Yudenich fled abroad. The Entente hastily withdrew its troops from the Land of Soviets. The Red Army drove them out of Archangel and Murmansk. The peoples of the Ukraine and North Caucasus threw off the yoke of the landlords and capitalists, of the tsarist generals and foreign usurpers. The Red Army helped them to become equal citizens of the Land of the Soviets.

In the Crimea, however, *General Wrangel was still in occupation at the head of*[94] the remnants of Denikin's forces still remained[95]. And in the west, Poland, carrying out the orders of the Entente, was mustering forces for another attack on Soviet Russia.

[**FIGURE 106:**] ~~Semen Budyonny.~~ [Figure 106 was replaced by Figure 107 to match Figure 104 in the 1937 Russian edition. Compare RGASPI, f. 558, op. 11, d. 1584, l. 102 and KRATKII KURS ISTORII SSSR, 179]

[**FIGURE 107:**] *Semen Budyonny.* [Figure 107 replaced Figure 106 to match Figure 104 in the 1937 Russian edition. Compare RGASPI, f. 558, op. 11, d. 1584, l. 102 and KRATKII KURS ISTORII SSSR, 179; also SH, 213]

59. ~~The End of the Civil War.~~ *War against the Polish Pans. The Rout of Wrangel*[96]

The war with White Poland. The year 1920 arrived. The Entente continued to wage war against the Soviet Republic. This time it instigated Poland against the Soviets.

At the end of 1918 Poland was restored as an independent state. The Great Proletarian Revolution granted the Polish people the right to secede from Russia. The Polish pans who were in power in Poland did not appreciate this. In 1919 they captured Minsk, the capital of Byelorussia, and a ~~big piece of land on the right bank~~ *part*[97] of the Ukraine.

The Council of People's Commissars repeatedly called upon the Poles to put a stop to their encroachment upon Soviet territory and violence against the peaceful Byelorussian and Ukrainian people and offered to conclude peace with them, but the Polish pans refused to hear of it. They dreamed of conquering the Ukraine right up to the Black Sca, ~~of returning themselves the estates that had been seized from the Polish and other landowners in Byelorussia and the Ukraine~~[98]. The Entente supplied the Poles with guns; machine guns and rifles. France provided them with 135 airplanes and sent her best military experts to help them. **In the spring of 1920** the Poles went to war against Soviet Russia and captured Kiev. Crossing the Dniepr, the Polish army made ready to capture the Ukraine, east of the Dniepr. Their aim was to join with the remnants of Denikin's army in the Crimea under the command of Baron Wrangel, who was also a henchman of the Entente.

Units of the Red Army were quickly withdrawn from ~~all the~~ *various*[99] fronts in order to muster an army to strike at the Polish aggressors. Budyonny's cavalry army was transferred from the Caucasian front. By means of forced marches these bold horsemen crossed a thousand kilometres almost without leaving saddle. Budyonny's cavalry broke through into the rear of the Polish army and struck at it near Kiev. The Poles fled, closely pursued by the Red Army. Soon, Byelorussia was cleared of Polish troops and the Red Army was approaching Warsaw, the capital of Poland. But Warsaw was not captured; the Red Army retreated.

Notwithstanding the retreat of the Soviet forces the Poles suffered such heavy losses in the war that they were unable to resume the offensive and offered to conclude peace with Soviet Russia. To this the Soviet Government agreed and the war was brought to an end **in the autumn of 1920.** The lands of Byelorussia and the Ukraine which had been captured by the Polish pans were restored; but sections of the Byelorussian and Ukrainian people are und the yoke of Poland to this day.

In this war the Red Army taught the Polish pans a lesson which they still remember.

The rout of Wrangel. One important enemy still remained, however. This was Wrangel. Assisted by the Entente, Wrangel built ~~very~~[100] strong fortifications on the Isthmus of Perekop, in the Crimea. The Bolshevik Party and the Soviet Government commissioned M. Frunze to lead the campaign against Wrangel. In conjunction with ~~Comrades Stalin and~~ Voroshilov *and Blucher*[101] he carefully drew up his plan of campaign.

Stubborn battles were fought. Defeated in the Ukraine, Wrangel took up his positions behind his fortifications in the Crimea. On the night of November 7, the third anniversary of the proletarian revolution, Comrade

[**FIGURE 108:**] *Vasili Blucher.* [Figure 108 was added to the 1937 Russian edition after Stalin noted in the margins "*A portrait of V. K. Blucher needs to be added.*" See RGASPI, f. 558, op. 11, d. 1584, l. 103; also Zhdanov: f. 77, op. 1, d. 854, l. 92. Also SH, 213. Figure 108 was deleted from all subsequent editions after his purge in late 1938—see Appendix]

[**FIGURE 109:**] Michael Frunze (1885–1925). [SH, 217]

Frunze gave the order to storm Perekop, Wrangel's stronghold. The Red forces advanced over ~~boggy~~ territory that afforded no cover whatever. The Whiteguards bombarded the Red Army men with heavy guns and rained a hail of machine gun bullets down upon them. The heroic Red Army men *under the leadership of Comrade Blucher*[102] marched ~~in water up to their knees. The water rose and threatened to drown them. But the Red Army~~[103] in impregnable ranks against the concrete fortifications of the Whites. Amidst a hurricane of bursting shells and flying bullets they broke into the enemy's trenches and drove him out. The battle of Perekop ended in the victory of the Red Army. The Whiteguards fled in panic. Wrangel and the remnants of his forces took ship, and fled across the Black Sea to his protectors, the Entente.

Neither the Poles nor Wrangel could help the Entente to crush Soviet rule in our country.

The third and last Entente campaign suffered defeat, as did the first two.

The establishment of Soviet rule in Central Asia and Trans-Caucasia. During the Civil War the population of Central Asia suffered great privation. The foreign usurpers, the BAIS, as the kulaks were called in Central Asia, and mullahs, or Mohammedan priests, organized robber bands known as BASMACHI. The Basmachi robbed the people and set fire to their villages. Lenin and Stalin sent large forces of the Red Army under the leadership of M. Frunze and V. Kuibyshev to the aid of the toilers of Central Asia. Fighting in the deserts and rocky mountains, the Red Army exterminated these Basmachi brigands and freed Central Asia from the rule of its oppressors.

In 1920 the Uzbek toilers rose in revolt against the rule of the Khan of Khiva. They achieved victory over the khan's forces and established the rule of the people. The rebellion in Khiva was followed by a rebellion in Bukhara. There, the toilers, to whose aid the Red Army came, overthrew the emir, and also established the rule of the people. At this time, also, the Turkmens liberated themselves from the power of their English and Socialist-Revolutionary executioners.

Trans-Caucasia was under the rule of the bourgeoisie *nationalists— the Georgian Mensheviks, the Armenian Dashnaks and the Azerbaidjan Mussavatists*[104]—who were assisted by the Entente. In the spring of 1920 the workers and peasants of Trans-Caucasia rose in rebellion. The Red Army under the leadership of Comrades Ordjonikidze, Kirov and Mikoyan came to their aid. The rule of the bourgeoisie was overthrown and the Trans-Caucasian peoples—Azerbaidjan, Armenia and Georgia—joined the friendly family of nations of the Land of Soviets.

The principal enemies of the workers and peasants were now defeated and driven from Soviet territory. The Soviet Government was able to achieve victory over the foreign and Russian capitalists because at the head of the toilers marched the Communist Party. The Party united the workers and peasants ~~and all the people~~[105] for the fight against their enemies and made use of ~~the great riches~~ *all the resources*[106] of the country for the purpose of crushing these enemies.

In the fight to thwart the plans of the interventionists great assistance

[**FIGURE 110:**] Valerian Kuibyshev (1888–1935). [SH, 218]

[**FIGURE 111:**] *Gregory (Sergo) Ordjonikidze (1886–1937).* [Figure 111 was added to the 1937 Russian edition after Stalin wrote into the margins: "*It's necessary to paste here a portrait of Com[rade] Ordjonikidze.*" RGASPI, f. 558, op. 11, d. 1584, l. 1040b. Also SH, 219]

was rendered the Soviet Republic by the workers of Germany, England and France. They hindered the shipment by land and sea of arms and munitions that were to be used in the fight against the Soviets. They demanded that the war against the Soviet Republic be stopped, and waged a struggle under the slogan of "Hands off Soviet Russia."

Having defeated the interventionists, the toilers of the Soviet Union *could now turn to peaceful labours, they*[107] could now set to work to build Socialism, to heal the wounds inflicted by the World War and the Civil War.

XIV

The Victors Build a Joyous Country of Socialism *The Turn to Peaceful Labour. Economic Restoration of the Country*[1]

60. *Economic*[2] Restoration and the Formation of the U.S.S.R.

Lenin's plan for terminating economic chaos. The World War and the Civil War imposed upon the country by the Entente and the counter-revolutionaries had brought the country to a state of economic collapse. Many factories and mills were idle; there was no fuel or raw materials for them. The railways were jammed with disabled locomotives and broken cars. In many places the bridges and railway tracks had been blown up by the Whites and needed repairs or had to be built anew. Industry was turning out only one-fifth of the goods that were turned out before the war.

The peasants' fields were badly tilled. Much of the cattle had been taken away during the tsar's war, and much of it was exterminated during the Civil War. Agricultural production amounted to only a half of what was produced in 1914. The country was starving.

During the Civil War private trade was prohibited. The peasants, who were accustomed to trade, were discontented because of this. The bourgeoisie and the kulaks, playing on this discontent, instigated the peasants in a number of places to rise against the Soviet Government.[3]

The Bolshevik Party and the Soviet Government resolved to introduce a number of measures to improve the economic situation in the country.

In 1921 Comrade Lenin proposed the following plan. During the Civil War the peasants gave up all their surplus grain to meet the needs of industry, the workers and the Red Army. This expressed the military alliance between the workers and peasants in the fight against the landlords and factory owners. Now an alliance was needed for the economic restoration of the country and to build Socialism. Lenin therefore proposed that the peasants cease to give up all their surplus grain, but pay a definite tax *in kind, that is, in agricultural produce*,[4] and dispose of all the produce that is left at their own discretion. To carry this out it was necessary to permit private trade. Therefore, said Lenin, private manufacturers, ~~craftsmen~~[5] and traders must be permitted to ~~start their own businesses~~ *open small factories and shops*[6]. Let the private manufacturers and traders manufacture and sell goods for the time being. In the meantime we will rapidly become strong and squeeze out private capital, and when the time comes we will completely abolish the remnants of the capitalists and kulaks in our country. Lenin's plan was adopted. This plan was known as the New Economic Policy, or N.E.P., for short.

To hasten the economic restoration of the country the Communist Party introduced SUBBOTNIKS, as it did during the Civil War. During these subbotniks, which were held on Saturday (SUBBOTA in Russian) afternoons or Sundays, voluntary unpaid work was done for the benefit of the country. All the toilers took part in these subbotniks.

Lenin's plan was quite successful. In the course of three or four years the country was put on its feet again. The factories began working again, and the work of the railways greatly improved. Agriculture also recovered. The peasants brought their grain, meat and eggs to market. They began to plant sugar beet and flax, and increased their cotton crops. The sugar refineries and cotton mills in the country began to hum.

The workers and peasants were now able to obtain bread, sugar, textiles and other goods. Many state and cooperative stores were opened. These began to squeeze out the private traders.

Vladimir Ilyich Lenin, that mountain eagle, as Comrade Stalin called him, saw very far ahead. He said that the workers and peasants could easily overcome the economic chaos and live happy lives. To do that they must build factories to manufacture machines, and these machines must be driven by electricity. He repeatedly said that the country must be covered with a network of power stations. *A plan for the electrification of the country was drawn up.*[7] On Lenin's proposal the erection of the first big hydro-electric power station was started on the River Volkhov, near Leningrad (as Petrograd began to be called in 1924). This power station was completed in 1926, after Lenin's death, and provided electricity for the factories and

[**FIGURE 112:**] V. Lenin and J. Stalin in Gorki during Lenin's illness. [SH, 225]

mills in Leningrad. This enabled the industry of Leningrad, which was very important for the country, to be restored.

Power stations were also erected in other parts of the country: in the Urals, Ukraine and Trans-Caucasia.[8]

End of Japanese intervention. While the ~~entire~~[9] land of Soviets was engaged in the work of economic restoration, our rich region, the Far East, was still occupied by the Japanese, who had been there since 1918. But in 1922, the Red Army, together with the Siberian Partisans, at last put an end to the war in this region and liberated the whole of the Far East from the Japanese robbers and the Whiteguards. The Red Army, under the leadership of ~~P. Postyshev and~~[10] V. Blucher, gained brilliant victories over the Whites and Japanese in the battles of Spassk and Volochayevka. In the village of Volochayevka, the Whiteguards had built strong barbed wire defences. In the depth of the winter, amidst bitter frost, the Red fighters, in rags and almost barefooted, rushed at these defences, tore them down with their bare hands and hacked at them with their swords. The defences were captured. The Whites and Japanese fled.

In October **1922** the Red Army liberated Vladivostok.

The Japanese yoke in the Far East was overthrown.

But the toilers of Siberia and the Far East will long remember the violence and plunder of the Japanese army. The workers and peasants will never forget how the Japanese burned Red Partisans alive in locomotive furnaces. This is how the hero, Sergei Lazo, died for the liberation of the Far East.

The formation of the U.S.S.R. The whole country was now cleared of Whites *forces*[11] and interventionists. The country had to be safeguarded from future armed attack by bourgeois countries. The country had to be strengthened economically, and Socialism had to be built. Assistance had to be given to all the nationalities in the Land of Soviets to revive and develop their national culture. To do all this it was necessary to create a single union state. For this purpose, on the proposal of Lenin and Stalin, a congress of delegates from all the Union Republics was held in Moscow in **1922**. *This was the First*[12] *All-Union Congress of Soviets.*[13] At this congress the voluntary state federation of the peoples, *the union state known as*[14] the Union of Soviet Socialist Republics, or U.S.S.R., for short, was formed.

At first the U.S.S.R. consisted of a few Soviet Republics. They were the Russian[15] Soviet Federative Socialist Republic (R.S.F.S.R.), with its capital in Moscow; the Ukraine[16] Soviet Socialist Republic (Uk.S.S.R.) with its capital, first in Kharkov, and later in Kiev; the Byelorussian[17] Soviet Socialist Republic (B.S.S.R.), with its capital in Minsk. The Trans-Caucasian[18] Soviet Socialist Republics, namely, Azerbaidjan, Georgia and Armenia, formed one federation known as the Trans-Caucasian Soviet Federative Socialist Republic, with its capital in Tbilisi. Somewhat later, three independent Soviet Republics were formed in Central Asia. They were the Uzbek[19] Republic, with its capital in Tashkent; the Turkmen[20] Republic, with its capital in Ashkhabad; and the Tadjik[21] Republic, with its capital in Stalinabad. These republics became constituent parts of the U.S.S.R.

The peoples of the U.S.S.R. began to live as a friendly ~~and joyous~~[22]

family. Under tsarism many nationalities were becoming extinct; they were downtrodden and illiterate; but now they revived and began to build Socialism in fraternal alliance with all the other nationalities. The development of national culture made rapid progress in all the republics. Many schools, universities and libraries were opened; theaters were built, and many books began to be printed in the languages of the various nationalities. The nationalities of the U.S.S.R. which had not possessed an alphabet before now acquired one. The culture of the peoples blossomed forth.

61. Lenin Died, but His Cause Lives Forever

Death of Lenin. On **January 21, 1924**, at the age of 54, after a long and severe illness, the great Lenin passed away in Gorki, near Moscow. The toilers of the whole world had prepared for and brought about the proletarian revolution, and in the years of hardship had saved it from innumerable enemies. There passed away the man who had done more for humanity than anyone had done before.

The millions of toilers grieved their loss. During the bitter January frosts, long lines of toilers in Moscow filed past his bier to take a last fare-

[**FIGURE 113:**] The toilers of Moscow filing into the Hall of Columns to take their last farewell of Lenin. [SH, 227]

well of their great leader. Their hearts were filled with grief and also with a firm determination to continue marching along the path mapped out by Lenin.

Amidst the sounds of mournful music Lenin was buried at the Kremlin wall. There he lies today, in a marble mausoleum, in a glass coffin, with the Order of the Red Flag pinned to his breast.

And on visiting Moscow the toilers from all parts of our country go to the mausoleum in order that the image of the leader who had led the people to freedom and to a life of happiness may be imprinted in their memory.

Stalin's vow. On January 26, when delegates from all parts of the U.S.S.R. gathered at the Second All-Union Congress of Soviets, Comrade Stalin, *on the instructions of the Bolshevik Party,*[23] took a vow before the people in the name of the Party. He said:

"In departing from us, Comrade Lenin bequeathed to us the duty of holding aloft and guarding the purity of the great title of member of the Party. We vow to you, Comrade Lenin, that we will fulfil your behest with honour! . . .

"In departing from us, Comrade Lenin bequeathed to us the duty of

[**Figure 114:**] The Lenin Mausoleum in the Red Square, Moscow. [SH, 228]

guarding the unity of our Party like the apple of our eye. We vow to you, Comrade Lenin, that we will also fulfil this behest of yours with honour! . . .

"Only in our country have the oppressed and suppressed masses of toilers succeeded in throwing off the rule of the landlords and capitalists and in putting in its place the rule of the workers and peasants. . . .

"This titanic struggle was led by Comrade Lenin and his Party. . . .

"Lenin's name has become the name most beloved by the toiling and exploited masses.

"In departing from us, Comrade Lenin bequeathed to us the duty of guarding and strengthening the dictatorship of the proletariat. We vow to you, Comrade Lenin, that we will spare no effort to fulfil also this behest of yours with honour! . . .

"In departing from us, Comrade Lenin bequeathed to us the duty of strengthening with all our might the alliance between the workers and the peasants. We vow to you, Comrade Lenin, that we will fulfil also this behest of yours with honour! . . .

"Russians and Ukrainians, Bashkirs and Byelorussians, Georgians and Azerbaidjanians, Armenians and Daghestanians, Tatars and Kirghiz, Uzbeks and Turkmens—all are equally interested in strengthening the dictatorship of the proletariat. . . .

"Comrade Lenin tirelessly urged upon us the necessity of establishing a voluntary alliance of the peoples of our country, the necessity for their fraternal collaboration within the framework of a Union of Republics.

"In departing from us, Comrade Lenin bequeathed to us the duty of strengthening and expanding the Union of Republics. We vow to you, Comrade Lenin, that we will carry out also this behest of yours with honour! . . .

"More than once Lenin pointed out to us that the strengthening of the Red Army and the improvement of its condition is one of the most important tasks of our party. . . .

"Let us vow then, comrades, that we will spare no effort to strengthen our Red Army and our Red Navy." . . .

The last words of Comrade Stalin's vow were:

"We vow to you, Comrade Lenin, that we will not spare our lives to strengthen and expend the league of the toilers of the whole world—the Communist International!"[24]

~~Stalin traveled his entire revolutionary path hand in hand with Lenin. From the first steps of Soviet power, Stalin and Lenin struggled with all the enemies of the Soviet republic. He replaced Lenin when the latter passed away. Stalin to this day leads the toilers of the U.S.S.R. from victory to victory.~~[25]

Socialism is Built in the U.S.S.R. *The U.S.S.R. is the Land of Victorious Socialism*[1]

62. Socialist Industry. and the Construction of[2] Collective Farming

The building of Socialist industry. The old factories and mills that were restarted and the machinery with which they were equipped were obsolete. Besides, there were few of them, and the goods they produced were not enough to supply the needs of the country. The amount of pig iron produced was very little, and so also was the amount of oil and coal. Many kinds of goods which the country needed were not produced at all. They had to be imported from abroad.

In 1925, at the 14th Congress of the Communist Party, Comrade Stalin, *on the Party's instructions,*[3] declared that we must in a short period of time transform our agricultural country into an industrial country. To do this we must build many new factories and power stations. All the old mills and factories must be reconstructed and brought up to date. *We must build tractors, harvester-combines, automobiles, new machines for the factories, and airplanes.*[4] We must train large numbers of skilled workers and experts. We must overtake and surpass the most advanced capitalist countries, "otherwise they will trample on us." *All this is called industrialization.*[5]

~~The party and entire people began to fulfill the plan that was proposed by Stalin with as much heroism as they had defeated the enemies during the Civil War. The workers built new factories, railway lines, and electric stations; they began to extract from the earth more coal, oil and metal ore. For the improvement of agriculture, they began to build tractors and harvester-combines.~~[6]

This plan of building Socialism in our country, however, was opposed by the traitors who at that time were in the ranks of the Party: Trotsky, Zino-

Иосиф Виссарионович Сталин

[**FIGURE 115:**] JOSEPH STALIN. [Stalin objected to Figure 115 appearing on special glossy paper, crossed it out, and wrote into the margins: "*Provide an ordinary portrait.*" RGASPI, f. 558, op. 11, d. 1584, l. 109. Although Zhdanov agreed with Stalin's decision, he did not cross out the portrait in his copy of the text—see f. 77, op. 1, d. 854, ll. 97–98. Also SH, 233]

viev and Kamenev. They did all they possibly could to hinder the building of Socialist industry. *They said that it was impossible to build Socialist society in the U.S.S.R.*[7]

They said that the workers and peasants could not get on without capitalists and kulaks.[8]

The foreign bourgeoisie took advantage of the struggle they waged against the Party to spread lies about the Soviet Union and to fight against it. They bribed a number of the old specialists and the remnants of the Mensheviks and Socialist-Revolutionaries, and formed them into counter-revolutionary groups of wreckers for the purpose of disrupting the growing industry of the U.S.S.R. The wreckers spoiled machines and wrecked coal and iron mines. They blew up and set fire to factories, mills and power stations. The wreckers were caught and severely punished. But the Trotsky-ites continued to fight the Party and the people. The Party expelled the Trotskyites from its ranks. The people banished Trotsky from the Soviet Union, and he openly went into the service of the bourgeoisie.

In order to carry out the tasks which Comrade Stalin had set before the country, a plan of great works was drawn up in **1928**. This was known as the First Five-Year Plan of Socialist Construction.

The toilers of the Soviet Union of all nationalities started on this great work of construction with enthusiasm and set numerous examples of labour heroism. In the Land of Soviets work became a matter of honour and glory, a matter of valour and heroism. Day and night strenuous work was carried on at the construction jobs so as to accomplish the plan of great works.

In the factories and on the railways Socialist competition spread on a wide scale. The workers beat all world record in laying bricks and in erecting factory buildings.

On the banks of the River Tom, near the town of Kuznetsk, where formerly the Siberian Tatar khans reigned, the erection of the huge Stalin Steel Works was started in 1930 and completed towards the end of the First Five-Year Plan period.

On the site of the former Zaporozhskaya Sech, where the Dniepr Rapids surged, the huge Lenin Dniepr Power Station was built. The electricity produced at the Dniepr Power Station helped to develop many districts of the Ukraine. Thousands of hectares of formerly barren land-were made fertile; the Dniepr, which had been blocked by the rocks forming the rapids,

[**FIGURE 116:**] Blast furnaces at the Kuznetsk Iron and Steel Works. [SH, 235]

became navigable throughout its length, and many large mills and factories now producing goods the country needs are supplied with electricity from this station.

In 1930, across the arid steppe and desert, the Turkestan-Siberian Railway was built and now connects the wheat country of Siberia with flourishing Central Asia.

During the First Five-Year Plan period a particularly large number of factories were erected in the national republics. Scores of new factories were erected in Central Asia, Trans-Caucasia, Ukraine and Byelorussia.

All this enabled us to build Socialist industry, that is, industry without capitalists.[9]

Building collective farms. For peasant agriculture, steel horses, that is, tractors, were built. During the First Five Year Plan period the huge Dzerzhinsky Tractor Works were built in Stalingrad, and factories for building harvester-combines were erected in Saratov and Zaporozhye.

All this was needed for the purpose of organizing peasant farming along the most up-to-date scientific and technical lines.

It enabled us to organize the small individual peasant farms into large collective farms (KOLKHOZ). This was not an easy task. At first the peasants clung very tight to their small farm*s*.

But the Party succeeded in proving to ~~such a~~ *the* peasants[10], not only by arguments, but also by deeds the enormous advantages of large-scale collective farming over small individual farming. The Soviet Government sent numerous tractors, harvest–combines and other machinery into the rural districts. In 1929, large numbers of middle peasants followed the poor peasants into the collective farms. The kulaks, realizing that the collective farms would sweep them away, began furiously to resist the organization of collective farms. They murdered the leading collective farmers, spoiled collective farm machines and set fire to collective farm fields. In their fight against the collective farms the kulaks were supported by a small clique of traitors to the people, headed by Bukharin and Rykov. They, too, like the Trotskyites, were opposed to the Five-Year Plan.

The *Bolshevik* Party ~~under Comrade Stalin~~[11], however, crushed these traitors and helped the peasants to break the resistance of the kulaks and to destroy them.

The collective farms grew, became firmly established and began to advance rapidly towards a happy and prosperous life. In the collective farms the peasants began to plough more land. They gathered larger harvests. In the villages more schools, libraries and clubs were built. In 1932, more than half the peasant*s households*[12] in the country were organized in collective farms.

The First Five-Year Plan of Socialist Construction was completed in **1932**, that is to say, not in five years but in four.

All this enabled us to build Socialist agriculture, that is, agriculture without landlords and kulaks.[13]

The workers and peasants could celebrate their victory.

By fulfilling the First Five-Year Plan, the U.S.S.R. ~~entered into~~ *ensured the victory of*[14] Socialism.

The U.S.S.R. now manufactured machines, extracted metals, built tractors and airplanes, and greatly increased the output of coal and oil. The U.S.S.R. was transformed into an industrial country.

Three times more goods were now being produced than in tsarist Russia. In 1933 the U.S.S.R. caught up with and surpassed a number of European countries. It took second place in the world output of oil, second place in

[**FIGURE 117:**] A harvester-combine reaping a collective-farm field. [SH, 236]

the world output of steel, third place in the world output of pig iron, and fourth place in the world output of coal.

But the enemies of the U.S.S.R. within the country and abroad did everything to hinder the work of erecting factories. In 1929 the foreign capitalists incited China and compelled her to start war on the U.S.S.R. The troops of the Chinese generals and Whiteguards attacked our Far-Eastern frontiers. But our Far-Eastern Red Army was firm and strong and, under the leadership of V. Blucher, quickly routed the enemies. There were wreckers also within the country. In 1930 a large party of wreckers consisting of old engineers and Mensheviks and Socialist-Revolutionaries, was uncovered by the valiant chekists[15]. These wreckers wanted to bring back the capitalists to Russia. They were preparing for another war against the U.S.S.R. The wreckers were caught and severely punished by the Soviet Government. After this the workers and peasants began to strengthen and equip their Red Army more than ever, and to help the organizations concerned with the safety of the Soviet state to expose the enemies of the Soviet people.

Thus, through labour and struggle, was the First *Five-Year* Plan[16] of great work, drawn up by ~~Comrade Stalin~~ *the Bolshevik Party*[17], accomplished. ~~The power of the Soviet Union became invincible.~~[18]

63. The U.S.S.R—The Land of Socialism

~~Our socialist riches~~ *The cultural achievements*[19] **and the people of the Land of Socialism.** During the period of the First Five-Year Plan the face of our country ~~very~~[20] greatly changed. But the whole life of our country underwent still greater change during the period of the Second Five-Year Plan (**1933–1937**). On one-sixth of the globe, from the North Pole to the torrid steppes of Turkmenia, from the Baltic Sea to the Pacific Ocean, ~~socialism~~ *a new Socialist system* was built, *a new life was created, a life without exploitation or oppression, without capitalists or landlords, without merchants or kulaks*[21].

~~The whole country came to life.~~ *The country began to work in a new way.*[22] The people of the Land of Soviets brought to light the riches concealed in the bowels of the earth. Coal, oil, gold, platinum, iron ore and non-ferrous metals were now produced in quantities never produced before. In the rich forests of the U.S.S.R. people began to obtain huge quantities of the most varied kinds of timber. In our oceans, seas, lakes and rivers they began to catch sea animals and the most valuable kinds of fish in quantities never seen before. As a result of the Second Five-Year Plan over 220,000,000 hectares of Socialist fields are now supplying the country with increasing quantities of grain ~~and crops for technical use~~, *cotton, flax and sugar beet*[23]. ~~The moment is near when Comrade Stalin's objective of harvesting 7–8 billion poods of grain will be realized.~~[24] Our Socialist ~~plantations~~ *fields*[25], orchards and gardens are producing increasing quantities of tea, tangerines, lemons, oranges, apples, pears and grapes.

Scores of most up-to-date, huge mills and factories built by Soviet engineers and equipped with Soviet machines are year after year increasing their output and improving the quality of their manufactures. Hundreds of new factories have been built in branches of industry which did not exist in our country before. Our automobiles, tractors, harvester-combines, airplanes and machines for factories ~~have completely crowded out~~ *are in no way inferior to*[26] those manufactured abroad.

Our thousands of mills and factories ~~(see the map on page 214)~~[27] are now producing everything that is requires to supply human needs. Our country is illuminated by electricity. Over 14,000 power stations supply electricity to our mills and factories. Only the workers *and peasants*[28] of the U.S.S.R, who were liberated from the exploitation of the capitalists, could build up such a mighty industry *and mighty agriculture*[29] in so short a time. Solicitude for the welfare of the individual—the seven-hour day, high wages, rest homes, sanatoriums, safety measures in the factories, good houses, free technical and other education—all served to bring about an increase in the productivity of labour ever witnessed before. Work ceased to be a burden. ~~It became joyous creativity.~~[30]

New people of a special kind arose in the Soviet Union.

In the Donetz Basin, the coal miner, Alexei Stakhanov, hewed in one shift 102 tons of coal, which was over fourteen times the ordinary output. Alexei Stakhanov, the famous miner of the Donetz Basin.

In the automobile works in Gorky, forgeman Busygin forged in one shift 1,050 crankshafts instead of the ordinary output of 675.

The two weavers, Dusia and Maria Vinogradova, began to tend 144 looms instead of 10. The example of these advanced people, who were called Stakhanovites, was followed by hundreds and thousands of others.

The Stakhanov movement spread throughout the country; from industry it spread to agriculture. The collective farmers began to gather harvests of hith-

[**FIGURE 118:**] Alexei Stakhanov, the famous miner of the Donetz Basin. [SH, 239]

erto unseen dimensions. Maria Demchenko obtained 500 centners of sugar beet per hectare. In the course of the summer the women tractor drivers in Pasha Angelina's brigade ploughed over 1,000 hectares with a *each*[31] tractor.

In order to carry the mountains of goods produced by the factories and mills, the billions of poods of the products of agriculture and the millions of passengers who wanted to travel, it was necessary to improve the work of

[**Figure 119:**] Lazar Kaganovich. [SH, 240]

the transport system. In a short space of time Lazar Kaganovich, People's Commissar of Railways, set the railways running smoothly. The workers began to call him the "Iron Commissar."

Great canals were built, such as the White Sea and Baltic Canal, which connects the Baltic Sea with the White Sea, and the Moscow-Volga Canal. ~~There are no such canals anywhere else in the world.~~[32]

The Metropolitan, an underground railway of wonderful beauty, the finest in the world, was built in Moscow, the capital of the U.S.S.R.

Soviet airplanes fly higher and longer distances than any other. They opened the route to the hitherto unknown icy wastes of the Arctic and conquered the North Pole. There, a radio station has been installed. Soviet airmen discovered the hitherto unknown route from the U.S.S.R. to America via the North Pole. The names of the Soviet Arctic explorers and airmen, the heroes of the Soviet Union, Schmidt, Chkalov, Baidukov, Belyakov,

[**FIGURE 120:**] ~~The Route of the Moscow-North Pole Flight in May 1937.~~ [Cut by Stalin: RGASPI, f. 558, op. 11, d. 1584, l. 1140b. Also Zhdanov: f. 77, op. 1, d. 854, ll. 102–1020b.]

[**FIGURE 121:**] ~~Chkalov, Baidukov and Belyakov—the aviator Heroes of the Soviet Union who flew from Moscow to America across the North Pole in June 1937.~~ [Cut by Stalin: RGASPI, f. 558, op. 11, d. 1584, l. 1140b. Also Zhdanov: f. 77, op. 1, d. 854, ll. 102–1020b.]

[**FIGURE 122:**] ~~The ANT-25 plane that made the Moscow-America flight.~~ [Cut by Stalin: RGASPI, f. 558, op. 11, d. 1584, l. 1140b. Also Zhdanov: f. 77, op. 1, d. 854, ll. 102–1020b.]

Gromov, Yumashev, Danilin,[33] Vodopyanov, Molokov, Levanevsky, Slepnev and others are famous throughout the country.

New cities sprang up in the U.S.S.R. with fabulous speed—Stalinsk in Western Siberia, *Magnitogorsk in the Urals,*[34] Komsomolsk in the Far East, and others. Old towns were rebuilt, and became unrecognizable.

The capitals of the Soviet Republics and the big industrial centres, particularly, expanded and became beautiful. Old Moscow with its crooked streets is now being transformed into a splendid capital of the Soviet Union. Hundreds of fine buildings were erected and work was started on the magnificent Palace of Soviets, which will be the largest and highest building in the world. And this lofty edifice will be crowned with a statue of the leader of the proletariat, V. I. Lenin. This statue will be 100 metres high.

[**FIGURE 123:**] *Model of t*he Palace of Soviets. [Edit by Zhdanov: RGASPI, f. 77, op. 1, d. 854, l. 205. Also SH, 241]

[**FIGURE 124:**] New Moscow. [SH, 243]

Socialist culture.[35] The capitalist system was the grave of popular talent. In those times only a few individuals climbed to any height in art and science. Such a one was I. Michurin, the great horticulturist of our country. He grew many new kinds of fruits, fruits which do not fear the frost. Michurin apple trees blossom and bend with the weight of fruit in cold Siberia and the Far North. Only the Soviet Government appreciated the value of his scientific discoveries.

Another genius was the grandfather of Russian aviation, K. Tsiolkovsky. He designed an airplane thirteen years before the first airplane rose into the sky. He invented the metal dirigible airship several years before the first dirigible was built in Germany. But in tsarist Russia the value of these inventions was not appreciated. Only in the Land of Soviets were Tsiolkovsky's discoveries put to use.

Only under Lenin and Stalin the Soviet Government was the scientific work of Academician Ivan Pavlov extensively developed. Surrounded with the care of the Soviet people and ~~supported by Lenin and Stalin~~ *assisted by the Soviet Government*[36], Pavlov made many discoveries concerning human life.

In its numerous schools and universities our country trained thousands of new scientists from the ranks of the workers and peasants. Everybody, young and old, now receives free education. Every schoolboy and schoolgirl can take up any career he or she wishes. All the nationalities inhabiting the Soviet Union have been given the opportunity to study in their own language.

In no country in the world are so many books and newspapers published as in the U.S.S.R. Nowhere are there so many libraries as in our country.

In the U.S.S.R. popular talent has been developed to a very high degree. It has found an outlet in the theatre, in literature and in the cinema. Under the guidance of the Communist Party, this talent was nursed and encouraged by the great proletarian writer, Maxim Gorky, the personal friend of Lenin and Stalin. Inspired by the building of Socialism in our country, Gorky wrote unforgettable works of great beauty and feeling. Together with the whole people, Gorky took part in creating a life of happiness in our country.

Soviet musicians and actors are ~~the best in the world~~ *among the best masters of their art*[37]. At international competitions the first prizes were obtained by Soviet pianists and violinists.

Only in the Land of Socialism could such brave people arise who, loving

[**Figure 125:**] Maxim Gorky (1868–1916). [SH, 244]

their country, are ready to lay down their lives for it. At the 17th Congress of the Bolshevik Party ~~(which had grown by this time to more than 3 mil-lion members)~~[38], held in 1934, the great Stalin, leader of the peoples, said: "Everyone sees that the line of the Party has conquered," that is to say, that the path of victory which the Party had mapped out was the right one. And millions of toilers in the Soviet Union and abroad repeated Stalin's words: "The line of the Party has conquered."

The remnants of the parasite class, the capitalists and kulaks, were destroyed. The possibility of their reviving again was removed. The Party thus carried out Lenin's great behest. Under its leadership, the people ~~built socialism~~ *created a new Socialist system*[39].

64. Our Enemies and Friends ~~Beyond the Borders of the U.S.S.R.~~ *Abroad*[40]

The U.S.S.R. stands for peace, the fascists stand for war. The peoples of the Soviet Union are waging a heroic struggle for the happiness of all mankind. In the U.S.S.R. Socialism has been built. The Land of Soviets does not want alien territory, it does not want war. Our Government pursues an unswerving policy of peace with all the nations of the globe. It has concluded a number of peace treaties with many countries. In order to strengthen the peace of the world the U.S.S.R. joined the League of Nations, which was formed as far back as 1919. Treaties of mutual assistance against possible enemy attack have been concluded with Czechoslovakia and France.

"The U.S.S.R.," said Comrade Stalin, "does not think of threatening anyone, let alone of attacking anyone. We stand for peace and champion the cause of peace. But we are not afraid of threats and are ready to answer the instigators of war blow for blow."

These instigators of war are ~~the hireling dogs of the bourgeoisie,~~[41] the fascists, the worst enemies of all the working people. The fascists are in power in Germany and Italy. The fascist militarists of Japan are at one with them. The fascists mete out cruel punishment to the revolutionary workers *and peasants*[42] in their countries, and persecute all those who are not with them. ~~In Germany, the fascists have held the leader of the German proletariat, Comrade Telman, in prison for a number of years.~~[43]

[**FIGURE 126:**] ~~Ernst Telman—chief of the German communists~~
~~(born in 1886).~~ [Cut by Stalin: RGASPI, f. 558, op. 11, d. 1584,
l. 116ob. Also Zhdanov: f. 77, op. 1, d. 854, l. 104ob.]

~~The books of the best writers and scientists in the world are burned in~~
~~bonfires on the streets. The fascists have stoked nationalist hatred and the~~
~~oppression of the toilers to the extreme.~~[44]

Most of all the fascists hate our country, the Land of Socialism, the powerful bulwark of the peace, liberty and happiness of the whole of mankind.

The fascist militarists of Japan have seized Manchuria and other territory in China. They test the strength of our Far Eastern frontiers and every
time they are vigorously repulsed. The Japanese militarists are preparing
for war against us.

~~The Italian fascists defeated Abyssinia, burned and destroyed Abyssin-~~
~~ian towns and villages, killed thousands of the working people with poison~~
~~gas and transformed the country into its colony.~~

~~Fascist Germany and Italy are waging a war against the heroic Spanish~~
~~people. Alongside the mutinous Spanish generals, they use their troops, air-~~
~~planes, tanks and navies to destroy the towns and villages of Spain and to~~
~~kill and maim women, children and the elderly.~~

[**FIGURE 127:**] Sergei Kirov (1886–1934). [SH, 246]

~~There is a war in Spain. The toilers of Spain heroically struggle with the fascist attack, defending their liberty and their ancient culture against these savage monsters.~~[45]

In their preparations for a world war the fascists send their spies to all countries. Fascist spies also managed to penetrate the Soviet Union. Here they found active assistants in the persons of the ~~Trotskyites~~ *adherents of Trotsky and Rykov*[46]. That contemptible enemy of the people, the fascist agent Trotsky *and his contemptible friends Rykov and Bukharin,*[47] organized in the U.S.S.R. gangs of murderers, wreckers and spies. They foully murdered that ardent Bolshevik S. Kirov. They plotted to murder ~~Stalin, Voroshilov, Ordjonikidze, Kaganovich, Molotov and~~[48] other leaders of the proletariat, too. The fascist scoundrels, the Trotskyites *and Rykovites*[49], caused train collisions in the U.S.S.R., blew up and set fire to mines and factories, wrecked machines, poisoned workers, and did all the damage they possibly could. These enemies of the people had a definite program, which was to restore the *yoke of the*[50] capitalists and landlords in the U.S.S.R., to destroy the collective farms, to surrender the Ukraine to the Germans and the Far East to the Japanese, and to prepare for the defeat of the U.S.S.R. in the event of war.

These brigands were caught and punished as they deserved.

But as long as the U.S.S.R. is surrounded by countries in which capitalism reigns, spies and wreckers will continuously strive to penetrate our country and cause us harm. The eyes of the ~~border guards~~ *workers and peasants*[51] must be sharper than ever. ~~There have been many cases in which spies have been caught crossing the border with the aid of our valiant children.~~ *All the inhabitants of the Land of Soviets, young and old, must guard our frontiers with greater alertness than ever.*[52]

Spies worm their way into the mills and factories, into the big cities and villages. Every suspicious person must be carefully watched and every fascist agent must be caught.

The Red Army and our friends abroad. The Soviet Union is firmer and stronger than any other country in the world. Its strength lies in its Red Army which is equipped along the most up-to-date technical and scientific lines. It is famous for its marshals and commanders, and its heroic Red Army men.

The strength of the U.S.S.R. lies still more in the fact that the whole people, men and women, children, adults and aged, are ready to shed their last drop of blood for their dearly beloved country.

The Soviet Union is the Socialist Fatherland of the toilers of the whole world. Increasing numbers of workers, peasants and intellectuals abroad are fighting the warlike designs of the ~~bourgeoisie~~ *fascists*[53] against the Soviet Union. They are uniting in a United Popular Front to combat the fascists. *The workers in Germany, England, France, Italy, Japan, Poland and America sympathize with the U.S,S.R. and wish it success. They are the friends and comrades of the workers of the U.S.S.R. in the fight for peace, in the fight against fascism. Their support makes the U.S.S.R. mightier still.*[54]

~~In Spain, representatives of the Popular Anti-fascist Front lead the government. In France, the government is similarly dependent on the Popular Front. The working class of France created a combined trade union that has united together more than five million workers and they are waging a successful struggle with the French fascists.~~

[**FIGURE 128:**] Kliment Voroshilov. [SH, 247]

[**FIGURE 129:**] First of May parade of the Red Army
in the Red Square, Moscow. [SH, 248]

~~The Popular Anti-Fascist Front movement is growing in other countries as well.~~

~~In China, the entire people is rising up against the Japanese. Soviet power has been created in a large portion of China. It has a powerful Red Army of Chinese workers and peasants at its disposal. Chinese Soviets are working tirelessly to create an all-Chinese combined front of toilers that will fight for the liberation of China from its Japanese invaders.~~

[**Figure 130:**] ~~Georgy Dimitrov (born in 1882).~~ [Cut by Stalin: RGASPI, f. 558, op. 11, d. 1584, l. 1190b. Also Zhdanov: f. 77, op. 1, d. 854, l. 1060b]

~~The Comintern under Comrade Dimitrov, Comrade Stalin's loyal comrade-in-arms, leads the struggle of the toiling masses of the entire world against the fascists and against those who would incite a war.~~

~~The Soviet Union stands like a granite cliff in the front lines of the struggle for peace. The fascists are applying all their energies to touch off a world war, so that they might be able to in this way crush the rising proletarian revolution and hold on to power.~~

~~But they will not get away with it.~~[55]

65. The ~~Great Stalin~~ *New* Constitution *of the U.S.S.R.*[56]

The structure of our state. The Great Proletarian Revolution destroyed and abolished the hated tsarist ~~empire~~ *monarchy*[57] and its laws, which kept the workers and peasants in chains.

On the ruins of old Russia the liberated workers and peasants built their own state. This was the workers' *and peasants'*[58] state, the like of which had never been seen before. This state was called the Russian Soviet Federative Socialist Republic (R.S.F.S.R.).

For three years the Soviet Republic kept at bay the enemies who were attacking it from all sides. It defeated the landlords and capitalists, Russian and foreign, who had organized civil war against it. It helped all the oppressed nationalities *in old Russia*[59] to throw off the yoke of landlord and capitalist violence. It helped them to establish Soviet rule in their liberated lands. Soviet Republics arose and became firmly established in the Ukraine, Byelorussia, Central Asia and Trans-Caucasia. By the joint efforts of all these Soviet Republics all the enemies were finally defeated. The liberated nations proceeded to restore the industry which had been destroyed by the war. In 1922, under the leadership of ~~Lenin and Stalin~~ *the Bolshevik Party*[60], they formed the great Union of Soviet Socialist Republics. At first the U.S.S.R. consisted of four Union Republics; later on, three more were added.

Nowhere in the world was there such friendship and mutual confidence between various nationalities as in the U.S.S.R. In **1924** the free peoples of the U.S.S.R. ~~wrote~~ *adopted*[61] their[62] first Constitution (or fundamental law) of the U.S.S.R. In this Constitution they sealed all the victories the country had achieved. A long time elapsed. Industry was built up and greatly enlarged; collective farms and *state farms (sovkhoz)*[63] were organized; culture blossomed forth. *The remnants of the landlords, capitalists and kulaks were uprooted, the exploitation of the toilers and the oppression of the people were abolished. This means that*[64] Socialism ~~had been built~~ *has triumphed* in the U.S.S.R.[65]

In **1936** *a Commission headed by*[66] Comrade Stalin drew up a new Constitution for the U.S.S.R. This Constitution was submitted to the people for wide discussion and later ratified by the supreme authority of the Union, the All-Union Congress of Soviets. December 5, the day on which the Constitution was ratified, was declared a public holiday. In this Constitution are recorded the main achievements of the Land of Soviets during the first nineteen years of its existence.

In the former Constitution it was stated that our Republic was called a Socialist Republic because the working class was in power and was striving to build Socialism. In the new Constitution our state is called a Socialist state of the workers and peasants because, *in the main,*[67] Socialism has already been built in the U.S.S.R.

In the U.S.S.R. all power belongs to the toilers of town and country, to the Soviets of Toilers' Deputies.

The land, mineral deposits, factories, mines, mills, railways, the big apartment houses and the state farms are state property, the possession of the whole people. Parallel with state property there is cooperative and collective-farm property, property which belongs to the various collective farms and cooperative societies. The Constitution states that in the U.S.S.R. the law permits the small private economy of handicraftsmen and individual peasants, on the condition, however, that the handicraftsman or individual peasant works himself and does not exploit the labour of others. Our state was able to achieve all this because it abolished the *landlords*[68], capitalists *and kulaks,*[69] because it abolished the exploitation of man by man and eliminated private property as a tool and means of production[70].

In the U.S.S.R. all able-bodied persons must work. "He who does not work, neither shall he eat."

[**Figure 131:**] Emblem of the U.S.S.R. [SH, 251]

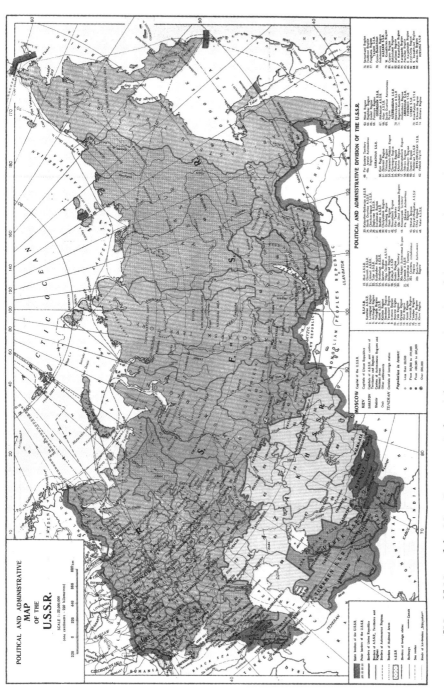

[MAP 6:] Map of the Most Important Industrial Construction Site of the First and Second Five-Year Plans in 11 Soviet Republics *Political and Administrative Map of U.S.S.R.* [SH, 252–253. Stalin crossed out an earlier map of Soviet industrial sites, wrote "Map of the Soviet Union" into the margins and then added "*Blow up the map and note on it all the union and autonomous republics.*" Compare RGASPI, f. 558, op. 11, d. 1584, l. 120 and KKISSSR, 212–213]

[MAP 7:] Political and Administrative Map of U.S.S.R. in Europe. [SH, 252–253. Later editorial addition—see KKISSSR, 216–217]

The U.S.S.R. is a voluntary and friendly federation of equal nationalities all enjoying equal rights. "And this friendship is a great thing: as long as it continues the peoples of our country will be free and invincible," said Comrade Stalin.

The U.S.S.R. is a voluntary federation of the following eleven *Union*[71] Republics possessing equal rights:

The Russian Soviet Federative Socialist Republic

The Ukrainian Soviet Socialist Republic

The Byelorussian Soviet Socialist Republic

The Azerbaidjan Soviet Socialist Republic

The Georgian Soviet Socialist Republic

The Armenian Soviet Socialist Republic

The Turkmen Soviet Socialist Republic

The Uzbek Soviet Socialist Republic

The Tadjik Soviet Socialist Republic

The Kirghiz Soviet Socialist Republic

The Kazakh Soviet Socialist Republic

The highest organ of state in the U.S.S.R. is the Supreme Soviet of the U.S.S.R. In the U.S.S.R. the Supreme Soviet alone has the right to pass laws. The Supreme Soviet sets up ~~in its meetings~~[72] the government of the U.S.S.R. called the Council of People's Commissars of the Union.

The local organs of state power are the Soviets of Toilers' Deputies. All the Soviets, the local Soviets, the Supreme Soviets *of the Union Republics and Autonomous Republics*[73], as well as the Supreme Soviet of the U.S.S.R., are elected by the citizens of the U.S.S.R. ~~who are more than 18 years old. This sort of election is called a direct election. In the U.S.S.R., no one is denied the right to vote in Soviet elections. Everyone—men and women, regardless of their nationality, may elect deputies, except for those who have been convicted of a crime or judged to be insane. Voting at elections takes place in secret and every citizen votes directly for the candidate to be elected to the Soviets. All citizens are equal in their right to vote~~ *on the basis of uni-*

[**FIGURE 132:**] Mikhail Ivanovich Kalinin. Chairman of
the All-Union Central Executive Committee and the All-
Russian Central Executive Committee. [SH, 253]

versal, equal and direct suffrage, with secret-ballot. All citizens of the U.S.S.R.,
male and female, who have reached the age of eighteen, irrespective of race, na-
tionality, religion, education, social origin, property status or past activities,
have the right to elect deputies and to be elected as deputies. Only the insane, and
those convicted to deprivation of the franchise by the courts, are excluded from
this right. This is called universal suffrage, because all have the right to vote. It
is called equal suffrage, because all citizens are equal in their right to vote. It is
called direct suffrage, because every citizen votes directly for the candidate to be
elected to the Soviets of Toilers' Deputies. Voting at elections takes place in secret;
every citizen has the right to vote for the candidate he wishes to be elected.[74]

The citizens of the U.S.S.R. are ensured the right to work, rest and lei-
sure, education, and *material*[75] security in old age.

Our state ensures these rights for all citizens.

In the Land of Socialism there is no unemployment, from which millions of workers in capitalist countries suffer.

Only in our country is there a seven-hour day, the shortest working day in the world.

Thousands of rest homes and sanatoriums are available to the toilers of our country. Every year all ~~laborers~~ *workers and office employees*[76] in the U.S.S.R. enjoy a vacation. Only in the U.S.S.R. can the toilers *really*[77] study and become educated. Instruction in all the educational establishments in the U.S.S.R. is free; many students are maintained by the state ~~with money to live~~[78] while they are studying. In the U.S. S.R care is taken of every person from the day he is born right up to old age.

For babies and young children, creches and kindergartens are provided. ~~All~~ The[79] aged and sick are provided for by the state. All citizens in the U.S.S.R.

[**FIGURE 133:**] Viacheslav Mikhailovich Molotov. Chairman of
the USSR Council of People's Commissars. [SH, 254]

are ensured the right of free speech, freedom of the press, freedom of assembly and street demonstrations.

But in addition to rights, every citizen of the U.S.S.R. has duties to the state. It is the duty of every citizen strictly to observe all[80] the laws *of the Soviet Union*[81], to maintain discipline, to perform his work honestly, to safeguard and strengthen Socialist property. Whoever encroaches upon Socialist property is an enemy of the people of the U.S.S.R.

Defence of the Fatherland against all enemies of the U.S.S.R. is the supreme duty of a citizen of the U.S.S.R. Whoever goes over to the enemy, whoever betrays the military secrets of the U.S.S.R. to the enemy, thereby betrays his country, betrays his people, and is punished as an enemy of the U.S.S.R.

The object of our great Socialist state is to create for all citizens a cultured, prosperous, free and happy life.

SUCH IS THE GREAT STALIN CONSTITUTION OF THE U.S.S.R.

In the U.S.S.R., Socialism, *in the main*,[82] has been built; here all toilers work for society according to their ability and receive from society according to the amount of work they perform.

The task that lies before our country is to build Communism, under which every worker will work for society according to his abilities, and will receive from society *all the things he requires, that is, will receive*[83] according to his needs.

The party, trade unions, komsomol and pioneers. The All-Union Communist Party (Bolsheviks) leads the socialist government. In it are combined all the most active and conscious citizens from the ranks of the working class and other toiling classes. The supreme organ of the party is the congress. In the intervening time between the party congresses, important issues are resolved by the Central Committee of the Communist Party of the Soviet Union (Bolsheviks) (C.C. C.P.S.U.[B.]) and the Political Bureau of the party's Central Committee). The best people in the party are elected to the Central Committee—people who are selflessly devoted to the cause of the Soviet people, the cause of the proletarian revolution. Members of the C.P.S.U.(B.) work at every end of our immense country. All of them share a single set of viewpoints, a single set of objectives. All of them act in unison, in harmony with one another, and in an organized way. All of them uphold a single line—the party line, and there is no power in existence that can turn a Bolshevik away from the correct party line. The C.P.S.U.(B.) enjoys the selfless support of the all of the toilers. The workers and peasants of our Union firmly know that their cause is in reliable hands. The growing well-being of the country's toilers demonstrates that the path chosen by the party is correct and leads to the ultimate victory, to communism.

The Bolshevik party, led by its chief, Comrade Stalin, is based on the mass organizations of the toilers that it directs.

The mass organizations of the toilers in the U.S.S.R. are trade unions. Trade unions appeared a long time ago; they existed even before the workers possessed power in our country. All workers and office employees in the U.S.S.R. may join them. Trade Unions unite 22 million people. Lenin and Stalin have always referred to the trade unions as schools of communism.

Soviet youth also possess their own organization—the All-Union Leninist Communist Youth League (A.L.C.Y.L.—the Komsomol). The komsomol originated in 1918. In all the years of its existence, it has marched in step alongside the C.P.S.U.(B.). It has earned the moniker first assistant to the party.

Children in the U.S.S.R. also possess their own organization. The Pioneer organization dates back to 1922.

The party and komsomol do everything, so that the pioneers grew up to be deserving citizens of our wondrous country.

Stalin is our beloved chief, father and teacher. The great continuer of Lenin's cause, Comrade Stalin has given his whole life and all his energies for the liberation of the toilers of the entire world. One of his comrades created a remarkable image of Comrade Stalin and his Bolshevik steadfastness, reminiscing about the time when Stalin was in prison: ". . . When the first unit of the Saliansk regiment was beating arrested 'politicals' in 1909 by making them run the gauntlet, Stalin walked through these lines, holding his head high despite the blows of the clubs, with a book in hand. And now, after two decades' time, Stalin walks at the head of the proletariat movement, through the hateful ranks of the world bourgeoisie, with the banner of Leninism and the liberation of the working class. For more than thirty years of his unwavering service to the cause of the working class, Stalin's rigorous devotion to the revolutionary's debt has allowed him to never duck his head or have his hands shake . . ."

As Comrade Kaganovich has said of Comrade Stalin:

"The engineer of the locomotive of the revolution, Stalin knows how to

ЧЛЕНЫ ПОЛИТБЮРО ЦК ВКП(б)

Сталин И. В. (род. в 1879 г.)   Молотов В. М. (род. в 1890 г.)

Ворошилов К. Е. (род. в 1881 г.)   Калинин М. И. (род. в 1875 г.)

Каганович Л. М. (род. в 1893 г.)   Орджоникидзе Г. К. (1886—1937 гг.)

[**FIGURE 134:**] Members of the C.P.S.U.(B.) Central Committee Politburo: J. V. Stalin (1879-), V. M. Molotov (1890-), K. E. Voroshilov (1881-), M. I. Kalinin (1875-), L. M. Kaganovich (1893-), G. K. Ordjonikidze (1886–1937). [Cut by Stalin: RGASPI, f. 558, op. 11, d. 1584, l. 123ob. Also Zhdanov: f. 77, op. 1, d. 854, l. 110ob]

124

ЧЛЕНЫ ПОЛИТБЮРО ЦК ВКП(б)

Коссиор С. В. (род. в 1889 г.)　　Микоян А. И. (род. в 1895 г.)

Андреев А. А. (род. в 1896 г.)　　Чубарь В. Я. (род. в 1891 г.)

СЕКРЕТАРИ ЦК ВКП(б)

Ежов Н. И. (род. в 1895 г.)　　Жданов А. А. (род. в 1896 г.)

[**Figure 135:**] ~~Members of the C.P.S.U.(B.) Central Committee Politburo:~~
~~S. V. Kossior (1889-), A. I. Mikoyan (1895-), A. A. Andreyev (1896-),~~
~~V. Ya. Chubar (1891-). C.P.S.U.(B.) Central Committee Secretaries:~~
~~N. I. Yezhov (1895-), A. A. Zhdanov (1896-).~~ [Cut by Stalin: RGASPI, f. 558,
op. 11, d. 1584, l. 124. Also Zhdanov: f. 77, op. 1, d. 854, l. 111. Kossior was
arrested in May 1938 and Chubar in July 1938. Yezhov was removed from
his post as NKVD chief in November 1938 and arrested in April 1939]

train and unite his cadres. The strength of our movement is in the unity of
our advance brigade, in the unity of our Leninist party and its Stalinist Central Committee, which lead our country from victory to victory. The train
of the revolution is steaming with precision and confidence, firmly holding
to its schedule. The results of the completion of this firm schedule for the
First and Second Five-Year Plans are visible in the growth of our industry,
in the villages, in the collective farms and the state farms, in the gigantic
industrial factories, in the mighty arsenal of our Red Army, in the improvement of the everyday material conditions of the toilers of our motherland,
in the Spartak competitions, in our schools, in every corner of our country,
where our bright new life is blooming, where the new man is growing strong
and rising up—the new man who will be victorious throughout the whole
world.[84]

[**FIGURE 136:**] A Pioneer. [Caption added and then cut along
with illustration by Stalin: RGASPI, f. 558, op. 11, d. 1584,
l. 125. Also Zhdanov, f. 77, op. 1, d. 854, l. 1170b.]

Chronological Table[1]

911 Treaty between Oleg and the Greeks.

988 Introduction of Christianity in Russ.

~~1113 Kievan uprising against the power of the princes, merchants and usurers.[2]~~

~~1136 Novgorod uprising against the power of the princes.[3]~~

1147 First reference to Moscow in annals.

1240 Conquest of the Russian principalities by Batu.

1242 Alexander Nevsky's victory over the German Knights ("The Battle of the Ice.").

1328–1341 Ivan Kalita, the first Grand Prince of Moscow.

1380 The Battle on Kulikovo Field.

1462–1505 Ivan III, Grand Prince of Moscow.

1480 Liberation of Russia from the Tatar-Mongolian yoke in the reign of Ivan III.[4]

1547 Ivan IV adopts the title of Tsar.

1581 Yermak's march to Western Siberia.

1606–1607 Rebellion of the peasants and Cossacks under the leadership of Bolotnikov.[5]

1612 Expulsion of the Poles from Moscow.

~~1648 Uprising in Moscow against the power of the tsar.[6]~~

1648 Rebellion of the Cossacks and peasants against the Polish yoke in the Ukraine under the leadership of Bogdan Khmelnitsky.

1649 The peasants become complete serfs.

1654 The Ukraine joins Russia.

1670–1671 The peasant revolt under the leadership of Stepan Razin.[7]

1682–1725 The reign of Peter I.

1703 Foundation of Petersburg (now Leningrad).

1707 Rebellion of the Cossacks and peasants under the leadership of Bulavin.[8]

1709 Defeat of the Swedes by Peter I at Poltava.

1721 ~~Peter I adopts the~~ Title[9] of Russian Emperor *adopted by Peter*[10].

1773–1775 Rebellion of the peasants, Cossacks and peoples of the Volga and Urals under the leadership of Pugachov.[11]

1789 Beginning of the French bourgeois revolution.

1801 Annexation of Georgia by Russia.

1812 Russia's war against Napoleon I.

1818–1883 Period of life of the great leader of the proletariat, Karl Marx.

1820–1895 Period of life of the great leader of the proletariat, Frederick Engels.

1825 The Decembrist rebellion.

1848 Bourgeois revolutions in France, Germany and Austria-Hungary.

1853–1856 The Crimean War.

1861 The Peasant Reform (abolition of serfdom).

1864 Marx and Engels found the First International.

1870–1924 Period of life of the great leader of the proletariat, Vladimir Ilyich Lenin.

1871 The Paris Commune.

1879 ~~Birthdate of Joseph Vissarionovich Stalin.~~[12]

1885 Strike at the Morozov Textile Mills in Orekhovo-Zuyevo.

1903 Formation of the Russian Social-Democratic Labour Party.

1905–1907 The first ~~Russian~~ *bourgeois*[13] revolution *in Russia*[14].

1912 Workers shot down in the Lena gold fields.

1912 The Bolshevik Russian Social-Democratic Labour Party takes final shape.

1914–1918 The World Imperialist War.

1917 (February) The second ~~Russian~~ *bourgeois*[15] revolution *in Russia*[16].

1917 (October) The Great October ~~Proletarian~~ *Socialist*[17] Revolution *in Russia*[18].

1917 The formation of the Russian Soviet Federative Socialist Republics.

1918 Organization of the Red Army.

1918 Defeat of the German interventionists in the Ukraine.

1918 Revolution in Germany and Austria-Hungary.

1919 Foundation of the Communist International.

1919 Defeat of ~~the first and second Entente campaigns~~ ([19]Kolchak, Denikin *and Yudenich*)[20].

1920 ~~Defeat of the third Entente campaign (Poland and Wrangel)~~ *War against the Polish pans and the defeat of Wrangel*[21].

1922 The defeat of the Japanese interventionists in the Far East.

1922 The formation of the Union of Soviet Socialist Republics.

1928–1932 Period of the First Five-Year Plan.

1933–1937 Period of the Second Five-Year Plan.

1934 The foul murder of S. Kirov by the enemies of the people, the Trotskyites.

1936 Ratification of the ~~Great Stalin~~ *new* Constitution *of the U.S.S.R.*[22]

Appendix:
Further Revisions to Stalin's Usable Past, 1937–1955

Despite the fanfare surrounding the release of Shestakov's SHORT HISTORY OF THE USSR in 1937, its position at the center of the canon was jeopardized from the start by the ongoing Great Purge. Panicky efforts to save the text during that year presaged a struggle over the course of the following two decades to keep this official view of the past in synch with the unpredictable present. The history of the textbook's often unacknowledged new editions and the radical nature of their editorial transformations testifies to the priority that the party leadership placed on the SHORT HISTORY. This historical revisionism also reveals the degree to which the Stalin-era propaganda state strived to continuously reshape Soviet society's historical imagination.

The first signs of crisis in the new historical canon appeared just as the SHORT HISTORY was beginning to restructure curriculums in public schools and adult indoctrination courses all across the USSR in 1937. Commissar of Education Andrei Bubnov, who was credited in the text with assisting Stalin in the Bolsheviks' 1917 seizure of power, was arrested on October 17 of that year on charges of anti-Soviet terrorism. Three months later, in early 1938, Marshal Alexander Egorov, who figured into Shestakov's account of the civil war, was dismissed from his post as First Deputy Commissar of Defense and arrested for ostensibly taking part in a rightist counterrevolutionary conspiracy. Later that May, Stanislav Kosior, a Ukrainian party boss mentioned in the text in connection with the lead-up to the October 1917 uprising, was likewise arrested. Five months later, another prominent marshal who figured into the textbook's account of the civil war—Vasily Bliukher—was arrested in connection with another supposed rightist military conspiracy.

Such developments jeopardized Shestakov's SHORT HISTORY, as such arrests could transform even the most important of books overnight from catechism into contraband. The official censor, Glavlit, was under strict instructions to remove from circulation any printed material, pictorial representation, or statuary that made reference to purge victims, and history texts were particularly vulnerable in this regard.[1] For that reason, the Commissariat of Education and the Red Army's political directorate worked to censor copies of the SHORT HISTORY that were in use in schools and political study circles in order to prevent them from being seized by Glavlit. In one case, detailed orders were telegraphed to local authorities instructing them to "ink-out or paste-over the picture of the enemy of the people Egorov on page 178."[2] Andrei Zhdanov personally struck out a picture of Bliukher from a 1938 copy of the Shestakov galleys that already had eliminated mention of Egorov, Bubnov, and Kosior.[3] Surviving copies of the SHORT HISTORY today reveal not only the blacked-out names of Bubnov, Kosior, Egorov, and Bliukher but also newspaper clippings glued over portraits of the latter two.[4]

Contrary to expectations, the conclusion to the purges' bloodletting in 1939 did not necessarily stabilize the situation on the textbook front. This was because in the wake of the signing of the Molotov-Ribbentrop pact with Nazi Germany that August, orders were given to delete invectives directed against "fascists" from the public school curriculum. Surviving copies of the Shestakov text reveal teachers to have inked out all mention of "fascists" in chapter 15, replacing them with the term "imperialists" in the margins.[5] Such political and historiographic instability halted a planned second edition of the Shestakov text in early 1940 and vastly complicated simultaneous work under way on more sophisticated history narratives ranging from Anna Pankratova's advanced textbook to readers on ancient, medieval, and modern world history.[6] Most would appear too late for the start of the 1940–1941 school year.

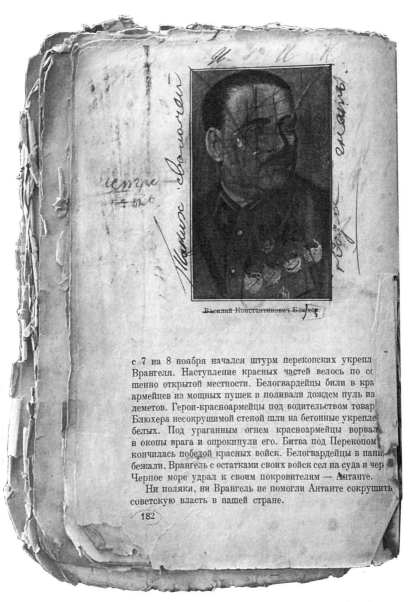

[**Figure 137:**] A page from the 1937 Short History with a defaced portrait of Vasily Bliukher flanked by the handwritten note: "We need to know such bastards." Collection of the author.

The 1938 English edition. The English translation of Shestakov's
Short History that lies at the center of this critical edition managed to
capture in type some of the ad hoc editing described previously when it
was sent to press in late 1938. Aside from deleting all mention of Egorov
from the text, this edition replaced its portrait of the fallen marshal with
a new picture of the Civil War martyr Sergei Lazo, who died early enough
in the Soviet period to ensure that he would never risk subsequent expo-
sure as an enemy of the people. Bubnov was likewise stripped from the
text in an editorial maneuver that required the deletion of all of Stalin's
other collaborators in October 1917, leaving him in exclusive command of
the party organization that supposedly coordinated the Bolshevik seizure
of power. This editing also replaced an illustration based on a 1935 painting
by Svarog featuring Stalin, Bubnov, Yakov Sverdlov, Felix Dzerzhinsky, and

[**Figure 138:**] Alexander Yakovlevich Parkhomenko. Hero of the
Civil War. [Istoriia SSSR: Kratkii kurs (1941), 182]

Moisei Uritsky with a more anodyne drawing of Vladimir Lenin flanked by Stalin and a handful of anonymous Red Guards. Kosior, it should be said, mysteriously escaped deletion from the text, despite his arrest in May 1938; Bliukher remained in the text because he was arrested only after the book was published.[7]

The 1941 edition. Sent to press on December 12, 1940, the second Russian edition of the SHORT HISTORY emerged under a slightly new title reminiscent of the recently published 1938 SHORT COURSE on party history.[8] Aside from this minor correction, it also reproduced all of the political editing of the 1938 English edition described earlier. Mention of Kosior and Bliukher was removed as well, with the latter's portrait being replaced by one of the lesser-known Alexander Parkhomenko.[9]

Aside from that, the 1941 edition also interpolated a handful of new elements into the domestic narrative. According to Shestakov, during the Time of Troubles, "the Russian people produced many heroes" including Ivan Susanin, a peasant who in 1612 misled a detachment of Polish troops advancing on Moscow into an intractable forest—a feat that he paid for with his life. Susanin was likely inserted into the text in connection with the rehabilitation of Mikhail Glinka's nineteenth-century opera A LIFE FOR THE TSAR during these years. In more recent history, the new edition offered a rewritten narrative on the 1937–1938 purges that captured the full breadth of the omnipresent conspiracy that had supposedly linked the left and right opposition with nationalists in the republics and capitalists abroad.[10]

The 1941 edition also reflected the changing diplomatic realities of the last prewar years. In 1937, chapter 11 had laid special blame for the start of World War I on Germany, insofar as Berlin had supposedly looked upon Britain, France, and Russia "with particular hatred" on account of their colonial empires. This gratuitous language disappeared from the SHORT HISTORY after the USSR's signing of the Molotov-Ribbentrop nonaggression treaty with Nazi Germany in August 1939. Similar motives likely explain editing in chapter 13 that deleted descriptions of the Brest-Litovsk treaty as "humiliating" and the German occupation of Ukraine as being marked by the repression of local Bolsheviks. Still another passage was cut from the 1937 edition that mourned the loss of territory to Poland in 1920, perhaps because the USSR had just avenged this indignity by dismembering that country with its new Nazi allies.[11]

Such editing foreshadowed the interpolation of an entirely new four-page subsection in chapter 15, justifying the signing of the Nazi-Soviet pact and the acquisition of new territory that accompanied it. Framing the events within the context of Soviet defense policy, the textbook explained that the USSR was committed to peace through strength and had demonstrated this position both through military clashes with Japan in 1938–1939 and the signing of the recent nonaggression treaty with Germany. Then, after Germany attacked Poland that September, the USSR ostensibly felt compelled to intervene after the Polish government collapsed in order to defend the country's Ukrainian and Belorussian minorities. According to Shestakov, the eastern regions of Poland subsequently petitioned to join the USSR in order to unify with the Ukrainian and Belorussian Soviet republics.[12]

According to the SHORT HISTORY, Britain and France's declaration of war against Nazi Germany in support of Poland in September 1939 triggered the start of a "second imperialist war" that directly threatened Soviet security. Seeking to strengthen its defensive positions, the USSR signed nonaggression pacts with Lithuania, Latvia, and Estonia and sought a similar agreement with Finland, complete with security guarantees for Leningrad. Finnish resistance resulted in what Shestakov described as a defensive conflict with Finland in 1939–1940 to provide the northern capital with a better security perimeter and Finnish-speaking Karelians with a republic of their own. Duplicity on the part of the Baltic states in defiance of the new nonaggression treaties then supposedly led the USSR to demand political changes in these states that would restore the alliances. According to the SHORT HISTORY, these demands led Lithuania, Latvia, and Estonia to formally petition to join the USSR as new Soviet republics. The territorial acquisitions were followed by more adjustments in the southwest when Soviet diplomats asked Romania to return territory in Bessarabia and Northern Bukovina that had been occupied in 1918. Bucharest's agreement to this request, according to Shestakov, led to the peaceful formation of yet another new Soviet republic—Moldavia—and stronger security perimeter for the USSR.[13]

Amid these tectonic shifts, the SHORT HISTORY made a series of more subtle changes to its discussion of revolutionary working class movements abroad. As noted above, in 1937, Stalin had deleted most of the textbook's discussion of the Comintern and reduced the attention that it paid to the oppression of ordinary working people in fascist Germany, Spain, and China. That said, he preserved mention of the USSR's leadership of the anti-fascist Popular Front and its coalition of international leftist organizations. Now, in 1941, in the wake of the Molotov-Ribbentrop Pact, not only was more commentary on the Comintern cut, but all mention of the Popular Front disappeared from the text as well.

Similar editing revised warnings about fascists in 1937 to focus on war-mongers in 1941.[14] Aside from these moments of political pragmatism, the 1941 edition offered new commentary on other key moments in Soviet history. Expectations for world revolution between 1917 and 1920 were lowered as mention of a "revolution" in Germany in 1919 was downgraded to an "uprising." And the SHORT HISTORY's account of the Great Purges was expanded to broaden the scale of the antiparty conspiracy (both in chronological terms and in terms of membership) and its impacts (regarding the number of Bolsheviks allegedly assassinated by the conspirators).[15]

All in all, the changes to the 1941 edition were designed to resolve issues that had likely confounded Soviet propagandists since 1937. That said, the fact that this new edition was approved for publication only in late 1940 meant that it did not make it into classrooms before the end of the school year in May 1941.[16] Needless to say, much of the new editing was then rendered obsolete only a month later when Nazi Germany attacked the USSR on June 22, 1941.

The 1945 edition. Although the Nazi attack made mockery of the 1941 edition of the Shestakov text, a new edition would not make it to press until the conclusion of the war in 1945. Worse, wartime exigencies precluded even normal print runs of the 1941 edition, leaving many classrooms to quietly make do with the original 1937 text. The reasons for this negligence in regard to the canon are a bit unclear. True, Shestakov died of natural causes in June 1941, just after the start of the war, but later editions of his text would be issued without him through 1955. Perhaps a better explanation for the lack of an updated edition is that Stalin, Zhdanov, and other ideological authorities were too busy to participate the revision process, leaving the editorial board at the State Instructional-Pedagogical Publishing House confused over how to narrate the war. Evidence suggests that only in 1945 did the publishers finally develop a new edition for release that fall.[17]

This first postwar edition of the SHORT HISTORY offered a thoroughly revised narrative for a redesigned public school curriculum. Stressing the thousand-year pedigree of Russian statehood, the textbook began with an introduction that included two new sentences hailing Soviet society's history of rebuffing foreign attackers. The most recent experience with German and Japanese invaders, the textbook averred, had left the USSR mightier than ever before. Earlier lines forecasting a rapid growth of socialist prosperity were deleted to accommodate this new militancy.[18]

Within the SHORT HISTORY's first few chapters, the stress of the narrative was altered to downplay early Slavic underdevelopment and reinforce the deep history of regional state building. Although this did not lead the SHORT HISTORY to alter its account of how the Varangians eventually took power in the region, it did describe them as encountering more local Slavic resistance. This editing was then complemented by an interpolation that characterized the Varangian conquest as little more than a pyrrhic victory: "The Varangian princes and their retinues did not have a more advanced culture than the Slavs; they quickly intermixed with the Slavs and adopted their language, faith, naming traditions, and customs."[19]

After the decline of Kiev, the textbook stressed the prosperity of Novgorod in part by moving an illustration to this section depicting foreign merchants unloading wares at the city's wharves that had originally appeared later in the book. At the same time, detail about how the local Veche counterbalanced the city's prince and nobles was deleted, as were discussions of popular restiveness during these years. This editing combined to suggest that the region was distinguished by stability and economic growth rather than what Shestakov had originally described as an unusually democratic political order.[20]

In chapter 3's treatment of the so-called Tatar-Mongol yoke, the new edition made several important interpretive changes. Discussion was cut of the Orthodox Church's support for the region's new overlords. Accompanying commentary was also deleted about how parish clergy counselled the local Slavic population to obey their new Tatar masters. This editing likely stemmed from the recent wartime rehabilitation of the church and the reestablishment of the Moscow Patriarchate in 1943. Similar editing anachronistically promoted Alexander Nevsky as a "great Russian military commander," reflecting how he had been celebrated during World War II. Even more striking were two revisions that replaced detail about Muscovite campaigns again the Poles and Lithuanians at the end of the fourteenth century with an account of how those neighbors had allied with Muscovy in 1410 against the Teutonic knights at the Battle of Grunwald. Such editorial decisions did not lead to the deletion of other material in the chapter about the geopolitical rivalry between Muscovy and the nascent Polish-Lithuanian Commonwealth, but they did provide an anachronistic precedent for these peoples' alliance against another German enemy between 1941 and 1945.[21]

The 1945 edition also promoted Russian state building by revising its characterization of Ivan Kalita. If Shestakov in 1937 had cast the prince as a greedy medieval warlord who sought personal profit during his service as a Tatar vassal, Stalin had altered this characterization to stress his supported for the Muscovite cause. Now, in 1945, the editors of the textbook unknowingly edited Stalin's interpolation in order to further strengthen Kalita's identity as a statist:

> Thus, ~~resorting to every means,~~ Kalita gathered the disunited Russian principalities into a single state with Moscow its centre.[22]

Descendants of Kalita enjoyed the same treatment. Prince Dmitry Donskoi, for instance, earned the moniker "exceptional military commander" for his defeat of Tatar forces at the 1380 Battle of Kulikov Field. Also worthy of note is the 1945 edition's reframing of the battle itself, in flagrantly anachronistic terms:

> *The Battle of Kulikov Field has the greatest historical importance: it united the Russian people in the struggle for their national independence, inspired them to believe in their own strength, and upset the monolithic Tatar Yoke.*[23]

Although the editors made no substantial changes to the 1945 edition's fourth chapter—"The Rise of the Russian National State"—they did alter the narrative on Ivan the Terrible in chapter 5. Cutting down the account of how the boyars had emotionally abused the future tsar in his minority, they recharacterized the nature of the tsar's changes in governance at the start of his reign. Rejecting the notion that Ivan had impetuously declared himself autocrat and ruled while "ignoring the boyars," this edition described Ivan as making the rational decision to choose his own advisors. According to the new passage, Ivan, "not trusting the boyars, turned to rely on the lower nobility and landowners." Later in the chapter, the editors reiterated Ivan's commitment to the centralization of state power instead of personalistic rule. In the section concerning the Oprichnina, they revised several key sentences:

> After the first defeats in the war, Ivan discovered that he was being betrayed by the big patrimonial boyars. These traitors went into the service of the Poles and Lithuanians. Tsar Ivan ~~hated the boyars, who lived in their patrimonies like little tsars and tried to limit his autocratic power~~ *waged a harsh struggle with the boyars, who opposed the unification of the country and the strengthening of the tsar's autocratic power.* ~~He began to banish and execute the rich and strong boyars~~ *He executed many of the boyars and their supporters, while banishing others to distant regions of the state. He confiscated their lands and distributed it to the smaller pomeshchiks (the lesser nobility).* He thought it necessary to fight the boyars in order to crush these little tsars *that these boyars were* and to strengthen ~~his position as sole ruler~~ *the central power.* To fight the boyars he recruited from among the pomeshchiks a special force, several thousand strong. This force he called the OPRICHNIKS.

Such editing had the effect of edging Ivan's estate-representative monarchy closer to absolutism than Shestakov or Stalin had ever intended.[24]

Additional changes were made to descriptions of Ivan's military campaigns to further support the notion of rational, pragmatic rule. Details of the fall of Kazan concerning the popular defense of the city and its subsequent destruction were deleted to keep the narrative focused on state building. And Ivan's unsuccessful campaigns in the Baltics against the Germanic Teutonic knights were recast as initially successful until the Poles, Swedes and Danes combined forces to cheat him of victory. This editing left the textbook's overall evaluation of Ivan's reign mixed, but clearly favoring his status as a progressive state builder.[25]

Chapter 6 underwent revisions reflective of the same sort of state-building priorities, albeit on a more minor scale. First, although the leitmotif of backwardness late in the chapter was designed to set up the Petrine revolution detailed in chapter 7, embarrassing facts about seventeenth-century Muscovite governance were nevertheless eliminated from the text. In particular, discussion of the chaotic bureaucracy was cut, as was apparently gratuitous commentary on bribe-taking. The 1945 edition also muted earlier printings' hyperbole about how traditional peasant healers had mistreated the sick, how the church had tortured dissidents, and how the state had pacified commoners with alcohol. Deletion of such detail allowed the editors to make the case that modernization was more concerned with the affairs of state than social or cultural development.[26]

The editing of chapter 6 also revealed a subtle recharacterization of tensions in the western borderlands. Most notably, in describing Ukrainian restiveness under the Polish-Lithuanian Commonwealth in the mid-1600s, commentary was cut concerning the economic exploitation that had catalyzed the tensions. This reframed the conflict from a socioeconomic one into something focusing on national identity. This same agenda likely explains why some negative details about the serf-owning Cossack hetman Bogdan Khmelnitsky were deleted from the text. Ultimately, such editorial changes transformed the complex Khmelnitsky into an iconic national hero who sought Muscovite shelter for his Cossack elites and their Ukrainian subjects.[27]

Editorial work on 1945's version of chapter 7 also reflected the more general theme of Russian martial strength. Detail was added to the textbook's commentary on the 1709 Battle of Poltava to stress that the Swedish forces were defeated specifically "by the Russian regular army." "Peter's own role" in the battle, the text averred, "was especially notable." Several pages later, more detail was added about military victories under Catherine the Great. "Especially celebrated," according to the SHORT HISTORY, was the Seven Years' War, "when German forces were defeated and the city of Berlin was captured in 1760." This stress on Russian military valor was complemented by the deletion of less flattering commentary, first on Peter's Dagestan campaign and the popular resistance that it catalyzed, and then on Catherine's suppression of Bashkir resistance during the Pugachev rebellion. Although these changes were not as revisionist as those in chapter 5, they did serve to enhance the reputation of Russian military might.[28]

Similar priorities were advanced elsewhere in the chapter to rehabilitate elements of eighteenth-century Russian imperialism. First, the polarizing subchapter heading "Catherine II Conquers New Lands and Subjugates New Peoples" was sanitized to "Catherine II Conquers New Lands." Second, prejudicial detail on the acquisition of Crimea was deleted, including Catherine's bribing of the Tatar nobility and her Russian landlords' abuse of Tatar commoners. Third, the arresting description of Catherine's partitioning of Poland as a "seizure" of Polish lands was cut. Fourth, Russian imperialism in Kazakhstan was recast as less of a conquest and more of an invitation to empire by local elites.[29] Finally, the editors concluded the chapter by cutting a bitterly anti-imperialist line about how the eighteenth century had seen Poles, Crimean Tatars, Azerbaidzhanis, and the Kazakhs join "the numerous peoples groaning under the rule of tsarism." This is not to say that the chapter now read as a thoroughgoing apologia for Russian colonialism, but it did attempt to normalize one of the most unsavory aspects of tsarist rule.[30]

Revisions to chapter 8 advanced this active reframing of Russian imperialism into the nineteenth century. Insofar as Stalin's objections to special criticism of the so-called Russian gendarme had been published after the 1941 edition of the SHORT HISTORY went to press, the editors corrected chapter 8's title from "Tsarist Russia, the Gendarme of Europe" to the less polarizing "Tsarist Russia at the End of the XVIII and First Half of the XIX Centuries." When the chapter turned to Alexander I's epic conflict with Napoleon, Shestakov's reference—"The War of 1812 with Napoleon"—was transformed in three places into the tsarist-era term "The Patriotic War of 1812" to evoke a closer association with the 1941–1945 conflict, which was known in the USSR as "The Great Patriotic War." Other elements were added to the chapter to reinforce this sense of patriotism. An illustration of Napoleon on Red Square in Moscow in 1812 was replaced by a reproduction of Roman Volkov's famous 1813 portrait of Kutuzov. This was accompanied by a new character sketch of the general that descried him as Suvorov's favorite pupil and credited him with saving the Russian army from certain defeat in 1812 (something that Shestakov had originally attributed to the Russian winter). Textual interpolations stressed the fact that the Russian army enjoyed the support of the whole society, including Ukrainians, Belorussians, Tatars, Bashkirs, and others. This impression of unity was then reinforced by the addition of a reproduction of Illarion Prianishkinov's 1874 canvas depicting the Grande Armée's retreat from Russia.[31]

Curiously, the 1945 version of chapter 8 did not go to similar lengths to sanitize the history of the Crimean War. Criticizing the general staff and its equipping of the army, the chapter conceded that the war had exposed the weaknesses of the empire and its armed forces. That said, the editors felt it necessary to differentiate this underwhelming performance from the steady valor of the common soldier. Deleting a defeatist phrase about how "Russian soldiers died in hundreds every day" at Sevastopol, they replaced it with the statement that "Russian soldiers fought heroically, stubbornly defending the city." They also interpolated into this section mention of how this dogged defense of the port had been coordinated by the famous Admiral Pavel Nakhimov, after whom officer academies and a new military decoration had been named between 1943 and 1944.[32]

The editors of the 1945 edition made fewer changes to chapters 9 and 10. Aside from stylistic corrections, they added one line to chapter 9 about how Russia's 1877 war with the Ottoman empire liberated two Slavic peoples in the Balkans—the Serbs and Bulgarians—and gave Romania its independence. Such commentary was likely designed to foreshadow the Soviet Union's 1944–1945 campaigns in the region. Mention of Vasily Surikov was likewise added to a discussion of the realist painter Ilya Repin to bolster the ranks of Russian artists engaged in civic activism. In chapter 10, only one substantial change was made to soften a demoralizing description of the Japanese army "routing" the tsarist army at Mukden in 1905.[33]

More alterations were made to chapter 11 concerning World War I. Early in the chapter, a subheading was corrected from the negative-sounding "Defeat of Russia in the War" to the more neutral "Tsarist Russia at War." Commentary that had been cut from the 1941 edition about how prewar Germany had looked with envy upon on British, French, and Russian colonies was restored. Similarly, France's ambitions in regard to Alsace-Lorraine were normalized from "seizing" the region to "returning" lands that "had been occupied by Germany" in 1871. Detail was also added that stressed the Austro-Hungarian and German role in starting the war while deleting other commentary implicating the Second International.[34]

Deeper into the chapter, positive mention was added about the Russian general Alexei Brusilov's successful 1916 offensive against Austro-Hungary, which was described as forcing Germany to redeploy troops in a way that provided relief to the British, French, and Italians on the western front. This positive coverage was carefully balanced by material on how the Russian general staff and tsarist court proved unable to take advantage of this "Brusilov breakthrough," in part because they failed to supply the front with sufficient arms and equipment. Fascinatingly, if the 1937 edition had blamed part of Russia's poor performance in the war on the fact that the tsarina and her ministers and generals had leaked military secrets to the Germans, the 1945 edition claimed only that German spies had infiltrated the government and general staff.[35]

Chapters 12, 13, and 14 largely escaped editing in 1945. Aside from a few stylistic changes, the only real alteration in chapter 12 involved the shortening of a statement regarding how Trotsky, Kamenev, and Zinoviev had tried to sabotage the October 1917 seizure of power. Deleting any speculation regarding motive, the new passage stressed only the treachery itself, as if to say that the explanation was irrelevant. In chapter 13, four major corrections acted to displace the civil war from the center of the Soviet period's historical narrative. First, portraits of Semen Budenny, Valery Kuibyshev, and Sergo Orzhonidikze were shifted to chapter 15, while Parkhomenko was deleted entirely. Second, the Caucasus conspiracy that led to the execution of the legendary twenty-six Baku commissars, which the 1937 edition had breathlessly blamed on the "Mussavatists, the enemies of the Azerbaidzhani people, along with the Mensheviks and SRs," was now attributed more generically to local nationalists and foreigners. (Editing later in the chapter revised mention of Georgian Mensheviks, SRs, Armenian Dashnaks, and Azerbaidzhani Mussavatists in a similar fashion.) Third, discussion of revolutionary tensions across Europe in 1919 was scaled back in 1945 to focus just on Germany and Hungary, in order to lower expectations for this unrest. Fourth, information on the Comintern's international significance was cut, insofar as the institution had been shuttered by Stalin in 1943. More material on the Comintern was deleted from Stalin's famous eulogy at Lenin's funeral, which was prominently featured in chapter 14.[36]

Chapter 15 inevitably endured major revisions in 1945, inasmuch as it had to be expanded to cover World War II. That said, its prewar sections also underwent considerable editing. Perhaps most striking is the deletion of some of the chapter's triumphalism. Its title was revised in 1945 from "The USSR is the Land of Victorious Socialism" to the more modest "The Stalinist Five-Year Plans and the Great Patriotic War." Other hyperbole about accomplishing "the plan of great works" was also deleted, as was mention that Lazar Kaganovich had thoroughly transformed rail transportation "in short order." Detail on unrealized policy targets was also deleted, such as promises of free higher education, "mountains of goods" and "billions of poods of products of agriculture." Most dramatic was the deletion of a series of ambitious predictions about the material goals of socialist construction:

> ~~The object of our great Socialist state is to create for all citizens a cultured, prosperous, free and happy life.~~
> ~~Such is the great Stalin Constitution of the U.S.S.R.~~
> ~~In the U.S.S.R., Socialism, in the main, has been built; here all toilers work for society according to their ability and receive from society according to the amount of work they perform.~~
> ~~The task that lies before our country is to build Communism, under which every worker will work for society according to his abilities, and will receive from society all the things he requires, that is, will receive according to his needs.~~

The deletion of text like this rendered socialism less utopian and communism's promise of prosperity further away.[37]

Later in the chapter, the textbook's account of the Great Purges and their aftermath was again revised. As before, the text affirmed the leftist Trotskyites' and rightist Bukharinites' connection to foreign espionage agencies, under whose direction they had engaged in economic wrecking and plotted the defeat and partitioning of the USSR. Curiously, however, these groups were now stripped of their "fascist" label and the accusation that they had planned to assassinate the Soviet leadership. Perhaps such details seemed unnecessarily hyperbolic in the wake of the war.[38]

Discussion of Soviet foreign policy in the SHORT HISTORY also underwent a major change in 1945. This included the deletion of a series of paragraphs about the USSR's antiwar position in the late 1930s, including a quotation on the subject by Stalin. Such prewar statements now probably looked naïve or foolish in retrospect. Another long paragraph from the 1937 edition about how the USSR was the fatherland of the world proletariat and enjoyed the support of German, British, French, Italian, Japanese, Polish, and American workers—material that had been dropped from the 1941 edition—was rewritten to suggest that the USSR enjoyed social support in countries ranging from Britain and the United States to Czechoslovakia, Yugoslavia, Poland, China, and Iran.[39]

Although the 1945 edition retained mention of the Molotov-Ribbentrop Pact, it downgraded expectations for this pact by explicitly describing Adolf Hitler as a warmonger with plans for world domination and the enslavement of all non-Aryans. Ignoring the dictator's genocidal fixation on Judeo-Bolshevism, the textbook averred that "most of all, Hitler wanted to enslave all the Slavs—Czechoslovaks, Poles, Belorussians, Ukrainians, Russians, and others." This edition also detailed the USSR's prewar annexation of Polish territory, the Baltic states, and Bessarabia, but with less detail, triumphalism, and connection to the Molotov-Ribbentrop treaty. Much the same approach governed a newly sober discussion of the Soviet-Finnish war and the formation of the Karelian Soviet Socialist Republic.[40]

Elsewhere, a new stress on prewar patriotism was revealed in the addition of commentary noting that through their hard work, the Soviet people had "strengthened their beloved Motherland." This anticipated a much more grim subsection about how the USSR did not desire conflict but was

[**FIGURE 139:**] Kliment Yefremovich Voroshilov. [ISSSR (1945), 250]

[**FIGURE 140:**] Semen Mikhailovich Budenny. [ISSSR (1945), 251]

prepared to go to war to defend its independence—a prophesy of sorts reinforced by the anachronistic updating of portraits of Kliment Voroshilov and Budenny to depict them in their wartime uniforms.[41]

Such editing anticipated the interpolation of a substantial new section to chapter 15 on World War II, referred to in Soviet parlance as the Great Patriotic War. This section began with a discussion of the Germans' treacherous violation of the Nazi-Soviet nonaggression treaty on June 22, 1941. Stalin, the SHORT HISTORY averred, responded immediately to this surprise attack by rallying the peoples of the USSR together in the defense of the country. At his command, Soviets of all ethnicities fought at the front, served in partisan detachments behind German lines and worked in the rear in the name of victory. This commentary drew attention to a handful of emblematic Soviet heroes ranging from the soldiers Alexander Matrossov and Torunsabaev to the pilots Nikolai Gastello and Gazret Aliev. Also detailed was the semimythical role that twenty-eight guards from the Panfilov regiment played in the defense of Moscow.[42]

Acknowledgment was also made of the United States' and Britain's contributions to the war effort—in terms of both Lend-Lease and the opening of the second front in North Africa in 1942 and Normandy in 1944. Explanation was also added about why the USSR had been left to fight the Nazis single-handedly until mid-1944 (that the United States and Great Britain ostensibly had been unprepared for war until then). The text concluded with passing mention of the USSR's contribution to the defeat of Japan before crediting victory in 1945 to the Soviet people. Here, it singled out the Russians for their role in the war, obliquely quoting Stalin's infamous russocentric postwar toast hailing "the Russian people, who are the most outstanding of all the nations who inhabit the Soviet Union."[43]

A substantial addition to the SHORT HISTORY, this new section of chapter 15 was also graced with an array of new illustrations, ranging from portraits of Stalin and Georgy Zhukov to pictures of Soviet tanks in Berlin, fireworks in Moscow, and the official victory medal inscribed with Stalin's profile and the slogan "Our Cause Was Just and We Were Victorious."[44] As is evident from this description, although chapter 15 advanced a statist agenda that it shared with the rest of the textbook, it was much more explicit than previous chapters in its celebration of popular agency and grassroots activism.

[**FIGURE 141:**] Supreme Commander and Generalissimo Joseph Vissarionovich Stalin. [ISSR (1945), 265]

[**FIGURE 142:**] Marshal of the Soviet Union Georgy Konstantinovich Zhukov. [ISSR (1945), 269]

The 1947 edition. Only a handful of revisions were made to the SHORT HISTORY two years later when several million more volumes of the text were ordered from the publisher.[45] Much of this editing picked up on earlier efforts to soften the imperialist nature of tsarist-era Russian expansionism. Terms referring to the "seizure" (ZAKHVAT) of territory were downgraded to the less pejorative "conquest" (ZAVOEVANIE) or the effectively neutral "incorporation" (PRISOEDINENIE) of new lands.[46]

Within the text's account of the Soviet period, pragmatism and caution over excessively utopian expectations for socialism factored into 1947's editing. In chapter 15's commentary on the new social contract embodied in the 1936 Stalin Constitution, for instance, a line about how the state would "take care of the old and sick" was changed to the more modest assurance that it would "provide aid" to them. Similar caution governed the edition's coverage of the start of postwar reconstruction. Here, attention was given to the 1946 elections, the announcement of a new Five-Year Plan, the renaming of commissariats as ministries, and Nikolai Shvernik's appointment as chair of the USSR Supreme Soviet. Despite the addition of a new portrait of

[**FIGURE 143:**] Chair of the Presidium of the USSR Supreme
Soviet Nikolai Mikhailovich Shvernik.
[ISSR (1947), 274]

Shvernik to flank this new commentary, it was a lifeless and schematic coda
to the SHORT HISTORY's dynamic account of the war.[47]

The 1951 edition. Several important revisions were made to the SHORT
HISTORY when a new print run was authorized in April 1951.[48] Most important was a veritable coup regarding the application of the "lesser evil"
thesis to the tsarist empire's annexation of the Caucasus in the nineteenth
century. What had been referred to in earlier editions as a "conquest" was
now described more favorably as an "incorporation" justified by Russia's
willingness to defend the region against Ottoman and Persian depredation.
No longer the lesser of two evils, this annexation was characterized as a
wholly positive and progressive historical development:

> *Incorporation of the peoples of the Caucasus into Russia allowed them to grow
> closer to the Russian people. They became acquainted with the advanced Russian
> culture. Subsequently, the peoples of the Caucasus would struggle alongside the
> Russian people against the tsar, landlords, and capitalists.*[49]

Equally stunning was the edition's turnabout in regard to the characterization of the Dagestani imam Shamil, who had been described positively since 1937 as the leader of his highlander people's resistance to tsarist imperialism. Now, instead of a freedom fighter, Shamil was described as a pawn of local anti-Russian elites and an agent of Ottoman and British imperialism. Alleged to have incited Muslims against their Russian neighbors, Shamil was held responsible for a long and bloody rebellion. In the end, the SHORT HISTORY averred, Shamil's followers finally grasped his treachery and deserted him, leading to his defeat. This allowed Russia to complete its benevolent incorporation of the Caucasus into its empire.[50]

When the text turned to the second half of the nineteenth century, it expanded the narrative's pantheon of prerevolutionary heroes. Alluding to Lenin's maxim that in every capitalist society, there was a democratic nation as well as a reactionary one, the SHORT HISTORY not only invoked artists like Lev Tolstoi, Repin, and Surikov but also now added to their ranks a host of new scientists. Discussion of the chemist Dmitry Mendeleev was complemented by detail on Ivan Sechenov, a researcher who focused on the human brain. Nikolai Zhukovsky was credited with discoveries that made flight possible. And Alexander Popov was hailed for inventing the radio. Portraits of Mendeleev and Popov flanked discussions that anticipated a similar focus on the accomplishments of Soviet science detailed in chapter 15. Such commentary reflected a new postwar fixation with prerevolutionary Russian cultural primacy and was clearly meant to demonstrate tsarist-era society to have been advanced rather than underdeveloped.[51]

When the text turned to the Soviet period, it left much of the previous editions' commentary in place. Predictably, more material on the Comintern was cut. This edition also broadened its predecessors' attempts to rein in unrealistic, hyperbolic commentary about Soviet socialism, resulting in the deletion of claims of how the economy was now be able to "produce everything that people need for their lives." Reckless talk about the war, too, was cut, such as the claim that "people happily gave up their lives for the motherland."[52]

More significant changes also affected the text's commentary on the war—particularly the allied alliance. Although earlier postwar discussions had credited the United States and Great Britain with Lend-Lease and the eventual opening of the second front, Cold War tensions during the early

1950s now made this impossible. Such discussions were therefore replaced by a more partisan assessment of the allies' contributions to the war effort:

> *England and the United States of America delayed opening a second front against the German forces in Europe in every way possible for three years. But when the enormous victories of the Soviet Army made it clear that the Soviet Union might completely defeat the enemy alone, occupy Germany and liberate all of western Europe, including France, England and the USA opened a second front in Europe.*

This bitter revisionism also muzzled any discussion about the combined allied assault on Germany between 1944 and 1945 and Japan after that—editing that effectively gave the USSR sole credit for winning the war. A different sort of revisionism resulted in the deletion of mention of Zhukov and Ivan Konev, insofar as these generals had fallen from official favor in the late 1940s. Zhukov's disgrace was signaled by the fact that his portrait was replaced by a new one of Nikolai Bulganin.[53]

[**FIGURE 144:**] Nikolai Aleksandrovich Bulganin. [ISSR (1951), 280]

The 1954 edition. More changes were made to the first post-Stalin edition of the SHORT HISTORY before it was sent to press in October 1953 some six months after the dictator's death.[54] Editing in the early chapters of the text continued to tone down the colonial nature of Russian expansionism, with instances of "seizure" and "conquest" being replaced by "incorpora-tion" and even "unification" (VOSSEDINENIE). Particularly worthy of note was this edition's new treatment of Khmelnitsky's seventeenth-century up-rising, which was reframed as an "emancipatory war against the oppression of the Polish pans." Here, the 1954 text credited Khmelnitsky with assem-bling a peasant fighting force (instead of a Cossack one) that consisted not only of Ukrainians but also of Belorussians and Poles. This had the effect of bolstering the hetman's reputation in three important ways. First, it cut mention of Khmelnitsky's status as a serf-owning landlord committed to the Cossack elite. Second, it deleted acknowledgment of the hetman's will-ingness to consider a Polish alliance. Third, it crossed out of the narrative all traces of Khmelnitsky's more humble rival Maxim Krivonos.

Such editing led to a thorough recasting of the 1654 annexation of Ukraine itself. Overturning Zhdanov's original characterization of Khmel-nitsky's decision to align with Russia as the lesser of two evils, the SHORT HISTORY now described this choice in wholly positive terms. "The Ukrai-nians," the textbook averred, "saw their salvation from foreign invaders in unification with the great Russian people." This notion of a joyous reunion of Slavic peoples was then reinforced by the deletion of all discussion of how the Ukrainian peasantry subsequently found Russian rule to include a more exploitative form of serfdom than they had ever experienced before.[55] Similar editing in the next chapter also reframed the acquisition of left-bank Ukraine and Crimea under Catherine the Great as an "incorporation" rather than a "conquest."[56]

Few changes of note were made to the text's treatment of the Soviet period. Predictably, the 1954 edition expanded earlier commentary on the postwar period, replacing detail on the 1946 elections, the 1947 Five-Year Plan and Shvernik's promotion with new attention to the 1952 Nineteenth Party Congress and the second postwar Five-Year Plan. Its portrait of Shvernik was replaced by one of Georgy Malenkov, flanked by an updated one of Voroshilov. Central to these new interpolations were several solemn new paragraphs about Stalin's death in March 1953. Commentary balanced the text's overall stress on postwar state building with mention of how the Soviet people rallied tightly around the communist party after the dicta-tor's passing. The SHORT HISTORY then concluded by assuring its read-ership that the country would henceforth be led by people like Malenkov

[**Figure 145:**] Chair of the Presidium of the USSR Supreme Soviet Kliment Yefremovich. Voroshilov [ISSR (1954), 280]

[**Figure 146:**] Chair of the USSR Council of Ministers Georgy Maksimilianovich Malenkov. [ISSR (1954), 281]

and Voroshilov, "Lenin and Stalin's faithful and experienced students and comrades-in-arms."[57]

1955 edition. A handful of additional changes were made to what was to be the final edition of the SHORT HISTORY before it was sent to press in June 1955.[58] Most interesting was the deletion of propagandistic rhetoric in the introduction claiming that "there is only one Socialist country in the world" and that "in no other country in the world is there such friendship among the various peoples"—editing needed to acknowledge the progressive character of the USSR's new eastern European satellites and the People's Republic of China. Other changes were more routine. Another usage of "incorporation" in regard to the colonization of Ukraine was switched to "unification." Continuing Cold War tensions provoked the interpolation of the United States into a list of foreign interventionists during the civil war. And discussion of domestic politics at the end of the textbook was altered to reflect the ongoing struggle for power among Stalin's former comrades in arms. Commentary on Malenkov was replaced by new material on Nikita Khrushchev, with Khrushchev's portrait displacing Malenkov's. New pictures of Voroshilov and Bulganin in civilian dress replaced older ones of them in uniform as space was again made for a portrait of Khrushchev ally

[**FIGURE 147:**] First Secretary
of the Communist Party of the
Soviet Union Nikita Sergeevich
Khrushchev. [ISSR (1955), 279]

[**FIGURE 148:**] Chair of the
Presidium of the USSR Supreme
Soviet Nikolai Aleksandrovich.
Bulganin. [ISSSR (1955), 281]

Shvernik. These images flanked new paragraphs reaffirming the USSR's commitment to heavy industry and noting how it would facilitate the expansion of agriculture and light industry. The text concluded with a statement about how the working people of the Soviet motherland were steadily advancing toward communism under the wise guidance of the party.[59]

In the chronological table at the end of the book, minor but telling changes were also made. Another instance of "incorporation" was replaced by "unification," while Polish suzerainty over Ukraine before 1654 was recharacterized as "Polish Noble Rule." Most amusingly, mention was added to the table of Stalin's birth and death dates, restoring entries that, as noted earlier, the general secretary had originally struck out with the slur "Bastards!" in 1937.[60]

In print for nearly twenty years and withdrawn from the curriculum only after Khrushchev condemned Stalin in his Secret Speech, the SHORT HIS-TORY acquired a significance that is difficult to overstate. Functioning as the singular Soviet history text between 1937 and 1941, it defined not only the elementary school curriculum but also the official line on the history of the USSR as reflected in more advanced textbooks, monographs, and scholarly articles. This, in turn, governed the depiction of historical events and history itself in the press, literature, theater, film, and museum exhibitions throughout the USSR. Even after other, more advanced histories of the USSR began to be published between 1940 and 1941, the Shestakov text continued to serve as a bellwether of change in the official line. As the preceding pages have demonstrated, between 1941 and 1955, the text reflected important shifts in the way that certain subjects were to be treated, particularly concerning Russian imperialism, the Comintern, the purges, the Molotov-Ribbentrop Pact, and the wartime alliance.

But if the SHORT HISTORY sometimes functioned as a Stalinist palimpsest of sorts, for much of the rest of the period the themes that it promoted in 1937 remained canonical elements of the Soviet usable past into the mid-1950s. A thousand years of state building and progressive leadership were celebrated, as was a russocentric historical narrative that made little more than incidental mention of the many other ethnicities that populated the region over the course of a millennium.

Although subsequent work on Soviet history between the mid-1950s and late 1980s brought nuance to the excesses of this Stalinist statism and russocentrism, mainstream historians struggled to challenge the hegemony of the official line. More dynamic work followed in the 1990s after the fall of the USSR, when post-Soviet historians took advantage of the collapse of the state's monopoly over the past to experiment with alternate approaches to writing national history as well as a more grassroots regional focus on the historical events themselves. That said, official concerns about patriotic mobilization and the establishment of a "Russian national idea" since 2000 under Vladimir Putin have led not only to a rehabilitation of many elements of Soviet history but also to a reinvestment in themes like statism, vanguardism, and russocentrism that today seem strikingly reminiscent of what defined Stalin's usable past nearly a century ago.

Notes

Introduction

1. KRATKII KURS ISTORII SSSR, ed. A. V. Shestakov (Moscow: Gosudarstvennoe uchebno-pedagogicheskoe izd-vo, 1937).

2. Van Wyck Brooks, "On Creating a Usable Past," DIAL 64 (1918): 337–341; Henry Steele Commager, THE SEARCH FOR A USABLE PAST AND OTHER ESSAYS IN HISTORIOGRAPHY (New York: Knopf, 1967), 3–27. This approach to mobilizational propaganda distinguishes between traditionalism (the rehabilitation of older political and social practices in order to support traditional political and social norms) and neotraditionalism (the co-opting of older political and social practices to advance new, modern objectives). Compare Nicholas Timasheff, THE GREAT RETREAT: THE GROWTH AND DECLINE OF COMMUNISM IN RUSSIA (New York: E. P. Dutton & Co., 1946) and David L. Hoffmann, "Was There a Great Retreat from Soviet Socialism?" KRITIKA 5, no. 4 (2004): 651–674.

3. A. A. Zhdanov's most important copy of the Shestakov galleys is at Rossiiskii gosudarstvennyi arkhiv sotsial'no-politicheskoi istorii (hereafter RGASPI), fond (hereafter f.) 77, opis (hereafter op.) 1, delo (hereafter d.) 854, list (hereafter l.) 1–118. On Zhdanov's outsized role, see David Brandenberger, NATIONAL BOLSHEVISM: STALINIST MASS CULTURE AND THE FORMATION OF MODERN RUSSIAN NATIONAL IDENTITY, 1931–1956 (Cambridge, MA: Harvard University Press, 2002), 50–53, 258–259; Russia's leading specialist on the text reached similar conclusions about Zhdanov's role in the editing of the text. See A. M. Dubrovskii, "'Veskii uchebnik' i arkhivnye materialy," in ARKHEOGRAFICHESKII EZHEGODNIK ZA 1996 (Moscow: Izd-vo Akademii nauk, 1998), 181–195; A. M. Dubrovskii, "A. A. Zhdanov v rabote nad shkol'nym uchebnikom istorii," in OTECHESTVENNAIA KUL'TURA I ISTORICHESKAIA NAUKA XVIII–XX VEKOV: SBORNIK STATEI (Briansk: BGU, 1996), 128–143.

4. See RGASPI, 558, op. 11, d. 1584; op. 3, dd. 374, 375.

5. Aside from my NATIONAL BOLSHEVISM, the best studies of this campaign are A. N. Artizov, "V ugodu vzgliadam vozhdia (konkurs 1936 g. na uchebnik po istorii SSSR)" KENTAVR 1 (1991): 125–135; A. M. Dubrovskii, ISTORIK I VLAST': ISTORICH-ESKAIA NAUKA V SSSR I KONTSEPTSIIA ISTORII FEODAL'NOI ROSSII V KONTEK-STE POLITIKI I IDEOLOGII, 1930–1950 GG. (Briansk: BGU, 2005), 170–304; A. M. Dubrovskii, VLAST' I ISTORICHESKAIA MYSL' V SSSR (1930–1950 GG.) (Moscow: Rosspen, 2017), 139–249; V. V. Tikhonov, POLEZNOE PROSHLOE: ISTORIIA V STA-LINSKOM SSSR (Moscow: Novoe literaturnoe obozrenie, 2023), 99–125.

6. Stalin was known to have criticized Pokrovsky and his materialist, schematic approach to history during the early 1930s, well before he was denounced in public. See diary entry from April 7, 1934 in Georgi Dimitrov, DNEVNIK (9 MART 1933–6 FEVUARI 1949) (Sofia: Universitetsko izdatelstvo "Sv. Kliment Okhridski," 1997), 101; Em. Iaroslavsky to Stalin (8 December 1938), RGASPI, f. 89, op. 8, d. 630, l. 25.

7. RGASPI, f. 17, op. 3, d. 942, ll. 7–8; f. 17, op. 120, d. 358, l. 72.

8. Arkhiv Rossiiskoi akademii nauk (hereafter Arkhiv RAN), f. 350, op. 1, d. 906, ll. 1–3ob. For more on this critical source, see A. M. Dubrovskii and D. L. Branden-berger, "'Grazhdanskoi istorii u nas net': Ob odnom vystuplenii I. V. Stalina vesnoi 1934 goda," in PROBLEMY OTECHESTVENNOI I VSEMIRNOI ISTORII (Briansk: BGU, 1998), 96–101.

9. Brandenberger, NATIONAL BOLSHEVISM, 27–37; David Brandenberger, PRO-PAGANDA STATE IN CRISIS: SOVIET IDEOLOGY, INDOCTRINATION, AND TERROR UNDER STALIN, 1927–1941 (New Haven, CT: Yale University Press, 2011), 67–119.

10. RGASPI, f. 17, op. 120, d. 358, l. 72; Gosudarstvennyi arkhiv Rossiiskoi feder-atsii (hereafter GARF), f. 2306, op. 69, d. 2177, ll. 1–3.

11. GARF, f. 2306, op. 69, d. 2177, ll. 11–12.

12. Diary entry from March 23, 1934, in DNEVNIK ISTORIKA S. A. PIONTKOVSK-OGO, ed. A. L. Litvin, A. M. Dubrovskii, and D. L. Brandenberger (Kazan: Kazan State University Press, 2009), 505–507. Piontkovsky also noted that in Stalin's attack on the schematic texts he took a passing shot at Pokrovsky, saying "all this mess stems from the time of Pokrovsky's influence."

13. A. I. Gukovskii, "Kak ia stal istorikom," ISTORIIA SSSR 6 (1965): 97.

14. GARF, f. 2306, op. 69, d. 2177, ll. 56ob-57.

15. D. Osipov, "Skelety v shkole," PRAVDA, April 5, 1934, 1.

16. "Za podlinnuiu istoriiu—protiv skholastiki i abstraktsii," ZA KOMMUNIS-TICHESKOE PROSVESHCHENIE, April 10, 1934, 1; [A. Z.] Ionnisiani, "Bez ucheta is-toricheskoi obstanovki, faktov i lits," ZA KOMMUNISTICHESKOE PROSVESHCHENIE, April 24, 1934, 3.

17. "O prepodavanii grazhdanskoi istorii v shkolakh SSSR," PRAVDA, May 16, 1934, 1. New pedagogues were needed because most teachers in the mid-1930s had entered the profession during NEP and were unfamiliar with anything but social studies. See TRUD V SSSR: STATISTICHESKII SPRAVOCHNIK (Moscow: TsSU SSSR, 1936), 323.

These changes in the history curriculum were accompanied by a reorganization of the public school system itself. Early in 1934, the Seventeenth Party Congress had mandated the establishment of universal seven-year education, and on May 15 a joint decree of the Central Committee and the Council of People's Commissars unveiled a bifurcated system in which primary schools (grades one through four) would feed into both "complete" and "incomplete" secondary schools. Complete secondary education—preparing those bound for higher education—continued through tenth grade, while incomplete secondary schools terminated after the seventh grade. See "O strukture nachal'noi i srednei shkoly v SSSR," PRAVDA, May 16, 1934, 1; SOBRANIE ZAKONOV I RASPORIAZHENII SSSR 47 (1935): art. 391.

18. "O vvedenii v nachal'noi i nepolnoi srednei shkole elementarnogo kursa vseobshei istorii i istorii SSSR," published in SPRAVOCHNIK PARTIINOGO RABOTNIKA, no. 9 (Moscow: Partizdat, 1935), 137. For background, see GARF, f. 2306, op. 69, d. 2177. In 1940, further courses on modern history were added to the curriculum of eighth through tenth grade in complete secondary schools, basically translating into more material on the prerevolutionary period. See PROGRAMMY SREDNEI SHKOLY: ISTORIIA SSSR, NOVAIA ISTORIIA (Moscow: Uchpedgiz, 1940).

19. Compare George Enteen, THE SOVIET SCHOLAR-BUREAUCRAT: M. N. POKROVSKII AND THE SOCIETY OF MARXIST HISTORIANS (University Park: Pennsylvania State University Press, 1978), 189 and Timasheff, THE GREAT RETREAT to Hoffmann, "Was There a Great Retreat from Soviet Socialism?"

20. RGASPI, f. 17, op. 3, d. 942, l. 7; f. 17, op. 120, d. 358, l. 72.

21. "O prepodavanii grazhdanskoi istorii v shkolakh SSSR."

22. Brandenberger, PROPAGANDA STATE IN CRISIS, 98–109.

23. I. I. Mints's Moscow brigade consisted of E. A. Morokhovets, M. V. Nechkina, V. E. Syroechkovsky, and B. E. Syroechkovsky; Malyshev's Leningrad group included V. N. Bernadsky, I. V. Gittis, T. S. Karpova, and L. I. Feldman. For the preliminary composition of the textbook brigades not detailed here, see SPRAVOCHNIK PARTIINOGO RABOTNIKA, 137. The composition of the two brigades working on the elementary history of the USSR texts was not published. Generally, see RGASPI, f. 17, op. 120, d. 358, ll. 72–73.

24. PERVYI VSESOIUZNYI S"EZD SOVETSKIKH PISATELEI, 1934: STENOGRAFICHESKII OTCHET (Moscow: Sovetskii pisatel', 1934), 18.

25. The party bosses' review process, taking place in Sochi, was in all likelihood dominated by Stalin. One possibly apocryphal account has Kirov protesting: "But Joseph Vissarionovich, what kind of historian am I?" Stalin's answer—"Don't worry—sit down and listen!" set the tone for the collaborative effort. See S. Krasnikov, SERGEI MIRONOVICH KIROV: ZHIZN' I DEIATEL'NOST' (Moscow: Gosizdat, 1964), 196.

26. RGASPI, f. 558, op. 1, d. 3156.

27. See RGASPI, f. 558, op. 1, d. 3156. For Stalin's views on the "international gendarme" moniker, see I. Stalin, "O stat'e Engel'sa 'Vneshniaia politika russkogo tsarizma,'" BOL'SHEVIK 9 (1941): 3–4; A. Latyshev, "Kak Stalin Engel'sa svergal," ROSSIISKAIA GAZETA, December 22, 1992, 4.

28. RGANI, f. 3, op. 33, d. 56, ll. 28–32.

29. RGASPI, f. 558, op. 3, d. 217, l. 1. See the page proofs to ELEMENTARNYI KURS ISTORII SSSR DLIA NACHAL'NOI SHKOLY, ed. I. I. Mints, E. A. Morokhovets, M. V. Nechkina, B. E. Syroechkovskii, and V. E. Syroechkovskii, at f. 558, op. 3, d. 217–218.

30. RGASPI, f. 558, op. 3, d. 217, ll. 86–87.

31. Rossiiskii gosudarstvennyi arkhiv noveishei istorii (hereafter RGANI), f. 3, op. 33, d. 56, ll. 64–66ob. See the page proofs to ELEMENTARNYI KURS ISTORII SSSR: UCHEBNIK DLIA NACHAL'NOI SHKOLY, ed. Z. B. Lozinskii, V. N. Bernadskii, I. V. Gittis, T. S. Karpova, and L. I. Fel'dman, at RGASPI, f. 558, op. 3, dd. 189–190.

32. RGANI, f. 3, op. 33, d. 56, ll. 92–103.

33. A. N. Artizov, "Shkola Pokrovskogo i sovetskaia istoricheskaia nauka (konets 1920-kh—1930-e gody)" (Doctoral diss., Gosudarstvennaia akademiia sfery byta i uslug, 1998), 123–124; Artizov, "V ugodu vzgliadam vozhdia," 127. Stalin's copy of Vanag's page proofs does not appear to have survived.

34. RGASPI, f. 17, op. 120, d. 356, ll. 108–113, here 110–111.

35. For Stalin's endorsement of Bystriansky's review, see RGANI, f. 3, op. 33, d. 56, ll. 155–164, here 155.

36. For instance, although Bystriansky was prescient to note the progressive nature of Russian state-building, he also demanded more attention to be cast on the history of the non-Russian peoples than would ultimately be reflected in the official narrative. See RGASPI, f. 17, op. 120, d. 356, ll. 108–113.

37. The group consisted of Bubnov, Bystriansky, K. Ya. Bauman, N. I. Bukharin, G. S. Fridliand, P. O. Gorin, Ya. A. Yakovlev, F. U. Khodzhaev, I. M. Lukin, K. B. Radek, A. S. Svanidze, and V. P. Zatonsky.

38. RGASPI, f. 17, op. 120, d. 358, ll. 1–3.

39. RGANI, f. 3, op. 33, d. 56, l. 129. The commission consisted of Bubnov, Bauman, Bystriansky, Bukharin, Gorin, Yakovlev, Khodzhaev, Lukin, Radek, Svanidze, and Zatonsky. Only Fridliand did not get a permanent appointment. See RGASPI, f. 558, op. 1, d. 3156, l. 8.

40. For Zhdanov's manuscript with signs of Stalin's editing, see RGASPI, f. 558, op. 11, d. 3156, ll. 9–12; on Bukharin, see David Brandenberger, "Politics Projected into the Past: What Precipitated the 1936 Campaign Against N. M. Pokrovskii," in REINTERPRETING REVOLUTIONARY RUSSIA: ESSAYS IN HONOR OF JAMES D. WHITE, ed. Ian Thatcher (London: Routledge, 2006), 202–214.

41. "V Sovnarkome Soiuza SSR i TsK VKP(b)," PRAVDA, 27 January 1936, 2–3.

42. [N. I. Bukharin,] "Nuzhna li nam marksistskaia istoricheskaia nauka? (O nekotorykh sushchestvenno vazhnykh, no nesostoiatel'nykh vzgliadakh tov. M. N. Pokrovskogo)," IZVESTIIA, January 27, 1936, 3–4; [K. B. Radek,] "Prepodavanie istorii v nashei shkole," PRAVDA, January 27, 1936, 1; I. Stalin, A. Zhdanov, S. Kirov, "Zamechaniia po povodu konspekta uchebnika po 'Istorii SSSR,'" PRAVDA, January 27, 1936, 2; V. A. Bystrianskii, "Kriticheskie zamechaniia ob uchebnikakh po istorii SSSR," PRAVDA, February 1, 1936, 2–3.

43. A. N. Artizov, "Kritika M. N. Pokrovskogo i ego shkoly," ISTORIIA SSSR 1 (1991): 102–121; Enteen, THE SOVIET SCHOLAR-BUREAUCRAT, 187–199. The 1936 press campaign against Pokrovsky, timed with the landmark publication of Stalin,

Zhdanov, and Kirov's 1934 observations, created the impression that the anti-Pokrovsky line had been officially sanctioned two years earlier than it actually had. See M. V. Nechkina, "Vopros o M. N. Pokrovskom v postanovleniiakh partii i pravitel'stva 1934-1938 gg. o prepodavanii istorii i istoricheskoi nauki," Istoricheskie zapiski 118 (1990): 232-246, esp. 236-239.

44. A. A. Chernobaev, "Professor s pikoi," ili Tri zhizni istorika M. N. Pokrovskogo (Moscow: Politizdat, 1992), 203; Artizov, "Kritika M. N. Pokrovskogo," 110.

45. Tsentral'nyi gosudarstvennyi arkhiv istoriko-politicheskikh dokumentov goroda Sankt-Peterburga (hereafter TsGAIPD SPb), f. 24, op. 2v, d. 1829, l. 93. Musabekov is a term of art for someone of non-Slavic background. I am grateful to Sarah Davies for this reference.

46. Arkhiv RAN, f. 638, op. 2, d. 105, l. 25. For memoirs dealing with the confusion caused by the denunciation of the Pokrovsky "school," see E. V. Gutnova, "Na istfake," Vestnik Moskovskogo universiteta (Seriia 8 Istoriia) 6 (1993): 73.

47. Zhdanov seems to have developed the idea for the competition, although he subsequently gave Stalin formal credit. See RGASPI, f. 558, op. 1, d. 3156, l. 8, 12; f. 77, op. 1, d. 571, l. 22.

48. The jury's preliminary composition included Zhdanov, Bauman, Bubnov, Bukharin, Bystriansky, Gorin, Yakovlev, Khodzhaev, Svanidze, and Zatonsky. See RGASPI, f. 17, op. 120, d. 358, l. 4. For Bukharin's communiqué, see f. 17, op. 120, d. 359, ll. 9-12; also f. 77, op. 1, d. 829, ll. 12-15.

49. "Ob organizatsii konkursa na luchshii uchebnik dlia nachal'noi shkoly po elementarnomu kursu istorii SSSR," Pravda, March 4, 1936, 1.

50. "V Sovnarkome Soiuza SSR i TsK VKP(b)." As noted above, the publication of the 1934 observations in 1936 likely confused its readership, insofar as Vanag's advanced history of the USSR project had been abandoned and terms used in the memo—particularly "Russia—prison of the peoples" and "Russia—the international gendarme"—sounded uncomfortably Pokrovskyian.

51. "Znat' i liubit' istoriiu svoei Rodiny," Pravda, March 7, 1936, 1.

52. RGASPI, f. 17, op. 120, d. 359, ll. 185-189, 158-164; also f. 17, op. 120, d. 365, ll. 235-238. Despite his interest in the competition, Bulgakov never submitted his manuscript. See Ia. S. Lur'e and V. M. Paneiakh, "Rabota M. A. Bulgakova nad kursom istorii SSSR," Russkaia literatura 3 (1988): 183-193; Otdel rukopisei Rossiiskoi gosudarstvennoi biblioteki (hereafter OR RGB), f. 552.

53. RGASPI, f. 77, op. 3, d. 113, ll. 16-17.

54. See RGASPI, f. 17, op. 120, d. 359, ll. 10-11; also f. 77, op. 1, d. 829, ll. 12-15. The etatist emphasis of this manuscript contradicts the notion that Bukharin resisted "the neo-nationalistic rehabilitation of czarism." See Stephen Cohen, Bukharin and the Bolshevik Revolution: A Political Biography, 1888-1938 (New York: Oxford University Press, 1973), 358, 468-469.

55. RGASPI, f. 17, op. 120, d. 359, ll. 185-189, 158-164; also f. 17, op. 120, d. 365, ll. 235-238.

56. Artizov, "V ugodu vzgliadam vozhdia," 130; A. N. Artizov, "Sud'by istorikov shkoly M. N. Pokrovskogo (seredina 1930-kh godov)," Voprosy istorii 7 (1994): 37–38.

57. Although Zhdanov's early December 1936 comment seems to be the first mention of the "lesser-evil" theory, Nechkina attributed it to Stalin—see M. V. Nechkina, "K itogam diskussii o periodizatsii istorii sovetskoi istoricheskoi nauki," Istoriia SSSR 2 (1962): 74. Many have followed Nechkina's attribution, e.g., Lowell Tillett, The Great Friendship: Soviet Historians on the Non-Russian Nationalities (Chapel Hill: University of North Carolina Press, 1969), 45–46 and n. 19. On the Stalinist approach to the history of Ukraine, see David Brandenberger, "'Basically, It's a History of the Russian State': Russocentrism, Etatism and the Ukrainian Question in Stalin's Editing of the 1937 Short History of the USSR," Nationalities Papers (forthcoming).

58. RGASPI, f. 17, op. 120, d. 359, ll. 13–14.

59. Artizov, "Sud'by istorikov," 47; Artizov, "V ugodu vzgliadam vozhdia," 130–131. The history of the Shestakov brigade's work between 1936 and 1937 is best described in Dubrovskii, "'Veskii uchebnik' i arkhivnye materialy," 181–195.

60. Enormous amounts of material remain unstudied—see RGASPI, f. 17, op. 120, d. 361–365; GARF, f. 2306, op. 70, d. 2421; RGANI, f. 3, op. 33, dd. 39–58.

61. This analysis first appeared in S. V. Bakhrushin, "K voprosu o kreshchenii Rusi," Istorik-Marksist 2 (1937): 40–77. Generally, see A. M. Dubrovskii, S. V. Bakhrushin i ego vremia (Moscow: Izd-vo Universiteta "Druzhby narodov," 1992), 87–88.

62. RGASPI, f. 17, op. 120, d. 359, ll. 18–33; f. 17, op. 120, d. 359, ll. 167–184.

63. RGASPI, f. 17, op. 120, d. 359, ll. 34–48.

64. RGASPI, f. 17, op. 120, d. 360, l. 140. Ironically, Vinogradov had been one of Pokrovsky's professors.

65. Rossiiskii gosudarstvennyi voennyi arkhiv (hereafter RGVA), f. 9, op. 29s, d. 323, ll. 110, 115.

66. See RGASPI, f. 17, op. 120, d. 359, ll. 131–140, published as "Postanovlenie zhiuri pravitel'stvennoi komissii po konkursu na luchshii uchebnik dlia 3 i 4 klassov srednei shkoly po istorii SSSR," Pravda, August 22, 1937, 2. See also f. 17, op. 120, d. 359, ll. 49–63, 118–129 and Dubrovskii, Vlast' i istoricheskaia mysl' v SSSR, 241–250.

67. Shestakov's brigade included N. G. Tarasov, N. D. Kuznetsov, A. S. Nifontov, D. N. Nikiforov, N. D. Firsov, and possibly A. Kazakov. Early consultants to the project included B. A. Gardanov, Iu. V. Gote, Z. G. Grinberg, A. I. Kazachenko, D. Ia. Kin, and S. A. Nikitin. See RGASPI, f. 588, op. 3, d. 374, l. 2.

68. Artizov, "V ugodu vzgliadam vozhdia," 133.

69. Many of the senior scholars worked in collaboration with younger Marxists, the latter essentially serving as political commissars, policing what was really a return to the old state school of imperial historiography. Konstantin Shteppa, Russian Historians and the Soviet State (New Brunswick, NJ: Rutgers

University Press, 1962), esp. 179; A. L. Sidorov, "Nekotorye razmyshleniia o trude i opyte istorika," Istoriia SSSR 3 (1964): 132; Enteen, The Soviet Scholar-Bureaucrat, 190–191, 198.

70. List reformatted. Arkhiv RAN, f. 638, op. 2, d. 105, ll. 17–18.

71. For the reviews, see RGANI, f. 3, op. 33, d. 58, ll. 67-96, published in Istoriiu v shkolu: Sozdanie pervykh sovetskikh uchebnikov, ed. S. Kudriashov (Moscow: Vestnik Arkhiva prezidenta, 2008), 247–257.

72. See RGASPI, f. 558, op. 3, dd. 374, 375.

73. See, for instance, Druzhinin's diary entry from June 16, 1937: "Dnevnik Nikolaia Mikhailovicha Druzhinina," Voprosy istorii 6 (1997): 102.

74. Arkhiv RAN, f. 638, op. 2, d. 105, l. 16.

75. For the individual reviews, see Bakhrushin's (dated June 19, 1937): RGASPI, f. 17, op. 120, d. 365, ll. 44, 45–51, 52–73; Bazilevich's (dated June 19): ll. 33–39, 40–430b; Bernadskii's (undated): 90–95, 96–100, 128–132; Bystriansky's (undated): ll. 101–102, 103–106; Grekov's (undated), ll. 108–117, 118–127; Druzhinin's (dated June 17): ll. 133–138, 139–145; Picheta's (undated): ll. 167–169. Bakhrushin wrote a supplement to his review on July 7 (ll. 74–87); Bazilevich wrote a supplement on July 3: ll. 22–28, 29–320b; Morokhovets wrote another on November 17 (Nauchnyi arkhiv Instituta Rossiiskoi istorii Rossiiskoi akademii nauk [hereafter NA IRI RAN], f. 1, op. 1, d. 5a, ll. 53–55); and Veselovsky competed his own on November 25 (Arkhiv RAN, f. 638, op. 1, d. 48, ll. 23–31. The review by Bykhovskaia does not appear to have survived. Generally, see Dubrovskii, "'Veskii uchebnik' i arkhivnye materialy," 181–195; Dubrovskii, Vlast' i istoricheskaia mysl' v SSSR, 231–233.

76. Druzhinin received a copy of the galleys from Zhdanov's office for vetting on July 1, 1937. See "Dnevnik Nikolaia Mikhailovicha Druzhinina," Voprosy istorii 1 (1997): 122.

77. For Bubnov's review, dated July 13, 1937, see RGASPI, f. 77, op. 1, d. 847, ll. 6–27, esp. 13, 15–16.

78. For Zatonsky's review, dated July 2, 1937, see RGASPI, f. 77, op. 1, d. 847, ll. 3–5. Ironically, the sections in the manuscript that Zatonsky had criticized for their tokenist treatment of non-Russian minorities were pared down even further before the final typesetting began. On the reediting, compare chap. 1 of the May 1937 draft at f. 558, op. 3, d. 374 with the edition published in September 1937. Similar concerns had been expressed earlier that spring by Bauman—see f. 17, op. 120, d. 359, ll. 176–179.

79. Na prieme u Stalina: Tetradi (zhurnaly) zapisei lits, priniiatykh I. V. Stalinym (1924–1953 gg). Spravochnik, ed. A. A. Chernobaev (Moscow: Novyi khronograf, 2008), 214–215. Stalin's dacha appointment book has never been declassified.

80. Although Zhdanov's working copy of the publishers' galleys was apparently not preserved, the recopied version with marks in his hand is at RGASPI, f. 77, op. 1, d. 854.

81. RGASPI, f. 17, op. 120, d. 373, ll. 334, 628, 143, 1440b, 608a–608a ob, 123–1230b.

82. Artizov, "V ugodu vzgliadam vozhdia," 130, 134; Artizov, "Kritika M. N.

Pokrovskogo," 108; and Artizov "Sud'by istorikov," 34–48. The fate of Shestakov's competitors was similarly grim. Gorin's brigade ceased work on their draft after Gorin was arrested in July, joining other historians associated with the competition in NKVD detention such as Dubrovsky, Grave, Fridliand, and V. M. Friedlin. Vanag's former group, now working under Pankratova, also stalled, as did Mints's and Gudoshnikov's. Only Pankratova would succeed in publishing anything, and that only in 1940. On the purges, see Artizov, "Sud'by istorikov," 37, 43; Artizov, "V ugodu vzgliadam vozhdia," 130, 134. On Pankratova's work, see RGASPI, f. 17, op. 125, d. 26, l. 30; O. M. Shchodra, "Prepodavanie istorii SSSR v Moskovskom Gosudarstvennom Universitete (1934–1941)," VESTNIK MOSKOVSKOGO UNIVERSITETA (SERIIA 8—ISTORIIA) 6 (1986): 15–24; "Dnevnik Nikolaia Mikhailovicha Druzhinina," VOPROSY ISTORII 10, 12 (1997): 88–92, 100–106; 63, 66–76, 81; A. M. Pankratova, S. V. Bakhrushin, K. V. Bazilevich, and A. V. Fokht, eds., ISTORIIA SSSR: UCHEBNIK DLIA SREDNEI SHKOLY, 3 vols. (Moscow: Uchpedgiz, 1940).

83. KRATKII KURS ISTORII SSSR, ed. A. V. Shestakov (Moscow: Uchpedgiz, 1937).

84. Shestakov did not fully realize the importance of these new statist priorities until he saw Stalin's editing. Thereafter, he spoke frequently about the issue in public. See, for instance, the materials in his personal archive cited in N. V. Tikhomirov, "Problema mezhnatsional'nykh otnoshenii v kontseptsii Russkogo gosudarstva v otechestvennoi istoriografii 1930-kh—nachala 1950-kh godov," VESTNIK GUMANITARNOGO OBRAZOVANIIA 4 (2020): 101–110, esp. 103, 105.

85. Shestakov likely did not appreciate the centrality of russocentrism to the new historical line until after he saw how Stalin had transformed his narrative. That said, he quickly became a major advocate of the concept—see the discussion of his advocacy in Tikhomirov, "Problema mezhnatsional'nykh otnoshenii v kontseptsii Russkogo gosudarstva v otechestvennoi istoriografii 1930-kh—nachala 1950-kh godov," 103, 105–106. For a different point of view, see V. V. Tikhonov, "'Natsional'nye' istorii narodov SSSR: nauchnye siuzhety i politicheskie praktiki," in SOVETSKII NATSIONAL'NYI PROEKT V 1920-E–1940-E GG.: IDEOLOGIIA I PRAKTIKA, ed. D. A. Amanzholova et al. (Moscow: Novyi khronograf, 2021), 461–465.

86. Shestakov, a specialist in prerevolutionary agrarian history, was forced to contradict elements of his own scholarship to downplay the historical importance of these uprisings in the SHORT HISTORY. See, e.g., A. V. Shestakov, OCHERKI PO SEL'SKOMU KHOZIAISTVU I KREST'IANSKOMU DVIZHENIIU V GODY VOINY I PERED OKTIABREM 1917 G. (Leningrad: "Priboi," 1927).

87. V. Ilyn [Lenin], "Kriticheskie zametki po national'nomu voprosu," PROSVESHCHENIE 10 (1913): 95–105; 11 (1913): 55–59; 12 (1913): 56–64; V. I. Lenin, "O natsional'noi gordosti velikorossov," SOTSIAL-DEMOKRAT, December 12, 1914.

88. This reversal of the 1920s valorization of peasant rebels like Bolotnikov, Razin, Bulavin, Pugachev, and Shamil forced the Commissariat of Education to scramble to help teachers adapt to the new line. See Arkhiv RAN, f. 638, op. 3, d. 333, ll. 47–49, 65; S. Liuboshits, "Anekdoticheskie dialogi," UCHITEL'SKAIA GAZETA, February 7, 1938, 3; A. Fokht, "Istoriia SSSR i politicheskoe vospitanie uchashchikhsia," UCHITEL'SKAIA GAZETA, March 23, 1938, 2.

89. "Bol'shaia pobeda na istoricheskom fronte," Istoricheskii zhurnal 8 (1937): 6; V. Losev, "Kratkii kurs istorii SSSR," Istoricheskii zhurnal 9 (1937): 98; A. K., "Kratkii kurs istorii SSSR," Bol'shevik 17 (1937): 84–96.

90. "Boevaia programma dal'neishego pod"ema istoricheskoi nauki," Istorik-Marksist 3 (1937): 146.

91. A. K., "Kratkii kurs istorii SSSR," 85–86; also "Bol'shaia pobeda na istoricheskom fronte," 7.

92. For use of the textbook in study circles, see RGVA, f. 9, op. 29s, d. 355, ll. 15–17, 18–20; A. Fedorov, "O podgotovke mladshikh politrukov," Propagandist i agitator RKKA 12 (1938): 9; "Programmy eksternata za [sic] Voenno-politicheskoe uchilishche v 1939 godu," Propagandist i agitator RKKA 15 (1939): 40; "Literatura k XX godovshchine Krasnoi Armii," Propaganda i agitatsiia 3 (1938): 64.

For reprinted excerpts of the Shestakov text for adults, see Kak rabochie i krest'iane zavoevali vlast' i postroili sotsialisticheskoe obshchestvo (Moscow: Partizdat, 1937); Vspomogatel'nyi material k izucheniiu istorii VKP(b), no. 1 (Leningrad: Lenoblizdat, 1938), 86–92, 92–106; Vspomogatel'nyi material k izucheniiu istorii VKP(b), no. 2 (Leningrad: Lenoblizdat, 1938), 180–184, 185–196.

For supplemental instructional texts that elaborated on the Shestakov textbook, see A. V. Shestakov, ed., Materialy k teme "Nasha rodina v dalekom proshlom" (Leningrad: Izdanie Politicheskogo upravleniia KBF, 1938); A. V. Shestakov, ed., Materialy k teme "Vostochnaia Evropa pod vlast'iu mongol'skikh zavoevatelei" (Leningrad: Izdanie Politicheskogo upravleniia KBF, 1938); A. V. Shestakov, ed., Materialy k teme "Sozdanie russkogo national'nogo gosudarstva" (Leningrad: Izdanie Politicheskogo upravleniia KBF, 1938); A. V. Shestakov, ed., Materialy k teme "Rasshirenie russkogo gosudarstva" (Leningrad: Izdanie Politicheskogo upravleniia KBF, 1938); A. V. Shestakov, ed., Materialy k teme "Krest'ianskie voiny i vosstaniia ugnetennykh narodov v XVII veke" (Leningrad: Izdanie Politicheskogo upravleniia KBF, 1938); A. V. Shestakov, ed., Materialy k teme "Rasshirenie russkogo gosudarstva" (Leningrad: Izdanie Politicheskogo upravleniia KBF, 1938); A. V. Shestakov, ed., Materialy k teme "Krest'ianskie voiny i vosstaniia ugnetennykh narodov v XVII veke: Khoziaistvo, gosudarstvennyi stroi, kul'tura i byt v Rossii vo vtoroi polovine XVII veka" (Leningrad: Izdanie Politicheskogo upravleniia KBF, 1938); A. V. Shestakov, ed., Materialy k teme "Rossiia XVIII veka—Imperiia pomeshchikov i kuptsov: Petr I i ero reformy" (Leningrad: Izdanie Politicheskogo upravleniia KBF, 1938), and others.

93. Shteppa, Russian Historians and the Soviet State, 128–129.

94. Ibid., 126–127.

95. A. Shestakov, "Kak prepodavat' istoriiu SSSR po novomu uchebniku," Istoricheskii zhurnal 9 (1937): 79–80. On the inaccessibility of the text, see N. V. Tikhomirov, "'Bol'she dlia uchitelei goditsia': Kritika pervogo uchebnika istorii SSSR sovetskim nauchno-pedagogicheskim soobshchestvom," Vestnik Mariisk-

OGO GOSUDARSTVENNOGO UNIVERSITETA: SERIIA "ISTORICHESKIE NAUKI. IU-RIDICHESKIE NAUKI" 8, no. 1 (2022): 81–90.

96. Print run of the text figures are compiled from a survey of weekly editions of KNIZHNAIA LETOPIS' between 1937 and 1941. See also GARF, f. 2306, op. 69, d. 2782, l. 26; RGASPI, f. 17, op. 125, d. 26, l. 27.

97. ISTORIIA SSSR: UCHEBNIK DLIA SREDNEI SHKOLY. Generally, see N. V. Tikhomirov, "Otrazhenie bor'by za novuiu kontseptsiiu istorii SSSR v programmakh kursov istorii dlia VUZov (1930-e gg)," VESTNIK MARIISKOGO GOSUDARSTVEN-NOGO UNIVERSITETA: SERIIA "ISTORICHESKIE NAUKI. IURIDICHESKIE NAUKI" 7, no. 1 (2021): 88–95.

98. For evidence of the sway that this textbook had even over the academic establishment, see NA IRI RAN, f. 1, op. 1, d. 11, ll. 72–116, cited in INSTITUT ISTORII AKADEMII NAUK SSSR V DOKUMENTAKH I MATERIALAKH, no. 1 (Moscow: Institut Rossiiskoi istorii RAN, 2016), 239–286.

99. Almost nothing is known about the textbook's translation into English or its anonymous translators.

100. For Stalin's editing, see RGASPI, f. 558, op. 11, d. 1584 (his fleeting commentary on the first set of Shestakov publisher's galleys from June 1937 is not represented in this edition—see f. 558, op. 3, dd. 374, 375).

101. For Zhdanov's copy of the galleys, where most of the needed edits to the text are recorded in the handwriting of one of his assistants, see RGASPI, f. 77, op.1, d. 854. Zhdanov's preliminary editing has not survived.

102. For Zhdanov's August copies of the third set of publisher's galleys, see RGASPI, f. 17, op. 120, d. 373, ll. 121–242, 608–727.

103. June 1977 interview with Isaak Mints, summarized in Robert Tucker, STALIN IN POWER: THE REVOLUTION FROM ABOVE, 1929–1941 (New York: Norton, 1990), 531–532. More generally, see I. I. Mints, "Podgotovka Velikoi proletarskoi revoliutsii: k vykhodu pervogo toma 'Istorii grazhdanskoi voiny v SSSR,'" BOL'SHEVIK 21 (1935): 15–30; I. I. Mints, "Stalin v grazhdanskoi voine: mify i fakty," VOPROSY ISTORII 11 (1989): 48.

104. Such editing reveals Shestakov's manuscript to have been strikingly undertheorized when it landed on Stalin's desk during the summer of 1937. Once published, however, the SHORT HISTORY and its author played a major role in shaping the party's historical line. See A. N. Fuks, "Formirovanie sovetskoi monokontseptsii otechestvennoi istorii i ee otrazhenie v shkol'nom uchebnike A. V. Shestakova," VESTNIK MOSKOVSKOGO GOSUDARSTVENNOGO OBLASTNOGO UNIVERSITETA. SERIIA: "ISTORIIA I POLITICHESKIE NAUKI" 2 (2009): 104–113.

105. On Lenin's understanding of socialism in one country, see Erik van Ree, BOUNDARIES OF UTOPIA—IMAGINING COMMUNISM FROM PLATO TO STALIN (New York: Routledge, 2015).

106. Vasily Svarog painted an oil version of this picture featuring Stalin, Kaganovich, Molotov, Andrei Andreev, Mikhail Kalinin, and Kliment Voroshilov for the 1939 New York World's Fair.

107. Many of the brigade members that Zhdanov deleted would be consumed in

the purges during the coming year—see Artizov, "Sud'by istorikov," 37, 43; Artizov, "V ugodu vzgliadam vozhdia," 130, 134.

108. Stalin's citation of the number fifty was rather arbitrary. If Soviet ethnographers considered there to be about 120 nationalities in the USSR in the mid-1930s, Stalin announced in a speech in 1936 that these nationalities had been consolidated into about sixty groups. Compare Francine Hirsch, EMPIRE OF NATIONS: ETHNOGRAPHIC KNOWLEDGE AND THE MAKING OF THE SOVIET UNION (Ithaca, NY: Cornell University Press, 2005), 277; and I. V. Stalin, DOKLAD O PROEKTE KONSTITUTSII SOIUZA SSR. KONSTITUTSIIA /OSNOVNOI ZAKON/ SOIUZA SOVETSKIKH SOTSIALISTICHESKIKH RESPUBLIK (Moscow: Partizdat, 1937), 60.

109. Shestakov's earlier draft had included more detail on Central Asian, Siberian, Kazakh, Bulgar, Greek, Mari, Urdmut, Mordva, and Lithuanian tribes, as well as pictures of Shota Rustaveli and Tigran the Great. See RGASPI, f. 558, op. 3, d. 374, ll. 5–14.

110. Marlene Laruelle, "The Concept of Ethnogenesis in Central Asia: Political Context and Institutional Mediators (1940–50)," KRITIKA 9, no. 1 (2008): 169–188. Although a Marxist, Stalin displayed a primordial, essentialist understanding of national identity that was grounded in stereotypes—see Erik Van Ree, "Heroes and Merchants: Stalin's Understanding of National Character," KRITIKA 8, no. 1 (2007): 41–65.

111. Curiously, B. B. Piotrovsky was awarded a Stalin prize for his work on Urartu in 1946 even though he denied Stalin's direct link between the medieval state and Georgia. See B. B. Piotrovskii, ISTORIIA I KUL'TURA URARTU (Yerevan: Izd-vo Akademii nauk ArSSR, 1944), 338. On Stalin's long-standing interest in Urartu, see V. V. Tikhonov, "Stalinskaia premiia kak instrument konstruirovaniia obshchei istorii narodov SSSR," ISTORICHESKII ZHURNAL: NAUCHNYE ISSLEDOVANIIA 2 (2016): 178–179; B. S. Ilizarov, POCHETNYI AKADEMIK STALIN I AKADEMIK MARR (Moscow: Veche, 2012), 372–377.

112. Shestakov's earlier draft had been less articulate about the Slavs' primordial roots in the region. See RGASPI, f. 558, op. 3, d. 374, l. 14.

113. Shestakov thus endorsed the so-called Norman theory that credited the Varangians with the foundation of east Slavic statehood—an idea that enjoyed broad supported among Soviet historians at the time. This view was contested by partisans of a more autochthonic interpretation in the 1940s. See, e.g., B. A. Rybakov, "Ranniaia kul'tura vostochnykh slavian," ISTORICHESKII ZHURNAL 11–12 (1943): 73–80; V. V. Mavrodin, BOR'BA S NORMANIZMOM V RUSSKOI ISTORICHESKOI NAUKE (Leningrad: Vsesoiuznoe obshchestvo po rasprostraneniiu politicheskikh i nauchnykh znanii, 1949).

114. Shestakov's later draft paid more attention to state building in Kiev Rus than his earlier one. See RGASPI, f. 558, op. 3, d. 374, ll. 14–19, 21.

115. Shestakov's later draft paid more attention to the progressive nature of Kiev Rus's conversion than his earlier one. See RGASPI, f. 558, op. 3, d. 374, ll. 18–19. See note 61.

116. This presentism was absent in Shestakov's earlier manuscript—see RGASPI, f. 558, op. 3, d. 374, l. 18.

117. Shestakov's view that Kiev Rus possessed a slave-owning mode of production contradicted that of other ranking historians like B. D. Grekov, who argued that eastern Slavic society had somehow skipped over that Marxist phase of development. Shestakov was later vindicated when Stalin sided with him in the 1938 SHORT COURSE on party history. See B. D. Grekov, "Byla li Drevniaia Rus' rabovladel'cheskim obshchestvom?" BOR'BA KLASSOV 3 (1935): 70–71; ISTORIIA VSESOIUZNOI KOMMUNISTICHESKOI PARTII (BOL'SHEVIKOV) (Moscow: Partizdat, 1938), 119–120.

118. On the evolution of the concept of the Russian national state, see A. L. Iurganov, RUSSKOE NATSIONAL'NOE GOSUDARSTVO. ZHIZNENNYI MIR ISTORIKOV EPOKHI STALINIZMA (Moscow: RGGU, 2011), esp. 15–226; N. V. Tikhomirov, "Otrazhenie problem mezhnatsional'nykh otnoshenii v Russkom feodal'nom gosudarstve XVI veka v shkol'nykh uchebnikakh istorii SSSR (konets 1930-kh—nachalo 1960-kh godov)," VESTNIK RIAZANSKOGO GOSUDARSTVENNOGO UNIVERSITETA IMENI S. A. ESENINA 2 (2022): 76–86.

119. Stalin had outlined this chronology for the transition of Muscovy from a national to a multinational empire at the Tenth Party Congress in 1921. See I. V. Stalin, "Ob ocherednykh zadachakh partii v natsional'nom voprose," in MARKSIZM I NATSIONAL'NO KOLONIAL'NYI VOPROS: SBORNIK STATEI I RECHI (Moscow: Partizdat, 1937), 73–74. See also N. V. Tikhomirov, "Otrazhenie protsessa tsentralizatsii russkogo gosudarstva v shklol'nikh uchebnikakh istorii kontsa 1930-kh—nachala 1950-kh gg.," VESTNIK MARIISKOGO GOSUDARSTVENNOGO UNIVERSITETA. SERIIA "ISTORICHESKIE NAUKI. IURIDICHESKIE NAUKI" 6, no. 4 (2020): 401–406.

120. On the rehabilitation of Ivan the Terrible, see David Brandenberger and Kevin M. F. Platt, "Terribly Pragmatic: Rewriting the History of Ivan IV's Reign," in EPIC REVISIONISM: RUSSIAN HISTORY AND LITERATURE AS STALINIST PROPAGANDA, ed. Kevin M. F. Platt and David Brandenberger (Madison: University of Wisconsin Press, 2006), 157–178.

121. RGASPI, f. 17, op. 120, d. 373, ll. 143, 1440b, 628.

122. Curiously, Stalin had used the expression "the landlords' and merchants' national state" in regard to Peter the Great and his heirs in a 1931 interview with the Emil Ludwig. See I. V. Stalin, "Beseda s nemetskim pisatelem Emilem Liudvigom," BOL'SHEVIK 8 (1932): 30.

123. After the war, Stalin became much more critical of Peter for his reliance on foreign expertise. See, for instance, "Stalin, Molotov, i Zhdanov o 2-i serii fil'ma 'Ivan Groznyi': Zapis' Sergeia Eizenshteina i Nikolaia Cherkasova," MOSKOVSKIE NOVOSTI, August 7, 1988, 8–9; K. Simonov, GLAZAMI CHELOVEKA MOEGO VREMENI: RAZMYSHLENIIA O I. V. STALINE (Moscow: Novosti, 1988), 129, 133.

124. As elsewhere in Stalin-era propaganda, the term "political terror" was consistently used to describe the actions of non-Bolshevik movements—the French Jacobins, the Russian Socialist-Revolutionaries, the White Guards, and so on. This explains why the party leadership never used the neologism "Great Terror" to describe the purges of the 1930s

125. This is a reference to Lenin's position on the redeemability of the "democratic" half of every nation—see note 87.

126. Zhdanov's interpolation about Russia as the "Gendarme of Europe" made it into the SHORT HISTORY despite Stalin's 1934 objection to the way that historians had traditionally singled out the 19th century empire as uniquely reactionary—see note 27.

127. This is a reference to Lenin's position on the redeemability of the "democratic" half of every nation—see note 87.

128. This is a reference to Lenin's position on the redeemability of the "democratic" half of every nation—see note 87.

129. Mention of Zinovy Litvin-Sedoi was apparently not deleted for political reasons.

130. Stalin was more explicit about the lack of coordination between revolts in the center and on the periphery in the 1938 SHORT COURSE on party history. See David Brandenberger and Mikhail Zelenov, eds., STALIN'S MASTER NARRATIVE: A CRITICAL EDITION OF THE HISTORY OF THE COMMUNIST PARTY OF THE SOVIET UNION (BOLSHEVIKS): SHORT COURSE (New Haven, CT: Yale University Press, 2019), 215.

131. At first glance, both edits would seem progressive, as if the general secretary wanted to supply more detail about women within the party leadership, in more gender-neutral terms. That said, one should probably read them in more cynical terms, insofar as they both subtly demoted Krupskaia, who was surprisingly outspoken about her disapproval of Stalin's rule during the mid-to-late 1930s.

132. In April 1937, Stalin explained this conduct of the Mensheviks, SRs, and other socialist oppositionists to Em. Yaroslavsky and P. N. Pospelov. According to Stalin, after these compromising parties were defeated by the Bolsheviks, they became embittered and conspired to seek revenge with aid from capitalist paymasters both at home and abroad. See RGASPI, f. 558, op. 11, d. 1217, ll. 26–28.

133. In 1924, Stalin outlined a conventionally internationalist, Leninist combination of factors that led to the October 1917 victory—three external circumstances, six internal conditions and four special features of the Bolshevik movement, as well as two particular aspects of the revolution itself. Beginning with the external circumstances, Stalin argued that World War I had provided a key precondition for the Bolsheviks' success, inasmuch as it had distracted the major imperialist powers from the challenge that the party posed to the international order. By the time that these powers grasped the scale of the Bolshevik threat, the party had already undermined their ability to preempt the revolution by mobilizing their own workers in its defense. This both shielded the revolutionary republic and stimulated additional unrest throughout the industrial and colonial world.

Domestically, the conditions that contributed to the 1917 victory stemmed from the party's vanguard role in uniting disaffected workers and peasants while at the same time neutralizing the revolution's weak, disorganized opponents. Elements of this story stemmed from the war's disruption of the Russian home front, but other dimensions related to the Bolsheviks' own "special features"—their concern for public opinion, their willingness to patiently build a mass movement, and their resolve to do much of this work within the context of a grassroots struggle for control of the soviets.

Two particular aspects of the revolution, according to Stalin, were also essential to a full appreciation of 1917. First, he stressed the importance of the worker-peasant alliance, which had allowed for a thorough-going revolution without requiring the domino effect outlined by Trotsky's "permanent revolution." Second, he noted that 1917 had confirmed Lenin's law on uneven economic and political development, whereby worker-peasant insurrections were more likely to succeed on the periphery of the industrial world than at its center. See I. V. Stalin, "Oktiabr'skaia revoliutsiia i taktika russkikh kommunistov," in NA PUTIAKH K OKTIABRIU, ed. I. Stalin, 1st ed. (Moscow: Gosudarstvennoe izdatel'stvo 1925), vii–lvi.

134. David Brandenberger, "Stalin's Rewriting of 1917," RUSSIAN REVIEW 76, no. 4 (2017): 667–689.

135. On the contours of party conspiracy thinking in 1936–1938, see David Brandenberger, "Ideological Zig Zag: Official Explanations for the Great Terror, 1936–1938," in THE ANATOMY OF TERROR: POLITICAL VIOLENCE UNDER STALIN, ed. James Harris (Oxford: Oxford University Press, 2013), 143–160.

136. In this, Shestakov followed the retreat from internationalism already visible in Stalin's editing of the 1935 HISTORY OF THE CIVIL WAR IN THE USSR. See M. V. Zelenov and D. Brandenberger, eds., "ISTORIIA GRAZHDANSKOI VOINY V SSSR" (1935). ISTORIIA TEKSTA I TEKST ISTORII (Moscow: ROSSPEN, 2017), 17, 462–492.

137. On the broader shift away from internationalism in general and the Comintern in particular, see David Brandenberger, "The Fate of Interwar Soviet Internationalism: A Case Study of the Editing of Stalin's 1938 Short Course on the History of the ACP(b)," REVOLUTIONARY RUSSIA 29, no. 1 (2016): 1–27.

138. Brandenberger, PROPAGANDA STATE IN CRISIS.

139. Party historians pursued similar strategies in early 1937—see chapter 7 of Brandenberger, PROPAGANDA STATE IN CRISIS.

140. B. E. Kalmykov's reputation was intact in 1937 when Stalin struck his name from the text. He was, however, arrested in 1938 and executed in 1940.

141. Postyshev was dismissed from his position as secretary of the Kiev regional party committee in January 1937 and as second secretary of the Ukrainian communist party in March. He then served in semi-disgrace in the Kuibyshev regional party committee until his arrest in February 1938 and execution a year later.

142. Deletion of the Comintern from the text likely stemmed from Stalin's shift away from internationalism during the second half of the 1930s and the arrest of key members of the Comintern leadership during the summer of 1937. See Brandenberger, "The Fate of Interwar Soviet Internationalism," 1–27.

143. Insofar as Shestakov and his brigade completed their prototype textbook in June 1937 and Stalin and Zhdanov finished their editing that July, the SHORT HISTORY was published too early provide full detail about the omnipresent conspiracy that would later link the left and right opposition together with nationalists in the

republics and capitalists abroad. See Brandenberger, "Ideological Zig Zag," 143–160.

144. Olga Velikanova, MASS POLITICAL CULTURE UNDER STALINISM: POPULAR DISCUSSION OF THE SOVIET CONSTITUTION (New York: Palgrave, 2018); David Brandenberger, "Nesostoiavshiesia sostiazatel'nye vybory 1937 goda," in ISTORIIA VYBOROV V ROSSII: SBORNIK MATERIALOV MEZHDUNARODNOI NAUCHNOI KONFERENTSII, 16–17 SENTIABRIA 2011 G., ed. V. P. Zhuravlev et al. (St. Petersburg: Izd-vo LGU im. Pushkina, 2011), 110–121.

145. Brandenberger, NATIONAL BOLSHEVISM.

Title Page

1. Stalin: RGASPI, f. 558, op. 11, d. 1584, l. 4. Also Zhdanov: f. 77, op. 1, d. 854, l. 1a.

2. Stalin: RGASPI, f. 558, op. 11, d. 1584, l. 4.Also Zhdanov: f. 17, op. 120, d. 373, ll. 123, 608a.

3. Later editorial addition.

4. Zhdanov: RGASPI, f. 17, op. 120, d. 373, ll. 608a ob, 123ob.

Table of Contents

1. Stalin: RGASPI, f. 558, op. 11, d. 1584, l. 5. Also Zhdanov: f. 77, op. 1, d. 854, l. 1.

2. Zhdanov: RGASPI, f. 77, op. 1, d. 854, l. 50b.

3. Stalin: RGASPI, f. 558, op. 11, d. 1584, l. 130b. Also Zhdanov: f. 77, op. 1, d. 854, l. 80b.

4. Stalin: RGASPI, f. 558, op. 11, d. 1584, l. 17. Also Zhdanov: f. 77, op. 1, d. 854, l. 12.

5. Stalin: RGASPI, f. 558, op. 11, d. 1584, l. 210b. Also Zhdanov: f. 77, op. 1, d. 854, l. 150b.

6. Stalin: RGASPI, f. 558, op. 11, d. 1584, l. 430b. Also Zhdanov: f. 77, op. 1, d. 854, l. 360b.

7. Stalin: RGASPI, f. 558, op. 11, d. 1584, l. 570b. Also Zhdanov: f. 77, op. 1, d. 854, l. 490b.

8. Stalin: RGASPI, f. 558, op. 11, d. 1584, l. 64. Also Zhdanov: f. 77, op. 1, d. 854, l. 54.

9. Stalin: RGASPI, f. 558, op. 11, d. 1584, l. 660b. Also Zhdanov: f. 77, op. 1, d. 854, l. 560b

10. Stalin: RGASPI, f. 558, op. 11, d. 1584, l. 700b. Also Zhdanov: f. 77, op. 1, d. 854, l. 600b.

11. Stalin: RGASPI, f. 558, op. 11, d. 1584, l. 700b. Also Zhdanov: f. 77, op. 1, d. 854, l. 600b.

12. Stalin: RGASPI, f. 558, op. 11, d. 1584, l. 780b. Also Zhdanov: f. 77, op. 1, d. 854, l. 1680b.

13. Stalin: RGASPI, f. 558, op. 11, d. 1584, l. 83. Also Zhdanov: f. 77, op. 1, d. 854, l. 73.

14. Stalin: RGASPI, f. 558, op. 11, d. 1584, l. 83. Also Zhdanov: f. 77, op. 1, d. 854, l. 73.

15. Stalin: RGASPI, f. 558, op. 11, d. 1584, l. 860b. Also Zhdanov: f. 77, op. 1, d. 854, l. 760b.

16. Stalin: RGASPI, f. 558, op. 11, d. 1584, l. 86ob. Also Zhdanov: f. 77, op. 1, d. 854, l. 76ob.

17. Stalin: RGASPI, f. 558, op. 11, d. 1584, l. 90. Also Zhdanov: f. 77, op. 1, d. 854, l. 79.

18. Stalin: RGASPI, f. 558, op. 11, d. 1584, l. 95. Also Zhdanov: f. 77, op. 1, d. 854, l. 84.

19. Stalin: RGASPI, f. 558, op. 11, d. 1584, l. 99ob. Also Zhdanov: f. 77, op. 1, d. 854, l. 88ob.

20. Stalin: RGASPI, f. 558, op. 11, d. 1584, l. 102ob. Also Zhdanov: f. 77, op. 1, d. 854, l. 91ob.

21. Stalin: RGASPI, f. 558, op. 11, d. 1584, l. 105. Also Zhdanov: f. 77, op. 1, d. 854, l. 94.

22. Stalin: RGASPI, f. 558, op. 11, d. 1584, l. 105. Also Zhdanov: f. 77, op. 1, d. 854, l. 94.

23. Stalin: RGASPI, f. 558, op. 11, d. 1584, l. 110. Also Zhdanov: f. 77, op. 1, d. 854, l. 98.

24. Stalin: RGASPI, f. 558, op. 11, d. 1584, l. 110. Also Zhdanov: f. 77, op. 1, d. 854, l. 98.

25. Stalin: RGASPI, f. 558, op. 11, d. 1584, l. 116. Also Zhdanov: f. 77, op. 1, d. 854, l. 104.

26. Stalin: RGASPI, f. 558, op. 11, d. 1584, l. 119. Also Zhdanov: f. 77, op. 1, d. 854, l. 107.

27. Stalin deleted this list, which is not reproduced in the present critical edition. See RGASPI, f. 558, op. 11, d. 1584, ll. 125ob-126. Also Zhdanov: f. 77, op. 1, d. 854, l. 117, 112.

28. Later editorial addition.

Maps

1. In the 1937 edition, Stalin shortened the title and replaced the adjectival ethnonym "Russian" (RUSSKOE) with the more general adjective "*Russian*" (*ROSSIIS-KOE*). RGASPI, f. 558, op. 11, d. 1584, l. 27.

2. In the 1937 Russian edition, Stalin replaced the adjectival ethnonym "Russian" (RUSSKOE) with the more generic adjective "*Russian*" (*ROSSIISKOE*), corrected the time frame to 1917 and replaced the term "Tsardom" in the legend with "*State*" twice. Later editing replaced 1917 with 1914. Compare RGASPI, f. 558, op. 11, d. 1584, l. 45 and KRATKII KURS ISTORII SSSR, 74-75.

3. Stalin crossed out an earlier map of Soviet industrial sites, wrote "*Map of the Soviet Union*" into the margins and then added "*Blow up the map and note on it all the union and autonomous republics.*" RGASPI, f. 558, op. 11, d. 1584, l. 120.

4. Later editorial addition.

Introduction

1. Stalin: RGASPI, f. 558, op. 11, d. 1584, l. 5. Also Zhdanov: f. 77, op. 1, d. 854, l. 1.

2. Stalin: RGASPI, f. 558, op. 11, d. 1584, l. 5. Also Zhdanov: f. 77, op. 1, d. 854, l. 1.

3. Stalin: RGASPI, f. 558, op. 11, d. 1584, l. 5. Zhdanov proposed the correction "are becoming ~~richer~~ *more remarkable*"—see f. 77, op. 1, d. 854, l. 1.

4. Stalin: RGASPI, f. 558, op. 11, d. 1584, l. 5. Also Zhdanov: f. 77, op. 1, d. 854, l. 1.

5. Stalin: RGASPI, f. 558, op. 11, d. 1584, l. 5. Also Zhdanov: f. 77, op. 1, d. 854, l. 1.

6. Stalin: RGASPI, f. 558, op. 11, d. 1584, l. 5. Also Zhdanov: f. 77, op. 1, d. 854, l. 1.

7. Stalin: RGASPI, f. 558, op. 11, d. 1584, l. 5ob. Also Zhdanov: f. 77, op. 1, d. 854, l. 10b.

8. Stalin: RGASPI, f. 558, op. 11, d. 1584, l. 5ob. Also Zhdanov: f. 77, op. 1, d. 854, l. 10b.

I: Our Country in the Distant Past

1. Zhdanov: RGASPI, f. 77, op. 1, d. 854, l. 2.

2. Zhdanov: RGASPI, f. 77, op. 1, d. 854, l. 2.

3. Zhdanov: RGASPI, f. 77, op. 1, d. 854, l. 2.

4. Zhdanov: RGASPI, f. 77, op. 1, d. 854, l. 2.

5. Zhdanov: RGASPI, f. 77, op. 1, d. 854, l. 2ob.

6. Zhdanov: RGASPI, f. 77, op. 1, d. 854, l. 2ob.

7. Zhdanov: RGASPI, f. 77, op. 1, d. 854, l. 2ob.

8. Zhdanov: RGASPI, f. 77, op. 1, d. 854, l. 2ob. In the 1937 Russian edition, "the skins of animals" is rendered as "the hides of cattle." See ISTORIIA SSSR: KRATKII KURS, 6.

9. Zhdanov: RGASPI, f. 77, op. 1, d. 854, l. 2ob.

10. Zhdanov: RGASPI, f. 77, op. 1, d. 854, l. 2ob.

11. Zhdanov: RGASPI, f. 77, op. 1, d. 854, l. 2ob.

12. Zhdanov: RGASPI, f. 77, op. 1, d. 854, ll. 2ob-3. At the end of this passage, Zhdanov composed and then deleted two final sentences: "*During these wars, the clans captured people and enslaved them. The slaves were owned by the entire clan and worked as all other members did.*"

13. Zhdanov: RGASPI, f. 77, op. 1, d. 854, ll. 3–3ob. At the end of this passage, Zhdanov composed and then deleted two final sentences: "*Especially wealthy became the chiefs of the most warlike and strong tribes, who made raids on their neighbors, captured prisoners, and forced them to become slaves and work when they themselves did nothing.*"

14. Zhdanov: RGASPI, f. 77, op. 1, d. 854, l. 3. Zhdanov initially proposed deleting this entire paragraph and then restored most of it to the text, writing "*necessary*" in the margins.

15. Zhdanov: RGASPI, f. 77, op. 1, d. 854, l. 3ob.

16. Zhdanov: RGASPI, f. 77, op. 1, d. 854, ll. 3–3ob. The term "Kings" was added to the 1938 English edition due to translator error. Compare ISTORIIA SSSR: KRATKII KURS, 7; A SHORT HISTORY OF THE U.S.S.R.,12.

17. Zhdanov: RGASPI, f. 77, op. 1, d. 854, l. 3.

18. Zhdanov: RGASPI, f. 77, op. 1, d. 854, l. 4.

19. Zhdanov: RGASPI, f. 77, op. 1, d. 854, l. 3ob.

20. Stalin: RGASPI, f. 558, op. 11, d. 1584, l. 7ob. Also Zhdanov: f. 77, op. 1, d. 854, l. 3ob.

21. Stalin: RGASPI, f. 558, op. 11, d. 1584, l. 70b. Also Zhdanov: f. 77, op. 1, d. 854, l. 30b.

22. Stalin: RGASPI, f. 558, op. 11, d. 1584, l. 70b. Also Zhdanov: f. 77, op. 1, d. 854, l. 30b.

23. Stalin: RGASPI, f. 558, op. 11, d. 1584, l. 70b. Also Zhdanov: f. 77, op. 1, d. 854, l. 30b.

24. Zhdanov: RGASPI, f. 77, op. 1, d. 854, l. 30b.

25. Zhdanov proposed inserting and then deleted an additional sentence: "*Later in the Trans-Caucasus, two large states arose—Georgia and Armenia*." See RGASPI, f. 77, op. 1, d. 854, l. 30b.

26. Stalin: RGASPI, f. 558, op. 11, d. 1584, l. 70b. Also Zhdanov: f. 77, op. 1, d. 854, l. 30b.

27. Zhdanov: RGASPI, f. 77, op. 1, d. 854, l. 30b.

28. Zhdanov: RGASPI, f. 77, op. 1, d. 854, l. 30b.

29. Zhdanov: RGASPI, f. 77, op. 1, d. 854, l. 30b.

30. Zhdanov: RGASPI, f. 77, op. 1, d. 854, l. 30b.

31. Zhdanov: RGASPI, f. 77, op. 1, d. 854, l. 30b.

32. Zhdanov: RGASPI, f. 77, op. 1, d. 854, ll. 30b, 8a.

33. Zhdanov: RGASPI, f. 77, op. 1, d. 854, l. 30b.

34. Zhdanov: RGASPI, f. 77, op. 1, d. 854, l. 30b.

35. Zhdanov: RGASPI, f. 77, op. 1, d. 854, l. 4.

36. Stalin: RGASPI, f. 558, op. 11, d. 1584, l. 9. Also Zhdanov: f. 77, op. 1, d. 854, l. 4.

37. Zhdanov: RGASPI, f. 77, op. 1, d. 854, l. 4.

38. Zhdanov: RGASPI, f. 77, op. 1, d. 854, l. 4.

39. Zhdanov: RGASPI, f. 77, op. 1, d. 854, l. 40b.

40. Zhdanov: RGASPI, f. 77, op. 1, d. 854, l. 40b.

41. Zhdanov: RGASPI, f. 77, op. 1, d. 854, l. 40b.

42. Zhdanov: RGASPI, f. 77, op. 1, d. 854, l. 40b.

43. Zhdanov: RGASPI, f. 77, op. 1, d. 854, l. 40b.

44. Zhdanov: RGASPI, f. 77, op. 1, d. 854, l. 40b.

45. Zhdanov: RGASPI, f. 77, op. 1, d. 854, l. 40b

46. Zhdanov: RGASPI, f. 77, op. 1, d. 854, l. 40b

47. Zhdanov: RGASPI, f. 77, op. 1, d. 854, l. 40b.

48. Zhdanov: RGASPI, f. 77, op. 1, d. 854, l. 40b.

49. Zhdanov: RGASPI, f. 77, op. 1, d. 854, l. 40b.

50. Zhdanov: RGASPI, f. 77, op. 1, d. 854, l. 40b.

51. Zhdanov: RGASPI, f. 77, op. 1, d. 854, l. 40b.

52. Zhdanov: RGASPI, f. 77, op. 1, d. 854, 1. 5.

53. Zhdanov: RGASPI, f. 77, op. 1, d. 854, 1. 5.

54. Zhdanov: RGASPI, f. 77, op. 1, d. 854, 1. 5.

55. Zhdanov: RGASPI, f. 77, op. 1, d. 854, 1. 5.

56. Zhdanov: RGASPI, f. 77, op. 1, d. 854, 1. 5.

57. Zhdanov: RGASPI, f. 77, op. 1, d. 854, 1. 5.

58. Zhdanov: RGASPI, f. 77, op. 1, d. 854, 1. 5.

59. Zhdanov: RGASPI, f. 77, op. 1, d. 854, l. 5.
60. Zhdanov: RGASPI, f. 77, op. 1, d. 854, l. 5.
61. Zhdanov: RGASPI, f. 77, op. 1, d. 854, l. 5.

II: The Kiev State

1. Zhdanov: RGASPI, f. 77, op. 1, d. 854, l. 50b.
2. Zhdanov: RGASPI, f. 77, op. 1, d. 854, l. 50b.
3. Zhdanov: RGASPI, f. 77, op. 1, d. 854, l. 50b.
4. Zhdanov: RGASPI, f. 77, op. 1, d. 854, l. 50b.
5. Zhdanov: RGASPI, f. 77, op. 1, d. 854, l. 50b
6. Zhdanov: RGASPI, f. 77, op. 1, d. 854, l. 50b.
7. Zhdanov: RGASPI, f. 77, op. 1, d. 854, l. 50b
8. Zhdanov: RGASPI, f. 77, op. 1, d. 854, ll. 50b-6.
9. Zhdanov: RGASPI, f. 77, op. 1, d. 854, l. 6.
10. Zhdanov: RGASPI, f. 77, op. 1, d. 854, l. 6.
11. Zhdanov: RGASPI, f. 77, op. 1, d. 854, l. 6
12. Zhdanov: RGASPI, f. 77, op. 1, d. 854, l. 6.
13. Zhdanov: RGASPI, f. 77, op. 1, d. 854, l. 6.
14. Zhdanov: RGASPI, f. 77, op. 1, d. 854, l. 6.
15. Zhdanov: RGASPI, f. 77, op. 1, d. 854, l. 60b.
16. Zhdanov: RGASPI, f. 77, op. 1, d. 854, l. 7.
17. Zhdanov: RGASPI, f. 77, op. 1, d. 854, l. 60b.
18. Zhdanov: RGASPI, f. 77, op. 1, d. 854, l. 60b.
19. Zhdanov: RGASPI, f. 77, op. 1, d. 854, l. 60b
20. Zhdanov: RGASPI, f. 77, op. 1, d. 854, l. 60b.
21. Zhdanov: RGASPI, f. 77, op. 1, d. 854, l. 7.
22. Zhdanov: RGASPI, f. 77, op. 1, d. 854, l. 7.
23. Zhdanov: RGASPI, f. 77, op. 1, d. 854, l. 7.
24. Zhdanov: RGASPI, f. 77, op. 1, d. 854, l. 70b.
25. Zhdanov: RGASPI, f. 77, op. 1, d. 854, l. 70b.
26. Zhdanov: RGASPI, f. 77, op. 1, d. 854, l. 70b.
27. Zhdanov: RGASPI, f. 77, op. 1, d. 854, l. 70b.
28. Zhdanov: RGASPI, f. 77, op. 1, d. 854, l. 8.
29. Zhdanov: RGASPI, f. 77, op. 1, d. 854, l. 8.
30. Zhdanov: RGASPI, f. 77, op. 1, d. 854, l. 8.
31. Zhdanov: RGASPI, f. 77, op. 1, d. 854, l. 8.
32. Zhdanov: RGASPI, f. 77, op. 1, d. 854, l. 8.

33. In the Russian original, Zhdanov corrected this word to "*fell*"; this nuance was lost in the 1938 English edition due to translator error. See RGASPI, f. 77, op. 1, d. 854, l. 8; compare Istoriia SSSR: Kratkii kurs, 17; A Short History of the U.S.S.R., 23.

34. Zhdanov: RGASPI, f. 77, op. 1, d. 854, l. 8.
35. Zhdanov: RGASPI, f. 77, op. 1, d. 854, l. 8.
36. Zhdanov: RGASPI, f. 77, op. 1, d. 854, l. 8.

37. Stalin: RGASPI, f. 558, op. 11, d. 1584, l. 130b. Also Zhdanov: f. 77, op. 1, d. 854, l. 80b.

38. Zhdanov: RGASPI, f. 77, op. 1, d. 854, l. 80b.

39. Zhdanov: RGASPI, f. 77, op. 1, d. 854, l. 80b.

40. Stalin: RGASPI, f. 558, op. 11, d. 1584, l. 130b. Also Zhdanov: f. 77, op. 1, d. 854, l. 80b.

41. Zhdanov: RGASPI, f. 77, op. 1, d. 854, l. 80b.

42. Zhdanov: RGASPI, f. 77, op. 1, d. 854, l. 80b.

43. Stalin: RGASPI, f. 558, op. 11, d. 1584, l. 130b. Also Zhdanov: f. 77, op. 1, d. 854, l. 80b.

44. Zhdanov: RGASPI, f. 77, op. 1, d. 854, l. 80b.

45. Stalin: RGASPI, f. 558, op. 11, d. 1584, l. 130b. Also Zhdanov: f. 77, op. 1, d. 854, l. 80b. Zhdanov initially proposed a different title for the subsection: "**The Social Order in the Principality of Kiev.**"

46. Stalin: RGASPI, f. 558, op. 11, d. 1584, l. 14. Also Zhdanov: f. 77, op. 1, d. 854, l. 9.

47. Stalin: RGASPI, f. 558, op. 11, d. 1584, l. 14. Also Zhdanov: f. 77, op. 1, d. 854, l. 9.

48. Stalin: RGASPI, f. 558, op. 11, d. 1584, l. 14. Also Zhdanov: f. 77, op. 1, d. 854, l. 9.

49. Zhdanov: RGASPI, f. 77, op. 1, d. 854, l. 9.

50. Zhdanov: RGASPI, f. 77, op. 1, d. 854, l. 9.

51. Stalin: RGASPI, f. 558, op. 11, d. 1584, l. 140b. Also Zhdanov: f. 77, op. 1, d. 854, l. 90b.

52. Stalin: RGASPI, f. 558, op. 11, d. 1584, l. 140b. Also Zhdanov: f. 77, op. 1, d. 854, l. 90b.

53. Zhdanov's correction "the oppressed ~~common people~~ *poor*" in the 1937 Russian edition was not reflected in the 1938 English edition due to translator error. See RGASPI, f. 77, op. 1, d. 854, l. 90b; compare Istoriia SSSR: Kratkii kurs, 20; A Short History of the U.S.S.R., 26.

54. Zhdanov: RGASPI, f. 77, op. 1, d. 854, l. 90b.

55. Zhdanov: RGASPI, f. 77, op. 1, d. 854, l. 90b.

56. Zhdanov: RGASPI, f. 77, op. 1, d. 854, l. 90b.

57. Zhdanov: RGASPI, f. 77, op. 1, d. 854, l. 90b. Here, Zhdanov wrote in the margins that the passage ought to be *"simpler."*

58. Zhdanov: RGASPI, f. 77, op. 1, d. 854, l. 90b.

59. Zhdanov: RGASPI, f. 77, op. 1, d. 854, l. 90b.

60. Zhdanov: RGASPI, f. 77, op. 1, d. 854, l. 10.

61. Zhdanov: RGASPI, f. 77, op. 1, d. 854, l. 10.

62. Stalin: RGASPI, f. 558, op. 11, d. 1584, l. 15. Also Zhdanov: f. 77, op. 1, d. 854, l. 10.

63. Zhdanov: RGASPI, f. 77, op. 1, d. 854, l. 10.

64. Zhdanov: RGASPI, f. 77, op. 1, d. 854, l. 10.

65. Zhdanov: RGASPI, f. 77, op. 1, d. 854, l. 10.

66. Zhdanov: RGASPI, f. 77, op. 1, d. 854, ll. 10–100b.

67. Zhdanov: RGASPI, f. 77, op. 1, d. 854, ll. 10.

68. Stalin: RGASPI, f. 558, op. 11, d. 1584, l. 15. Also Zhdanov: f. 77, op. 1, d. 854, l. 10.

69. Zhdanov: RGASPI, f. 77, op. 1, d. 854, l. 100b.

70. Zhdanov: RGASPI, f. 77, op. 1, d. 854, l. 100b.

71. Stalin: RGASPI, f. 558, op. 11, d. 1584, l. 150b. Also Zhdanov: f. 77, op. 1, d. 854, l. 100b.

72. Stalin: RGASPI, f. 558, op. 11, d. 1584, l. 150b. Also Zhdanov: f. 77, op. 1, d. 854, l. 100b.

73. Zhdanov: RGASPI, f. 77, op. 1, d. 854, l. 11.

74. Zhdanov: RGASPI, f. 77, op. 1, d. 854, l. 11.

75. Zhdanov: RGASPI, f. 77, op. 1, d. 854, l. 11.

76. Zhdanov: RGASPI, f. 77, op. 1, d. 854, l. 11.

77. Zhdanov: RGASPI, f. 77, op. 1, d. 854, l. 11.

78. Zhdanov: RGASPI, f. 77, op. 1, d. 854, l. 11.

79. Zhdanov: RGASPI, f. 77, op. 1, d. 854, l. 11.

80. Zhdanov: RGASPI, f. 77, op. 1, d. 854, l. 11.

81. Zhdanov: RGASPI, f. 77, op. 1, d. 854, l. 110b.

82. Zhdanov: RGASPI, f. 77, op. 1, d. 854, l. 110b.

83. Zhdanov: RGASPI, f. 77, op. 1, d. 854, l. 110b.

84. Zhdanov: RGASPI, f. 77, op. 1, d. 854, l. 110b.

85. Zhdanov: RGASPI, f. 77, op. 1, d. 854, l. 110b.

86. Zhdanov: RGASPI, f. 77, op. 1, d. 854, l. 110b.

87. Zhdanov: RGASPI, f. 77, op. 1, d. 854, l. 110b.

88. Zhdanov: RGASPI, f. 77, op. 1, d. 854, l. 110b.

89. Zhdanov: RGASPI, f. 77, op. 1, d. 854, l. 110b

III: Eastern Europe under the Rule of the Mongol Conquerers

1. Stalin: RGASPI, f. 558, op. 11, d. 1584, l. 17. Also Zhdanov: f. 77, op. 1, d. 854, l. 12.

2. Zhdanov: RGASPI, f. 77, op. 1, d. 854, l. 12.

3. Stalin: RGASPI, f. 558, op. 11, d. 1584, l. 170b. Also Zhdanov: f. 77, op. 1, d. 854, l. 120b.

4. Zhdanov: RGASPI, f. 77, op. 1, d. 854, l. 120b.

5. Zhdanov: RGASPI, f. 77, op. 1, d. 854, l. 120b.

6. Stalin: RGASPI, f. 558, op. 11, d. 1584, l. 170b. Also Zhdanov: f. 77, op. 1, d. 854, l. 120b.

7. Stalin: RGASPI, f. 558, op. 11, d. 1584, l. 170b. Also Zhdanov: f. 77, op. 1, d. 854, l. 120b.

8. Stalin: RGASPI, f. 558, op. 11, d. 1584, l. 170b. Also Zhdanov: f. 77, op. 1, d. 854, l. 120b.

9. Zhdanov's correction "The Khan of the Golden Horde began to rule over the

conquered lands as a ~~tsar~~ *lord*" was not fully captured in the 1938 English edition. See RGASPI, f. 77, op. 1, d. 854, l. 120b; compare Istoriia SSSR: Kratkii kurs, 27; A Short History of the U.S.S.R., 34.

10. Stalin: RGASPI, f. 558, op. 11, d. 1584, l. 19. Also Zhdanov: f. 77, op. 1, d. 854, l. 13.

11. Stalin: RGASPI, f. 558, op. 11, d. 1584, l. 19. Also Zhdanov: f. 77, op. 1, d. 854, l. 13.

12. Stalin: RGASPI, f. 558, op. 11, d. 1584, l. 19. Also Zhdanov: f. 77, op. 1, d. 854, l. 13.

13. Zhdanov: RGASPI, f. 77, op. 1, d. 854, l. 13.

14. Stalin: RGASPI, f. 558, op. 11, d. 1584, l. 20. Also Zhdanov: f. 77, op. 1, d. 854, l. 14.

15. Zhdanov: RGASPI, f. 77, op. 1, d. 854, l. 14.

16. Stalin: RGASPI, f. 558, op. 11, d. 1584, l. 20. Also Zhdanov: f. 77, op. 1, d. 854, l. 14.

17. Zhdanov: RGASPI, f. 77, op. 1, d. 854, l. 14.

18. Stalin: RGASPI, f. 558, op. 11, d. 1584, l. 20. Also Zhdanov: f. 77, op. 1, d. 854, l. 14.

19. Stalin: RGASPI, f. 558, op. 11, d. 1584, l. 20. Also Zhdanov: f. 77, op. 1, d. 854, l. 14.

20. Stalin: RGASPI, f. 558, op. 11, d. 1584, l. 20. Also Zhdanov: f. 77, op. 1, d. 854, l. 14.

21. Zhdanov: RGASPI, f. 77, op. 1, d. 854, l. 14.

22. Zhdanov: RGASPI, f. 77, op. 1, d. 854, l. 14.

23. Stalin's correction of "empire" to "state" was not incorporated in the 1938 English edition due to translator error. See RGASPI, f. 558, op. 11, d. 1584, l. 200b. Also Zhdanov: f. 77, op. 1, d. 854, l. 140b; compare Istoriia SSSR: Kratkii kurs, 30; A Short History of the U.S.S.R., 38.

24. Zhdanov: RGASPI, f. 77, op. 1, d. 854, ll. 140b–15.

25. Zhdanov: RGASPI, f. 77, op. 1, d. 854, l. 140b–15.

26. Zhdanov: RGASPI, f. 77, op. 1, d. 854, l. 15

IV: The Rise of the Russian National State

1. Stalin: RGASPI, f. 558, op. 11, d. 1584, l. 210b. Also Zhdanov: f. 77, op. 1, d. 854, l. 150b.

2. Zhdanov: RGASPI, f. 77, op. 1, d. 854, l. 150b.

3. Zhdanov: RGASPI, f. 77, op. 1, d. 854, l. 150b.

4. Stalin: RGASPI, f. 558, op. 11, d. 1584, l. 210b. Also Zhdanov: f. 77, op. 1, d. 854, l. 150b.

5. Zhdanov: RGASPI, f. 77, op. 1, d. 854, l. 150b.

6. Zhdanov: RGASPI, f. 77, op. 1, d. 854, l. 150b.

7. Zhdanov: RGASPI, f. 77, op. 1, d. 854, l. 150b.

8. Zhdanov: RGASPI, f. 77, op. 1, d. 854, l. 16.

9. Stalin: RGASPI, f. 558, op. 11, d. 1584, l. 22. Also Zhdanov: f. 77, op. 1, d. 854, l. 16.

10. Stalin: RGASPI, f. 558, op. 11, d. 1584, l. 22. Also Zhdanov: f. 77, op. 1, d. 854, l. 16.

11. Zhdanov: RGASPI, f. 77, op. 1, d. 854, l. 16.

12. Stalin: RGASPI, f. 558, op. 11, d. 1584, l. 22ob. Also Zhdanov: f. 77, op. 1, d. 854, l. 16.

13. Zhdanov: RGASPI, f. 77, op. 1, d. 854, l. 16.

14. Zhdanov: RGASPI, f. 77, op. 1, d. 854, l. 17. Zhdanov wrote in the margins "*D. S. N.*," which may mean "*Provide modern [terminological] names.*"

15. Zhdanov: RGASPI, f. 77, op. 1, d. 854, l. 17.

16. Zhdanov: RGASPI, f. 77, op. 1, d. 854, l. 17.

17. Zhdanov: RGASPI, f. 77, op. 1, d. 854, l. 17ob.

18. Zhdanov: RGASPI, f. 77, op. 1, d. 854, l. 17ob.

19. Zhdanov: RGASPI, f. 77, op. 1, d. 854, l. 17ob.

V: The Expansion of the Russian State

1. Zhdanov: RGASPI, f. 77, op. 1, d. 854, l. 18.

2. Zhdanov: RGASPI, f. 77, op. 1, d. 854, l. 18.

3. Zhdanov initially proposed cutting this paragraph. He then wrote in the margins that it should be moved to the end of the chapter along with the illustration of Ivan Fedorov (Figure 22). Later, he concluded that the paragraph should be left in place. See RGASPI f. 77, op. 1, d. 854, ll. 18–18ob. See note 16 below.

4. Stalin: RGASPI, f. 558, op. 11, d. 1584, l. 24ob. Also Zhdanov: f. 77, op. 1, d. 854, l. 18ob.

5. Zhdanov: RGASPI, f. 77, op. 1, d. 854, l. 18ob.

6. Stalin: RGASPI, f. 558, op. 11, d. 1584, l. 25. Also Zhdanov: f. 77, op. 1, d. 854, l. 19.

7. Stalin: RGASPI, f. 558, op. 11, d. 1584, l. 25ob. Also Zhdanov: f. 77, op. 1, d. 854, l. 19ob.

8. Zhdanov: RGASPI, f. 77, op. 1, d. 854, l. 19ob.

9. Zhdanov: RGASPI, f. 77, op. 1, d. 854, l. 19ob.

10. Stalin: RGASPI, f. 558, op. 11, d. 1584, l. 25ob. Also Zhdanov: f. 77, op. 1, d. 854, l. 20.

11. Zhdanov: RGASPI, f. 77, op. 1, d. 854, l. 20. In the 1937 Russian edition, this paragraph ended on Zhdanov's instruction with the line "*It was at that time that the adage 'So much for St. George's Day, granny!' originated.*" The proverb was not incorporated into the 1938 English edition, presumably for stylistic reasons. Compare Istoriia SSSR: Kratkii kurs, 41; A Short History of the U.S.S.R., 50. Zhdanov also made a reference to Bazilevich in the margins before crossing out the note.

12. Stalin: RGASPI, f. 558, op. 11, d. 1584, l. 26. Also Zhdanov: f. 77, op. 1, d. 854, l. 20.

13. Stalin: RGASPI, f. 558, op. 11, d. 1584, l. 26. Also Zhdanov: f. 77, op. 1, d. 854, l. 20.

14. Stalin: RGASPI, f. 558, op. 11, d. 1584, l. 26. Also Zhdanov: f. 77, op. 1, d. 854, l. 20.

15. Stalin: RGASPI, f. 558, op. 11, d. 1584, l. 26ob. Also Zhdanov: f. 77, op. 1, d. 854, l. 20.

16. Zhdanov initially noted in the margins that this would be a good place for the chapter's material on Ivan Fedorov, augmented by something from Bakhrushin's assessment of the text. Zhdanov then crossed the note out. See RGASPI, f. 77, op. 1, d. 854, l. 200b. See note 3 above.

VI: The Peasant Wars and Revolts of the Oppressed Peoples in the 17th Century

1. Zhdanov: RGASPI, f. 77, op. 1, d. 854, l. 21.

2. Stalin: RGASPI, f. 558, op. 11, d. 1584, l. 28. Also Zhdanov: f. 77, op. 1, d. 854, l. 21.

3. Stalin: RGASPI, f. 558, op. 11, d. 1584, l. 28. Also Zhdanov: f. 77, op. 1, d. 854, l. 21.

4. Stalin: RGASPI, f. 558, op. 11, d. 1584, l. 28ob. Also Zhdanov: f. 77, op. 1, d. 854, l. 21ob.

5. Stalin: RGASPI, f. 558, op. 11, d. 1584, l. 28ob. Also Zhdanov: f. 77, op. 1, d. 854, l. 21ob.

6. Stalin: RGASPI, f. 558, op. 11, d. 1584, l. 29. Also Zhdanov: f. 77, op. 1, d. 854, l. 22.

7. Stalin: RGASPI, f. 558, op. 11, d. 1584, l. 29. Also Zhdanov: f. 77, op. 1, d. 854, l. 22.

8. Stalin: RGASPI, f. 558, op. 11, d. 1584, l. 29. Also Zhdanov: f. 77, op. 1, d. 854, l. 22.

9. Stalin: RGASPI, f. 558, op. 11, d. 1584, l. 29. Also Zhdanov: f. 77, op. 1, d. 854, ll. 22–22ob.

10. Stalin: RGASPI, f. 558, op. 11, d. 1584, l. 28. Also Zhdanov: f. 77, op. 1, d. 854, l. 22ob.

11. Stalin: RGASPI, f. 558, op. 11, d. 1584, l. 29. Also Zhdanov: f. 77, op. 1, d. 854, l. 22ob.

12. Stalin: RGASPI, f. 558, op. 11, d. 1584, l. 29. Also Zhdanov: f. 77, op. 1, d. 854, l. 22ob.

13. Zhdanov: RGASPI, f. 77, op. 1, d. 854, l. 22ob.

14. Zhdanov: RGASPI, f. 77, op. 1, d. 854, l. 22ob.

15. Zhdanov: RGASPI, f. 77, op. 1, d. 854, l. 22ob.

16. Stalin deleted this word in the 1937 Russian edition; it appeared in the 1938 English edition due to translator error. See RGASPI, f. 558, op. 11, d. 1584, l. 30. Also Zhdanov: f. 77, op. 1, d. 854, l. 23; compare Istoriia SSSR: Kratkii kurs, 46; A Short History of the U.S.S.R., 57.

17. Zhdanov: RGASPI, f. 77, op. 1, d. 854, l. 23.

18. Stalin: RGASPI, f. 558, op. 11, d. 1584, l. 30ob. Also Zhdanov: f. 77, op. 1, d. 854, l. 23ob.

19. Zhdanov: RGASPI, f. 77, op. 1, d. 854, l. 23ob.

20. The 1937 Russian text's note that the Zemsky Sobor assembled "in Moscow"

was dropped from the 1938 English edition due to translator error. Compare ISTO-RIIA SSSR: KRATKII KURS, 48; A SHORT HISTORY OF THE U.S.S.R., 60.

21. Zhdanov wrote a note in the margins about incorporating something from Bubnov's assessment of the text. See RGASPI, f. 77, op. 1, d. 854, l. 240b. For Bubnov's assessment, see f. 77, op. 1, d. 847, ll. 1–28.

22. Stalin: RGASPI, f. 558, op. 11, d. 1584, l. 310b. Also Zhdanov: f. 77, op. 1, d. 854, l. 240b.

23. Stalin: RGASPI, f. 558, op. 11, d. 1584, l. 310b. Also Zhdanov: f. 77, op. 1, d. 854, l. 240b.

24. Stalin: RGASPI, f. 558, op. 11, d. 1584, l. 32. Also Zhdanov: f. 77, op. 1, d. 854, l. 240b.

25. Stalin: RGASPI, f. 558, op. 11, d. 1584, l. 32. Also Zhdanov: f. 77, op. 1, d. 854, l. 25.

26. Zhdanov: RGASPI, f. 77, op. 1, d. 854, l. 25.

27. Zhdanov: RGASPI, f. 77, op. 1, d. 854, l. 25.

28. Zhdanov: RGASPI, f. 77, op. 1, d. 854, l. 250b.

29. Stalin: RGASPI, f. 558, op. 11, d. 1584, l. 330b. Also Zhdanov: f. 77, op. 1, d. 854, l. 260b

30. Stalin: RGASPI, f. 558, op. 11, d. 1584, l. 34. Also Zhdanov: f. 77, op. 1, d. 854, l. 27.

31. Stalin: RGASPI, f. 558, op. 11, d. 1584, l. 34. Also Zhdanov: f. 77, op. 1, d. 854, l. 27.

32. Stalin: RGASPI, f. 558, op. 11, d. 1584, l. 34. Also Zhdanov: f. 77, op. 1, d. 854, l. 27.

33. Stalin: RGASPI, f. 558, op. 11, d. 1584, l. 34. Also Zhdanov: f. 77, op. 1, d. 854, l. 27.

34. Stalin: RGASPI, f. 558, op. 11, d. 1584, l. 32. Also Zhdanov: f. 77, op. 1, d. 854, l. 27.

35. Stalin: RGASPI, f. 558, op. 11, d. 1584, l. 35. Also Zhdanov: f. 77, op. 1, d. 854, l. 28. Stalin's addition of "*on the side*" to the 1937 Russian edition did not appear in the 1938 English edition due to translator error. Compare ISTORIIA SSSR: KRATKII KURS, 56; A SHORT HISTORY OF THE U.S.S.R., 69.

36. Later edit: Zhdanov: RGASPI, f. 77, op. 1, d. 854, l. 280b. Zhdanov's addition of "*foreign*" to the 1937 Russian edition did not appear in the 1938 English edition due to translator error. Compare ISTORIIA SSSR: KRATKII KURS, 57; A SHORT HISTORY OF THE U.S.S.R., 70.

37. Stalin: RGASPI, f. 558, op. 11, d. 1584, l. 350b. Also Zhdanov: f. 77, op. 1, d. 854, l. 280b.

38. Stalin: RGASPI, f. 558, op. 11, d. 1584, l. 36. Also Zhdanov: f. 77, op. 1, d. 854, l. 29.

39. Stalin: RGASPI, f. 558, op. 11, d. 1584, l. 36. Also Zhdanov: f. 77, op. 1, d. 854, l. 29.

40. Zhdanov: RGASPI, f. 77, op. 1, d. 854, l. 290b.

41. Stalin: RGASPI, f. 558, op. 11, d. 1584, l. 360b. Also Zhdanov: f. 77, op. 1, d. 854, l. 290b.

42. Stalin: RGASPI, f. 558, op. 11, d. 1584, l. 360b. Also Zhdanov: f. 77, op. 1, d. 854, l. 290b.

43. Stalin: RGASPI, f. 558, op. 11, d. 1584, l. 360b. Also Zhdanov: f. 77, op. 1, d. 854, l. 290b.

VII: Russia in the 18th Century. The Empire of the Landlords and Merchants

1. Stalin: RGASPI, f. 558, op. 11, d. 1584, l. 37. Also Zhdanov: f. 77, op. 1, d. 854, l. 30.

2. Stalin: RGASPI, f. 558, op. 11, d. 1584, l. 37. Also Zhdanov: f. 77, op. 1, d. 854, l. 30.

3. Stalin: RGASPI, f. 558, op. 11, d. 1584, l. 370b. Also Zhdanov: f. 77, op. 1, d. 854, l. 300b.

4. Stalin: RGASPI, f. 558, op. 11, d. 1584, l. 38. Also Zhdanov: f. 77, op. 1, d. 854, l. 300b.

5. Zhdanov: RGASPI, f. 77, op. 1, d. 854, l. 31.

6. Stalin: RGASPI, f. 558, op. 11, d. 1584, l. 380b. Also Zhdanov: f. 77, op. 1, d. 854, l. 310b.

7. Stalin: RGASPI, f. 558, op. 11, d. 1584, l. 380b. Also Zhdanov: f. 77, op. 1, d. 854, l. 310b.

8. Zhdanov: RGASPI, f. 77, op. 1, d. 854, l. 310b.

9. Zhdanov: RGASPI, f. 77, op. 1, d. 854, l. 310b.

10. Zhdanov: RGASPI, f. 77, op. 1, d. 854, l. 310b.

11. Zhdanov: RGASPI, f. 77, op. 1, d. 854, l. 310b.

12. Zhdanov: RGASPI, f. 77, op. 1, d. 854, l. 310b.

13. Zhdanov: RGASPI, f. 77, op. 1, d. 854, l. 32.

14. Zhdanov: RGASPI, f. 77, op. 1, d. 854, l. 32.

15. Stalin: RGASPI, f. 558, op. 11, d. 1584, l. 39. Also Zhdanov: f. 77, op. 1, d. 854, l. 32.

16. Stalin: RGASPI, f. 558, op. 11, d. 1584, l. 39. Also Zhdanov: f. 77, op. 1, d. 854, l. 32.

17. Stalin: RGASPI, f. 558, op. 11, d. 1584, l. 390b. Also Zhdanov: f. 77, op. 1, d. 854, l. 320b.

18. Stalin: RGASPI, f. 558, op. 11, d. 1584, l. 390b. Also Zhdanov: f. 77, op. 1, d. 854, l. 320b.

19. Zhdanov: RGASPI, f. 77, op. 1, d. 854, l. 320b.

20. Stalin: RGASPI, f. 558, op. 11, d. 1584, l. 390b. Also Zhdanov: f. 77, op. 1, d. 854, l. 320b.

21. Zhdanov: RGASPI, f. 77, op. 1, d. 854, l. 33.

22. Zhdanov: RGASPI, f. 77, op. 1, d. 854, l. 33.

23. Stalin: RGASPI, f. 558, op. 11, d. 1584, l. 40. Also Zhdanov: f. 77, op. 1, d. 854, l. 33.

24. Stalin: RGASPI, f. 558, op. 11, d. 1584, l. 40. Also Zhdanov: f. 77, op. 1, d. 854, l. 33.

25. Zhdanov: RGASPI, f. 77, op. 1, d. 854, l. 34.

26. Zhdanov: RGASPI, f. 77, op. 1, d. 854, l. 34.

27. Zhdanov: RGASPI, f. 77, op. 1, d. 854, l. 35.

28. Zhdanov: RGASPI, f. 77, op. 1, d. 854, l. 35.

29. Zhdanov: RGASPI, f. 77, op. 1, d. 854, l. 36.

30. Zhdanov: RGASPI, f. 77, op. 1, d. 854, l. 36.

31. Stalin: RGASPI, f. 558, op. 11, d. 1584, l. 73. Also Zhdanov: f. 77, op. 1, d. 854, l. 36.

32. Zhdanov: RGASPI, f. 77, op. 1, d. 854, l. 36.

33. Stalin: RGASPI, f. 558, op. 11, d. 1584, l. 43. Also Zhdanov: f. 77, op. 1, d. 854, l. 36.

34. Stalin: RGASPI, f. 558, op. 11, d. 1584, l. 43ob. Also Zhdanov: f. 77, op. 1, d. 854, l. 36ob.

35. Stalin: RGASPI, f. 558, op. 11, d. 1584, l. 43ob. Also Zhdanov: f. 77, op. 1, d. 854, l. 36ob.

36. Zhdanov: RGASPI, f. 77, op. 1, d. 854, l. 36ob.

37. Stalin: RGASPI, f. 558, op. 11, d. 1584, l. 43ob. Also Zhdanov: f. 77, op. 1, d. 854, l. 36ob.

38. Zhdanov: RGASPI, f. 77, op. 1, d. 854, l. 36ob.

39. Zhdanov: RGASPI, f. 77, op. 1, d. 854, l. 37.

40. Stalin: RGASPI, f. 558, op. 11, d. 1584, l. 44. Also Zhdanov: f. 77, op. 1, d. 854, l. 37.

41. Stalin added *"of the Poles"* to the 1937 Russian edition; this edit was not reflected the 1938 English edition due to translator error. See RGASPI, f. 558, op. 11, d. 1584, l. 44. Also Zhdanov: f. 77, op. 1, d. 854, l. 37. Compare ISTORIIA SSSR: KRATKII KURS, 73; A SHORT HISTORY OF THE U.S.S.R., 90.

42. Zhdanov: RGASPI, f. 77, op. 1, d. 854, l. 37.

43. Zhdanov: RGASPI, f. 77, op. 1, d. 854, l. 37.

44. Stalin: RGASPI, f. 558, op. 11, d. 1584, l. 44. Also Zhdanov: f. 77, op. 1, d. 854, l. 37.

45. Stalin: RGASPI, f. 558, op. 11, d. 1584, l. 44. Also Zhdanov: f. 77, op. 1, d. 854, l. 37.

46. In the 1937 Russian edition, this expression reads "subjected to Russian rule," which more accurately reflects the chapter's differentiation of the empire's ruling classes from its subjects. See ISTORIIA SSSR: KRATKII KURS, 74.

47. Stalin: RGASPI, f. 558, op. 11, d. 1584, l. 44ob. Also Zhdanov: f. 77, op. 1, d. 854, l. 37ob.

48. Stalin: RGASPI, f. 558, op. 11, d. 1584, l. 44ob. Also Zhdanov: f. 77, op. 1, d. 854, l. 37ob.

49. Stalin: RGASPI, f. 558, op. 11, d. 1584, l. 44ob. Also Zhdanov: f. 77, op. 1, d. 854, l. 37ob.

VIII: Tsarist Russia—the Gendarme of Europe

1. Zhdanov: RGASPI, f. 77, op. 1, d. 854, l. 38.

2. Stalin: RGASPI, f. 558, op. 11, d. 1584, l. 46. Also Zhdanov: f. 77, op. 1, d. 854, l. 38.

3. Stalin: RGASPI, f. 558, op. 11, d. 1584, l. 46ob. Also Zhdanov: f. 77, op. 1, d. 854, l. 38ob.

4. Stalin: RGASPI, f. 558, op. 11, d. 1584, l. 46ob. Also Zhdanov: f. 77, op. 1, d. 854, l. 38ob.

5. Stalin: RGASPI, f. 558, op. 11, d. 1584, l. 46ob. Also Zhdanov: f. 77, op. 1, d. 854, l. 38ob.

6. Stalin: RGASPI, f. 558, op. 11, d. 1584, l. 46ob. Also Zhdanov: f. 77, op. 1, d. 854, l. 38ob.

7. Stalin: RGASPI, f. 558, op. 11, d. 1584, l. 47. Also Zhdanov: f. 77, op. 1, d. 854, l. 38ob.

8. Stalin: RGASPI, f. 558, op. 11, d. 1584, l. 47. Also Zhdanov: f. 77, op. 1, d. 854, l. 38ob.

9. Stalin: RGASPI, f. 558, op. 11, d. 1584, l. 47. Also Zhdanov: f. 77, op. 1, d. 854, l. 39.

10. Stalin: RGASPI, f. 558, op. 11, d. 1584, l. 47. Also Zhdanov: f. 77, op. 1, d. 854, l. 39.

11. Zhdanov: RGASPI, f. 77, op. 1, d. 854, l. 39.

12. Zhdanov: RGASPI, f. 77, op. 1, d. 854, l. 39.

13. Zhdanov: RGASPI, f. 77, op. 1, d. 854, l. 39.

14. Stalin: RGASPI, f. 558, op. 11, d. 1584, l. 47ob. Also Zhdanov: f. 77, op. 1, d. 854, l. 39ob.

15. Stalin: RGASPI, f. 558, op. 11, d. 1584, l. 47ob. Also Zhdanov: f. 77, op. 1, d. 854, l. 39ob.

16. Stalin's edit in the 1937 Russian edition was more explicitly critical of the revanche: "At this time, Napoleon Bonaparte staged a coup d'etat *against the revolution* and declared himself supreme ruler of the country." RGASPI, f. 558, op. 11, d. 1584, l. 47ob. Also Zhdanov: f. 77, op. 1, d. 854, l. 39ob. See ISTORIIA SSSR: KRATKII KURS, 78–79.

17. Zhdanov: RGASPI, f. 77, op. 1, d. 854, l. 39ob.

18. Zhdanov: RGASPI, f. 77, op. 1, d. 854, l. 40.

19. Zhdanov: RGASPI, f. 77, op. 1, d. 854, l. 40.

20. Stalin: RGASPI, f. 558, op. 11, d. 1584, l. 48. Also Zhdanov: f. 77, op. 1, d. 854, l. 40.

21. Zhdanov: RGASPI, f. 77, op. 1, d. 854, l. 40.

22. Zhdanov: RGASPI, f. 77, op. 1, d. 854, l. 40.

23. Zhdanov: RGASPI, f. 77, op. 1, d. 854, l. 40.

24. Stalin: RGASPI, f. 558, op. 11, d. 1584, l. 49. Also Zhdanov: f. 77, op. 1, d. 854, l. 41.

25. Zhdanov: RGASPI, f. 77, op. 1, d. 854, l. 41.

26. Zhdanov: RGASPI, f. 77, op. 1, d. 854, l. 41.

27. Zhdanov: RGASPI, f. 77, op. 1, d. 854, l. 41.

28. Stalin: RGASPI, f. 558, op. 11, d. 1584, l. 49. Also Zhdanov: f. 77, op. 1, d. 854, l. 41.

29. Stalin: RGASPI, f. 558, op. 11, d. 1584, l. 49. Also Zhdanov: f. 77, op. 1, d. 854, l. 41.

30. Stalin: RGASPI, t. 558, op. 11, d. 1584, l. 49. Also Zhdanov: f. 77, op. 1, d. 854, l. 41.

31. Stalin: RGASPI, f. 558, op. 11, d. 1584, l. 49ob. Also Zhdanov: f. 77, op. 1, d. 854, l. 41ob.

32. Stalin: RGASPI, f. 558, op. 11, d. 1584, l. 49ob. Also Zhdanov: f. 77, op. 1, d. 854, l. 41ob.

33. Stalin: RGASPI, f. 558, op. 11, d. 1584, l. 49ob. Also Zhdanov: f. 77, op. 1, d. 854, l. 41ob.

34. Stalin: RGASPI, f. 558, op. 11, d. 1584, l. 49ob. Also Zhdanov: f. 77, op. 1, d. 854, l. 41ob.

35. Zhdanov: RGASPI, f. 77, op. 1, d. 854, l. 41ob.

36. Zhdanov: RGASPI, f. 77, op. 1, d. 854, l. 42.

37. Zhdanov: RGASPI, f. 77, op. 1, d. 854, l. 42.

38. Zhdanov: RGASPI, f. 77, op. 1, d. 854, l. 42.

39. Zhdanov: RGASPI, f. 77, op. 1, d. 854, l. 42.

40. Zhdanov: RGASPI, f. 77, op. 1, d. 854, l. 42.

41. Zhdanov: RGASPI, f. 77, op. 1, d. 854, l. 42ob. Zhdanov wrote in the margins the Russian abbreviation "D. S. P." for unclear reasons.

42. Zhdanov: RGASPI, f. 77, op. 1, d. 854, l. 42ob.

43. Zhdanov: RGASPI, f. 77, op. 1, d. 854, l. 42ob.

44. Stalin initially deleted "and thousands" from this parenthetical statement. Subsequently, the entire statement was excised from the English translation due to translator error. See RGASPI, f. 558, op. 11, d. 1584, l. 51. Also Zhdanov: f. 77, op. 1, d. 854, l. 43. Compare ISTORIIA SSSR: KRATKII KURS, 85; A SHORT HISTORY OF THE U.S.S.R., 104.

45. Stalin: RGASPI, f. 558, op. 11, d. 1584, l. 51ob. Also Zhdanov: f. 77, op. 1, d. 854, l. 43ob.

46. Stalin: RGASPI, f. 558, op. 11, d. 1584, l. 51ob. Also Zhdanov: f. 77, op. 1, d. 854, l. 43ob.

47. Stalin: RGASPI, f. 558, op. 11, d. 1584, l. 51ob. Also Zhdanov: f. 77, op. 1, d. 854, l. 43ob.

48. Stalin: RGASPI, f. 558, op. 11, d. 1584, l. 53. Also Zhdanov: f. 77, op. 1, d. 854, l. 45.

49. Zhdanov: RGASPI, f. 77, op. 1, d. 854, l. 45.

50. Zhdanov: RGASPI, f. 77, op. 1, d. 854, l. 45ob.

51. Stalin: RGASPI, f. 558, op. 11, d. 1584, l. 53ob. Also Zhdanov: f. 77, op. 1, d. 854, l. 45ob.

52. Stalin: RGASPI, f. 558, op. 11, d. 1584, l. 53ob. Also Zhdanov: f. 77, op. 1, d. 854, l. 45ob.

53. Stalin: RGASPI, f. 558, op. 11, d. 1584, l. 530b. Also Zhdanov: f. 77, op. 1, d. 854, l. 450b.

54. Stalin: RGASPI, f. 558, op. 11, d. 1584, l. 530b-54. Also Zhdanov: f. 77, op. 1, d. 854, ll. 450b-46.

55. Stalin: RGASPI, f. 558, op. 11, d. 1584, l. 530b. Also Zhdanov: f. 77, op. 1, d. 854, l. 46.

56. Stalin: RGASPI, f. 558, op. 11, d. 1584, l. 540b. Also Zhdanov: f. 77, op. 1, d. 854, l. 460b.

57. Stalin: RGASPI, f. 558, op. 11, d. 1584, l. 540b. Also Zhdanov: f. 77, op. 1, d. 854, l. 460b.

58. Stalin: RGASPI, f. 558, op. 11, d. 1584, l. 540b. Also Zhdanov: f. 77, op. 1, d. 854, l. 460b.

59. Stalin: RGASPI, f. 558, op. 11, d. 1584, l. 540b. Also Zhdanov: f. 77, op. 1, d. 854, l. 460b.

60. Stalin: RGASPI, f. 558, op. 11, d. 1584, l. 540b. Also Zhdanov: f. 77, op. 1, d. 854, l. 460b.

61. Stalin: RGASPI, f. 558, op. 11, d. 1584, l. 55. Also Zhdanov: f. 77, op. 1, d. 854, l. 47.

62. Stalin: RGASPI, f. 558, op. 11, d. 1584, l. 55. Also Zhdanov: f. 77, op. 1, d. 854, l. 47.

63. Stalin: RGASPI, f. 558, op. 11, d. 1584, l. 55. Also Zhdanov: f. 77, op. 1, d. 854, l. 47.

64. Stalin: RGASPI, f. 558, op. 11, d. 1584, l. 55. Also Zhdanov: f. 77, op. 1, d. 854, l. 47.

65. Stalin: RGASPI, f. 558, op. 11, d. 1584, l. 55. Also Zhdanov: f. 77, op. 1, d. 854, l. 47.

66. Stalin: RGASPI, f. 558, op. 11, d. 1584, l. 55.

67. Zhdanov: RGASPI, f. 77, op. 1, d. 854, l. 47.

68. Zhdanov's proposed corrections to this sentence—"The revolution spread to ~~Hungary, which was~~ part of the ~~Austrian~~ *Austro-Hungarian* Empire"—were dismissed. See RGASPI, f. 77, op. 1, d. 854, ll. 47–470b.

69. Stalin: RGASPI, f. 558, op. 11, d. 1584, l. 550b. Also Zhdanov: f. 77, op. 1, d. 854, l. 470b.

70. Zhdanov: RGASPI, f. 77, op. 1, d. 854, l. 48.

71. Zhdanov: RGASPI, f. 77, op. 1, d. 854, l. 48.

72. Stalin: RGASPI, f. 558, op. 11, d. 1584, l. 56. Also Zhdanov: f. 77, op. 1, d. 854, l. 48.

73. Zhdanov: RGASPI, f. 77, op. 1, d. 854, l. 48.

74. Zhdanov: RGASPI, f. 77, op. 1, d. 854, l. 48.

75. Zhdanov: RGASPI, f. 77, op. 1, d. 854, l. 48.

76. Zhdanov: RGASPI, f. 77, op. 1, d. 854, l. 48.

77. Stalin: RGASPI, f. 558, op. 11, d. 1584, l. 560b. Also Zhdanov: f. 77, op. 1, d. 854, l. 480b.

78. Zhdanov: RGASPI, f. 77, op. 1, d. 854, l. 480b.

79. Zhdanov: RGASPI, f. 77, op. 1, d. 854, l. 48ob.

80. Zhdanov: RGASPI, f. 77, op. 1, d. 854, l. 48ob.

81. Stalin: RGASPI, f. 558, op. 11, d. 1584, l. 56ob. Also Zhdanov: f. 77, op. 1, d. 854, l. 48ob.

82. Stalin: RGASPI, f. 558, op. 11, d. 1584, l. 57. Also Zhdanov: f. 77, op. 1, d. 854, l. 49.

IX: The Growth of Capitalism in Tsarist Russia

1. Stalin: RGASPI, f. 558, op. 11, d. 1584, l. 57ob. Also Zhdanov: f. 77, op. 1, d. 854, l. 49ob.

2. Stalin: RGASPI, f. 558, op. 11, d. 1584, l. 57ob. Also Zhdanov: f. 77, op. 1, d. 854, l. 49ob.

3. Stalin: RGASPI, f. 558, op. 11, d. 1584, l. 57ob. Also Zhdanov: f. 77, op. 1, d. 854, l. 49ob.

4. Zhdanov: RGASPI, f. 77, op. 1, d. 854, l. 49ob.

5. Zhdanov: RGASPI, f. 77, op. 1, d. 854, l. 49ob.

6. Stalin: RGASPI, f. 558, op. 11, d. 1584, l. 58. Also Zhdanov: f. 77, op. 1, d. 854, l. 50.

7. In later editing, Zhdanov added "sanguinary battles were fought *with the peasants* in which hundreds were killed and wounded." This editing was not reflected in the 1938 English edition of the textbook. See RGASPI, f. 77, op. 1, d. 854, l. 50. Compare Istoriia SSSR: Kratkii kurs, 98; A Short History of the U.S.S.R., 119.

8. Stalin: RGASPI, f. 558, op. 11, d. 1584, l. 58. Also Zhdanov: f. 77, op. 1, d. 854, l. 50.

9. Stalin altered the term "revolutionary" (revoliutsioner) to "*populist* revolutionary" (narodnicheskii revoliutsioner); his expression was changed in the text's English translation to "revolutionary *democrat*." RGASPI, f. 558, op. 11, d. 1584, l. 58. Also Zhdanov: f. 77, op. 1, d. 854, l. 50. Compare Istoriia SSSR: Kratkii kurs, 98; A Short History of the U.S.S.R., 119.

10. Stalin deleted the word "all" from this sentence, but it was retained for unclear reasons. RGASPI, f. 558, op. 11, d. 1584, l. 58ob.

11. Zhdanov: RGASPI, f. 77, op. 1, d. 854, l. 50ob.

12. Stalin altered the term "revolutionaries" (revoliutsionerami) to "*populist* revolutionaries" (narodnicheskimi revoliutsionerami) in the 1937 Russian edition; it was rendered as "~~revolutionaries~~ revolutionary democrats" in the 1938 English edition. RGASPI, f. 558, op. 11, d. 1584, l. 58ob. Also Zhdanov: f. 77, op. 1, d. 854, l. 50ob. Compare Istoriia SSSR: Kratkii kurs, 98; A Short History of the U.S.S.R., 120.

13. Zhdanov: RGASPI, f. 77, op. 1, d. 854, l. 50ob.

14. Stalin altered the term "revolutionary" (revoliutsionera) to "*populist* revolutionary" (narodnicheskogo revoliutsionera); his expression was changed in the text's English translation to "revolutionary *democrat*." RGASPI, f. 558, op. 11, d. 1584, l. 58ob. Also Zhdanov: f. 77, op. 1, d. 854, l. 50ob. Compare Istoriia SSSR: Kratkii kurs, 98; A Short History of the U.S.S.R., 120.

15. Zhdanov: RGASPI, f. 77, op. 1, d. 854, l. 500b.

16. Stalin underlined the word "village." RGASPI, f. 558, op. 11, d. 1584, l. 59.

17. Stalin underlined the word "volost elder." RGASPI, f. 558, op. 11, d. 1584, l. 59.

18. Zhdanov: RGASPI, f. 77, op. 1, d. 854, l. 51.

19. The word "also" was added to the 1938 English edition by translator error. See A Short History of the U.S.S.R., 121.

20. Stalin: RGASPI, f. 558, op. 11, d. 1584, l. 590b. Also Zhdanov: f. 77, op. 1, d. 854, l. 510b.

21. Stalin: RGASPI, f. 558, op. 11, d. 1584, l. 590b. Also Zhdanov: f. 77, op. 1, d. 854, l. 510b.

22. Stalin: RGASPI, f. 558, op. 11, d. 1584, l. 590b. Also Zhdanov: f. 77, op. 1, d. 854, l. 510b.

23. Stalin: RGASPI, f. 558, op. 11, d. 1584, l. 590b. Also Zhdanov: f. 77, op. 1, d. 854, l. 510b.

24. Stalin: RGASPI, f. 558, op. 11, d. 1584, l. 590b. Also Zhdanov: f. 77, op. 1, d. 854, l. 510b.

25. Zhdanov: RGASPI, f. 77, op. 1, d. 854, l. 510b.

26. Zhdanov: RGASPI, f. 77, op. 1, d. 854, l. 510b.

27. Stalin: RGASPI, f. 558, op. 11, d. 1584, l. 590b. Also Zhdanov: f. 77, op. 1, d. 854, l. 510b.

28. Stalin: RGASPI, f. 558, op. 11, d. 1584, l. 60. Also Zhdanov: f. 77, op. 1, d. 854, l. 52.

29. Zhdanov: RGASPI, f. 77, op. 1, d. 854, l. 52.

30. Zhdanov: RGASPI, f. 77, op. 1, d. 854, l. 52.

31. Stalin corrected this phrase to "*noble* Russia" (DVORIANSKOI ROSSIEI) in the 1937 Russian edition; it was rendered as "*landlord* Russia" in the 1938 English translation due to translator error. RGASPI, f. 558, op. 11, d. 1584, l. 590b. See also Zhdanov, f. 77, op. 1, d. 854, l. 52. Compare ISTORIIA SSSR: KRATKII KURS, 102; A Short History of the U.S.S.R., 124.

32. Zhdanov: RGASPI, f. 77, op. 1, d. 854, l. 52.

33. Zhdanov: RGASPI, f. 77, op. 1, d. 854, l. 52.

34. Zhdanov: RGASPI, f. 77, op. 1, d. 854, l. 520b.

35. Stalin: RGASPI, f. 558, op. 11, d. 1584, l. 600b. Also Zhdanov: f. 77, op. 1, d. 854, l. 520b.

36. Stalin: RGASPI, f. 558, op. 11, d. 1584, l. 600b. Also Zhdanov: f. 77, op. 1, d. 854, l. 520b.

37. Zhdanov: RGASPI, f. 77, op. 1, d. 854, l. 520b. Here, Zhdanov wrote in the margins "*Bessarabia?*" and then crossed it out.

38. Stalin: RGASPI, f. 558, op. 11, d. 1584, l. 600b. Also Zhdanov: f. 77, op. 1, d. 854, l. 520b.

39. Zhdanov: RGASPI, f. 77, op. 1, d. 854, l. 520b.

40. Zhdanov: RGASPI, f. 77, op. 1, d. 854, l. 53.

41. Stalin: RGASPI, f. 558, op. 11, d. 1584, l. 62. Also Zhdanov: f. 77, op. 1, d. 854, l. 53.

42. Stalin: RGASPI, f. 558, op. 11, d. 1584, l. 62. Also Zhdanov: f. 77, op. 1, d. 854, l. 53.

43. Stalin: RGASPI, f. 558, op. 11, d. 1584, l. 62. Also Zhdanov: f. 77, op. 1, d. 854, l. 53.

44. Stalin: RGASPI, f. 558, op. 11, d. 1584, l. 62. Also Zhdanov: f. 77, op. 1, d. 854, l. 53.

45. Stalin stressed the armed nature of this National Guard in the Russian version of the text. RGASPI, f. 558, op. 11, d. 1584, l. 62. Also Zhdanov: f. 77, op. 1, d. 854, l. 53.

46. Stalin: RGASPI, f. 558, op. 11, d. 1584, l. 62. Also Zhdanov: f. 77, op. 1, d. 854, l. 53.

47. Zhdanov: RGASPI, f. 77, op. 1, d. 854, l. 53ob.

48. Stalin: RGASPI, f. 558, op. 11, d. 1584, l. 62ob. Also Zhdanov: f. 77, op. 1, d. 854, l. 53ob.

49. Stalin: RGASPI, f. 558, op. 11, d. 1584, l. 62ob. Also Zhdanov: f. 77, op. 1, d. 854, l. 53ob.

50. Stalin referred to the Commune in this interpolation as the "*Paris* Commune" in the 1937 Russian edition; it was rendered differently in the 1938 English translation for stylistic reasons. RGASPI, f. 558, op. 11, d. 1584, l. 62ob. Also Zhdanov: f. 77, op. 1, d. 854, l. 53ob. Compare ISTORIIA SSSR: KRATKII KURS, 104; A SHORT HISTORY OF THE U.S.S.R., 127.

51. Stalin: RGASPI, f. 558, op. 11, d. 1584, l. 64. Also Zhdanov: f. 77, op. 1, d. 854, l. 54.

52. Stalin: RGASPI, f. 558, op. 11, d. 1584, l. 64. Also Zhdanov: f. 77, op. 1, d. 854, l. 54.

53. Zhdanov: RGASPI, f. 77, op. 1, d. 854, l. 54.

54. Zhdanov: RGASPI, f. 77, op. 1, d. 854, l. 54.

55. Stalin: RGASPI, f. 558, op. 11, d. 1584, l. 64. Also Zhdanov: f. 77, op. 1, d. 854, l. 54.

56. This sentence was shortened from "In 1876, after the fall of the Paris Commune, the First International ceased to exist" in the 1938 English edition due to translator error. Compare ISTORIIA SSSR: KRATKII KURS, 106; A SHORT HISTORY OF THE U.S.S.R., 129.

57. Stalin: RGASPI, f. 558, op. 11, d. 1584, l. 64. Also Zhdanov: f. 77, op. 1, d. 854, l. 54.

58. Stalin: RGASPI, f. 558, op. 11, d. 1584, l. 64. Also Zhdanov: f. 77, op. 1, d. 854, l. 54.

59. Stalin: RGASPI, f. 558, op. 11, d. 1584, l. 64. Also Zhdanov: f. 77, op. 1, d. 854, l. 54.

60. Zhdanov: RGASPI, f. 77, op. 1, d. 854, l. 54.

61. Stalin: RGASPI, f. 558, op. 11, d. 1584, l. 64ob. Also Zhdanov: f. 77, op. 1, d. 854, l. 54ob.

62. Zhdanov: RGASPI, f. 77, op. 1, d. 854, l. 54ob.

63. Zhdanov: RGASPI, f. 77, op. 1, d. 854, l. 54ob. Zhdanov wrote in the margins: "*Provide the modern administrative names*" and then crossed it out the note.

64. Stalin: RGASPI, f. 558, op. 11, d. 1584, l. 64ob. Also Zhdanov: f. 77, op. 1, d. 854, l. 540b.

65. Stalin: RGASPI, f. 558, op. 11, d. 1584, l. 65. Also Zhdanov: f. 77, op. 1, d. 854, l. 55.

66. Stalin: RGASPI, f. 558, op. 11, d. 1584, l. 65. Also Zhdanov: f. 77, op. 1, d. 854, l. 55.

67. Stalin: RGASPI, f. 558, op. 11, d. 1584, l. 65ob. Also Zhdanov: f. 77, op. 1, d. 854, l. 55ob.

68. Stalin: RGASPI, f. 558, op. 11, d. 1584, l. 65ob. Also Zhdanov: f. 77, op. 1, d. 854, l. 55ob.

69. Stalin added *"tsar* Alexander II" to the 1937 Russian text that was not reflected in the 1938 English edition due to translator error. See RGASPI, f. 558, op. 11, d. 1584, l. 65ob. Also Zhdanov: f. 77, op. 1, d. 854, l. 55ob. Compare Istoriia SSSR: Kratkii kurs, 109; A Short History of the U.S.S.R., 132.

70. Stalin: RGASPI, f. 558, op. 11, d. 1584, l. 65ob. Also Zhdanov: f. 77, op. 1, d. 854, l. 55ob.

71. Stalin: RGASPI, f. 558, op. 11, d. 1584, l. 65ob. Also Zhdanov: f. 77, op. 1, d. 854, l. 55ob.

72. Stalin: RGASPI, f. 558, op. 11, d. 1584, l. 65ob. Also Zhdanov: f. 77, op. 1, d. 854, l. 55ob.

73. Stalin: RGASPI, f. 558, op. 11, d. 1584, l. 65ob. Also Zhdanov: f. 77, op. 1, d. 854, l. 55ob.

74. Stalin: RGASPI, f. 558, op. 11, d. 1584, l. 65ob. Also Zhdanov: f. 77, op. 1, d. 854, l. 55ob.

75. Stalin: RGASPI, f. 558, op. 11, d. 1584, l. 65ob. Also Zhdanov: f. 77, op. 1, d. 854, l. 55ob.

76. Stalin: RGASPI, f. 558, op. 11, d. 1584, l. 66. Also Zhdanov: f. 77, op. 1, d. 854, l. 56.

77. This sentence was shortened from the 1937 Russian text "He began writing his ~~notable~~ works when he was still a young man" in the 1938 English edition, eliding Stalin's correction. See RGASPI, f. 558, op. 11, d. 1584, l. 66; also Zhdanov: f. 77, op. 1, d. 854, l. 56. Compare Istoriia SSSR: Kratkii kurs, 109; A Short History of the U.S.S.R., 133.

78. Zhdanov: RGASPI, f. 77, op. 1, d. 854, l. 56.

79. Zhdanov: RGASPI, f. 77, op. 1, d. 854, l. 56.

80. Zhdanov: RGASPI, f. 77, op. 1, d. 854, l. 56.

81. Zhdanov: RGASPI, f. 77, op. 1, d. 854, l. 56ob.

82. Zhdanov: RGASPI, f. 77, op. 1, d. 854, l. 56ob.

83. Stalin: RGASPI, f. 558, op. 11, d. 1584, l. 66ob. Also Zhdanov: f. 77, op. 1, d. 854, l. 56ob

84. Stalin: RGASPI, f. 558, op. 11, d. 1584, l. 66ob. Also Zhdanov: f. 77, op. 1, d. 854, l. 56ob

85. Stalin: RGASPI, f. 558, op. 11, d. 1584, l. 66ob. Also Zhdanov: f. 77, op. 1, d. 854, l. 56ob

86. Stalin: RGASPI, f. 558, op. 11, d. 1584, l. 68. Also Zhdanov: f. 77, op. 1, d. 854, l. 58.

87. Stalin: RGASPI, f. 558, op. 11, d. 1584, l. 68. Also Zhdanov: f. 77, op. 1, d. 854, l. 58.

88. Stalin: RGASPI, f. 558, op. 11, d. 1584, l. 68. Also Zhdanov: f. 77, op. 1, d. 854, l. 58.

89. Stalin: RGASPI, f. 558, op. 11, d. 1584, l. 68. Also Zhdanov: f. 77, op. 1, d. 854, l. 58.

90. Stalin: RGASPI, f. 558, op. 11, d. 1584, l. 68. Also Zhdanov: f. 77, op. 1, d. 854, l. 58.

91. Stalin: RGASPI, f. 558, op. 11, d. 1584, l. 68. Also Zhdanov: f. 77, op. 1, d. 854, l. 58.

92. Stalin: RGASPI, f. 558, op. 11, d. 1584, l. 68ob. Also Zhdanov: f. 77, op. 1, d. 854, l. 58ob.

93. Stalin: RGASPI, f. 558, op. 11, d. 1584, l. 68ob. Also Zhdanov: f. 77, op. 1, d. 854, l. 58ob

94. Stalin: RGASPI, f. 558, op. 11, d. 1584, l. 68ob. Also Zhdanov: f. 77, op. 1, d. 854, l. 58ob.

95. Stalin: RGASPI, f. 558, op. 11, d. 1584, l. 68ob. Also Zhdanov: f. 77, op. 1, d. 854, l. 58ob.

96. Stalin: RGASPI, f. 558, op. 11, d. 1584, l. 68ob. Also Zhdanov: f. 77, op. 1, d. 854, l. 58ob.

97. Stalin: RGASPI, f. 558, op. 11, d. 1584, l. 69ob. Also Zhdanov: f. 77, op. 1, d. 854, l. 59ob.

98. Stalin: RGASPI, f. 558, op. 11, d. 1584, l. 69ob. Also Zhdanov: f. 77, op. 1, d. 854, l. 59ob.

99. Stalin: RGASPI, f. 558, op. 11, d. 1584, ll. 69ob-70. Also Zhdanov: f. 77, op. 1, d. 854, ll. 59ob-60.

X: The First Bourgeois Revolution in Russia

1. Stalin: RGASPI, f. 558, op. 11, d. 1584, l. 70ob. Also Zhdanov: f. 77, op. 1, d. 854, l. 60ob.

2. Stalin: RGASPI, f. 558, op. 11, d. 1584, l. 70ob. Also Zhdanov: f. 77, op. 1, d. 854, l. 60ob.

3. Zhdanov: RGASPI, f. 77, op. 1, d. 854, l. 60ob.

4. Zhdanov: RGASPI, f. 77, op. 1, d. 854, l. 61.

5. Zhdanov: RGASPI, f. 77, op. 1, d. 854, l. 61.

6. Zhdanov: RGASPI, f. 77, op. 1, d. 854, l. 61.

7. Stalin: RGASPI, f. 558, op. 11, d. 1584, l. 71ob. Also Zhdanov, f. 77, op. 1, d. 854, l. 61ob.

8. Stalin: RGASPI, f. 558, op. 11, d. 1584, l. 71ob. Also Zhdanov: f. 77, op. 1, d. 854, l. 61ob.

9. Stalin: RGASPI, f. 558, op. 11, d. 1584, l. 71ob. Also Zhdanov: f. 77, op. 1, d. 854, l. 61ob.

10. Stalin: RGASPI, f. 558, op. 11, d. 1584, l. 710b. Also Zhdanov: f. 77, op. 1, d. 854, l. 610b.

11. Stalin: RGASPI, f. 558, op. 11, d. 1584, l. 710b. Also Zhdanov: f. 77, op. 1, d. 854, l. 610b.

12. Stalin: RGASPI, f. 558, op. 11, d. 1584, l. 710b. Also Zhdanov: f. 77, op. 1, d. 854, l. 610b.

13. Stalin: RGASPI, f. 558, op. 11, d. 1584, l. 710b. Also Zhdanov: f. 77, op. 1, d. 854, l. 610b.

14. Stalin: RGASPI, f. 558, op. 11, d. 1584, l. 710b. Also Zhdanov: f. 77, op. 1, d. 854, l. 610b.

15. Stalin: RGASPI, f. 558, op. 11, d. 1584, ll. 710b-72. Also Zhdanov: f. 77, op. 1, d. 854, l. 62.

16. Zhdanov: RGASPI, f. 77, op. 1, d. 854, l. 62.

17. Stalin: RGASPI, f. 558, op. 11, d. 1584, l. 72. Also Zhdanov: f. 77, op. 1, d. 854, l. 62.

18. Stalin: RGASPI, f. 558, op. 11, d. 1584, l. 72. Also Zhdanov: f. 77, op. 1, d. 854, l. 62.

19. Stalin: RGASPI, f. 558, op. 11, d. 1584, l. 72. Also Zhdanov: f. 77, op. 1, d. 854, l. 62.

20. Stalin: RGASPI, f. 558, op. 11, d. 1584, l. 72. Also Zhdanov: f. 77, op. 1, d. 854, l. 62.

21. Stalin: RGASPI, f. 558, op. 11, d. 1584, l. 72. Also Zhdanov: f. 77, op. 1, d. 854, l. 62.

22. Zhdanov: RGASPI, f. 77, op. 1, d. 854, l. 62.

23. Zhdanov: RGASPI, f. 77, op. 1, d. 854, l. 620b.

24. The 1937 Russian edition describes this defeat as "a rout"; the English translation was softened by translator error. Compare Istoriia SSSR: Kratkii kurs, 122; A Short History of the U.S.S.R., 147.

25. Stalin corrected this term to "the *tsarist* Russian navy" in the 1937 Russian edition; this edit was not reflected in the 1938 English edition due to translator error. RGASPI, f. 558, op. 11, d. 1584, l. 720b. Also Zhdanov: f. 77, op. 1, d. 854, l. 620b. Compare Istoriia SSSR: Kratkii kurs, 122; A Short History of the U.S.S.R., 147.

26. Zhdanov: RGASPI, f. 77, op. 1, d. 854, l. 620b.

27. Zhdanov: RGASPI, f. 77, op. 1, d. 854, l. 620b.

28. Stalin: RGASPI, f. 558, op. 11, d. 1584, l. 73. Also Zhdanov: f. 77, op. 1, d. 854, l. 63.

29. Stalin: RGASPI, f. 558, op. 11, d. 1584, l. 73. Also Zhdanov: f. 77, op. 1, d. 854, l. 63.

30. Stalin: RGASPI, f. 558, op. 11, d. 1584, l. 74. Also Zhdanov, f. 77, op. 1, d. 854, l. 64.

31. Stalin: RGASPI, f. 558, op. 11, d. 1584, l. 74. Also Zhdanov, f. 77, op. 1, d. 854, l. 64.

32. Zhdanov: RGASPI, f. 77, op. 1, d. 854, l. 64.

33. Zhdanov: RGASPI, f. 77, op. 1, d. 854, l. 64.

34. Zhdanov: RGASPI, f. 77, op. 1, d. 854, l. 64.

35. Zhdanov: RGASPI, f. 77, op. 1, d. 854, l. 64ob.

36. Here, Zhdanov proposed adding the following conclusion: "*For the first time peasant uprisings had taken on a more organized character. This organization was a characteristic that the peasant revolutionary movement had received from the working class which had been strengthened in its many-year struggle by the Bolshevik party, which had inspired and forged the progressive people of the working class.*" Stalin apparently rejected the interpolation. See RGASPI, f. 77, op. 1, d. 854, l. 64ob.

37. Stalin: RGASPI, f. 558, op. 11, d. 1584, l. 74ob. Also Zhdanov: f. 77, op. 1, d. 854, l. 64ob.

38. Stalin: RGASPI, f. 558, op. 11, d. 1584, l. 76. Also Zhdanov: f. 77, op. 1, d. 854, l. 66.

39. Zhdanov: RGASPI, f. 77, op. 1, d. 854, l. 66.

40. Zhdanov: RGASPI, f. 77, op. 1, d. 854, l. 66.

41. Zhdanov: RGASPI, f. 77, op. 1, d. 854, l. 66.

42. Zhdanov: RGASPI, f. 77, op. 1, d. 854, l. 66.

43. Stalin struck out the word "largely" from the 1937 Russian edition; this edit was not retained in the 1938 English edition due to translator error. See RGASPI, f. 558, op. 11, d. 1584, l. 76ob; also Zhdanov: f. 77, op. 1, d. 854, l. 66ob. Compare ISTO-RIIA SSSR: KRATKII KURS, 130; A SHORT HISTORY OF THE U.S.S.R., 156.

44. Stalin: RGASPI, f. 558, op. 11, d. 1584, l. 76ob. Also Zhdanov: f. 77, op. 1, d. 854, l. 66ob.

45. Stalin: RGASPI, f. 558, op. 11, d. 1584, l. 76ob. Also Zhdanov: f. 77, op. 1, d. 854, l. 66ob.

46. Stalin: RGASPI, f. 558, op. 11, d. 1584, l. 77. Also Zhdanov: f. 77, op. 1, d. 854, l. 67.

47. Stalin: RGASPI, f. 558, op. 11, d. 1584, l. 77. Also Zhdanov: f. 77, op. 1, d. 854, l. 67.

48. Stalin: RGASPI, f. 558, op. 11, d. 1584, l. 77. Also Zhdanov: f. 77, op. 1, d. 854, l. 67.

49. Stalin: RGASPI, f. 558, op. 11, d. 1584, l. 77ob. Also Zhdanov: f. 77, op. 1, d. 854, l. 67ob.

50. Stalin: RGASPI, f. 558, op. 11, d. 1584, l. 77ob. Also Zhdanov: f. 77, op. 1, d. 854, l. 67ob

51. Stalin: RGASPI, f. 558, op. 11, d. 1584, l. 78. Also Zhdanov: f. 77, op. 1, d. 854, l. 68.

52. Stalin underlined the term "oppressors." RGASPI, f. 558, op. 11, d. 1584, l. 78.

53. Stalin underlined 7,000, perhaps unsure of its accuracy. RGASPI, f. 558, op. 11, d. 1584, l. 78.

54. Stalin underlined "up in arms." RGASPI, f. 558, op. 11, d. 1584, l. 77.

55. Zhdanov: RGASPI, f. 77, op. 1, d. 854, l. 68.

56. Stalin: RGASPI, f. 558, op. 11, d. 1584, l. 77. Also Zhdanov: f. 77, op. 1, d. 854, l. 68.

57. Stalin: RGASPI, f. 558, op. 11, d. 1584, l. 78ob. Also Zhdanov: f. 77, op. 1, d. 854, l. 168ob.

58. Stalin underlined the subheading before editing it. See RGASPI, f. 558, op. 11, d. 1584, l. 78ob; also Zhdanov: f. 77, op. 1, d. 854, l. 68ob.

59. Zhdanov: RGASPI, f. 77, op. 1, d. 854, l. 69.

60. Zhdanov: RGASPI, f. 77, op. 1, d. 854, l. 69

61. Stalin underlined "irons." RGASPI, f. 558, op. 11, d. 1584, l. 79.

62. Zhdanov: RGASPI, f. 77, op. 1, d. 854, l. 69.

63. Stalin: RGASPI, f. 558, op. 11, d. 1584, l. 79ob. Also Zhdanov: f. 77, op. 1, d. 854, l. 69ob.

64. Stalin: RGASPI, f. 558, op. 11, d. 1584, l. 79ob. Also Zhdanov: f. 77, op. 1, d. 854, l. 69ob.

65. Stalin: RGASPI, f. 558, op. 11, d. 1584, l. 79ob. Also Zhdanov: f. 77, op. 1, d. 854, l. 69ob.

66. Zhdanov proposed that this sentence be rewritten as "~~Each peasant could claim~~ *The peasants could take* the lands ~~he~~ *that they* occupied *as private property*, quit the community and become ~~an~~ independent farmer*s*." He then crossed his correction out and wrote "*Restore the initial text.*" See RGASPI, f. 77, op. 1, d. 854, l. 70.

67. Zhdanov proposed adding a short paragraph following this one: "*Quitting the community was possible only for the rich peasant kulaks.*" He then crossed it out. See RGASPI, f. 77, op. 1, d. 854, l. 70.

68. Stalin: RGASPI, f. 558, op. 11, d. 1584, l. 80. Also Zhdanov: f. 77, op. 1, d. 854, l. 70.

69. Stalin: RGASPI, f. 558, op. 11, d. 1584, l. 80. Also Zhdanov: f. 77, op. 1, d. 854, l. 70.

70. Zhdanov: RGASPI, f. 77, op. 1, d. 854, l. 70.

71. Stalin: RGASPI, f. 558, op. 11, d. 1584, l. 80ob-82ob. Also Zhdanov: f. 77, op. 1, d. 854, ll. 70ob-71.

72. Stalin: RGASPI, f. 558, op. 11, d. 1584, l. 80ob-81. Also Zhdanov: f. 77, op. 1, d. 854, ll. 70ob-71.

73. Stalin: RGASPI, f. 558, op. 11, d. 1584, l. 81. Also Zhdanov: f. 77, op. 1, d. 854, l. 71.

74. Stalin underlined "were published." RGASPI, f. 558, op. 11, d. 1584, l. 82.

75. Stalin underlined "guided." RGASPI, f. 558, op. 11, d. 1584, l. 82.

76. Stalin underlined "escaped several times." RGASPI, f. 558, op. 11, d. 1584, l. 82.

77. Stalin: RGASPI, f. 558, op. 11, d. 1584, l. 82ob. Also Zhdanov: f. 77, op. 1, d. 854, l. 72ob.

78. Stalin: RGASPI, f. 558, op. 11, d. 1584, l. 82ob. Also Zhdanov: f. 77, op. 1, d. 854, l. 72ob.

79. Stalin: RGASPI, f. 558, op. 11, d. 1584, l. 82ob. Also Zhdanov: f. 77, op. 1, d. 854, l. 72ob.

80. Zhdanov: RGASPI, f. 77, op. 1, d. 854, l. 72ob.

XI: The Second Bourgeois Revolution in Russia

1. Stalin: RGASPI, f. 558, op. 11, d. 1584, l. 83. Also Zhdanov: f. 77, op. 1, d. 854, l. 73.

2. Stalin: RGASPI, f. 558, op. 11, d. 1584, l. 83. Also Zhdanov: f. 77, op. 1, d. 854, l. 73.

3. The 1937 Russian edition rendered this subtitle as "The Defeat of Russia in the War." Compare ISTORIIA SSSR: KRATKII KURS, 144; A SHORT HISTORY OF THE U.S.S.R., 172.

4. Stalin: RGASPI, f. 558, op. 11, d. 1584, l. 83. Also Zhdanov: f. 77, op. 1, d. 854, l. 73.

5. Stalin: RGASPI, f. 558, op. 11, d. 1584, l. 83. Also Zhdanov: f. 77, op. 1, d. 854, l. 73.

6. Stalin: RGASPI, f. 558, op. 11, d. 1584, l. 83. Also Zhdanov: f. 77, op. 1, d. 854, l. 73.

7. Stalin: RGASPI, f. 558, op. 11, d. 1584, l. 83. Also Zhdanov: f. 77, op. 1, d. 854, l. 73.

8. Stalin: RGASPI, f. 558, op. 11, d. 1584, l. 83. Also Zhdanov: f. 77, op. 1, d. 854, l. 73.

9. Stalin: RGASPI, f. 558, op. 11, d. 1584, l. 83. Also Zhdanov: f. 77, op. 1, d. 854, l. 73.

10. Stalin: RGASPI, f. 558, op. 11, d. 1584, l. 83. Also Zhdanov: f. 77, op. 1, d. 854, l. 73.

11. Stalin: RGASPI, f. 558, op. 11, d. 1584, l. 83ob. Also Zhdanov: f. 77, op. 1, d. 854, l. 73ob.

12. Stalin: RGASPI, f. 558, op. 11, d. 1584, l. 83ob. Also Zhdanov: f. 77, op. 1, d. 854, l. 73ob.

13. Stalin: RGASPI, f. 558, op. 11, d. 1584, l. 83ob. Also Zhdanov: f. 77, op. 1, d. 854, l. 73ob.

14. Stalin: RGASPI, f. 558, op. 11, d. 1584, l. 84. Also Zhdanov: f. 77, op. 1, d. 854, l. 74.

15. Stalin's "~~exiled to~~ *sent to live in*" correction in the 1937 Russian edition was not reflected in the 1938 English edition due to translator error. See RGASPI, f. 558, op. 11, d. 1584, l. 84; also Zhdanov: f. 77, op. 1, d. 854, l. 74. Compare ISTORIIA SSSR: KRATKII KURS, 146; A SHORT HISTORY OF THE U.S.S.R., 175.

16. Stalin: RGASPI, f. 558, op. 11, d. 1584, l. 84. Also Zhdanov: f. 77, op. 1, d. 854, l. 74.

17. Stalin: RGASPI, f. 558, op. 11, d. 1584, l. 84. Also Zhdanov: f. 77, op. 1, d. 854, l. 74.

18. Stalin: RGASPI, f. 558, op. 11, d. 1584, l. 84. Also Zhdanov: f. 77, op. 1, d. 854, l. 74.

19. Stalin: RGASPI, f. 558, op. 11, d. 1584, l. 84. Also Zhdanov: f. 77, op. 1, d. 854, l. 74.

20. Stalin: RGASPI, f. 558, op. 11, d. 1584, l. 84. Also Zhdanov: f. 77, op. 1, d. 854, l. 74.

21. Stalin: RGASPI, f. 558, op. 11, d. 1584, l. 84. Also Zhdanov: f. 77, op. 1, d. 854, l. 74ob

22. Stalin: RGASPI, f. 558, op. 11, d. 1584, l. 84ob. Also Zhdanov: f. 77, op. 1, d. 854, l. 74ob.

23. Stalin: RGASPI, f. 558, op. 11, d. 1584, l. 84ob. Also Zhdanov: f. 77, op. 1, d. 854, l. 74ob.

24. Stalin: RGASPI, f. 558, op. 11, d. 1584, l. 84ob. Also Zhdanov: f. 77, op. 1, d. 854, l. 74ob.

25. Stalin: RGASPI, f. 558, op. 11, d. 1584, l. 85. Also Zhdanov: f. 77, op. 1, d. 854, l. 75.

26. Stalin: RGASPI, f. 558, op. 11, d. 1584, l. 85. Also Zhdanov: f. 77, op. 1, d. 854, l. 75.

27. Stalin: RGASPI, f. 558, op. 11, d. 1584, l. 85. Also Zhdanov: f. 77, op. 1, d. 854, l. 75.

28. Stalin added the terminological clarification "(*separate peace*)" to the Russian text. This clarification was lost in the 1938 English edition due to translator error. See RGASPI, f. 558, op. 11, d. 1584, l. 85; also Zhdanov: f. 77, op. 1, d. 854, l. 75. Compare Istoriia SSSR: Kratkii kurs, 148; A Short History of the U.S.S.R., 177.

29. Stalin: RGASPI, f. 558, op. 11, d. 1584, l. 85. Also Zhdanov: f. 77, op. 1, d. 854, l. 75.

30. Stalin: RGASPI, f. 558, op. 11, d. 1584, l. 85. Also Zhdanov: f. 77, op. 1, d. 854, l. 75.

31. Stalin: RGASPI, f. 558, op. 11, d. 1584, l. 85. Also Zhdanov: f. 77, op. 1, d. 854, l. 75.

32. Stalin: RGASPI, f. 558, op. 11, d. 1584, l. 85. Also Zhdanov: f. 77, op. 1, d. 854, l. 75.

33. Stalin: RGASPI, f. 558, op. 11, d. 1584, l. 85. Also Zhdanov: f. 77, op. 1, d. 854, l. 75.

34. Stalin: RGASPI, f. 558, op. 11, d. 1584, l. 85. Also Zhdanov: f. 77, op. 1, d. 854, l. 75.

35. Stalin: RGASPI, f. 558, op. 11, d. 1584, l. 85ob. Also Zhdanov: f. 77, op. 1, d. 854, l. 75ob.

36. Stalin: RGASPI, f. 558, op. 11, d. 1584, l. 85ob. Also Zhdanov: f. 77, op. 1, d. 854, l. 75ob.

37. Stalin: RGASPI, f. 558, op. 11, d. 1584, l. 85ob. Also Zhdanov: f. 77, op. 1, d. 854, l. 75ob.

38. Stalin: RGASPI, f. 558, op. 11, d. 1584, l. 85ob. Also Zhdanov: f. 77, op. 1, d. 854, l. 75ob.

39. Stalin: RGASPI, f. 558, op. 11, d. 1584, l. 85ob. Also Zhdanov: f. 77, op. 1, d. 854, l. 75ob.

40. Stalin: RGASPI, f. 558, op. 11, d. 1584, l. 85ob. Also Zhdanov: f. 77, op. 1, d. 854, l. 75ob.

41. Stalin: RGASPI, f. 558, op. 11, d. 1584, l. 85ob. Also Zhdanov: f. 77, op. 1, d. 854, l. 75ob.

42. Stalin: RGASPI, f. 558, op. 11, d. 1584, l. 85ob. Also Zhdanov: f. 77, op. 1, d. 854, l. 75ob.

43. Stalin: RGASPI, f. 558, op. 11, d. 1584, l. 85ob. Also Zhdanov: f. 77, op. 1, d. 854, l. 75ob.

44. Stalin: RGASPI, f. 558, op. 11, d. 1584, l. 85ob. Also Zhdanov: f. 77, op. 1, d. 854, l. 75ob.

45. Stalin: RGASPI, f. 558, op. 11, d. 1584, l. 85ob. Also Zhdanov: f. 77, op. 1, d. 854, l. 75ob.

46. Stalin: RGASPI, f. 558, op. 11, d. 1584, l. 85ob. Also Zhdanov: f. 77, op. 1, d. 854, l. 75ob.

47. Zhdanov: RGASPI, f. 77, op. 1, d. 854, l. 76.

48. Stalin: RGASPI, f. 558, op. 11, d. 1584, l. 86. Also Zhdanov: f. 77, op. 1, d. 854, l. 76.

49. Stalin deleted "World"; it reappeared in the 1938 English edition due to translator error. See RGASPI, f. 558, op. 11, d. 1584, l. 86; also Zhdanov: f. 77, op. 1, d. 854, l. 76. Compare Istoriia SSSR: Kratkii kurs, 150; A Short History of the U.S.S.R., 180.

XII: The Great October Socialist Revolution in Russia

1. Stalin: RGASPI, f. 558, op. 11, d. 1584, l. 86ob. Also Zhdanov: f. 77, op. 1, d. 854, l. 76ob.

2. Stalin: RGASPI, f. 558, op. 11, d. 1584, l. 86ob. Also Zhdanov: f. 77, op. 1, d. 854, l. 76ob.

3. Later editorial correction. Mention of Bubnov appeared in the 1937 Russian edition but was deleted from the 1938 English edition after his arrest in October 1937. Mention of S. V. Kosior was retained despite his arrest in May 1938. Compare Istoriia SSSR: Kratkii kurs, 151; A Short History of the U.S.S.R., 181.

4. Stalin: RGASPI, f. 558, op. 11, d. 1584, l. 86ob. Also Zhdanov: f. 77, op. 1, d. 854, l. 76ob.

5. Stalin: RGASPI, f. 558, op. 11, d. 1584, l. 86ob. Also Zhdanov: f. 77, op. 1, d. 854, l. 76ob.

6. Stalin: RGASPI, f. 558, op. 11, d. 1584, l. 86ob. Also Zhdanov: f. 77, op. 1, d. 854, l. 76ob.

7. Stalin: RGASPI, f. 558, op. 11, d. 1584, l. 86ob. Also Zhdanov: f. 77, op. 1, d. 854, l. 76ob.

8. Stalin: RGASPI, f. 558, op. 11, d. 1584, l. 86ob. Also Zhdanov: f. 77, op. 1, d. 854, l. 76ob.

9. Stalin: RGASPI, f. 558, op. 11, d. 1584, l. 87. Also Zhdanov: f. 77, op. 1, d. 854, l. 77.

10. Stalin: RGASPI, f. 558, op. 11, d. 1584, l. 87. Also Zhdanov: f. 77, op. 1, d. 854, l. 77.

11. Stalin: RGASPI, f. 558, op. 11, d. 1584, l. 87ob. Also Zhdanov: f. 77, op. 1, d. 854, l. 77ob.

12. Stalin: RGASPI, f. 558, op. 11, d. 1584, l. 87ob. Also Zhdanov: f. 77, op. 1, d. 854, l. 77ob.

13. Zhdanov: RGASPI, f. 77, op. 1, d. 854, l. 77ob.

14. Stalin: RGASPI, f. 558, op. 11, d. 1584, l. 87ob. Also Zhdanov: f. 77, op. 1, d. 854, l. 77ob.

15. Stalin: RGASPI, f. 558, op. 11, d. 1584, l. 87ob. Also Zhdanov: f. 77, op. 1, d. 854, l. 77ob.

16. Stalin: RGASPI, f. 558, op. 11, d. 1584, l. 87ob. Also Zhdanov: f. 77, op. 1, d. 854, l. 77ob.

17. Stalin: RGASPI, f. 558, op. 11, d. 1584, l. 87ob. Also Zhdanov: f. 77, op. 1, d. 854, l. 77ob.

18. Stalin: RGASPI, f. 558, op. 11, d. 1584, l. 88. Also Zhdanov: f. 77, op. 1, d. 854, l. 78.

19. Stalin: RGASPI, f. 558, op. 11, d. 1584, l. 88. Also Zhdanov: f. 77, op. 1, d. 854, l. 78.

20. Stalin: RGASPI, f. 558, op. 11, d. 1584, l. 88ob. Also Zhdanov: f. 77, op. 1, d. 854, l. 78ob.

21. Stalin: RGASPI, f. 558, op. 11, d. 1584, l. 88ob. Also Zhdanov: f. 77, op. 1, d. 854, l. 78ob.

22. Stalin: RGASPI, f. 558, op. 11, d. 1584, l. 88ob. Also Zhdanov: f. 77, op. 1, d. 854, l. 78ob.

23. Stalin: RGASPI, f. 558, op. 11, d. 1584, l. 88ob. Also Zhdanov: f. 77, op. 1, d. 854, l. 78ob.

24. Stalin: RGASPI, f. 558, op. 11, d. 1584, l. 88ob. Also Zhdanov: f. 77, op. 1, d. 854, l. 78ob.

25. Stalin: RGASPI, f. 558, op. 11, d. 1584, l. 88ob. Also Zhdanov: f. 77, op. 1, d. 854, l. 78ob.

26. Stalin: RGASPI, f. 558, op. 11, d. 1584, l. 88ob. Also Zhdanov: f. 77, op. 1, d. 854, l. 78ob.

27. Zhdanov: RGASPI, f. 77, op. 1, d. 854, l. 78ob.

28. Stalin: RGASPI, f. 558, op. 11, d. 1584, l. 88ob. Also Zhdanov: f. 77, op. 1, d. 854, l. 78ob.

29. Stalin: RGASPI, f. 558, op. 11, d. 1584, l. 88ob. Also Zhdanov: f. 77, op. 1, d. 854, l. 78ob.

30. Stalin: RGASPI, f. 558, op. 11, d. 1584, l. 88ob. Also Zhdanov: f. 77, op. 1, d. 854, l. 78ob.

31. Stalin: RGASPI, f. 558, op. 11, d. 1584, l. 90. Also Zhdanov: f. 77, op. 1, d. 854, l. 79.

32. Stalin: RGASPI, f. 558, op. 11, d. 1584, l. 90. Also Zhdanov: f. 77, op. 1, d. 854, l. 79.

33. Stalin: RGASPI, f. 558, op. 11, d. 1584, l. 90. Also Zhdanov: f. 77, op. 1, d. 854, l. 79.

34. Stalin: RGASPI, f. 558, op. 11, d. 1584, l. 90. Also Zhdanov: f. 77, op. 1, d. 854, l. 79.

35. Stalin: RGASPI, f. 558, op. 11, d. 1584, l. 90. Also Zhdanov: f. 77, op. 1, d. 854, l. 79

36. Stalin: RGASPI, f. 558, op. 11, d. 1584, l. 90. Also Zhdanov: f. 77, op. 1, d. 854, l. 79.

37. Stalin: RGASPI, f. 558, op. 11, d. 1584, l. 90. Also Zhdanov: f. 77, op. 1, d. 854, l. 79.

38. Stalin: RGASPI, f. 558, op. 11, d. 1584, l. 90. Also Zhdanov: f. 77, op. 1, d. 854, l. 79.

39. Stalin: RGASPI, f. 558, op. 11, d. 1584, l. 90. Also Zhdanov: f. 77, op. 1, d. 854, l. 79.

40. Stalin: RGASPI, f. 558, op. 11, d. 1584, l. 90. Also Zhdanov: f. 77, op. 1, d. 854, l. 79.

41. Stalin: RGASPI, f. 558, op. 11, d. 1584, l. 90. Also Zhdanov: f. 77, op. 1, d. 854, l. 79.

42. Stalin: RGASPI, f. 558, op. 11, d. 1584, l. 90. Also Zhdanov: f. 77, op. 1, d. 854, l. 79.

43. Later interpolation into the 1938 English edition. See note 44 below.

44. This sentence in the 1937 Russian edition was deleted from the 1938 English edition after Bubnov's purge in October 1937. Compare ISTORIIA SSSR: KRATKII KURS, 157; A SHORT HISTORY OF THE U.S.S.R., 188. See note 43 above.

45. Stalin: RGASPI, f. 558, op. 11, d. 1584, l. 90ob. Also Zhdanov: f. 77, op. 1, d. 854, l. 79ob.

46. Stalin: RGASPI, f. 558, op. 11, d. 1584, l. 90ob. Also Zhdanov: f. 77, op. 1, d. 854, l. 79ob.

47. Stalin: RGASPI, f. 558, op. 11, d. 1584, l. 91. Also Zhdanov: f. 77, op. 1, d. 854, l. 80.

48. Zhdanov proposed deleting the word "proletarian," but Stalin apparently did not agree. RGASPI, f. 77, op. 1, d. 854, l. 80.

49. Later editorial addition.

50. Stalin: RGASPI, f. 558, op. 11, d. 1584, l. 91. Also Zhdanov: f. 77, op. 1, d. 854, l. 80.

51. Zhdanov: RGASPI, f. 77, op. 1, d. 854, l. 80ob.

52. Stalin: RGASPI, f. 558, op. 11, d. 1584, l. 91ob. Also Zhdanov: f. 77, op. 1, d. 854, l. 80ob.

53. Stalin: RGASPI, f. 558, op. 11, d. 1584, l. 92ob. Also Zhdanov: f. 77, op. 1, d. 854, l. 81ob.

54. Stalin: RGASPI, f. 558, op. 11, d. 1584, l. 92ob. Also Zhdanov: f. 77, op. 1, d. 854, l. 81ob.

55. Stalin: RGASPI, f. 558, op. 11, d. 1584, l. 92ob. Also Zhdanov: f. 77, op. 1, d. 854, l. 81ob.

56. Stalin: RGASPI, f. 558, op. 11, d. 1584, l. 92ob. Also Zhdanov: f. 77, op. 1, d. 854, l. 81ob.

57. Stalin: RGASPI, f. 558, op. 11, d. 1584, l. 92ob. Also Zhdanov: f. 77, op. 1, d. 854, l. 81ob.

58. Stalin: RGASPI, f. 558, op. 11, d. 1584, l. 92ob. Also Zhdanov: f. 77, op. 1, d. 854, l. 81ob.

59. Stalin wrote "*completely*" in the margins. RGASPI, f. 558, op. 11, d. 1584, l. 92ob.

60. Stalin: RGASPI, f. 558, op. 11, d. 1584, l. 92ob. Also Zhdanov: f. 77, op. 1, d. 854, l. 81ob.

61. Stalin: RGASPI, f. 558, op. 11, d. 1584, l. 94. Also Zhdanov: f. 77, op. 1, d. 854, l. 82.

62. Stalin's actual phrasing in the 1937 Russian edition is stronger: "*Without these reasons, the October revolution would not have been victorious.*" RGASPI, f. 558, op. 11, d. 1584, ll. 94–94ob. Also Zhdanov: f. 77, op. 1, d. 854, l. 82. Compare ISTORIIA SSSR: KRATKII KURS, 161; A SHORT HISTORY OF THE U.S.S.R., 193.

63. Stalin: RGASPI, f. 558, op. 11, d. 1584, l. 94. Also Zhdanov: f. 77, op. 1, d. 854, l. 82.

64. Stalin: RGASPI, f. 558, op. 11, d. 1584, l. 94. Also Zhdanov: f. 77, op. 1, d. 854, l. 82.

65. Stalin: RGASPI, f. 558, op. 11, d. 1584, l. 94. Also Zhdanov: f. 77, op. 1, d. 854, l. 82.

66. Stalin: RGASPI, f. 558, op. 11, d. 1584, l. 94ob. Also Zhdanov: f. 77, op. 1, d. 854, l. 82ob.

67. Stalin: RGASPI, f. 558, op. 11, d. 1584, l. 94ob. Also Zhdanov: f. 77, op. 1, d. 854, l. 82ob.

68. Stalin: RGASPI, f. 558, op. 11, d. 1584, l. 94ob. Also Zhdanov: f. 77, op. 1, d. 854, l. 82ob.

69. Stalin: RGASPI, f. 558, op. 11, d. 1584, l. 94ob. Also Zhdanov: f. 77, op. 1, d. 854, l. 82ob.

70. Stalin: RGASPI, f. 558, op. 11, d. 1584, l. 94ob-95. Also Zhdanov: f. 77, op. 1, d. 854, l. 82ob.

XIII: Military Intervention. The Civil War

1. Stalin: RGASPI, f. 558, op. 11, d. 1584, l. 95. Also Zhdanov: f. 77, op. 1, d. 854, l. 84.

2. Stalin: RGASPI, f. 558, op. 11, d. 1584, l. 95. Also Zhdanov: f. 77, op. 1, d. 854, l. 84. Zhdanov initially proposed deleting "Russian," but Stalin overruled him.

3. Stalin: RGASPI, f. 558, op. 11, d. 1584, l. 95. Also Zhdanov: f. 77, op. 1, d. 854, l. 84.

4. Stalin: RGASPI, f. 558, op. 11, d. 1584, l. 95. Also Zhdanov: f. 77, op. 1, d. 854, l. 84.

5. Stalin: RGASPI, f. 558, op. 11, d. 1584, l. 95. Also Zhdanov: f. 77, op. 1, d. 854, l. 84.

6. Stalin: RGASPI, f. 558, op. 11, d. 1584, l. 95. Also Zhdanov: f. 77, op. 1, d. 854, l. 84.

7. Stalin: RGASPI, f. 558, op. 11, d. 1584, l. 95. Also Zhdanov: f. 77, op. 1, d. 854, l. 84.

8. Stalin. RGASPI, f. 558, op. 11, d. 1584, l. 95. Stalin wrote "*completely*" in the margins. Also Zhdanov: f. 77, op. 1, d. 854, l. 84.

9. Stalin deleted "*part of*" during his editing; it was restored later for unclear reasons. RGASPI, f. 558, op. 11, d. 1584, l. 95. Also Zhdanov: f. 77, op. 1, d. 854, l. 84.

10. Stalin's editing of this phrase, "the haughty German generals ~~and officers~~," was incorrectly rendered in the 1938 English translation due to translator error. See RGASPI, f. 558, op. 11, d. 1584, l. 95; also Zhdanov: f. 77, op. 1, d. 854, l. 84. Compare ISTORIIA SSSR: KRATKII KURS, 165; A SHORT HISTORY OF THE U.S.S.R., 197.

11. Stalin: RGASPI, f. 558, op. 11, d. 1584, l. 95. Also Zhdanov: f. 77, op. 1, d. 854, l. 84.

12. Stalin: RGASPI, f. 558, op. 11, d. 1584, l. 95. Also Zhdanov: f. 77, op. 1, d. 854, l. 84.

13. Stalin: RGASPI, f. 558, op. 11, d. 1584, l. 95. Also Zhdanov: f. 77, op. 1, d. 854, l. 84.

14. Stalin: RGASPI, f. 558, op. 11, d. 1584, l. 95. Also Zhdanov: f. 77, op. 1, d. 854, l. 84.

15. Stalin: RGASPI, f. 558, op. 11, d. 1584, l. 95. Also Zhdanov: f. 77, op. 1, d. 854, ll. 84–83.

16. Stalin: RGASPI, f. 558, op. 11, d. 1584, l. 95. Also Zhdanov: f. 77, op. 1, d. 854, l. 84.

17. Stalin: RGASPI, f. 558, op. 11, d. 1584, l. 95. Also Zhdanov: f. 77, op. 1, d. 854, l. 83.

18. Stalin: RGASPI, f. 558, op. 11, d. 1584, l. 95. Also Zhdanov: f. 77, op. 1, d. 854, l. 83.

19. Stalin: RGASPI, f. 558, op. 11, d. 1584, l. 95. Also Zhdanov: f. 77, op. 1, d. 854, l. 83.

20. Stalin: RGASPI, f. 558, op. 11, d. 1584, l. 95ob. Also Zhdanov: f. 77, op. 1, d. 854, l. 84ob.

21. Stalin: RGASPI, f. 558, op. 11, d. 1584, l. 95ob. Also Zhdanov: f. 77, op. 1, d. 854, l. 84ob

22. Stalin: RGASPI, f. 558, op. 11, d. 1584, ll. 95ob-97. Also Zhdanov: f. 77, op. 1, d. 854, ll. 84ob-83ob.

23. Later editorial addition: the word "First" was inserted into the 1938 English edition for stylistic reasons. Compare Istoriia SSSR: Kratkii kurs, 167; A Short History of the U.S.S.R., 199.

24. Stalin: RGASPI, f. 558, op. 11, d. 1584, l. 95ob. Also Zhdanov: f. 77, op. 1, d. 854, l. 84ob.

25. Stalin: RGASPI, f. 558, op. 11, d. 1584, l. 95ob. Also Zhdanov: f. 77, op. 1, d. 854, l. 84ob.

26. Stalin: RGASPI, f. 558, op. 11, d. 1584, l. 96. Also Zhdanov: f. 77, op. 1, d. 854, l. 85.

27. Stalin: RGASPI, f. 558, op. 11, d. 1584, l. 96. Also Zhdanov: f. 77, op. 1, d. 854, l. 85.

28. Stalin: RGASPI, f. 558, op. 11, d. 1584, l. 96. Also Zhdanov: f. 77, op. 1, d. 854, l. 85.

29. Stalin: RGASPI, f. 558, op. 11, d. 1584, l. 96ob. Also Zhdanov: f. 77, op. 1, d. 854, l. 85ob

30. Stalin: RGASPI, f. 558, op. 11, d. 1584, l. 96ob. Also Zhdanov: f. 77, op. 1, d. 854, l. 85ob.

31. Stalin: RGASPI, f. 558, op. 11, d. 1584, l. 96ob. Also Zhdanov: f. 77, op. 1, d. 854, l. 85ob.

32. Stalin: RGASPI, f. 558, op. 11, d. 1584, l. 96ob. Also Zhdanov: f. 77, op. 1, d. 854, l. 85ob.

33. Stalin: RGASPI, f. 558, op. 11, d. 1584, l. 96ob. Also Zhdanov: f. 77, op. 1, d. 854, l. 85ob.

34. Stalin: RGASPI, f. 558, op. 11, d. 1584, l. 96ob. Also Zhdanov: f. 77, op. 1, d. 854, l. 85ob.

35. Stalin: RGASPI, f. 558, op. 11, d. 1584, l. 96ob. Also Zhdanov: f. 77, op. 1, d. 854, l. 85ob.

36. Stalin: RGASPI, f. 558, op. 11, d. 1584, l. 97. Also Zhdanov: f. 77, op. 1, d. 854, l. 86.

37. Stalin: RGASPI, f. 558, op. 11, d. 1584, l. 97. Also Zhdanov: f. 77, op. 1, d. 854, l. 86.

38. Stalin: RGASPI, f. 558, op. 11, d. 1584, l. 97. Also Zhdanov: f. 77, op. 1, d. 854, l. 86.

39. Stalin: RGASPI, f. 558, op. 11, d. 1584, l. 97. Also Zhdanov: f. 77, op. 1, d. 854, l. 86.

40. Stalin: RGASPI, f. 558, op. 11, d. 1584, l. 97. Also Zhdanov: f. 77, op. 1, d. 854, l. 86.

41. Stalin: RGASPI, f. 558, op. 11, d. 1584, l. 97ob. Also Zhdanov: f. 77, op. 1, d. 854, l. 86ob.

42. Stalin: RGASPI, f. 558, op. 11, d. 1584, l. 97ob. Also Zhdanov: f. 77, op. 1, d. 854, l. 86ob.

43. Stalin: RGASPI, f. 558, op. 11, d. 1584, l. 97ob. Also Zhdanov: f. 77, op. 1, d. 854, l. 86ob.

44. Stalin: RGASPI, f. 558, op. 11, d. 1584, l. 97ob. Also Zhdanov: f. 77, op. 1, d. 854, l. 86ob.

45. Stalin: RGASPI, f. 558, op. 11, d. 1584, l. 97ob. Also Zhdanov: f. 77, op. 1, d. 854, l. 86ob.

46. Stalin: RGASPI, f. 558, op. 11, d. 1584, l. 97ob. Also Zhdanov: f. 77, op. 1, d. 854, l. 86ob.

47. Stalin: RGASPI, f. 558, op. 11, d. 1584, l. 97ob. Also Zhdanov: f. 77, op. 1, d. 854, l. 86ob.

48. Stalin: RGASPI, f. 558, op. 11, d. 1584, l. 97ob. Also Zhdanov: f. 77, op. 1, d. 854, l. 86ob.

49. Stalin: RGASPI, f. 558, op. 11, d. 1584, l. 97ob. Also Zhdanov: f. 77, op. 1, d. 854, l. 86ob.

50. Stalin: RGASPI, f. 558, op. 11, d. 1584, l. 97ob. Also Zhdanov: f. 77, op. 1, d. 854, l. 86ob.

51. Stalin: RGASPI, f. 558, op. 11, d. 1584, l. 97ob. Also Zhdanov: f. 77, op. 1, d. 854, l. 86ob.

52. Stalin: RGASPI, f. 558, op. 11, d. 1584, l. 98. Also Zhdanov: f. 77, op. 1, d. 854, l. 87.

53. Stalin: RGASPI, f. 558, op. 11, d. 1584, l. 98. Also Zhdanov: f. 77, op. 1, d. 854, l. 87.

54. Stalin: RGASPI, f. 558, op. 11, d. 1584, l. 98. Also Zhdanov: f. 77, op. 1, d. 854, l. 87.

55. Stalin: RGASPI, f. 558, op. 11, d. 1584, l. 98. Also Zhdanov: f. 77, op. 1, d. 854, l. 87.

56. Stalin: RGASPI, f, 558, op, 11, d. 1584, l. 98. Also Zhdanov: f. 77, op 1, d 854, l. 87.

57. Stalin: RGASPI, f. 558, op. 11, d. 1584, l. 98. Also Zhdanov: f. 77, op. 1, d. 854, l. 87.

58. Stalin: RGASPI, f. 558, op. 11, d. 1584, l. 98. Also Zhdanov: f. 77, op. 1, d. 854, l. 87.

59. Stalin: RGASPI, f. 558, op. 11, d. 1584, l. 98ob. Also Zhdanov: f. 77, op. 1, d. 854, l. 87ob.

60. Stalin: RGASPI, f. 558, op. 11, d. 1584, l. 98ob. Also Zhdanov: f. 77, op. 1, d. 854, l. 87ob.

61. Stalin: RGASPI, f. 558, op. 11, d. 1584, l. 98ob. Also Zhdanov: f. 77, op. 1, d. 854, l. 87ob.

62. Stalin: RGASPI, f. 558, op. 11, d. 1584, l. 98ob. Also Zhdanov: f. 77, op. 1, d. 854, l. 87ob.

63. Stalin: RGASPI, f. 558, op. 11, d. 1584, l. 99. Also Zhdanov: f. 77, op. 1, d. 854, l. 88.

64. Stalin: RGASPI, f. 558, op. 11, d. 1584, l. 99. Also Zhdanov: f. 77, op. 1, d. 854, l. 88.

65. Stalin: RGASPI, f. 558, op. 11, d. 1584, l. 99. Also Zhdanov: f. 77, op. 1, d. 854, l. 88.

66. Stalin: RGASPI, f. 558, op. 11, d. 1584, l. 99. Also Zhdanov: f. 77, op. 1, d. 854, l. 88.

67. Stalin: RGASPI, f. 558, op. 11, d. 1584, l. 99. Also Zhdanov: f. 77, op. 1, d. 854, l. 88.

68. Stalin: RGASPI, f. 558, op. 11, d. 1584, l. 99ob. Also Zhdanov: f. 77, op. 1, d. 854, l. 88ob.

69. Stalin: RGASPI, f. 558, op. 11, d. 1584, l. 99ob. Also Zhdanov: f. 77, op. 1, d. 854, l. 88ob

70. Stalin: RGASPI, f. 558, op. 11, d. 1584, l. 99ob. Also Zhdanov: f. 77, op. 1, d. 854, l. 88ob.

71. Stalin: RGASPI, f. 558, op. 11, d. 1584, l. 99ob. Also Zhdanov: f. 77, op. 1, d. 854, l. 88ob.

72. Stalin: RGASPI, f. 558, op. 11, d. 1584, l. 99ob. Also Zhdanov: f. 77, op. 1, d. 854, l. 88ob.

73. Stalin: RGASPI, f. 558, op. 11, d. 1584, l. 99ob. Also Zhdanov: f. 77, op. 1, d. 854, l. 88ob.

74. Stalin: RGASPI, f. 558, op. 11, d. 1584, l. 99ob. Also Zhdanov: f. 77, op. 1, d. 854, l. 88ob.

75. Stalin: RGASPI, f. 558, op. 11, d. 1584, l. 99ob. Also Zhdanov: f. 77, op. 1, d. 854, l. 89.

76. Stalin: RGASPI, f. 558, op. 11, d. 1584, l. 99ob. Also Zhdanov: f. 77, op. 1, d. 854, l. 89.

77. Stalin: RGASPI, f. 558, op. 11, d. 1584, l. 99ob. Also Zhdanov: f. 77, op. 1, d. 854, l. 89.

78. Zhdanov: f. 77, op. 1, d. 854, l. 89ob.

79. Stalin: RGASPI, f. 558, op. 11, d. 1584, l. 101. Also Zhdanov: f. 77, op. 1, d. 854, l. 90.

80. Stalin: RGASPI, f. 558, op. 11, d. 1584, l. 101. Also Zhdanov: f. 77, op. 1, d. 854, l. 90.

81. Stalin: RGASPI, f. 558, op. 11, d. 1584, l. 101. Also Zhdanov: f. 77, op. 1, d. 854, l. 90.

82. Stalin: RGASPI, f. 558, op. 11, d. 1584, l. 101. Also Zhdanov: f. 77, op. 1, d. 854, l. 90.

83. Later editorial correction: Stalin's interpolation into the 1937 Russian edition *"and together with the commander of the front Comrade A. Egorov"* was deleted from all subsequent editions after Egorov's 1938 purge. See RGASPI, f. 558, op. 11, d. 1584, l. 101; also Zhdanov: f. 77, op. 1, d. 854, l. 90. Compare Istoriia SSSR: Kratkii kurs, 177 and A Short History of the U.S.S.R., 212.

84. Stalin: RGASPI, f. 558, op. 11, d. 1584, l. 101. Also Zhdanov: f. 77, op. 1, d. 854, l. 90.

85. Stalin: RGASPI, f. 558, op. 11, d. 1584, l. 101ob. Also Zhdanov: f. 77, op. 1, d. 854, l. 90ob.

86. Stalin: RGASPI, f. 558, op. 11, d. 1584, l. 101ob. Also Zhdanov: f. 77, op. 1, d. 854, l. 90ob.

87. Stalin: RGASPI, f. 558, op. 11, d. 1584, l. 101ob. Also Zhdanov: f. 77, op. 1, d. 854, l. 90ob.

88. Stalin removed the second textual mention of Egorov in 1937, presumably to eliminate redundancy. RGASPI, f. 558, op. 11, d. 1584, l. 101ob. Also Zhdanov: f. 77, op. 1, d. 854, l. 90ob.

89. Stalin: RGASPI, f. 558, op. 11, d. 1584, l. 101ob. Also Zhdanov: f. 77, op. 1, d. 854, l. 90ob.

90. Stalin: RGASPI, f. 558, op. 11, d. 1584, l. 101ob. Also Zhdanov: f. 77, op. 1, d. 854, l. 90ob.

91. Stalin: RGASPI, f. 558, op. 11, d. 1584, l. 102. Also Zhdanov: f. 77, op. 1, d. 854, l. 91.

92. Stalin: RGASPI, f. 558, op. 11, d. 1584, l. 102ob. Also Zhdanov: f. 77, op. 1, d. 854, l. 91ob.

93. Stalin: RGASPI, f. 558, op. 11, d. 1584, l. 102ob. Also Zhdanov: f. 77, op. 1, d. 854, l. 91ob

94. Stalin: RGASPI, f. 558, op. 11, d. 1584, l. 102ob. Also Zhdanov: f. 77, op. 1, d. 854, l. 91ob.

95. Stalin: RGASPI, f. 558, op. 11, d. 1584, l. 102ob. Also Zhdanov: f. 77, op. 1, d. 854, l. 91ob.

96. Stalin: RGASPI, f. 558, op. 11, d. 1584, l. 1020b. Also Zhdanov: f. 77, op. 1, d. 854, l. 910b.

97. Stalin: RGASPI, f. 558, op. 11, d. 1584, l. 1020b. Also Zhdanov: f. 77, op. 1, d. 854, l. 910b.

98. Stalin: RGASPI, f. 558, op. 11, d. 1584, l. 1020b. Also Zhdanov: f. 77, op. 1, d. 854, l. 910b.

99. Stalin: RGASPI, f. 558, op. 11, d. 1584, l. 103. Also Zhdanov: f. 77, op. 1, d. 854, l. 92.

100. Stalin: RGASPI, f. 558, op. 11, d. 1584, l. 103. Also Zhdanov: f. 77, op. 1, d. 854, l. 92.

101. Stalin crossed out his own name and wrote in "*Bliukher.*" See RGASPI, f. 558, op. 11, d. 1584, l. 103; also Zhdanov: f. 77, op. 1, d. 854, l. 92.

102. Stalin: RGASPI, f. 558, op. 11, d. 1584, l. 1030b; also Zhdanov: f. 77, op. 1, d. 854, l. 920b.

103. Stalin: RGASPI, f. 558, op. 11, d. 1584, l. 1030b. Also Zhdanov: f. 77, op. 1, d. 854, l. 920b.

104. Stalin: RGASPI, f. 558, op. 11, d. 1584, l. 104. Also Zhdanov: f. 77, op. 1, d. 854, l. 93.

105. Stalin: RGASPI, f. 558, op. 11, d. 1584, l. 1040b. Also Zhdanov: f. 77, op. 1, d. 854, l. 930b.

106. Stalin: RGASPI, f. 558, op. 11, d. 1584, l. 1040b. Also Zhdanov: f. 77, op. 1, d. 854, l. 930b.

107. Stalin: RGASPI, f. 558, op. 11, d. 1584, l. 1040b. Also Zhdanov: f. 77, op. 1, d. 854, l. 930b.

XIV: The Turn to Peaceful Labour. Economic Restoration of the Country

1. Stalin: RGASPI, f. 558, op. 11, d. 1584, l. 105. Also Zhdanov: f. 77, op. 1, d. 854, l. 94. Stalin initially rewrote the chapter title as "*The Turn to Peaceful Labour for the Restoration of the Country's Economy.*"

2. Stalin: RGASPI, f. 558, op. 11, d. 1584, l. 105. Also Zhdanov: f. 77, op. 1, d. 854, l. 94.

3. Zhdanov proposed deleting this paragraph; Stalin overruled him. See RGASPI, f. 77, op. 1, d. 854, l. 94.

4. Stalin: RGASPI, f. 558, op. 11, d. 1584, l. 105. Also Zhdanov: f. 77, op. 1, d. 854, l. 940b.

5. Zhdanov: RGASPI, f. 77, op. 1, d. 854, l. 940b.

6. Stalin: RGASPI, f. 558, op. 11, d. 1584, l. 105. Also Zhdanov: f. 77, op. 1, d. 854, l. 940b.

7. Stalin: RGASPI, f. 558, op. 11, d. 1584, l. 105. Also Zhdanov: f. 77, op. 1, d. 854, l. 940b.

8. Zhdanov wrote into the margins "*D. S. N.*," which might mean "*Provide modern [terminological] names.*" See RGASPI, f. 77, op. 1, d. 854, l. 95.

9. Stalin: RGASPI, f. 558, op. 11, d. 1584, l. 106. Also Zhdanov: f. 77, op. 1, d. 854, l. 95.

10. Stalin: RGASPI, f. 558, op. 11, d. 1584, l. 106. Also Zhdanov: f. 77, op. 1, d. 854, l. 95.

11. Stalin: RGASPI, f. 558, op. 11, d. 1584, l. 106. Also Zhdanov: f. 77, op. 1, d. 854, l. 95.

12. The word "First" was added to the 1938 English edition as this set of sentences was being translated.

13. Stalin: RGASPI, f. 558, op. 11, d. 1584, l. 1060b. Also Zhdanov: f. 77, op. 1, d. 854, l. 950b.

14. Stalin: RGASPI, f. 558, op. 11, d. 1584, l. 1060b. Also Zhdanov: f. 77, op. 1, d. 854, l. 950b.

15. Stalin underlined "Russian." It was rendered with emphasis in the 1937 Russian edition but not in the 1938 English edition. See RGASPI, f. 558, op. 11, d. 1584, l. 107. Also Zhdanov: f. 77, op. 1, d. 854, l. 96. Compare Istoriia SSSR: Kratkii kurs, 190 and A Short History of the U.S.S.R., 226.

16. Stalin underlined "Ukraine." It was rendered with emphasis in the 1937 Russian edition but not in the 1938 English edition. See RGASPI, f. 558, op. 11, d. 1584, l. 107. Also Zhdanov: f. 77, op. 1, d. 854, l. 96. Compare Istoriia SSSR: Kratkii kurs, 190 and A Short History of the U.S.S.R., 226.

17. Stalin underlined "Byelorussian." It was rendered with emphasis in the 1937 Russian edition but not in the 1938 English edition. See RGASPI, f. 558, op. 11, d. 1584, l. 107. Also Zhdanov: f. 77, op. 1, d. 854, l. 96. Compare Istoriia SSSR: Kratkii kurs, 190 and A Short History of the U.S.S.R., 226.

18. Stalin underlined "Trans-Caucasian." It was rendered with emphasis in the 1937 Russian edition but not in the 1938 English edition. See RGASPI, f. 558, op. 11, d. 1584, l. 107. Also Zhdanov: f. 77, op. 1, d. 854, l. 96. Compare Istoriia SSSR: Kratkii kurs, 190 and A Short History of the U.S.S.R., 226.

19. Stalin underlined "Uzbek." It was rendered with emphasis in the 1937 Russian edition but not in the 1938 English edition. See RGASPI, f. 558, op. 11, d. 1584, l. 107. Also Zhdanov: f. 77, op. 1, d. 854, l. 96. Compare Istoriia SSSR: Kratkii kurs, 190 and A Short History of the U.S.S.R., 226.

20. Stalin underlined "Turkmen." It was rendered with emphasis in the 1937 Russian edition but not in the 1938 English edition. See RGASPI, f. 558, op. 11, d. 1584, l. 107. Also Zhdanov: f. 77, op. 1, d. 854, l. 96. Compare Istoriia SSSR: Kratkii kurs, 190 and A Short History of the U.S.S.R., 226.

21. Stalin underlined "Tadjik." It was rendered with emphasis in the 1937 Russian edition but not in the 1938 English edition. See RGASPI, f. 558, op. 11, d. 1584, l. 107. Also Zhdanov: f. 77, op. 1, d. 854, l. 96. Compare Istoriia SSSR: Kratkii kurs, 190 and A Short History of the U.S.S.R., 226.

22. Stalin: RGASPI, f. 558, op. 11, d. 1584, l. 107. Also Zhdanov: f. 77, op. 1, d. 854, l. 96.

23. Stalin: RGASPI, f. 558, op. 11, d. 1584, l. 1070b. Also Zhdanov: f. 77, op. 1, d. 854, l. 960b.

24. For Stalin's complete vow, see "Vtoroi s"ezd sovetov SSSR," Pravda, January 30, 1924, 6.

25. Stalin: RGASPI, f. 558, op. 11, d. 1584, l. 1080b. Also Zhdanov: f. 77, op. 1, d. 854, l. 970b.

XV: The U.S.S.R. is the Land of Victorious Socialism

1. Stalin: RGASPI, f. 558, op. 11, d. 1584, l. 110. Also Zhdanov: f. 77, op. 1, d. 854, l. 98. Stalin initially rewrote the chapter title as *"The Victorious Construction of Socialism. The New Constitution of the U.S.S.R."*

2. Stalin: RGASPI, f. 558, op. 11, d. 1584, l. 110. Also Zhdanov: f. 77, op. 1, d. 854, l. 98. In Russian, this subheading is less elegant: *"Socialist Industry. Collective Work in Agriculture (Collective Farms)."*

3. Stalin: RGASPI, f. 558, op. 11, d. 1584, l. 110. Also Zhdanov: f. 77, op. 1, d. 854, l. 98.

4. Stalin: RGASPI, f. 558, op. 11, d. 1584, l. 110. Also Zhdanov: f. 77, op. 1, d. 854, l. 98.

5. Stalin: RGASPI, f. 558, op. 11, d. 1584, l. 110. Also Zhdanov: f. 77, op. 1, d. 854, l. 98.

6. Stalin: RGASPI, f. 558, op. 11, d. 1584, l. 110. Also Zhdanov: f. 77, op. 1, d. 854, l. 98.

7. Stalin: RGASPI, f. 558, op. 11, d. 1584, l. 110. Also Zhdanov: f. 77, op. 1, d. 854, l. 980b.

8. Stalin: RGASPI, f. 558, op. 11, d. 1584, l. 110. Also Zhdanov: f. 77, op. 1, d. 854, l. 980b.

9. Stalin: RGASPI, f. 558, op. 11, d. 1584, l. 111. Also Zhdanov: f. 77, op. 1, d. 854, l. 99.

10. Stalin: RGASPI, f. 558, op. 11, d. 1584, l. 1110b. Also Zhdanov: f. 77, op. 1, d. 854, l. 990b

11. Stalin: RGASPI, f. 558, op. 11, d. 1584, l. 1110b. Also Zhdanov: f. 77, op. 1, d. 854, l. 990b.

12. Stalin: RGASPI, f. 558, op. 11, d. 1584, l. 112. Also Zhdanov: f. 77, op. 1, d. 854, l. 100.

13. Stalin: RGASPI, f. 558, op. 11, d. 1584, l. 112. Also Zhdanov: f. 77, op. 1, d. 854, l. 100.

14. Stalin: RGASPI, f. 558, op. 11, d. 1584, l. 112. Also Zhdanov: f. 77, op. 1, d. 854, l. 100.

15. Zhdanov: RGASPI, f. 77, op. 1, d. 854, l. 100.

16. Stalin: RGASPI, f. 558, op. 11, d. 1584, l. 112. Also Zhdanov: f. 77, op. 1, d. 854, l. 100.

17. Stalin: RGASPI, f. 558, op. 11, d. 1584, l. 112. Also Zhdanov: f. 77, op. 1, d. 854, l. 100.

18. Stalin: RGASPI, f. 558, op. 11, d. 1584, l. 112. Also Zhdanov: f. 77, op. 1, d. 854, l. 100.

19. Stalin: RGASPI, f. 558, op. 11, d. 1584, l. 112. Also Zhdanov: f. 77, op. 1, d. 854, l. 100.

20. Stalin: RGASPI, f. 558, op. 11, d. 1584, l. 112. Also Zhdanov: f. 77, op. 1, d. 854, l. 100.

21. Stalin: RGASPI, f. 558, op. 11, d. 1584, l. 112ob. Also Zhdanov: f. 77, op. 1, d. 854, l. 100ob.

22. Stalin: RGASPI, f. 558, op. 11, d. 1584, l. 112ob. Also Zhdanov: f. 77, op. 1, d. 854, l. 100ob.

23. Stalin: RGASPI, f. 558, op. 11, d. 1584, l. 112ob. Also Zhdanov: f. 77, op. 1, d. 854, l. 100ob.

24. Stalin: RGASPI, f. 558, op. 11, d. 1584, l. 112ob. Also Zhdanov: f. 77, op. 1, d. 854, l. 100ob.

25. Stalin: RGASPI, f. 558, op. 11, d. 1584, l. 112ob. Also Zhdanov: f. 77, op. 1, d. 854, l. 100ob.

26. Stalin: RGASPI, f. 558, op. 11, d. 1584, l. 112ob. Also Zhdanov: f. 77, op. 1, d. 854, l. 100ob.

27. Stalin: RGASPI, f. 558, op. 11, d. 1584, l. 112ob. Also Zhdanov: f. 77, op. 1, d. 854, l. 100ob.

28. Stalin: RGASPI, f. 558, op. 11, d. 1584, l. 112ob. Also Zhdanov: f. 77, op. 1, d. 854, l. 100ob.

29. Stalin: RGASPI, f. 558, op. 11, d. 1584, l. 112ob. Also Zhdanov: f. 77, op. 1, d. 854, l. 100ob.

30. Stalin: RGASPI, f. 558, op. 11, d. 1584, l. 113. Also Zhdanov: f. 77, op. 1, d. 854, l. 101.

31. Stalin: RGASPI, f. 558, op. 11, d. 1584, l. 113. Also Zhdanov: f. 77, op. 1, d. 854, l. 101.

32. Stalin: RGASPI, f. 558, op. 11, d. 1584, l. 113. Also Zhdanov: f. 77, op. 1, d. 854, l. 101.

33. Stalin: RGASPI, f. 558, op. 11, d. 1584, l. 113ob. Also Zhdanov: f. 77, op. 1, d. 854, l. 101ob.

34. Stalin: RGASPI, f. 558, op. 11, d. 1584, l. 113ob. Also Zhdanov: f. 77, op. 1, d. 854, l. 101ob.

35. Stalin: RGASPI, f. 558, op. 11, d. 1584, l. 114. Also Zhdanov: f. 77, op. 1, d. 854, l. 102.

36. Stalin: RGASPI, f. 558, op. 11, d. 1584, l. 114. Also Zhdanov: f. 77, op. 1, d. 854, l. 102.

37. Zhdanov: RGASPI, f. 77, op. 1, d. 854, l. 103ob.

38. Stalin: RGASPI, f. 558, op. 11, d. 1584, l. 115ob. Also Zhdanov: f. 77, op. 1, d. 854, l. 103ob.

39. Stalin: RGASPI, f. 558, op. 11, d. 1584, l. 116. Also Zhdanov: f. 77, op. 1, d. 854, l. 104.

40. Stalin: RGASPI, f. 558, op. 11, d. 1584, l. 116. Also Zhdanov: f. 77, op. 1, d. 854, l. 104.

41. Stalin: RGASPI, f. 558, op. 11, d. 1584, l. 116. Also Zhdanov: f. 77, op. 1, d. 854, l. 104.

42. Stalin: RGASPI, f. 558, op. 11, d. 1584, l. 116. Also Zhdanov: f. 77, op. 1, d. 854, l. 104.

43. Stalin: RGASPI, f. 558, op. 11, d. 1584, l. 116. Also Zhdanov: f. 77, op. 1, d. 854, l. 104.

44. Stalin: RGASPI, f. 558, op. 11, d. 1584, l. 116. Also Zhdanov: f. 77, op. 1, d. 854, l. 104.

45. Stalin: RGASPI, f. 558, op. 11, d. 1584, ll. 116ob-117. Also Zhdanov: f. 77, op. 1, d. 854, ll. 104ob-105.

46. Stalin: RGASPI, f. 558, op. 11, d. 1584, l. 117. Also Zhdanov: f. 77, op. 1, d. 854, l. 105.

47. Stalin: RGASPI, f. 558, op. 11, d. 1584, l. 117. Also Zhdanov: f. 77, op. 1, d. 854, l. 105

48. Stalin: RGASPI, f. 558, op. 11, d. 1584, l. 117. Also Zhdanov: f. 77, op. 1, d. 854, l. 105.

49. Stalin: RGASPI, f. 558, op. 11, d. 1584, l. 117. Also Zhdanov: f. 77, op. 1, d. 854, l. 105.

50. Stalin: RGASPI, f. 558, op. 11, d. 1584, l. 117ob. Also Zhdanov: f. 77, op. 1, d. 854, l. 105ob.

51. Stalin: RGASPI, f. 558, op. 11, d. 1584, l. 117ob. Also Zhdanov: f. 77, op. 1, d. 854, l. 105.

52. Zhdanov: RGASPI, f. 77, op. 1, d. 854, l. 105.

53. Stalin: RGASPI, f. 558, op. 11, d. 1584, l. 117ob. Also Zhdanov: f. 77, op. 1, d. 854, l. 106.

54. Stalin: RGASPI, f. 558, op. 11, d. 1584, l. 118–118ob. Also Zhdanov: f. 77, op. 1, d. 854, l. 106.

55. Stalin: RGASPI, f. 558, op. 11, d. 1584, l. 118–119. Also Zhdanov: f. 77, op. 1, d. 854, ll. 106–107.

56. Stalin: RGASPI, f. 558, op. 11, d. 1584, l. 119. Also Zhdanov: f. 77, op. 1, d. 854, l. 107.

57. Stalin: RGASPI, f. 558, op. 11, d. 1584, l. 119. Also Zhdanov: f. 77, op. 1, d. 854, l. 107.

58. Stalin: RGASPI, f. 558, op. 11, d. 1584, l. 119. Also Zhdanov: f. 77, op. 1, d. 854, l. 107.

59. Stalin: RGASPI, f. 558, op. 11, d. 1584, l. 119. Also Zhdanov: f. 77, op. 1, d. 854, l. 107.

60. Stalin: RGASPI, f. 558, op. 11, d. 1584, l. 119. Also Zhdanov: f. 77, op. 1, d. 854, l. 107.

61. Zhdanov: RGASPI, f. 77, op. 1, d. 854, l. 107.

62. Zhdanov: RGASPI, f. 77, op. 1, d. 854, l. 107ob.

63. Stalin: RGASPI, f. 558, op. 11, d. 1584, l. 119ob. Also Zhdanov: f. 77, op. 1, d. 854, l. 107ob.

64. Stalin: RGASPI, f. 558, op. 11, d. 1584, l. 1190b. Also Zhdanov: f. 77, op. 1, d. 854, l. 1070b.

65. Stalin: RGASPI, f. 558, op. 11, d. 1584, l. 1190b. Also Zhdanov: f. 77, op. 1, d. 854, l. 1070b.

66. Stalin: RGASPI, f. 558, op. 11, d. 1584, l. 1190b. Also Zhdanov: f. 77, op. 1, d. 854, l. 1070b.

67. Stalin: RGASPI, f. 558, op. 11, d. 1584, l. 1190b. Also Zhdanov: f. 77, op. 1, d. 854, l. 1070b.

68. Stalin: RGASPI, f. 558, op. 11, d. 1584, l. 1190b. Also Zhdanov: f. 77, op. 1, d. 854, l. 1070b.

69. Stalin: RGASPI, f. 558, op. 11, d. 1584, l. 1190b. Also Zhdanov: f. 77, op. 1, d. 854, l. 1070b.

70. Stalin: RGASPI, f. 558, op. 11, d. 1584, l. 1190b. Also Zhdanov: f. 77, op. 1, d. 854, l. 1070b.

71. Stalin: RGASPI, f. 558, op. 11, d. 1584, l. 121. Also Zhdanov: f. 77, op. 1, d. 854, l. 108.

72. Stalin: RGASPI, f. 558, op. 11, d. 1584, l. 1210b. Also Zhdanov: f. 77, op. 1, d. 854, l. 1080b.

73. Stalin: RGASPI, f. 558, op. 11, d. 1584, l. 122. Also Zhdanov: f. 77, op. 1, d. 854, l. 109.

74. Zhdanov: RGASPI, f. 77, op. 1, d. 854, l. 109.

75. Stalin: RGASPI, f. 558, op. 11, d. 1584, l. 122. Also Zhdanov: f. 77, op. 1, d. 854, l. 109.

76. Zhdanov: RGASPI, f. 77, op. 1, d. 854, l. 1090b.

77. Stalin: RGASPI, f. 558, op. 11, d. 1584, l. 1220b. Also Zhdanov: f. 77, op. 1, d. 854, l. 1090b.

78. Stalin: RGASPI, f. 558, op. 11, d. 1584, l. 1220b. Also Zhdanov: f. 77, op. 1, d. 854, l. 1090b.

79. Stalin: RGASPI, f. 558, op. 11, d. 1584, l. 1220b. Also Zhdanov: f. 77, op. 1, d. 854, l. 1090b.

80. Stalin: RGASPI, f. 558, op. 11, d. 1584, l. 1220b. Also Zhdanov: f. 77, op. 1, d. 854, l. 1090b.

81. Stalin: RGASPI, f. 558, op. 11, d. 1584, l. 1220b. Also Zhdanov: f. 77, op. 1, d. 854, l. 1090b.

82. Stalin: RGASPI, f. 558, op. 11, d. 1584, l. 1220b. Also Zhdanov: f. 77, op. 1, d. 854, l. 1090b.

83. Stalin: RGASPI, f. 558, op. 11, d. 1584, l. 1220b. Stalin initially edited phrase to read: "every worker will work for society according to his abilities, *that is, work as much as he can,* and will receive according to his needs, that is, *all the things that he requires.*" See RGASPI, f. 558, op. 11, d. 1584, l. 1220b. Also Zhdanov: f. 77, op. 1, d. 854, l. 1090b.

84. Stalin: RGASPI, f. 558, op. 11, d. 1584, l. 1220b-1240b. Also Zhdanov: f. 77, op. 1, d. 854, ll. 1090b-1110b. The first quoted passage in this concluding section of the text was taken from an article by D. Z. Manuilsky, who based his 1929 account of Sta-

lin's experience with corporal punishment on those of the poet Demian Bedny and the eyewitness S. I. Vereshchak. Shestakov left the passage unattributed as neither Manuilsky nor Bedny were in good favor in 1937, nor was the former SR Vereshchak. See D. Z. Manuil'skii, "Stalin: k piadesiatiletiiu so dnia ego rozhdeniia," Kommunisticheskii Internatsional 52 (1929): 12; S. I. Vereshchak, "Stalin v tiur'me: Vospominaniia politicheskogo zakliuchennogo," Dni (Paris), January 22, 1928, 2; D. Bednyi, "S podlinnym verno," Pravda, December 20, 1929, 2. When Em. Yaroslavsky and P. N. Pospelov tried to insert a reference to the same event into their Short Course on party history during the following year, Stalin again deleted it. See David Brandenberger and Mikhail Zelenov, eds., Stalin's Master Narrative: A Critical Edition of the History of the Communist Party of the Soviet Union (Bolsheviks): Short Course (New Haven: Yale University Press, 2019), 245. For the speech from which Kaganovich's passage was taken, see "Priem rabotnikov zheleznodorozhnogo transporta v Kremle," Pravda, August 2, 1935, 1.

Chronological Table

1. Stalin deleted the galleys' "List of Words Requiring Explanation," which is not reproduced here. See RGASPI, f. 558, op. 11, d. 1584, l. 225ob-126. Also Zhdanov: f. 77, op. 1, d. 854, ll. 117, 112.

2. Stalin: RGASPI, f. 558, op. 11, d. 1584, l. 226ob. Also Zhdanov: f. 77, op. 1, d. 854, l. 112ob.

3. Stalin: RGASPI, f. 558, op. 11, d. 1584, l. 226ob. Also Zhdanov: f. 77, op. 1, d. 854, l. 112ob

4. Stalin underlined 1480 in pencil. RGASPI, f. 558, op. 11, d. 1584, l. 226ob

5. Stalin underlined 1606–1607 and "Bolotnikov" in pencil and placed a "X" in the margins. RGASPI, f. 558, op. 11, d. 1584, l. 226ob.

6. Stalin underlined "power of the tsar" in pencil and placed a question mark in the margins. The line was subsequently deleted. RGASPI, f. 558, op. 11, d. 1584, l. 226ob. Also Zhdanov: f. 77, op. 1, d. 854, l. 112ob.

7. Stalin placed a "X" in the margins. RGASPI, f. 558, op. 11, d. 1584, l. 226ob.

8. Stalin underlined "Bulavin" in pencil and placed an "X" in the margins. RGASPI, f. 558, op. 11, d. 1584, l. 226ob.

9. Zhdanov: RGASPI, f. 17, op. 120, d. 373, l. 240.

10. Zhdanov: RGASPI, f. 17, op. 120, d. 373, l. 240.

11. Stalin underlined "Pugachov" in pencil and placed an "X" in the margins. RGASPI, f. 558, op. 11, d. 1584, l. 226ob.

12. Stalin crossed out this line and wrote in the margins "Bastards!" RGASPI, f. 558, op. 11, d. 1584, l. 127. Zhdanov also deleted the line: f. 77, op. 1, d. 854, l. 113.

13. Zhdanov: RGASPI, f. 17, op. 120, d. 373, l. 240ob.

14. Zhdanov: RGASPI, f. 17, op. 120, d. 373, l. 240ob.

15. Zhdanov: RGASPI, f. 17, op. 120, d. 373, l. 240ob.

16. Zhdanov: RGASPI, f. 17, op. 120, d. 373, l. 240ob.

17. Zhdanov: RGASPI, f. 17, op. 120, d. 373, l. 240ob.

18. Zhdanov: RGASPI, f. 17, op. 120, d. 373, l. 2400b.

19. Zhdanov: RGASPI, f. 17, op. 120, d. 373, l. 2400b.

20. Zhdanov: RGASPI, f. 17, op. 120, d. 373, l. 2400b.

21. Zhdanov: RGASPI, f. 17, op. 120, d. 373, l. 2400b.

22. Stalin: RGASPI, f. 558, op. 11, d. 1584, l. 127. Also Zhdanov: f. 77, op. 1, d. 854, l. 113.

Appendix

1. See, for example, two 1938 issues of the official Glavlit bulletin: RGVA, f. 9, op., 35s, d. 92, ll. 34–35, 83.

2. RGVA, f. 9, op. 35s, d. 92, l. 120. Such orders, issued by military and Narkompros authorities and probably coordinated by Glavlit, do not seem to have been routinely preserved.

3. RGASPI, f. 17, op. 120, d. 373, ll. 99–990b, 1030b, 108, 157, 151.

4. Memoirists also recall censored textbooks in circulation during this period. See Nadezhda Mandel'shtam, Vospominaniia (New York: Izd–vo im. Chekhova, 1970), 366; Nina Nar, "The Campaign against Illiteracy and Semi-Illiteracy in the Ukraine, Caucasus, and Northern Caucasus, 1922–1941," in Soviet Education, ed. George L. Kline (London: Routledge & Kegan Paul, 1957), 149.

5. See Kratkii kurs istorii SSSR, 206–209 (author's personal collection). The State Instructional-Pedagogical Publishing House was also instructed in 1939 to change "fascist" to "bourgeois" in other textbooks. See GARF, f. 2306, op., 69, d. 2642, ll. 154–157.

6. Pankratova's Istoriia SSSR was also included in the list of texts undergoing last-minute reediting. See GARF, f. 2306, op. 69, d. 2640, ll. 1–3; f. 2306, op. 69, d. 2586, l. 250; f. 2306, op. 69, d. 2642, ll. 148–153.

7. Compare pp. 177–178, 151, and 157 in the 1937 edition to pp. 212, 181, and 188–189 in the 1938 edition. L. Z. Mekhlis was responsible for rephrasing the passage about Stalin's leadership of the revolutionary "fighting center"—see RGASPI, f. 558, op. 3, d. 1585, l. 86.

8. The 1937 title Kratkii kurs istorii SSSR (The Short Course on the History of the USSR) was revised as Istoriia SSSR: Kratkii kurs (History of the USSR: The Short Course).

9. Compare pp. 151, 157, 177–178, 182, 188 in the 1937 edition and the 1941 edition.

10. Compare pp. 47 and 206–208 in the 1937 edition and the 1941 edition.

11. Compare pp. 144, 166–167, and 188 in the 1937 edition and the 1941 edition.

12. See pp. 216–217 in the 1941 edition. Such commentary obscured the fact that the USSR and Nazi Germany had agreed aforehand to partition Poland in the case of war.

13. See pp. 217–220 in the 1941 edition. As above, such commentary obscured the fact that the USSR and Nazi Germany had agreed aforehand to divide Eastern Europe into separate spheres of influence.

14. Compare pp. 206–209 in the 1937 and 1941 edition.

15. Compare pp. 173, 166, 170, and 207 in the 1937 and 1941 edition.

16. KNIZHNIAIA LETOPIS' 10 (1941): 24; 13 (1941): 23; 14 (1941): 27.

17. The 1945 edition was signed over to press in November of that year.

18. Compare pp. 3–4 in the 1941and 1945 edition.

19. Compare pp. 10–13 in the 1941 edition with pp. 10–15 in the 1945 edition.

20. Compare pp. 21–22 in the 1941 edition with pp. 24–25 in the 1945 edition

21. Compare pp. 27, 23, and 29–31 in the 1941 edition with pp. 32, 26, and 35–37 in the 1945 edition.

22. Compare p. 29 in the 1941 edition with p. 35 in the 1945 edition.

23. Compare p. 29 in the 1941 edition with p. 35 in the 1945 edition.

24. Compare pp. 37 and 40 in the 1941 edition with pp. 43 and 46 in the 1945 edition.

25. Compare pp. 38 and 41 in the 1941 edition with pp. 44 and 48 in the 1945 edition.

26. Compare pp. 58–59 in the 1941 edition with pp. 68–70 in the 1945 edition.

27. Compare pp. 50–52 in the 1941 edition with pp. 59–61 in the 1945 edition. Deletion of compromising material on Khmelnitsky may have stemmed from the fact that the USSR introduced a new state military award named after him in 1943.

28. Compare pp. 63, 66, 63, and 69–70 in the 1941 edition with pp. 74, 79, 75, and 83 in the 1945 edition.

29. This partial rehabilitation of Russian imperialism was likely triggered by a major scandal revolving around a wartime book on Kazakh history that had been declared to be "anti-Russian" in 1944. See Brandenberger, NATIONAL BOLSHEVISM, 123–132; Dubrovskii, VLAST' I ISTORICHESKAIA MYSL' V SSSR, 339–382.

30. Compare pp. 72–74 in the 1941 edition with pp. 86–89 in the 1945 edition. Deletion of the word "Subjugates" led the editors of the 1945 edition to unknowingly delete a term that Stalin himself had interpolated into the text in 1937.

31. Compare pp. 75, 80–82 in the 1941 edition with pp. 90 and 96–99 in the 1945 edition. For Stalin's questioning of Russia's characterization as the "international gendarme," see Stalin, "O stat'e Engel'sa 'Vneshniaia politika russkogo tsarizma.'"

32. Compare pp. 95–96 in the 1941 edition with pp. 117–118 in the 1945 edition.

33. Compare pp. 102, 110, and 122 in the 1941 edition with pp. 127, 137, and 150 in the 1945 edition. The reason for chapter 10's deletion of E. D. Stasova is unclear, insofar as she had not fallen into disfavor.

34. Compare pp. 144–145, in the 1941 edition with pp. 175–176 in the 1945 edition. In editing the line about Alsace-Loraine, the editors unknowingly altered one of Stalin's 1937 interpolations.

35. Compare pp. 145–146 in the 1941 edition with pp. 176–177 in the 1945 edition.

36. Compare pp. 156–157, 171–172, 184, 173–174, and 193 in the 1941 edition with pp. 192, 210–211, 223, 212–214, and 235 in the 1945 edition. In editing the lines about the Mussavatists, the editors were unknowingly altering two of Stalin's 1937 interpolations.

37. Compare pp. 194, 200–202, and 215 in the 1941 edition with pp. 236, 244–247, and 261 in the 1945 edition. This deletion unknowingly eliminated two of Stalin's 1937 interpolations.

38. Compare pp. 206–207 in the 1941 edition with pp. 255–256 in the 1945 edition.

39. Compare pp. 206 and 216 in the 1941 edition and p. 209 in the 1937 edition with pp. 254 in the 1945 edition.

40. Compare pp. 216–220 in the 1941 edition with pp. 261–264 in the 1945 edition.

41. See p. 252 in the 1945 edition.

42. See pp. 264–268 in the 1945 edition. The story of Kazakh fighter Torunsabaev was evidently invented by Ilia Ehrenburg for an October 1942 article on the battlefield heroism of non-Russian soldiers in KRASNAIA ZVEZDA, as was V. I. Koroteev and A. Yu. Krivitsky's earlier story of the 28 Panfilov guards' heroic 1941 defense of Moscow.

43. See pp. 270–271 and 273–274 in the 1945 edition. See I. V. Stalin, "Vystuplenie I. V. Stalina na prieme v Kremle v chest' komanduiushchikh voiskami Krasnoi armii, 24 maia 1945 goda," in O VELIKOI OTECHEVENNOI VOINE SOVETSKOGO SOIUZA (Moscow: Gosudarstvennoe izdatel'stvo politicheskoi literatury, 1947), 197.

44. See pp. 270–274 in the 1945 edition.

45. KNIZHNIAIA LETOPIS' 14 (1946): 31. For an internal review of this edition that raked it over the coals for being out of step with postwar developments in Soviet historical politics, see RGASPI, f. 606, op. 1, d. 715, ll. 69–82. The editor is grateful to Kevin M. F. Platt for this citation.

46. Compare pp. 48 and 88 in the 1945 and 1947 editions.

47. Compare p. 261 in the 1945 and 1947 editions and see pp. 273–275 in the latter edition.

48. KNIZHNIAIA LETOPIS' 29 (1951): 42. The logic behind several editorial changes to the 1951 edition remains elusive. In one case, Stalin's 1937 labeling of the Jacobins as "petty bourgeois democrats" was crossed out, while in another case, Stalin's terming of Herzen as a "bourgeois democratic revolutionary" was downgraded to a mere "democrat." Compare pp. 92 and 119 of the 1947 edition with pp. 94 and 121 in the 1951 edition.

49. Compare pp. 108–111 in the 1947 edition with pp. 111–113 in the 1951 edition. This reversal was likely provoked by a revisionist article published by the first secretary of the Azerbaidzhani communist party that attacked the valorization of Shamil in 1950—see M. D. Bagirov, "K voprosu o kharaktere dvizhenii miuridizma i Shamilia," BOL'SHEVIK 13 (1950): 21–37. M. V. Nechkina followed up Bagirov's piece with a broader challenge to the "lesser evil" thesis that was greeted with controversy; Bagirov then broadened his attack on the concept in 1952 at the Nineteenth Party Congress. See M. V. Nechkina, "K voprosu o formule "naimen'shee zlo' (pis'mo v redaktsiiu)," VOPROSY ISTORII 4 (1951): 44–48; "Rech' tov. M. D. Bagirova," PRAVDA, October 7, 1952, 4–5.

50. Compare pp. 109–111 in the 1947 edition with pp. 112–113 in the 1951 edition.

51. Compare pp. 136–138 in the 1947 edition with pp. 139–141 in the 1951 edition. On Russian primacy, see, for instance, RASSKAZY O RUSSKOM PERVENTSVE, ed. V. Orlov (Moscow: Molodaia gvardiia, 1950).

52. Compare pp. 213–214, 245, and 252 in the 1947 edition with pp. 220, 252, and 275 in the 1951 edition.

53. Compare pp. 270–272 of the 1947 edition with pp. 277–279 in the 1951 edition.

54. KNIZHNIAIA LETOPIS' 15 (1954): 79. Curiously, the editors unknowingly deleted a line in this edition that Stalin had interpolated into the text in 1937 about how the Pugachev rebellion had failed because an "alliance between the working class and the peasantry was lacking." Compare p. 00 in the 1951 and 1954 editions.

55. Compare pp. 61–63 in the 1951 edition with the 1954 edition. This shift from "incorporation" to "unification" was part of a larger shift in the representation of tsarist-era colonialism from the "lesser evil thesis" to the so-called Great Friendship myth. As discussed above, Azerbaidzhani party boss Bagirov denounced the "lesser evil" theory in regard to the Caucasus between 1950 and 1952, demanding a more russocentric, apologetic interpretation of Russian colonialism. In October 1952, Ukrainian first party secretary L. G. Melnik echoed Bagirov's replacement of the traditional term "incorporation" with "unification" when he wrote to Stalin to propose celebrating the three hundredth anniversary of the Pereiaslav Treaty in 1954. Although Stalin ignored Melnik, his initiative was revived after the dictator's death by another Ukrainian first secretary, A. I. Kirchenko. His mid-1953 proposal—also framed in terms of "unification" rather than "incorporation"—won approval for the celebration during which the new "Great Friendship" paradigm governing Russian-Ukrainian historical relations was unveiled in January 1954. Fascinatingly, the 1954 edition of the SHORT HISTORY, sent to press in October 1953, anticipated much of this new language. On the Pereiaslav Treaty initiative, see "'Pologali by tselesobraznym otmetit' etu zamechatel'nuiu datu:' Kak gotovilos' prazdnovanie 300-letiia vossoedineniia Ukrainy s Rossiei (1952–1954gg)," ISTORICHESKII ARKHIV 4 (2002): 5–26; ISTORIIA SSSR: KRATKII KURS (1954), 61–63. See also G. A. Sanin, "O termine 'Vossoedinenie' Ukrainy s Rossiei,'" in NATSIONAL'NYI VOPROS V ISTORII ROSSII (Moscow: AIRO-XXI, 2015), 29–30 and SUPRA note 49.

56. Compare pp. 88–90 in the 1951 edition with the 1954 edition.

57. Compare pp. 279–282 in the 1951 and 1954 editions.

58. KNIZHNIAIA LETOPIS' 32 (1955): 68.

59. Compare pp. 3, 69, 214, and 281–282 in the 1954 and 1955 editions.

60. Compare pp. 283–284 in the 1954 and 1955 editions.

Index

Indexed entries include brief biographical and terminological information. In cases where the 1938 English translation of the SHORT HISTORY OF THE USSR textbook employed non-standard spellings of historical events and names, modern Russian transliterations have been supplied (see "A Note on Conventions," xix–xx).

STANFORD-HOOVER SERIES ON **AUTHORITARIANISM**

Edited by Paul R. Gregory and Norman Naimark

The Stanford–Hoover Series on Authoritarianism is dedicated to publishing peer-reviewed books for scholars and general readers that explore the history and development of authoritarian states across the globe. The series includes authors whose research draws on the rich holdings of the Hoover Library and Archives at Stanford University. Books in the Stanford–Hoover Series reflect a broad range of methodologies and approaches, examining social and political movements alongside the conditions that lead to the rise of authoritarian regimes, and is open to work focusing on regions around the world, including but not limited to Russia and the Soviet Union, Central and Eastern Europe, China, the Middle East, and Latin America. The Stanford–Hoover Series on Authoritarianism seeks to expand the historical framework through which scholars interpret the rise of authoritarianism throughout the twentieth century.

Mark Harrison, *Secret Leviathan:*
Secrecy and State Capacity under Soviet Communism
2023